Vino de Cocos, the Pilgrim Beverage

Vino de Cocos, the Pilgrim Beverage
Filipino Knowledge, Colonial Encounters and the Forgotten Origins of Mezcal

Paulina Machuca

Anabasis Project

"Le code de la propriété intellectuelle n'autorisant, aux termes des paragraphes 2° et 3° de l'article L122-5, d'une part, que les "copies ou reproductions strictement réservées à l'usage privé du copiste et non destinées à une utilisation collective" et, d'autre part, sous réserve du nom de l'auteur et de la source, que "les analyses et les courtes citations justifiées par le caractère critique, polémique, pédagogique, scientifique ou d'information", toute représentation ou reproduction intégrale ou partielle, faite sans consentement de l'auteur ou de ses ayants droit, est illicite (art. L122-4).

Cette représentation ou reproduction, par quelque procédé que ce soit, constituerait donc une contrefaçon sanctionnée par les articles L 335-2 et suivants du code de la propriété intellectuelle."

© **Anabasis Project, 2025**

Imprimé à la demande
Dépôt Légal : Novembre 2025
Image de couverture : Gervasio Gironella, *Álbum. Vistas de las Yslas Filipinas. Traces de sus abitantes*, Madrid, 1847, Biblioteca Nacional de España (hereinafter BNE), DIB/15/84, plate 45

Montage de couverture, mise en page et édition : Anabasis Project.
Titre original en espagnol : *El vino de cocos en la Nueva España. Historia de una transculturación en el siglo XVII*.
Traduction : Paul Kersey.
Cet ouvrage a fait l'objet d'une évaluation par les pairs en double aveugle.

ISBN relié : 978-2-487321-38-0
ISBN broché : 978-2-487321-39-7
ISBN ebook : 978-2-487321-40-3

Anabasis Project
52, Boulevard Gabriel Koenigs
31300, Toulouse, Haute-Garonne
France

www.anabasisproject.com

*To Thomas,
the light that illuminates my path
at the dawning of the day.*

PRESENTATION

It is with great pride and deep appreciation that I commend the publication of this important work on *lambanog*, the traditional Filipino distilled spirit derived from coconut. Books of this nature—deeply rooted in cultural memory and historical scholarship—are rare, and therefore all the more valuable.

This book is more than a chronicle of a time-honored craft; it is also a testament to the enduring cultural ties that bind the Philippines and Mexico—two nations connected not only by the vast Pacific Ocean, but by centuries of shared history, mutual influence, and vibrant exchange.

From the 16th to the 19th century, the Manila-Acapulco Galleon Trade served as a cultural and economic bridge that has tied the destinies of the Philippines and Mexico. The *lambanog* is a product of this beautiful convergence. This book thus offers more than an ethnographic record—it is a window into our interconnected past.

This publication also contributes to protecting the intangible legacy of generations of Filipino artists by preserving the history of the *lambanog*. It fills a critical gap, offering readers in both countries an opportunity to rediscover our shared, rich cultural and historical heritage. It is my hope that through this kind of research, it may help us better comprehend the legacies of our ancestors and fortify the cultural ties that still bind us today.

May this book inspire renewed appreciation, and dialogue around our common heritage, and may it serve as a foundation for further cultural diplomacy and cooperation between our two nations.

LILYBETH R. DEAPERA
Ambassador
Republic of the Philippines to the United Mexican States

Foreword

This book is an admirable initiative towards expanding the existing knowledge on the historical and cultural attributes of the *vino de cocos*. Through its historical methodology, it goes beyond the narrative of *lambanog* being only a local Filipino beverage.

Despite its geographical distance in the Pacific, Mexico and the Philippines share common cultural and historical ties. Notably, the role of the Acapulco-Manila galleon trade paved the way for economic and cultural exchanges of products, people, and customs throughout its transpacific journey. This contribution is one testimony of that notion.

As this investigation provides a new way of understanding the *vino de cocos*, it also contributes to the contemporary insights on the cultural and historical interconnectedness of both countries. The profound knowledge not only offers a new perspective on our shared history but also continues to recognize the mutual interrelation between the Asia-Pacific and Mexico.

May this research not only serve as a catalyst for strengthening cultural diplomatic relations, but also as an instrument for the broader understanding of shared experiences and cultural practices across the Pacific.

DANIEL HERNÁNDEZ JOSEPH

Ambassador of the United Mexican States to the Republic of the Philippines

PREFACE TO THE ENGLISH EDITION

The first edition of this book was originally published in 2018 by El Colegio de Michoacán, under the title *El vino de cocos en la Nueva España. Historia de una transculturación en el siglo XVII*. It was warmly received and, in 2019, received the Francisco Javier Clavijero Award from Mexico's Instituto Nacional de Antropología e Historia (INAH) in the category of "Best Research in National History and Ethnohistory." By 2020, it had sold out. Two of the sectors where it circulated most widely —among academics and the general public— showed great interest, respectively, in the sociocultural links between Mexico and the Philippines during the time of the Manila Galleon, and in the discussion of distilled beverages, especially mezcal and tequila. And there is good reason for this: on the one hand, my research contributes to the renewal of the historiography of transpacific studies by focusing, not on the circulation of merchandise, but on the movement of people across the Pacific Ocean and their capacity for agency as they introduced techniques and cultural practices into the places where they settled. On the other, the book appeared at a key moment for the field of "agave studies", which at the time was ensconced in heated debates over the origins of the first mezcals in Mexico, one side defending their pre-Hispanic development, the other seeking the answer in the post-conquest period. My position regarding the Filipino influence on the emergence of mezcals in Western Mexico has enriched those discussions and the intense, ongoing debates they have generated.

After 2018, I continued my study of the Filipino heritage in Mexico by examining the trajectories of some Filipinos who were active in *vino de cocos* production in the province of Colima. While El *vino de cocos en la Nueva España* called attention to several signatures in Baybayin, the ancient Filipino alphabet, I explored this topic in greater depth in an article published in 2022 and have incorporated my findings from that work into this edition.[1] Likewise, the account of the life of Francisca Martha, a *china criolla* who participated in *vino de cocos* production in Colima in the 17th century —discussed briefly in the first edition— is included here in its entirety, adapted from a chapter that appeared in 2016.[2] One of the reasons for including the complete trajectory of our *china criolla* in this edition is the resurgence of *vino de cocos* production in Colima that began in 2023, thanks to a project conceived by Jorge Velasco Rocha, a resident of that state, who named his brand *La china mestiza*, in honor of Francisca Martha. Without doubt, her story deserves to be included among the "minuscule lives" of the *vinateros* discussed herein, as a homage.

Finally, I have updated several papers that allowed me to anchor my research in the historiographical debate on global microhistory and have enhanced the maps and some illustrations. My hope is that, upon holding this book, readers will discover the same insights and, above all, feel some of the same emotions I felt during my studies and encounters with these humanities—while also perceiving the profound vibrations that still move me today.

INTRODUCTION

On December 15, 1600, in the days leading up to Christmas, a singular judicial investigation was underway in the remote Caxitlán Valley, jurisdiction of Colima, in New Spain, a small town on the road between the port of Salagua (today Manzanillo) and the villa of Colima, capital of the province of the same name. Graced by a temperate-humid climate, Caxitlán provided ideal conditions for cultivating tropical crops like cacao and coconut palms, the latter recently introduced from Oceania and the Philippines. However, certain "unhealthy" features, like excessively high temperatures, swarms of mosquitoes and other harmful insects, including scorpions, limited the presence of Spaniards. Colonial authorities and plantation owners preferred to reside in the capital, some fifty kilometers away. On that day, the visit by the Deputy of the *alcalde mayor* (provincial magistrate), Juan de Monroy, brought to light an event that shocked the valley's small population, for it turned out that four *chinos* had caused a disturbance in the town by inviting some local Indians to drink *vino de cocos*, an unknown, distilled drink with a high alcohol content.[3]

The judicial file provides some background on those four Asians: Domingo, a native of Manila, and Agustín, from Parañaque (some 20 km south of Manila), plied a trade that came to be known as *vinatero* (winemaker) or *maestro de hacer vino*; that is, experts in distilling *vino de cocos*. We learn only that Domingo was 30 years old, and that Agustín had a wife in the Philippines, whom he had not seen in six years. It was alleged that the other two *chinos* (Francisco Hernández, also 30, and Juan, 27) were accomplices in distributing the *vino de cocos*. An additional intriguing peculiarity in the file was that Juan signed his name in Asian characters; more precisely, in Baybayin, a pre-Hispanic writing system from the Philippine archipelago. That signature stands out as a rarity in archival documents from the Philippines and elsewhere.

The judicial process pursued against the four *chinos* accused of selling *vino de cocos* to Indians was the first of several cases from the 17th century that reveal how a group of Asian immigrants and their descendants—the vast majority of them Filipinos—were able to change various aspects of everyday life in the province of Colima, and how the coconut palm (*Cocos nucifera* L.), introduced first from the Solomon Islands in 1569 and then from the Philippines after 1571, modified extensive landscapes along Mexico's Pacific coastal fringe. Those Filipinos, *connoisseurs* of the millenarian trade of cultivating and exploiting coconut palms, not only participated in transforming the entire region, but also bestowed an identity upon it, as this book will show.

How I Came to This Research

The discovery of the document on the four *chinos* and my broader interest in the Filipino influence in Mexico have clear antecedents, for I was born in Colima, "the city of palm trees". As a little girl, I frolicked in the seemingly endless coconut palm plantations near the shores of the Pacific Ocean. I became accustomed to drinking coconut water in the morning to, as my father said, "eliminate parasites", while my mother always bought me a glass of *tuba* to drink as we strolled around the city center.[4] The woven reed roofs (*palapas*) of the restaurants along Colima's coastline formed part of the architectural imaginary I forged during my adolescence, until the day when, perhaps

Introduction

by fate, I discovered that the history of that panorama, the whole tradition in Colima of cultivating and exploiting coconut palms, had its roots far away on the other side of the Pacific. I felt compelled to tell that story.

The first text that sparked my interest was an undated typewritten document (c. 1995) that I stumbled upon in the Archivo Histórico del Municipio de Colima. Signed by Eigi Fuchigami, it bore the title, "Indios chinos en Colima, siglos XVI and XVII",[5] and presented a "brief summary" of the results of the author's research. In 28 pages, Fuchigami explained the importance of the Asians who settled in Colima in colonial times, especially in relation to the exploitation of palm trees to produce a distilled drink called *vino de cocos*. Unfortunately –perhaps deliberately?– he omitted all references from the file. At that time, the archival collections had not been formally cataloged, so it was very difficult to corroborate his affirmations.[6] Fuchigami's short study came to me as a kind of "revelation", a call for me to turn my attention to the role of the Asian population in Colima society, in part because his inquiries opened so many questions but provided so few answers. Was his an exhaustive exploration, or just a superficial study lost in a sea of uncatalogued colonial documents? Time would show that I had, in effect, found the starting point of a captivating story, unknown up to then in the historiography of New Spain.

This led to the publication, in 2009, of two studies in which I discussed the role that *indios chinos* played on the palm haciendas in Colima where *vino de cocos* was produced, and the emergence of an atypical figure in the apparatus of justice in New Spain: the *alcalde de chinos* [advocate of the Asians].[7] Those articles outlined the imprint of the Asian community on Colima's political-institutional and economic framework, but also raised new questions: how and when did those *chinos* and the coconut palm make their way to the Pacific region of New Spain?; what was the ecological base on which the palm haciendas were established?; how did the palm tree introduction impact the region's ecosystems?; was the province of Colima the only place where haciendas of this kind emerged, or did they extend into other areas of New Spain where Asians were present?; was *vino de cocos* a catalyst of local economies or only a complementary activity?; what kinds of labor relations were established between *chinos* and Spaniards?; was the technique for elaborating *vino de cocos* identical in the Philippines and New Spain?, and were the uses of the coconut palm on the Asian archipelago the same as in this area of the Americas?

A Perspective from Global Microhistory

I found that answering these questions demanded adopting a multiple approach that would allow me, on the one hand, to interweave the micro and macro scales in a kind of play between "extreme long-shots" and "close-ups", as Carlo Ginzburg proposed for microhistorical analyses[8] and, on the other, to elaborate an exhaustive analysis of local, non-serial –in reality, fragmentary– sources as I strove to reconstitute the lives of those immigrants from the other side of the Pacific who came on the Manila Galleon. A focus situated between the local and the global, distinct from the mainstream narrative surrounding the Galleon that focused on commercial flows and the circulation of civil and religious authorities and mercantile elites to concentrate, instead, on small-scale, local actors. We cannot dismiss the fact that, as Arturo Giraldez stated, "from a global perspective, Manila's founding implied that for the first time in the history of humanity the planet's landmasses were joined by uninterrupted interactions".[9] And it was, precisely, the voyages of the Manila Galleon that made those long-distance social interactions possible.

In an article published in 2010, Tonio Andrade pointed out that one of the weaknesses of global history, preoccupied as it always is with planetary structures and grand flows of capital, was that "we've tended to neglect the human dramas that make history come alive". Therefore, he continued, "I believe we should adopt microhistorical and biographical approaches to help populate our models and theories with real people, to write what one might call global microhistory".[10] This is exactly what I set out to do in my research by analyzing individuals' lives in global contexts. The term global microhistory appeared from the convergence of microhistory and global history. Emerging from the microhistory in vogue from the decade of 1980, this concept undertook exhaustive analyses of local sources and their context, while from global history, whose apogee began in the 1990s, it condensed the study of the large-scale economic and sociocultural interactions characteristic of the first globalization.[11] Following this premise, I would add that this book was written from the ground level perspective (*au ras du sol*):[12] first, the space where those people acted was somewhat marginalized compared to other urban centers in New Spain. The immigrants from the Manila Galleon who devoted their labors to producing *vino de cocos*, mainly in Colima but also around Acapulco, moved in rural agricultural spaces far from major urban areas. But these actors of that first globalization, these "small", often anonymous, people who so rarely appear in autobiographical narratives, also led "global lives", in the words of Miles Ogborn.[13]

Second, it is evident that responding to many of the questions posed above demands a multi-level approach: in biocultural terms, the introduction of the coconut palm along the coastal strip of the Mar del Sur (Pacific Ocean) triggered modifications and successions where the tree found especially favorable geographies. This phenomenon was accelerated by the arrival of Asians on the Galleon who, thanks to their ample familiarity with the cultivation and exploitation of the coconut palm, almost immediately succeeded in settling among the native population. At the anthropological level we can ask, what did the insertion of a distilled drink into a market dominated by fermented beverages signify in the early 17th century? Here, we cannot lose sight of the fact that *vino de cocos* was the first distillate to circulate widely in New Spain, as it found important markets in large cities and in the mining zones of the central-north region where it mitigated the effects of grueling workdays. At the socioeconomic level, *vino de cocos* emerged as an option when cacao production declined in the economies of the *alcaldías mayores* (provincial governments) of Colima and Los Motines early in the 17th century, and as a complementary productive activity in the *alcaldías mayores* of Zacatula and Acapulco in the same period. This explains why in the political sphere, and given the demand for alcoholic drinks in mining regions, from 1627 onwards the *ayuntamiento* (local governing council) of Colima convinced the Viceroy of New Spain to free production and commerce in this beverage, a situation that lasted into the decade of 1690. At the cultural level, over time the introduction of *vino de cocos* and the distillation technique led to the appearance of another drink: mezcal, a rival that would emerge victorious, as the historical and ethnohistorical sources discussed at the end of this book corroborate. Learning how to operate the Filipino-style still not only gave local people the opportunity to produce *vino de cocos*, but also served as the basis for distilling the fermented must of the cooked heads of agave plants, a resource widely exploited in the alimentary system of Mesoamerican society.

Having posited the central questions of my research, I had to identify the kinds of sources available. Archives in Colima were the main sources of information, complemented by those in Guadalajara and Mexico City. Archives in mining zones like Zacatecas, San Luis Potosí, Mazapil, and Sombrerete further supported my search, as did those in the ancient Bishopric of Michoacán, especially holdings in Morelia and Pátzcuaro. In Spain, the Archivo General de Indias in Sevilla supplied data relevant to my study, as did the repository at the Real Academia de la Historia in Madrid, though to a lesser degree. The main challenge I faced was the scarcity of information on the elaboration of *vino de cocos* in the *alcaldías mayores* of Zacatula and Acapulco so, as the reader will see, my references to those places are much less illustrative than those to Colima and Los Motines. This was due, in part, to the disappearance of documents from the 17th century but, above all, to the fact that *vino de cocos* production was never more than an ancillary activity there.

Follow the People, Follow the Plant, Follow the Technique: A Multi-Sited Ethnography

In addition to these issues regarding the historical sources, the circumstances of the historical objective and the scientific process raised an additional question: what challenges would I confront in researching the history of a drink that ceased to exist early in the 18th century in New Spain, but is still being produced in the Philippines today under the name *lambanog*? Unlike researchers interested in other alcoholic drinks –like sugarcane aguardiente or mezcal– I had no living witnesses in Colima who could orient me on the preparation and distilling processes, a predicament compounded by the fact that the historical sources were largely silent on this subject, leaving me unable to learn the details of diverse aspects related to this drink, such as: how did *vino de cocos* taste?; how many liters of *tuba* (the raw sap) were needed to obtain a liter of distillate?; and what was the nature of the fermentation process? Questions like these motivated me to undertake what George Marcus calls a "multi-sited ethnography".[14] I decided to go to the Philippine archipelago in search of answers that the documents I had combed through could not provide. In Luzon and the Visayas, among *manananggot, mananguete,*[15] and distilleries I found, thanks to ethnography, the most efficacious methodological tools for this type of research.[16]

That was the moment when my study methodology, originally based on a critical review of documental sources, swung sharply toward anthropology, and I began my fruitful fieldwork in the Philippines in 2012, 2013, and 2015 from an interdisciplinary focus that considerably enriched my results. As Marcus states, for the ethnographer interested in local changes in culture and society, "single-sited research can no longer be easily located in a world system perspective". For me, this affirmation became a route to be taken: follow the people, follow the plant, follow the technique.[17]

The motivation I received from *vino de cocos* and *tuba* producers in Luzon and the Visayas whet my appetite to return to Colima where, although *vino de cocos* was no longer produced,[18] some *tuberos* still exist. They have transformed their drink into a local, "native" tradition, completely unaware of its Filipino influence. During this "mobile ethnography" (to quote Marcus) between Luzon-Visayas and Colima, I produced the documentary film *Hacer tuba en México y Filipinas: cuatro siglos de historia compartida* ("Making tuba in Mexico and the Philippines: four centuries of shared history") that allowed me to reach a wider public.[19] This way of proceeding as a historian, how I combined the methodological tools of history and anthropology, became the "trademark" of this study, whose contents I present in the pages of this book.

Part I. Biocultural Transfers across the Pacific

In his seminal work on Columbian exchange, Alfred Crosby observed that the American continent underwent an unprecedented biological revolution in the 16th century, perhaps the most important one since the end of the Pleistocene, for it was at the dawn of that epoch that Old World plants, animals, and germs were brought to America, with their widely known consequences.[20] But exchanges continued in other ways as well: as Spanish colonization

INTRODUCTION

advanced, and the transpacific route was inaugurated (1565), the insular, continental façades established in the Hispanic Pacific region, especially tropical areas, with their maximum exponents in Mexico and the Philippines, underwent their own ecological revolution.

It was thanks to the Manila Galleon that innumerable tropical plants circulated in both directions, with species like the coconut palm, rice, tamarind, mangos, and diverse spices traveling to Acapulco, while corn, cacao, tobacco, and a wide variety of Mesoamerican fruits made their way to Manila. Calculations suggest that approximately 230 species of useful plants were exchanged in this way, carefully transported to resist the three-to-six-month voyage across the Pacific Ocean.[21] Without doubt, the transpacific route carried the second great wave of plants introduced into New Spain and, hence, constituted a second moment of enormous impact on the agricultural systems of ancient Mesoamerica.

Regarding the Mar del Sur coast of New Spain, the arrival of *Cocos nucifera* triggered one of the most significant ecological changes, not only in biological terms but also in the sociocultural sphere. A tree that grows and propagates quickly under favorable conditions, the coconut palm found an ideal niche in the warm-humid lands and sandy soils of this zone. In less than a century it became a reference across the landscape, a source of food, and an essential architectural material along the coast. These phenomena were made possible by the convergence of two elements: the systematic introduction of coconut tree seeds from the Philippines and Pacific islands, and the simultaneous arrival of numerous Asians –*indios chinos*– bearers of traditional knowledge of how to cultivate and exploit that tree.

Chapter 1, "The World the Coconut Palm Created", presents a cultural history of the coconut palm: its origins, dissemination, and introduction into New Spain. It is based mainly on Portuguese and Spanish sources that considered it the most profitable tree in the world. Over time, the arrival of *indios chinos* aboard the Galleon who identified with this millenarian tree established the initial conditions to produce a distilled beverage extracted from the sap of the coconut palm; this is the central theme of Chapter 2, "Vino de Cocos: A Traveling Technique from the Philippines to New Spain". The discussion focuses on the production process, material culture required, and *savoir faire* transferred from one side of the Pacific to the other, complemented by a description of the production areas where palm haciendas dotted the landscape. Cacao, a native tree whose cultivation expanded with the arrival of the Spanish, adopted *Cocos nucifera* as its "mother tree" that gave needed shade, replacing the *cacahuanantzin*, a Náhuatl word that means "mother of cacao".

Part II. Actors of the First Globalization: A View "from Below"

A topic long relegated by Mexican historiography concerned the role of the *indios chinos* who settled in New Spain after the transpacific aperture in the second half of the 16th century. Recent, valuable studies have shed light on the origin, settlement areas, and forms of insertion of that Asian population into New Spain. Chapter 3, "Francisca Martha and the *Indios Chinos* in the Mar del Sur", analyzes in detail how a *china criolla* successfully, and with distinction, inserted herself into the world of the palm haciendas devoted to distilling *vino de cocos*, a predominantly male domain. Chapter 4, "The Indios Chinos Vinateros: Rural Connections across the Pacific", offers a detailed study of how some Filipinos developed, with some success, in the *alcaldías mayores* of Colima and Los Motines, where their labors as *vinateros* came to be highly-valued and allowed them to adapt to the receiving society in diverse ways.

One particularly significant discovery involved the signatures of some *vinateros* in Baybayin, an ancient form of Filipino writing. This was a truly rare find in early colonial sources, both in and beyond the Philippines that, as I mentioned above, without doubt places a stamp on that moment of the history of the first globalization; that is, the encounter of various cultures that circulated bearing their mental universes. This is the focus of Chapter 5, "The *Vinateros* Who Signed in Baybayin". Chapter 6, "*Indian Vinateros* and Other Castes", reflects on the transfer of techniques and knowledges between Asian and American societies, especially those related to the extraction of *tuba* –a raw material gathered as sap from coconut palms; an element still very much alive in Colima culture today– for distillation. I was able to demonstrate historically that by the 1630s some Indians in Colima were also plying the trade of *vinatero*, "climbing palms like the *chinos*".

Part III. The Pilgrim Beverage

Vino de cocos was the first distilled beverage to enter the market of alcoholic drinks in New Spain –around the year 1598– and the first distillate to be produced, commercialized, and consumed across broad expanses of those territories, as it was transported from the Pacific Hot Lands to various urban areas and the northern mining zones of Zacatecas and Parral. In addition, the model of *vino de cocos* production led directly to the emergence of other distilled drinks, including mezcal, beverages that were later joined by others: *chinguiritos* (sugarcane aguardiente) and *vino de Parras*. In the late 17th century, competing in a market that offered various distilled drinks elaborated with more accessible raw materials and in places more strategic for satisfying demand in cities and mining zones, *vino de cocos* suffered a marked decline that led to its complete disappearance in the 18th century.

Chapter 7, "Prohibition, Apogee, and Decline of *Vino de Cocos*", recounts how this distillate transited from being banned to emerge as a drink authorized periodically by several Viceroys of New Spain. It traces how this drink went from being a pillar of the economies of provinces like Colima in the 1620-1640 period to experiencing a precipitous decrease in production in the ensuing decades. Chapter 8, "Commercial Routes of Vino de Cocos", highlights the success the drink enjoyed in the urban areas of Guadalajara, Valladolid, and Mexico City, and in numerous mining zones in central-north New Spain. Despite being legitimately licensed for trade, transport was not always exempt from prohibitions, especially because Viceregal policy regarding alcoholic drinks was characterized, in general, by ambiguity and a double discourse. This topic is examined in Chapter 9, "Vino de Cocos and Prohibitionist Policies", which closes the third and final section of the book.

This research ends with an Epilogue that poses the question of whether mezcal, the national drink of Mexico *par excellence*, is the heir of *vino de cocos*. The controversy that marks discussions of whether mezcal is a pre-Hispanic drink or one that appeared in colonial times thanks to the imported Asian-style still demands that I state my posture clearly: based on the historical sources I consulted it is clear that mezcal, in reality, emerged in western New Spain thanks to the Asian technique of distillation introduced by immigrants who arrived on the Manila Galleon. This means that we are dealing with a transcultural process, in Malinowski's words, "a transition between two cultures, both of which made important contributions" that proved capable of creating new realities.[22]

* * *

Though written for a broad public, Vino de Cocos, the Pilgrim Beverage. Filipino Knowledge, Colonial Encounters and the Forgotten Origins of Mezcal, adopts the methodological rigor of an academic study. It presents a new vision of the past by discovering a topic long neglected, unknown, even perhaps erased from the memory of the place where it originated. It seeks to open new horizons on the Pacific region and recognize the Asian legacy there, especially its Filipino roots. My hope is that through this book readers will travel back to the past and enter a world dominated by the heat of palm haciendas where the dreams of many Asian immigrants, and uncountable miners in the highlands, vanished with a swig of *vino de cocos*.[23]

PART I
BIOCULTURAL TRANSFERS ACROSS THE PACIFIC

1. THE WORLD THE COCONUT PALM CREATED

> When no other means of subsistence existed, the palm tree sufficed to ease men's hunger. All that was left was for God to raise men in those palms.
>
> —Sebastián de Vera, resident of Colima (1612)

INTRODUCTION

One belief in the mythology of the Visaya Indians, peoples who inhabit an archipelago in the central Philippines, was that the human race arose through the union of two coconuts. Regarding the origin of the universe, the Visaya knew neither the beginning nor the author. "[The tree] produced its fruits [and] two mature [coconuts] fell into the sea, on whose shores that stately palm stood". The coconuts rode the waves, at the mercy of capricious winds, until one day the sea in its fury flung them violently onto a crag. The coconuts suddenly opened and from one emerged a man, "the first man", called Laqui. From the smaller coconut arose a woman, named Baie. "All men descended from those two, the first parents of the human race". In these words, Jesuit Ignacio Alzina related the people's ancient belief of the origins of humankind in his *Historia de las islas e indios Visayas* in 1668. Alzina narrated the story of Laqui and Baie with complete incredulity and an air of irony not lacking in sarcasm: "this idea that we are grandchildren of the palms is not [imputed] to coconuts by any of the authors I have read who have written of this, and they are not a few".[24]

Was it perhaps the coconut's size and similarity to a human head, above all its three orifices that seem to mimic two eyes and a mouth, that led the Visaya to see in this fruit a divinity they traced back to the first birth? The Portuguese who sailed the waters of the Indian Ocean in the 16th century perceived such a morphological affinity but associated it with monkeys, so they are believed to be the first to call the fruit *coquo* or *côco*. In his *Coloquios dos simples e drogas da India* (1563), Garcia da Orta affirmed that authorship of the name belonged to those Lusitanian seamen, since the fruit's three orifices resembled the eyes and mouth of a monkey or some other animal,[25] similar to the mythical phantasm that scared misbehaving children or those who balked at going to bed.

The coconut palm (*Cocos nucifera* L.) has existed for millennia in diverse tropical populations on the Asian continent, providing entire societies not only with food and drink, but also shelter, clothing, and innumerable utensils for everyday life. This has led to it being called "the tree of life". Similar to Mesoamerican cosmogony which portrays humankind being created from corn –as mentioned in the *Popol Vuh* of the Quiché Maya– in the Visaya imaginary humans emerged from the coconut palm, the basis of the transcendence they attributed to that bounteous tree.

In the following pages we discuss the importance of the coconut palm in some Asian societies, especially India and the Philippines, before proceeding to an analysis of how the introduction of this tree impacted the coastal societies of New Spain in the second half of the 16th century through the aperture of transpacific trade with the Manila Galleon as its main protagonist. But before exploring these aspects in depth, we should clarify key botanical features of the palm tree to give the reader a better understanding of the origins of *vino de cocos*.

THE COCONUT PALM: SOME BOTANICAL FEATURES

The coconut palm is a member of the Arecaceae family. Its scientific name, *Cocos nucifera* L, was given in the 18th century by Carlos Linnaeus. He called them *cocos* because by that time the Portuguese name was in common use as far away as Europe, while *nucifera* refers to the nut or shell of its fruit. Today, this tree is found in tropical and subtropical regions on every continent, between 26° north-south latitude, and at altitudes as high as 1200 meters above sea level. It thrives in climates with limited seasonal fluctuations, average temperatures above 20°C, and mean annual precipitation around 1000-1800 mm, though it can withstand higher precipitation in soils with good drainage. It develops best in sandy, alluvial-type soils with organic matter and a pH of 5-8. To achieve optimal growth, minimum soil depth must be 80-100 cm. Due to its capacity to grow in sandy soils susceptible to flooding, the palm tree has developed important adaptive mechanisms, including an extensive root system that allows it to resist high winds.[26] Coconut palms are, in fact, often the only things left standing after a hurricane devastates a region.

Coconut palms begin to produce fruit 5-7 years after the seed is planted. Inflorescence occurs year-round. Trees can reach heights of 30 m and have leaves that measure as much as 5-6 m in length. They are differentiated by size as "dwarf" or "tall" trees. The former make up around 5% of all palm trees cultivated worldwide, located mainly on the outskirts of populated areas, which suggests that their presence may reflect a process of human selection since their fruits are closer to the ground and easier to exploit for domestic uses. Tall palms, in contrast, grow more quickly.

Many are exploited to obtain copra to produce oil or extract fiber from the shells.[27] This indicates clearly that palm trees undergo phenotypical changes as they are selected for cultivation by humans.

Illustration 1. Morphology of Cocos nucifera L.[28]

PALM TREE
(*Cocos nucifera* L.)

The palm tree's physiological hardiness allows it to tolerate saline soils, alkaline conditions, and occasional frosts, but plantations in coastal areas are usually established in sandy soils poor in organic matter. For this reason, in his *Tractado de las drogas y medicinas de las Indias Orientales* (published in Burgos in 1578), Cristóbal de Acosta affirmed that palm trees were fertilized with water, ash, and ox or carabao dung.[29] Ash and dung are rich in organic matter, so similar information appears in some botanical works, like the book on New Spain by the *protomédico* (physician) Francisco Hernández.[30] Today, the elements deemed essential for optimal nutrition of coconut trees are nitrogen, potassium, calcium, magnesium, sulfur, iron, and chlorine.[31]

According to recent research by Bee F. Gunn et al., the coconut palm originated independently in two basins, one in the Pacific Ocean, the other in the Indian Ocean. The trees must have evolved in those two regions and been domesticated simultaneously, culminating in two autonomous centers of domestication: a) from the Malacca peninsula to New Guinea; and b) southern India, including Sri Lanka, the Maldives, and the Laccadive Islands. These data reflect the latest research based on genetic analyses and archaeobotanical and historical sources, which suggest that coconut palms were being cultivated in southern India around 2500-3000 years ago.[32]

On the phenomenon of coconut palm domestication, Hugh C. Harries explains that humans were not interested in modifying the size of the fruit –already very large– or the number of fruits in each cluster, though these processes are evident in other vegetable species. Instead, human selection increased water and food content by as much as 50% compared to the endosperm of the original fruit, while substantially reducing the proportion of the hard outer shell that covers the skin from 70 to just 35%, the exact thickness necessary to protect the fruit and buffer the impact of falls from heights of 30 m.[33]

The other aspect of domestication evident in coconut trees is the form –phenotype– of the fruit, with two predominant types being recognized worldwide. The first is an oblong –or triangular– fruit with a large amount of husk for fiber. In Polynesian language, it is called *niu kafa*.[34] According to Harries, this kind of fruit is characterized by a high dissemination capacity through flotation, while its angular form impedes it from moving –as occurs with round coconuts– so it remains on land instead of rolling toward the sea. The fruits elongated shape and flat base allowed it to serve as a vessel or cup, similar to the way in which diverse American peoples used gourds (*Crescentia* and *Lagenaria*) as recipients. The second type is called *niu vai* in Polynesian. It is characterized by its round shape, bright color, and higher water content.[35]

Another characteristic of coconut palms is their high natural capacity for dispersion. According to Foale, through a process of natural selection, the coconut developed the means to disperse over vast oceanic areas and take firm root in perilous border regions between land and sea. It has also resisted, and adapted to, severe storms and periodic floods while casting its fruits into the oceans to spread to ever more distant lands.[36] Before the emergence of humans, Foale continued, the coconut had reached thousands of islands and continental shores across the tropical Pacific Ocean, from the islands of southeastern Asia to the coasts of the Indian Ocean. The Atlantic Ocean, however, missed out on this natural dissemination because no ocean currents connected it to the Indian Ocean. Thus, it was not until the 16th century that the palm tree was introduced into those regions, finally reaching the shores of the Atlantic thanks to European sailors, as we will see below.[37]

THE COCONUT TREE IN INDIA AND THE PHILIPPINES

Almost everything we know about the uses and handling of coconut palms by ancient societies in tropical Asia we owe to Arabic and European sources. There are, certainly, relevant archaeobotanical studies that have traced this tree for millennia, but the details, minutiae, and firsthand information on the multiple uses of the coconut palm were recorded by the Arabs, Portuguese, Spanish, Dutch, and English during their maritime expeditions along the route of the spice trade.[38]

In the 15th century, the Portuguese began to dominate the Atlantic; first by occupying the Madeiras and Azores, then gradually penetrating into the "eerie sea" and skirting the coasts of Africa. Don Enrique El *Navegante* (1394-1460), who earned this name by propelling Portugal's projects of maritime expansion, was a pillar of early European penetration into Asia. In a short time, he formed a group of astronomers, geographers, and able seamen in the period that began the apogee of the sailing vessels called *carabelas* (caravels). Under his auspices, the team ventured into Senegal, Cabo Verde, Guinea, and Sierra Leone, where they debunked the myth of the existence of sea monsters that attacked crews as they sought to sail further south. In that context, on July 8, 1497, a small but hopeful fleet departed from Lisbon *en route* to Calicut through the waters of the Indian Ocean. It was commanded by Vasco da Gama who sailed aboard the *São Gabriel*, accompanied by four other ships that carried some 150 seamen. As they prepared to head out, a crowd accompanied a procession through the streets of Lisbon to honor the crew. Those intrepid ocean adventurers, candles in hand, received absolution in the form of a bull that don Enrique had obtained for those who might meet their death in the conquests and discoveries undertaken in the name of the Portuguese Crown.[39] It took da Gama two years to complete the round trip between Lisbon and Calicut, though part of the route had been mapped years earlier by his compatriot, Bartolomeu Dias, who gave the Cape of Good Hope, the extreme southern tip of the African continent, its name.

In early March 1498, Vasco da Gama was close to Mozambique. Nicolau Coelho, the captain of one of the ships, was sure they had entered the territory of Muhammad because inhabitants spoke "the language of the Moors", wore turbans, and were governed by a sultan.[40] In those lands peopled, he assumed, by Mohammedan Muslims, he saw palm trees laden with fruits as large as melons with edible pulp inside that had a sweet flavor similar to hazelnuts.[41] Without doubt, he was referring to coconut palms, though his writings do not mention this name. On the fleet's return voyage from Calicut to Lisbon in September, 1498, people on an island in Indian territory called Angédive offered them the same fruits. That was the moment when the *Roteiro da viagem em descobrimento da India* recorded the word *coquos* in reference to those melon-sized fruits, possibly for the first time in history.[42] The viands that the governor and his people gave Da Gama included *coquo* fruit, among others.

In 1500, when the expedition led by the Portuguese Pedro Alvares Cabral returned to India, King don Manuel's heroic sailors piqued his curiosity by informing him of a strange tree from which diverse things could be extracted for human consumption. He shared that novelty with the Catholic Kings:

> And from these trees [coconut palms] and their fruit are made the following things: sugar, honey, oil, wine, water, vinegar, charcoal, and cordage for ships, and for everything else, and matting of which they make some sails for ships, and it serves them for everything they need. And the aforesaid fruit, in addition to what is thus made of it, is their chief food, particularly at sea.[43]

But don Manuel did not mention the name of "those trees" that Portuguese sailors described after crossing the Indian Ocean. Was the plant perhaps unknown to Europeans of the time? In reality, no, because in the 13th century Marco Polo had noted the existence of some "trees similar to [date] palms" that he decided to call "*noce dall'India*". He only mentioned that people extracted a liquor,

Part I

"white and red as wine and very perfect for drinking".⁴⁴ There can be no doubt that he was referring to the sap of the palm tree, with which people elaborated a fermented drink called *tuba*. But he did not give this much importance nor did he describe that palm tree –so similar to the date palm– so his brief mention passed unnoticed among the fabulous tales of rich spices and precious stones that this traveler made great efforts to disseminate. The name that Marco Polo chose may reflect the fact that the Arabs of the lands through which he had passed, called the fruit *narel* or *jausialindi*; that is, the "nut of India", since it was taken from there to the Strait of Ormuz in the form of copra; the substance we know today as grated coconut.

Thanks to the writings of the Moroccan Ibn Battuta, a Muslim who traveled through the Mideast and southeast Asia in the 14th century, we have the first description of the coconut palm and its benefits. Battuta spent almost a year and a half in the Maldives between 1344 and 1345, where he observed how coconut oil, milk, and honey were obtained. He also narrated the process of obtaining sap, which involved servants "climbing trees at dawn", though he did not clarify if the liquid obtained was consumed as a fermented or distilled drink.⁴⁵ A century and a half later, another Italian traveler, Ludovico de Varthema, undertook a voyage that would last almost five years and take him through the Mideast and southeast Asia. De Varthema yearned to form part of the first wave of western explorers to visit those exotic lands that held such fascination for Europeans. He is recognized as the first non-Muslim European to enter Mecca as a pilgrim; after his fellow countryman, Marco Polo, two centuries earlier, had performed the feat of completing the journey along the Silk Route with great success. This voyager from Bologna reached India around 1505, where he described the customs of the inhabitants, especially the uses and processing of what he considered "the most fructiferous tree in the world": the coconut palm.

De Varthema's description is the most complete European reference of his time. Although the Portuguese knew of the tree by then, the details of its use, the methods employed to distill *tuba*, and the nutritional importance of the tree for the people of India only became known with the publication of the *Itinerario de Ludovico de Varthema, bolognese*, in Rome in 1510, a work that later appeared in translations in Europe. That tireless traveler devoted an entire chapter of *Itinerario* to the palm tree, calling it "the best tree in the world", though he referred to it as *tenga*, a word from the local language.[46] De Varthema attributed a dozen benefits to the coconut palm, for it provided firewood, nuts to eat, ropes for sailing, thin textiles that, when dried, appeared to be made of silk, fuel of the greatest perfection, wine, water, sugar, and leaves for roofing houses.

From the decade of 1560 onwards, various European authors included information related to the palm tree in their writings. In his *Tercera década* (1563), João de Barros –recognized as one of the first great Portuguese historians– described innumerable benefits of the coconut palm in the Maldives, south of India.[47] In that same year, the physician and naturalist Garcia da Orta wrote in his *Coloquios dos simples e drogas da India* of the abundance of palm trees in the Maldives, boasting that the Portuguese had been the first to call the fruit *coquo* because of its three orifices that resembled the face of a monkey or other animal.[48] While traveling through Cape Verde in 1578, the Englishman Francis Drake mentioned that the palm trees there had no equal in Europe, and that the liquor extracted from its sap was "very good and flavorful" and inebriated men who drank it to excess. Referring to coconut fruit, he wrote that it was extremely good, delicate, delicious, and cordial.[49]

The Spanish came to know the fruit of the coconut physically in the first half of the 16th century when it was introduced into the Iberian Peninsula by the Portuguese. In his *Tractado de las drogas y medicinas de las Indias Orientales*

(1578), Cristóbal de Acosta confirmed that this fruit, which "the Portuguese call the coconut because of its three holes, was brought to Spain".[50] Thus, when they encountered the fruit in Spanish America they did not hesitate to apply its Portuguese name. Acosta based much of his description of the coconut palm on Portuguese sources, especially Garcia da Orta. As a result, while the Lusitanians were introducing coconut trees from the Indian region into Europe and America, the Spanish were doing the same with the tree from the Philippines.

Turning now to the Philippines, the first written references to the coconut tree there appear in Chau Ju-kua's chronicles of Chinese and Arab commerce in the 12th and 13th centuries, which mention the tree's importance as a food and beverage, and the use of the nut as a recipient. In the period prior to the arrival of the Spanish, natives in the Palawan region in the extreme west of the Philippines elaborated mats with coconut fiber that they traded with the Chinese for silks and porcelain objects.[51] A few centuries later, in the *Primo viaggio attorno al mondo* by Antonio de Pigafetta, the Vicentine chronicler of Fernando de Magallanes' expedition to the Philippines in 1521, described multiple uses of the palm tree on the Mariana Islands (Guam), known then as the *Islas Ladrones*. But it was not until the Spanish colonization of the Filipino archipelago that descriptions of *Cocos nucifera* multiplied. Works like the one by the Jesuit Francisco Ignacio Alzina on the history of the Visaya Indians (1668), devoted whole chapters to the bounties of the coconut tree, while in 1837 the Augustinian Manuel Blanco concentrated the knowledge on the palm tree accumulated up to that time in his *Flora de Filipinas*, adding his own observations, as we mention below (see Table 1).

In what seems to have been almost a contest, Europeans vied to coin the phrase that best sang the praises of the coconut palm. De Varthema referred to it as "the most fructiferous tree that exists in the world".[52] Father Alzina wrote, "with much reason we can say that the coconut palm takes the laurels among all trees, for it seems that nature deposited more prodigiously and liberally in her than in all others, and [...] most everything with which it is endowed provides in one sole trunk of this palm almost everything that is necessary for human life.[53] William Dampier penned that it was "possibly of all others the most generally serviceable to the conveniences, as well as the necessities of human life",[54] while Manuel Blanco affirmed that the coconut palm was "an excellent tree, among the most admirable and useful for man".[55] João de Barros wrote that it was one of the most beneficial things that God had given man for his sustenance,[56] and Garcia da Orta mentioned that it offered so many necessary things that no other tree gave even the sixth part.[57] In his *Historia del Gran Reyno de la China* –originally published in Rome in 1585–, Juan González de Mendoza observed that "among the notable things that our people have seen in those islands [the Philippines], the one that has most compelled them to admire and commit to memory, is a tree usually called the coconut palm".[58] One would be hard put, indeed, to find such praise for one specific plant in so many different languages!

THE USE AND MANAGEMENT OF THE COCONUT PALM IN ASIAN SOCIETIES

By the end of the 17th century, knowledge of the use and management of the coconut palm in Asian societies was current in Europe. In fact, at that time comparisons were made between two or more nations, from Goa, the Maldives, Sumatra, and Timor to the Philippines and the Mariana Islands. Dampier, for example, compared uses from Goa, the Maldives, Sumatra, and the Marianas. Broadly speaking, all those informants mentioned at least six areas of use, including food, medicine, housing, dress, navigation, and utensils (Table 1).

Part I

As a food, coconut trees provided not only food and drink, but also derived products like oil, vinegar, milk, fermented and distilled drinks, honey, and sugar. Father Alzina stated that the "meat" (pulp) of the coconut was grated and expressed to obtain a kind of thick white milk, similar to cow's milk, that could be substituted for almond milk. The Visaya Indians called this *natuc* and used it as an ingredient in a wide variety of local dishes that Spaniards on the archipelago soon incorporated into their own meals. According to Alzina, "the Spaniards prepare various dishes, especially rice, that is not inferior to that cooked in Spain with goat's and sheep's milk".[59] Dampier witnessed that English sailors also adopted that culinary practice. In both Southeast Asia and part of India, coconut milk was added to cooked rice, a custom that Europeans learned from the natives.[60] Copra, the hard, dry pulp of the coconut, could be carried on long voyages because it kept so well. Garcia da Orta's account affirms that copra was taken from India to the Strait of Ormuz, and from there Arabs traded it in other areas. In the 14th century, Ibn Battuta himself wrote that the honey extracted from coconut trees in the Maldives was sold to merchants from India, Yemen, and China to prepare sweets.[61]

Table 1. The coconut palm and its benefits, according to chroniclers (12th-19th centuries)[62]

Year	Source	Place	Uses observed
12th c.	Chau Ju-kua	The Philippines	Foods Fruit, water Utensils Gourds, mats
1344	Ibn Battuta	Maldives	Foods Fruit, water, milk, oil, honey Navigation Ropes for ships Utensils Spoons, fuel for lamps, hair conditioner
1505	Ludovico de Varthema	Calicut (India)	Foods Fruit, bread, oil, sugar, water, wine House Leaves for roofing Navigation Ropes for ships Utensils Fibers for clothing, firewood
1521	Antonio Pigafetta	Marianas	Foods Fruit, milk, oil, water, wine, vinegar House Leaves for roofing Utensils Fiber for lounge chairs and recipients, oil for personal care
1563	João de Barros	Maldives	Foods Fruit, oil, honey, wine, vinegar Navigation Ropes for ships Utensils Leaves for making paper
1563	Garcia da Orta	Maldives	Foods Fruit, copra, milk, sugar, water, wine, vinegar Navigation Wood, ropes, and caulking for ships Utensils Cups

PART I

Year	Source	Place	Uses observed
1598	John H. van Linschoten	India	Foods Drink, edibles, milk, oil, vinegar, wine House Construction materials Utensils Hats, ropes, cups, mats, fuel Navigation Construction of complete boats, ropes for ships, textiles for sails
1611	Blas de la Madre de Dios	The Philippines	Medicine Coconut water for fever; milk for hemorrhoids; tuba with eggs for asthma and the chest; vino de cocos with ground clove for colds, "buzzing in the ears", mange; oil for cough, erysipelas, dyschezia (constipation), vomiting blood, asthma, carnosities.
1668	F. Ignacio Alzina	The Philippines	Foods Fruit, milk, honey, oil, water, wine, vinegar House Wood for pillars Navigation Cloth for sails, caulking for ships Utensils Leaves for mats and brooms, cords for arquebus wicks, shell for plates, cups for chocolate, firewood, ash for soap, textiles for jackets, sacks, and saddlebags Medicine Tuba (sap) to reduce liver inflammation, cure urinary pain, eliminate pulmonary obstructions, and clean the stomach, oil to reduce inflammation, and as a laxative
1686	William Dampier	Marianas	Foods Fruit, milk, oil, water, wine Navigation Ropes for ships, cloth for sails Utensils Cups, plates, spoons
ca. 1670-1698	Ignacio Mercado	The Philippines	Foods Oil, honey, vinegar, wine Medicinal To treat the kidneys, as a laxative Utensils Vessels, cups, spoons, ropes, cable, mats, brooms, soap, fuel

Year	Source	Place	Uses observed
1837	Manuel Blanco	The Philippines	Foods Fruit, milk, sugar, water, wine, vinegar House Leaves for roofing Navigation Ropes and caulking for ships Utensils Pitchers, cups for chocolate, soap, dye, beads for rosaries Medicine Water and wine to cure tuberculosis, gonorrhea, hernias, and stomach ailments

Three types of drinks are obtained from the coconut palm: coconut water, fermented sap, and distilled sap. Coconut water was the most common one, as people had only to crack open the shell to obtain the liquid inside. A more complex technique was utilized to produce alcoholic drinks for it involved carefully cutting the buds or inflorescences on the trees. We will explore this technique in greater detail below, but it is important to elucidate this procedure. The sap was collected in small recipients twice a day. It was called çura in India, but *tuba* or *tubâ* in the Philippines. The liquid was left to ferment for a few days until an alcohol content of 6 to 8 degrees was obtained. If it fermented for a longer period it turned into vinegar. If a drink with higher content alcohol was desired, the *tuba* was distilled to reach a graduation above 40 degrees. That drink was called *arrak, alak, urraca* or *orraqua* –a word of Arabic origin– a name also known in the Philippines. The Spaniards, however, christened it as *vino de cocos*, a beverage equivalent to the drink known today as *lambanog*.

Coconut fiber had multiple uses, including making garments. Referring to India, de Varthema wrote that people made a kind of short pants (*bombachas*) with this fiber, which was similar to linen.[63] Antonio Pigafetta noted that women on the Ladrones Islands (Marianas) dressed in a thin, supple cloth made from palm tree bark[64] that also served to make sails for some ships and utensils for daily life, such as bags and nets for storing food. Father Alzina added that Spaniards used the fibers as matchlocks for their arquebuses.[65]

In addition to cloth for sails, coconut fiber was widely used to make several kinds of ropes and cords that were highly-valued by sailors because, as Garcia da Orta wrote, they were resistant to saltwater.[66] Sailors also used coconut oil to lubricate ropes,[67] fiber as a base for caulking their ships,[68] and burned shells as fuel. Europeans learned from the natives, adopted their practices, and adapted them so that hemp, which they were always struggling to obtain, was gradually replaced by fibers from Asia (such as abaca, *Musa textilis* L.), which they recognized as optimal materials for the nautical world.

In other references to palm trees and navigation, the Augustinian friar Juan González de Mendoza affirmed in his *Historia de las cosas más notables, ritos y costumbres del Gran Reyno de la China* (Roma, 1585) that the coconut palm was an admirable, bountiful, mysterious tree that served to make ropes, cords, sails, masts, and spikes for ships. Almost all the ships that passed through the Philippines were made of palm trees, and merchants on board traded blankets made "with great beauty and subtlety" from their bark. De Mendoza added that inhabitants of the Maldives survived thanks to the bounty of the coconut palm, which "has this and many other virtues, that I have mentioned, in part, because they are so noteworthy that they cause admiration among all those who pass through those parts, [I] refrain from saying more so as not to extend this".[69] An especially interesting fact is that João de Barros recorded how natives in the Maldives made paper from coconut fiber.[70]

The use of the coconut palm in architecture in southeast Asia is well known, especially for the roofs of *palapas*, a word brought to New Spain by Philippine immigrants aboard the Manila Galleon. Palm leaves served to cover the roofs of homes, and wood from the trunk served well as posts and pillars. Of course, those materials were combined with others from the region, as in the typical Filipino house called *bahay kubo*, which was completed with the *nipa* plant (*Nypa fruticans*). The practice of making mats and lounge chairs from the leaves was recorded in both the Philippines and the Marianas, where brooms were included. Nuts or shells were used mainly as recipients for numerous tasks and as plates, cups, spoons, and even cups for chocolate (*cocos chocolateros*), highly appreciated among well-off families in Spanish America. It is curious that when referring to the experience of the Visaya world Alzina mentioned that the cups made from coconut shells were known as *tecumates*;[71] that is, the Mesoamerican *tecomates*, from the Náhuatl word *tecomatl*, clear evidence that certain Nahuatlisms were introduced into the Philippines through the transpacific voyages of the Manila Galleon. Another use of the shell was to elaborate beads for rosaries, as mentioned by Manuel Blanco (see Table 1).

On the topic of personal grooming, Pigafetta observed that women in Guam used coconut oil –and sesame seed oil– to soften their skin and hair.[72] Referring to daily hygiene in the Philippines, Father Blanco stated that the burned shoots and leaves of palm trees were a source of "a very good lye" for making soap.[73] Alzina's observations of the Visaya islands included the comment that "the ashes of burned palms, which are no good for anything else, [are used] to make lye that, when mixed with a bit of lime, makes a lovely, hard white soap that cleans very well".[74]

Finally, the coconut palm and its derivatives were much appreciated in traditional Asian medicine, a subject on which the Spanish clergymen Alzina and Blanco wrote widely. Coconut water cured stomach ailments and eliminated "worms", while *tuba*, Alzina wrote:

> Is not only a widely offered, healthful drink as everyone knows from daily experience, but [also] a very good medi-

cine because it refreshes the blood, reduces liver inflammation, eliminates lung obstructions [and] softens the abdomen and its distensions [...] it is said to cure everything since many who find no [other] remedy for their chronic illnesses find it helps to drink said *tuba*.[75]

Tuba was highly esteemed on many Pacific islands, where natives used it to cure an illness called beriberi (*berber*), caused by a vitamin B deficiency, which causes swelling and weakening of the limbs. Thanks to the work *Conquista de las Molucas* by the Aragonese Bartolomé Leonardo Argensola, dedicated to King Felipe III in 1609, we know that natives in that region cured beriberi by ingesting a mixture of *vino de cocos*, cloves, and ginger:

> According to Juan de Barros, a serious historian, these islands [Moluccas] are pleasant to the sight, but unhealthy, [especially] for foreigners, who are susceptible to the beriberi disease that is common in that land. It swells the body [and] weakens the limbs, but with cloves and wine from the Philippines ingested with ginger, or with the use of a certain herb known to the natives, they are cured and return to health [...] the Dutch [add] lemon juice, a remedy found through fear and experience.[76]

This extract from Argensola –based on Juan de Barros' *Décadas*– and the previous references led us to reflect on the importance that the palm tree had not only for local societies but also for the Europeans who ventured into Asian waters over several centuries. It is well known that alcoholic beverages provided sailors with calories, but not nutrients, as they were stored in the liver in the form of fat.[77]

Many descriptions by Europeans, and even Arabs, compared the coconut palm to the date palm. The Moroccan traveler, Ibn Battuta, stated: "the coconut palm is similar to the date tree: the only difference between the two is that the fruits of the former are nuts and of the latter, dates".[78] The date palm was better known in the Middle East and Mediterranean region, where it rivaled the coconut tree in terms of cultural importance. Titus Burckhardt observed that the arrangement of the arches supported on columns in Arab architecture simulated the branches of a date palm, while the columns themselves resembled their trunks, as is evident in the famous mosque in Córdoba, Spain. For Arabs on the Peninsula, the date palm was "the symbol by antonomasia of the far away homeland... for an Arab, a palm tree is more than just a tree".[79] With those words we close the section on the "tree of marvels", whose bounties crossed to the other shore of the Pacific.

THE COCONUT PALM IN THE NEW WORLD

The arrival of *Cocos nucifera* L. to the American continent has generated one of the most passionate debates in the history of plants. In the late 19th century, the Swiss botanist Alphonse de Candolle affirmed, in his famous book *Origine des plantes cultivées*, that the origin of the coconut palm was an "obscure question" that excellent, renowned authors had resolved in different ways.[80] Indeed, while the scientific community recognizes the coconut palm as native to the Asian continent, in the early 20th century authors like the North American botanist Orator Fuller Cook suggested that *C. nucifera* was native to the American continent as well.[81] That hypothesis was later disproven, but it is widely accepted that the coconut palm did in fact exist in Central America when the Spaniards arrived in the early 16th century. But how did it get there? Could it have been without human help? And what role did the Spanish and Portuguese play in its expansion into America? These are the questions we try to answer in what follows.

Part I

The Polynesian Route

It is to Gonzalo Fernández de Oviedo, chronicler of Hispaniola, that we owe the first news of the coconut palm on the Central American strip. Oviedo traveled to the Indies with the Panama expedition led by Pedrarias Dávila in 1513, where he had the opportunity to gather firsthand information on the society and the environment where it developed. Upon his return from the second voyage to Indian lands in 1523, he published the *Sumario de la natural historia de las Indias*, in Toledo in 1526, where he described "these palms or coconuts" of which "there are many on the coast of the Mar del Sur, in the province of the cacique Chiman, many more in what they call Borica, and still many more on an island in the austral gulf in the sea at a hundred leagues or more off the coast of Peru".[82] Oviedo's description of the palm tree is quite detailed and similar to some given by authors from settings in Asia, so the information he provided has spurred controversy: where did he obtain it, and on what precise date did he "see" what he narrated? Here we need to tread cautiously.

The year 1514 is usually taken as the date when Oviedo "observed" those trees in the places mentioned above, but as Víctor Manuel Patiño has pointed out, at that time Panama had not yet been founded, the southern coast was little known, and the expedition to Borica had not taken place, though Oviedo mentioned all those places in his *Sumario*.[83] Moreover, in later editions –recalling that his complete works were published in several phases– we read his own testimony: "I wrote all those things according to what *reached me, and what I understood, and, in part, what I saw* of those coconuts, when I wrote the repertory published in Toledo in the year fifteen hundred and twenty-six".[84] At the end of his narrative, Oviedo admitted that "after I wrote the repertory I have mentioned, I was in the province and at the point of Borica, and ate some of those coconuts and took many on to Nicaragua".[85] This indicates that his firsthand information may actually have been taken from other authors –a common practice at the time– and that he may have only confirmed in situ some characteristics of the coconut palm.

Another author who noted the presence of coconut palms in Central America in the early colonial period was Pedro Mártir de Anglería. Referring to Gil González Dávila's expedition in Nicaragua, he wrote in his *Tercera década*:

> On October fourteenth of this year, 1516, the aforementioned Rodrigo Colmenares and one Francisco de la Puente came to see me [...] Colmenares left Darién after the return of the defeated. Both recounted, the latter having heard it, the former as an eyewitness, that there are various islands in the austral sea, to the west of the Ensenada of San Miguel and Rica Island, where trees grow and are cultivated that give fruits similar to that of Colocut [Calicut], which with Cochin and Camemori, form the Portuguese perfume fair, so it can be inferred that the lands which produce all kinds of aromatic substances begin not far from there.[86]

This extract generates two reflections: on the one hand, Anglería did not call the "coconut" by name; on the other, it is symptomatic that he mentioned "trees that give fruits similar to that of Calicut", for this remits us to Ludovico de Varthema's *Itinerario*, published in Rome in 1510, whose description of the palm tree was based on the area of Calicut (Kerala, India). It was not until the *Quinta década*, composed between 1521 and 1523, that Anglería actually named the fruits of the coconut palm:

> There [in Natá, Panama], a great abundance of coconuts is found, a fruit whose merits we mentioned above, especially in the austral region where the flow of the sea bathes broad plains, one of which it is said, has an extension of 2 leagues that are wet when the tide rises [but] dry when it ebbs. It is said that coconut trees are born and grow spontaneously in those parts, but not in others, unless transplanted when young. Some think that the ocean current drags seeds of [the] tree there from places unknown and affirm that they have been transported to Hispaniola and Cuba from other areas of the Indies where they are native, as was once said

of cinnamon [that went] from the islands to the continent, arriving in [areas of] the south.[87]

If these early colonial sources confirm the existence of coconut palms on the American continent then we are obliged to ask, when and how did they arrive? Specialists in *Cocos nucifera* agree that its seeds can be spread by ocean currents and germinate at their destination without human help, as long as the conditions they encounter are suitable. Seeds can float for up to 110 days and, with favorable currents, travel up to 4,800 km. This suggests that the palm tree arrived in Central America from Polynesia at some still undetermined time thanks to the equatorial current in the Pacific Ocean (Map 1).[88]

Map 1. Route of the Dispersion of the Coconut Palm toward the Americas

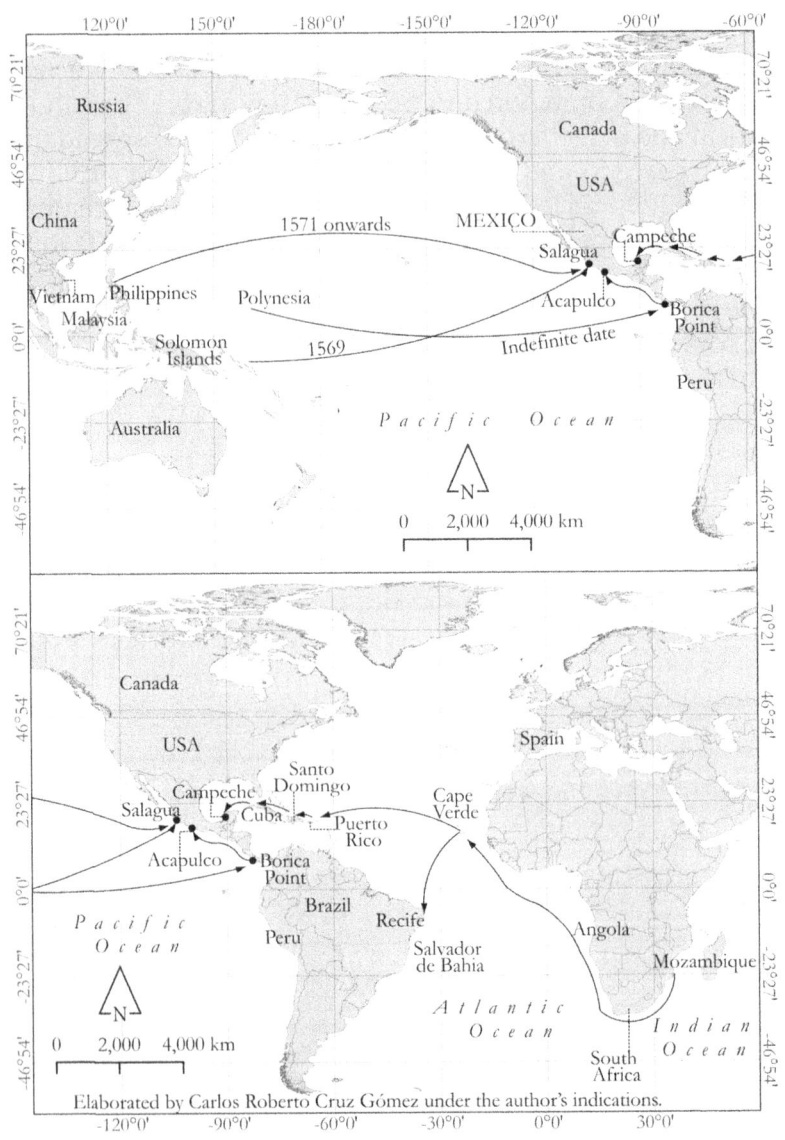

Elaborated by Carlos Roberto Cruz Gómez under the author's indications.

Part I

It is probable that some exemplars of coconut palms were sent from Central America to New Spain or, at least, that attempts were made to do so. While in Panama, Álvaro de Guijo sent a letter to Hernán Cortés, dated April 18th 1539, informing him that he was going to send him two dozen coconuts to be planted somewhere along the coast:

> I learned that *this fruit that we call coconut here does not exist there* [...] I sent one of my ships along the coast where one of these palms was and it brought back some two dozen [coconuts] that I send to you, my lord. You could have some of the more mature ones planted [...] in my view it would be good to [plant] them very shallow because they are born where the sea tends to [cover them...] if my lord feels he has been well served, on another occasion more could be sent [with] some seedlings.[89]

Here, Guijo confirms that reports had informed him of the absence of coconuts in New Spain, but also indicates that the tree had been introduced into Central America only a short time before. But were the seeds that he mentions in his letter really sent to New Spain and planted there? This is difficult to prove. Henry Bruman suggested the possibility that the seeds were carried on a ship called *San Lázaro* that sailed from Panama in April 1539 and would have arrived in Colima in June of that year, but this is a mere conjecture deduced from the dates on which the ship set out and other information that Cortés and Diego de Guinea, his agent in Oaxaca, exchanged. There is no firm evidence to confirm that those first coconut palms actually arrived and were planted in Colima.[90] Bruman's hypothesis is also based on a comment by Friar Alonso Ponce that he noticed numerous coconut palms while walking the streets of Colima in 1586, "a most beautiful and dazzling tree".[91] Bruman inferred that those trees must have been the ones brought from Panama in the 1530s, but he could not review documentation in Colima which points out, as we will see below, that in 1569 Álvaro de Mendaña brought coconut palm seeds through the port of Salagua (today

Manzanillo, Colima). Since palms begin to produce fruit after 5 to 7 years, there is sufficient time to think that the coconut palms that Friar Ponce saw were actually those brought by Mendaña.

In summary, as Víctor Manuel Patiño affirms, the fact that Spaniards only saw coconut palms in the geographic region of Central America tells us that the tree had arrived on the American continent only shortly before, and that its dispersion had barely begun at the time of European colonization: "one must conclude that these [American] nations knew this palm for at least four generations, without exploiting it".[92] Henry Bruman calculated that the coconut palm arrived some 200 years before Columbus' first voyages,[93] but Gunn et al. came to a bolder conclusion, arguing that the arrival of coconut palms in Central America may well have occurred around 2,250 years ago.[94] That date, however, seems unlikely because if this were the case the tree would certainly have spread into what is today the territory of Mexico over pre-Hispanic maritime and terrestrial trade routes that we know carried a continuous flow of plants like corn, pineapple, and annatto (*achiote*).[95] In addition, two thousand years of coexistence with a tree as bounteous as the coconut palm would have sufficed to generate a cultural attachment comparable to that of the Asian world, but no such phenomenon emerged in the Americas. It is important to keep in mind here information from the English sailor William Dampier who complained, in 1686, that while the coconut palm was of great utility and highly esteemed in the East, in the West Indies it was hardly exploited at all: "Yet this Tree, that is of such great use, and esteemed so much in the East Indies, is scarce regarded in the West Indies, for want of the knowledge of the benefit which it may produce. And it is partly for the sake of my Country-men, in our American Plantations, that I have spoken so largely of it".[96] Here, Dampier proclaims himself a promoter of the benefits of the coconut palm in the Caribbean region.

Part I

The African Route

A second route for the introduction of Cocos nucifera L. to the American continent was across the Atlantic Ocean, an incursion that would have involved Portuguese navigation routes. Hugh C. Harries traced its dispersion from Mozambique, in East Africa, around the Cape of Good Hope to Cape Verde, and then to Puerto Rico.[97] From there, it could have followed two paths: toward Brazil, or along the route to Santo Domingo, Cuba, Veracruz, Campeche, and Yucatán (Map 1). The Descripción de Puerto Rico, elaborated in 1582 by the governor and justicia mayor (chief justice) of the city of San Juan, reported the following:

> There are hens from Guinea as large as those of Castille [that] sing like partridges and have the same taste as partridge. They are black, with a few white tinges. They are not native, having been brought in the year forty-nine [1549] by Diego Corenço, canon of Cape Verde, who brought the coconut palms to this island that have multiplied abundantly since orders were given to make mills for sugar production.[98]

This means that the first coconut palms from Africa were introduced into Puerto Rico in 1549 and spread from there across the Caribbean islands until they reached the shores of the Gulf of Mexico. In the 1550s, the tree was reported in Campeche and was seen in Veracruz around 1580.[99] The alcalde mayor [provincial magistrate] of that city, don Álvaro Patiño de Ávila, highlighted this in his Descripción de la ciudad de Veracruz y su comarca: "coconuts from Guinea, brought here from Cape Verde, also grow extremely well in this land. And this does not seem illogical [for] it is a species of palm [tree], of which there is an incredible abundance throughout this region".[100] Without doubt, the coconut trees on the Atlantic coast came from Africa and soon spread along the shores of the Gulf of Mexico.

The Asian and Melanesian Route

On January 22, 1569, the celebrated sailor from León, Spain, Álvaro de Mendaña y Neira, landed in the port of Salagua, Colima, aboard the ship *Los Reyes* after over a year spent exploring the Pacific islands, especially the Solomons, sufficient time for him to study the flora and fauna there. The arrival of Mendaña and his crew on the coast of Colima caused great unrest among local inhabitants who mistook them for Lutherans. Once calm was restored, the sailors began to unload exotic products from those far-off islands, including coconut palm seeds. Chronicles of that period do not mention details of this episode, so it was not until 1612 that Francisco Toscano Gorjón, a resident of the villa of Colima for over 60 years, evoked the moment when "a guy named Avendaño" –referring to Mendaña– left the first coconut palm seeds in the port of Salagua.[101] This means that in the memory of people in Colima, Mendaña is seen as the man who introduced one of the region's most cherished natural treasures.

Before long, the coconut palm began to modify the coastal landscape of the Pacific region of New Spain as it spread south from Colima toward Acapulco. The earliest recording of the presence of coconut palms on the Pacific coast of New Spain occurred in 1577, precisely in Colima, when six trees grew in Diego Morán's hacienda in the Caxitlán Valley,[102] just a few leagues from the port of Salagua and, as we will discuss in the chapter on the palm haciendas, an especially fertile area for cultivating the tree. By 1580, coconut palms had been planted in the neighboring jurisdiction of Motines,[103] a fact which confirms that the route of dissemination ran southward.

But the introduction of coconut palms from the Solomon Islands was not the only case. Thanks to instructions issued in 1580 by Viceroy Martín Enríquez de Almansa to Cosme del Campo, the *factor* of the port of Acapulco and the official in charge of the office that oversaw voyages to the islands of the East or the Philippines, we know that:

PART I

> Coconuts and tamarinds have been brought from islands in the East to be planted in the port and province of Acapulco, and have begun to grow and produce quite well. Those already planted will be well-tended and more will be added so they multiply.[104]

In general, the cultivation of coconut palms spread from the port of Salagua along two southward routes: one followed the littoral of the Alima Valley to reach Maquilí and Zacatula, then Tecpan and Acapulco. The other was from Maquilí and the Alima Valley into the region called *Tierra Caliente* (Hot Lands), passing through Coalcomán, Tepalcatepec, and Apatzingán on the way to La Huacana.[105] The historical documentation available, therefore, allows us to affirm that the introduction of coconut palms in the Mar del Sur began in Colima in 1569 after Álvaro de Mendaña's voyage through the Solomon Islands and, from the 1570s, in the port of Acapulco, after arriving directly from the Philippines (Map 2).

Map 2. Coconut Palm Dispersion in the Pacific Region of New Spain

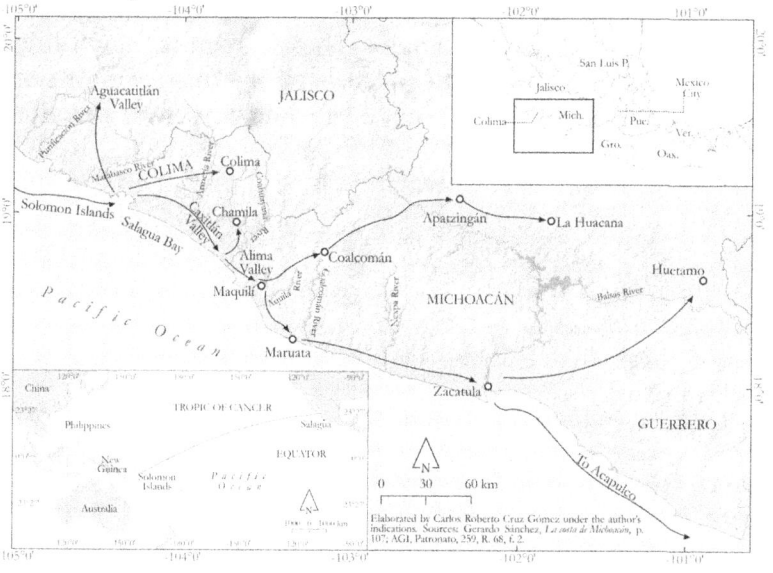

There are only minimal references to the cultivation practices of coconut palms after their arrival on the shores of the Mar del Sur, but we know that some people in Colima planted them in seedbeds. They first placed seeds in individual trays, allowed them to germinate, and then planted them in suitable sites. When Andrea Rosales, owner of a palm hacienda on the outskirts of the villa of Colima beside the Chiquito River, sold her property in 1691, she included a clause that bound the purchaser "to plant two hundred palm seedlings in the following year, then transplant them in places judged best for their cultivation, and tend them until they begin to produce".[106] This technique may have been practiced in other areas, but the dearth of sources does not allow us to affirm this.

COCONUT CULTURE AND ITS ROOTS IN THE MAR DEL SUR

If exploitation of coconut palms in diverse zones of the Mar del Sur began immediately, it was thanks to the presence of *indios chinos* (literally, "Chinese Indians"), especially people of Philippine origin, bearers from time immemorial of traditional knowledge of their care and uses. Table 2 shows the many benefits of these palms that residents of Colima enjoyed in 1612, a very early date when we consider that the tree was introduced in 1569 and began to give its first fruits from 1577 onward. Why did people in Colima begin to exploit it so quickly? The answer is, precisely, because Filipinos taught them how to utilize it for diverse facets of their daily lives, such as food, drink, medicine, and architecture.

Part I

Table 2. Benefits of the Coconut Palm according to Residents of Colima (1612)[107]

Resident	Age	Uses
Juan de Polonte (priest)	50	Food Oil, honey, vinegar, wine Medicine Cures phlegm, and gases, and heals wounds
Martín Alonso Enríquez	27	Food Oil, honey, wine, vinegar Medicine Cures illnesses and heals wounds
Juan García del Álamo	40	Food Oil, honey, vinegar, wine Medicine Cures phlegm, fever, and pain under the rib cage, and heals wounds
Hernán Gómez Machorro	-	Food Oil, honey, wine, and vinegar Medicine Cures colds, stomach pain, phlegm, gases, fever, and wounds
Matheo de Sepúlveda	60	Food Oil, honey, wine, vinegar Medicine Cures illnesses and pain under the rib cage
Juan Ruiz de Haro	50	Food Oil, honey, wine, vinegar Medicine Cures illnesses, heals wounds, and relieves pain and swelling
Sebastián de Vera	50	Food Oil, honey, wine, vinegar Navigation Boards, nails, topsails, sails, rigging, pitch, supplies, water for sailors, weapons for combat (observation from the Philippines) Medicine Cures illnesses, ague, and scorpion stings; the oil heals diverse wounds

Vino de Cocos, the Pilgrim Beverage

Resident	Age	Uses
Gabriel Muñoz	30	Food Oil, honey, wine, vinegar Medicine Cures illnesses, and heals wounds
Francisco Toscano Gorjón	90	Food Oil, honey, wine, vinegar Medicine Cures illnesses and heals wounds
Cristóbal de Herrera (physician)	60	Food Oil, honey, wine, vinegar Medicine Cures illnesses and evacuates the humors, is used in plasters, for sweating, infusions, and drinks
Hernando de Alarcón Vetancor	40	Food Oil, honey, milk, butter, wine, vinegar Medicine Cures illnesses, stomach pain, pain below the rib cage, and gases and heals wounds
Martín Hernández (physician)	45	Food Oil, honey, wine, vinegar Medicine Cures "severe, difficult" illnesses and heals wounds, cuts phlegm, and causes sweating to combat stings of scorpions and other vermin

Table 2 shows that the coconut palm immediately satisfied two basic needs for people in Colima: food and medicine. All these residents concurred that the oil, honey, and vinegar obtained from those trees served as substitutes for products that no longer arrived from Spain because of the long distance to Mexico City. Hernando de Alarcón Vetancor, for example, mentioned that butter and milk were also elaborated, "in small amounts for cooking rice".[108] This shows that Asian culinary practices also appeared on the tables of residents of Colima in the early 17th century.

But perhaps what those people mentioned most emphatically were the medicinal properties of the coconut palm and its derivatives, especially *tuba* and *vino de cocos*.

Part I

This was no accident, but something that circumstances demanded when the Real Audiencia of Mexico ordered that all palm trees in the jurisdiction be chopped down, alleging that the aguardiente produced from their sap was terribly harmful for people. But one resident, Sebastián de Vera, reported that he had witnessed how a negro (black) stung by a scorpion in a cacao orchard, "where they are most poisonous", was cured with *vino de cocos*.[109] He added:

> This witness [...] has seen how some *chinos* use the fruits of these palms oil, honey, and vinegar, to make an ointment with betony to heal wounds, both penetrating and old, when treating them with medicines from the dispensary brought for this did not heal them [...] so this oil is seen as a singular medicine of such benefit that when no other sustenance is available, the palm tree suffices for man, as Father Marín,[110] the venerable, learned Augustinian friar who [joined in] the conversion of Japan and the Great China, says in a book he composed and published on the grandeur of China; where in the Chapter that deals with the virtues of the palm tree [he writes] that [entire] boats are made from [it] tree because it [provides] boards, nails, topsails, sails, rigging, and pitch from a liquor made from it, supplies, water and weapons for combat; so people say *All that was left was for God to make men in those palm trees*.[111]

De Vera's testimony provides valuable historical data by confirming that *chinos* –that is, Filipinos– taught local people to extract the oil for use in both local cuisine and medicine. It is significant that de Vera, a nephew of don Santiago de Vera (governor of the Philippines from 1584 to 1590, and later President of the *Audiencia* of Nueva Galicia from 1593 to 1606) was familiar with the bounties of coconut palms in the Philippines. Clearly, people in Colima knew the category of the tree that was now growing in their midst.

Perhaps the area where coconut culture became most evident was architecture. According to Adolfo Gómez Amador, the most significant Filipino contribution to architecture was in the elaboration of roofs made of palm leaves, known as *palapas*, a word of Filipino origin that has endured in Mexico for centuries. Amador explained that the broad acceptance of the *palapa* along Mexico's coasts was due to "its suitability for local conditions, thanks to its similarity to the technology of the region and its morphology, so similar to the indigenous architecture of cultures [in western Mexico]".[112] The insertion of this type of architecture was due to at least three factors: a) its suitability for local geographic and climatic conditions; b) its similarity to the technology that existed in the region; and c) familiarity with the morphology of indigenous American and Filipino architecture.[113] As Amador pointed out, "in particular, construction techniques from the Philippines, lands exposed to earthquakes and hurricanes, adapted perfectly to lands in Colima subject to the same rigors of nature, to a quite similar climate, and a comparable landscape".[114]

In pre-Hispanic times in this coastal region, native palm trees –especially the genus *Orbingya*– supplied roofing material as their trunks "are often employed to build houses, though undoubtedly the greatest benefit is obtained from the leaves, the favored material for the roofs of homes".[115] Jerzy Rzedowski has written that leaves were also used to make hats, bags, mats, crafts, and utensils. Over time, the coconut palm progressively replaced the genus *Orbignya* (*cayaco* palm) along the Pacific coast because the ecological conditions that both require are so similar, but the coconut palm provides greater economic yield. The phenomenon of the displacement of the *cayaco* by the coconut palm is also visible in the state of Guerrero today, where the native tree has virtually disappeared due to the extensive cultivation of coconut palms.[116]

We do not know exactly when a type of protective outer garment (capote) made from the foliage of coconut palms –amply disseminated in southeast Asia– appeared in Colima, but from the very first moment it was known as a *china*. The capote, now on the verge of disappearing due to the introduction of plastic raincoats, provides additional evidence of Asian influence in the uses that local people made of this tree. It is symptomatic that this article of clothing was also called a *manga* in Colima, a word surely derived from the Filipino term *annanga*, used to refer to the capote (Photograph 1). While we cannot know for sure if people in New Spain made clothes from coconut fiber, there is evidence that similar garments were known in this area of the Pacific because an *alférez* (military officer) named Antonio Blanco, a resident of Coyuca, had among his possessions a pair of pants (*bombacha*) made of coconut linen "from China", adorned with fine stitching; and a resident of Manila was selling coconut cottons in Acapulco.[117] Juan Carlos Reyes argued that *angeo*, a kind of fibrous linen that grows at the base of palm tree leaves, was utilized in western Mexico to make sieves and saddles.[118]

Photograph 1. Raincoat Known as a China (Colima)

Left: an *annanga* in the Museo Crisologo Memorabilia (Ilocos Sur, the Philippines), photograph by Paulina Machuca. Right: a *china* from the collection at the Museo de Artes Populares "María Teresa Pomar" (Colima, Mexico), photograph by Florencio Amezcua Quiroz.

The art world did not escape from the wonders of the coconut palm. Once this tree appeared in the territory of New Spain, the nut of its fruit was coveted for making cups covered in silver called cocos chocolateros (Illustration 2). In his *Historia de las Plantas de la Nueva España*, Felipe II's physician, Francisco Hernández, wrote that from the nut "[they] produce the most beautiful cups, decorated with gold and silver [...] they have gained fame because they make the beverages most healthy and (through I know not what virtues) relieve paralysis and strengthen the nerves".[119] We found one of these cups listed in 1570 among the properties of doña Beatriz López, a resident of Colima, together with other objects from Asia. Unfortunately, we do not know their provenance.[120] In the 17th century, workshops in New Spain began to produce cocos chocolateros for markets both there and in Europe. At the same time, records of their existence in the property inventories of elites in Spanish America multiplied.[121] In 1755, for example, the inventory found upon the death of a Crown official named José de Laisequilla included 21 cocos chocolateros (or cocos de Indias), coated with silver. Laisequilla had worked in diverse *audiencias* in the Americas, allowing him to accumulate his collection.[122]

Illustration 2. Coco Chocolatero from San Luis Beltrán (ca. 1671)

Courtesy of the *Museu d'història de València*. Municipal government of Valencia. Photograph by Josep Manel Vert.

Final Reflections

In this chapter we have addressed the importance of the coconut palm in some Asian societies, especially in India and the Philippines, both recognized as centers of the origin and domestication of this tree that for millennia has provided food and drink, roofing material, medicines, and numerous utensils for daily life, so it became known as "the tree of life". Its importance transcended the utilitarian domain to become a symbolic, even mythical, element, as the creator of mankind in the cosmogony of peoples like the Visaya. But there are more examples, among them Ludovico de Varthema's narration of a well-known case from India where such enmity once existed between two kings that their animadversion resulted in the son of one of them being murdered. A slim possibility of reaching a peace accord between the enemy sovereigns persisted, but if one king were to cut down a coconut palm belonging to the other, all hope of peace would vanish forever.[123] Another is the fact that in the popular culture of the Maldives when people wish to emphasize the benefits of something, they say: "it is more fructiferous and bounteous than a palm tree".[124]

In the final years of the 17th century, upon the aperture of transpacific trade through the Manila Galleon, some of this *savoir faire* was taken from the distant Pacific shore to New Spain, where Mesoamerican culture had its own providential "tree of life": the maguey (*Agave* spp.), a plant comparable to the coconut palm in terms of utility and cultural importance. Suffice to recall that Francisco López de Gómara, author of the Historia de la conquista de México (1552), referred to the maguey (or *metl*) as a "good plant with so many uses and [widely] exploited by man",[125] and described its abundance in the lands of New Spain as being comparable to vineyards in Spain. He further observed that the maguey was a source of food, drink, medicine, shelter, dress, and utensils, virtually the same elements as the coconut palm.[126] This brought a convergence of botanical knowledge between the Asian and American worlds, complemented by the Mediterranean experience.

In ecological terms, the arrival of the coconut palm displaced some native palms and other trees called *cacahuanantzin* that gave the shade that cacao orchards required. In anthropological terms, the coconut tree provided people with food, drink, roofing material, and many utensils, but without doubt, the most highly-prized derivative in the 17th century was the aguardiente, *vino de* cocos. The coastal Pacific strip of New Spain witnessed the emergence of two new products, *tuba* and *vino de cocos*, that competed with pulque, at that time the "drink of the land", and even with wine from Castille. What were these two beverages of Asian origin, and how were they elaborated? This is the focus of the next chapter.

2. VINO DE COCOS: A TRAVELING TECHNIQUE FROM THE PHILIPPINES TO NEW SPAIN

> It is clear that our Filipinos, including our Visayans, do not lack [the means to cause] drunkenness, as they perhaps have more drinks that cause this than any other nation in the Universe.
>
> —Francisco Ignacio Alzina (1668)

INTRODUCTION

The exact dates of the genesis of the elaboration of *vino de cocos* in the Philippines and other areas around the Indian Ocean are unknown. On his voyage to Kerala (India) around 1505, the intrepid Italian explorer Ludovico de Varthema observed that inhabitants distilled a palm aguardiente so strong that simply inhaling its aroma, without imbibing a drop, "affected the brain" of whoever held it.[127] Varthema's description of the process of elaborating this "wine" —one of the earliest in European sources— coincides with many other versions related to *vino de cocos* written later that we find in the tales of Portuguese, Spanish, and English travelers, first in Asia, then in New Spain.[128]

As the process of Spanish colonization of the Philippines advanced, observers both civil and ecclesiastical reported the importance of *vino de cocos* on those islands and outlying areas. For example, in his *Historia de las cosas más notables, ritos y costumbres del gran Reino del China* (1585) the Augustinian friar Juan González de Mendoza wrote that *vino de cocos* "is drunk in all the islands [Philippines] and kingdoms of China". It was affordable and, in the absence of grape wine, the drink that circulated most widely in that region.[129]

This chapter is dedicated to analyzing the content of these descriptions with the objective of emphasizing that the techniques used to produce *vino de cocos* showed such similar patterns in places far distant from the Indian and Pacific Oceans that they probably arose from a common origin and were then dispersed along Indo-Pacific trade routes. The lines that follow are organized around two axes: the first examines European sources on *vino de cocos* in Asia that illustrate techniques, material culture, and forms of consumption; the second addresses the introduction of *vino de cocos* into New Spain and compares this to the Filipino context to establish similarities and differences between the two sides of the Pacific.

VINO DE COCOS IN THE SOCIETIES OF THE PHILIPPINES

We should inform readers that in this chapter they will encounter a direct dialogue between colonial historical sources and an ethnographic present that has allowed us to reconstruct the pieces of a long-dispersed puzzle. The analysis is written in the present tense because it deals with a process that has changed very little over several centuries.

The Technique for Extracting *Tuba*: The First Step

The process of obtaining sap from coconut palms begins when men –called *tuberos* or *manananggot/mananguete*– climb those trees. The *tuberos* first carve several cuts in the trunk of the tree to serve as steps. Those cuts are usually made in the shape of an "A" and their size must allow the *tubero* to place the soles of his feet securely, for if they do not, he risks slipping and falling from heights so great that the impact can be fatal. Due to this peril, some men reduce the danger by tying a rope around their backs and securing it to the tree. Since they have to collect sap from several coconut palms, it is common to see wooden or bamboo bridges constructed to interconnect various trees from which they will gather sap for *vino de cocos* production. This facilitates extraction while diminishing –but by no means eliminating– the risk of accidents as they climb up and down the trees (see Photograph 2).

In the second half of the 17th century, Father Alzina was amazed to see Visaya Indians scaling palm trees carrying tubes called *cañutos* full of sap, "with a nonchalance that causes admiration among those who are dumbfounded while watching them".[130] In the 18th century, Father Manuel Blanco, a writer more cautious in his affirmations, mentioned in his *Flora de Filipinas* that "when they collect *tuba* from many palms, the Indians make small bridges from tree-to-tree that they traverse with great agility, but not without terrible falls".[131] For good reason then, before beginning their ascent *tuberos* make offerings to Mankukutod, the protector of coconut palms.[132] In 1875, a German named Fedor Jagor, while traveling through Santa Cruz in the Philippine region of Laguna on the island of Luzon, noted that "since sap is gathered twice a day [...] it is necessary to [place] pairs of bamboo [stalks] from trunk-to-trunk to avoid the bother of continuously climbing up and down; thus the worker walks along the lower [stalk] supporting himself by the upper one that serves as a handrail".[133] It almost seems like Jagor's description was written in our time, for one can still see *tuberos* there walking along bamboo bridges just as their ancestors had done (Photograph 2).

Once aloft and facing the crown of the tree, the *tubero* has to choose and clean the spadix and remove all the dry leaves around it. He then bends the inflorescence slightly downward from its natural erect, vertical position to allow the sap to flow out into a recipient carefully placed to catch the liquid. Because the inflorescence is such a delicate part of the coconut palm, the *tubero* must twist and squeeze it slowly and gently, aided by bundles of thin leaves from the tree itself or cords of natural fibers available in the area, such as *abacá* (*Musa textilis*) or rattan (*Raphia* spp.). One false move in this delicate operation can detach the inflorescence, making it impossible to extract more sap (Photograph 3).

Photograph 2. Bamboo Bridges Among Palm Trees for Extracting Tuba

Tayabas, Quezon (Luzon, the Philippines) Photograph by Paulina Machuca

PART I

Photograph 3. Preparing the Inflorescence to Extract *Tuba*

A *Manananggot* from Bohol, central Visayas (the Philippines) Photograph by Paulina Machuca.

Once the inflorescence has been tied and bent downward, the *tubero* makes a fine cut using a special knife. An erratic cut will severely damage the inflorescence and reduce the amount of sap harvested, so handling the knife requires great dexterity. Reflecting this, people in the Philippines refer to the *tubero*'s trade as *manananggot*, which means "he who knows how to handle the knife, or *sanggot*". Immediately after making the cut, he places a small recipient under the inflorescence to collect the sap as it flows out. The cup, called *sahod* or *tukil*, is usually made of bamboo. In his *Estado de las Islas Filipinas en 1810*, Tomás de Comyn identified it as a *cañuto* (roughly, tube):

> *Vino de cocos* is a weak aguardiente obtained in the following manner. The crown of the tree that produces this fruit is adorned with rosettes or corollas, from whose center or calyx there emerges a fleshy shoot full of juice; the Indian cuts the end of this shoot, bends the rest of it laterally, introduces it into a large tube [*cañuto*] hanging from [his body], and retrieves it full of a smooth, rather viscous liquor that is purged from the tree in this way twice every twenty-four hours.[134]

Diverse varieties of bamboo of all sizes grow in the Philippines, so it is the preferred plant for use in the process of obtaining *vino de cocos*. Another recipient utilized, called a *kawit*, is made from a larger variety of bamboo than the *cañuto*. The *tuba* collected from all the trees is poured into the *kawit*, which has a wooden arm so it can be slung over the *tubero*'s back as he clambers up and down the trees, leaving both hands free to brace himself on the trunks without the recipient disturbing his movements (Illustration 3).

Part I

Illustration 3. Materials Used to Store *Tuba*

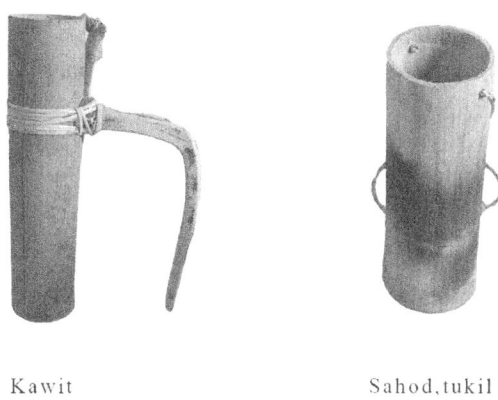

Kawit   Sahod, tukil

Source: Author's Collection.

The *tubero* (Illustration 4) has to repeat the procedure of cutting inflorescences twice a day year-round, once in the morning and again in the afternoon. Clearly, this trade demands great commitment and constancy. It is the *tubero*'s job throughout his lifetime since skipping either the morning or afternoon climb can severely deteriorate the productivity of the spadices. The amount of sap extracted depends on various factors: the skill of the *tubero*, the specific variety of coconut tree, and its age and nutritional condition. The younger and better-nourished the tree, the more *tuba* it produces. In addition to the name *tuba*, the juice is called *toddy* in other places where it is gathered.[135]

Illustration 4. A Filipino *Tubero* or *Indio Mananguetero* (1847)

Source: Gervasio Gironella, **Álbum.** Vistas de las Yslas Filipinas. *Trages de sus abitantes*, Madrid, 1847, Biblioteca Nacional de España (hereinafter BNE), DIB/15/84, plate 45.

Part I

Distilling *Tuba*: The Decisive Step

In the Philippines, the *vino de cocos* obtained by distilling *tuba* is called *lambanog*. Its alcohol content by volume ranges from 40-70%, depending on the number of distillations. This local name, however, rarely appears in Spanish sources from the early colonial period, where the beverage was called simply *uraca* or *arrach/arrak/alak*, a generic name for distilled drinks, according to its Arabic etymology. *Vino de cocos* is an alcoholic drink on the level of Japanese sake, Russian vodka, Brazilian *cachaça*, or, of course, Mexican tequila and mezcal. The *tuba* collected for distillation is stored in containers for around a week to give it the time it needs to reach an adequate state of fermentation; that is, the conversion of sugars into alcohol. According to Tomás de Comyn,

> This liquor, called *tuba* in that country's language, is left to ferment for eight days in a bucket, then the Indians distill it in their rustic stills that are nothing more than a few large cauldrons with a base of lead or tin, muddied joints and a tube, often made of simple cane, that deposits the aguardiente in jars, without passing through the coils of our common stills, through a bath in pools or ponds that contributes so much to correcting the vices of an overly accelerated evaporation.[136]

Comyn pointed out the need to let the *tuba* ferment for a week. Today, this step has been modified, as it is left to repose for only 3-5 days before distillation.[137] The microorganisms responsible for fermentation are present naturally in both the inflorescence and the bamboo recipient (*cañuto*), but the bees, ants, and other insects that inhabit palm trees also contribute (Photograph 4).

Photograph 4. Bees in Fermenting *Tuba* Must

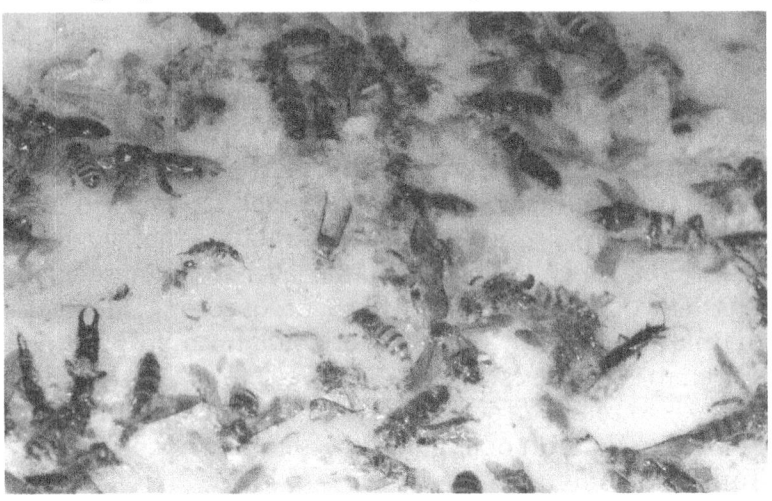

Tayabas, Quezon (Luzon, the Philippines) Photograph by Paulina Machuca

Fermentation is a key stage in the process of elaborating alcoholic drinks because it requires the participation of live beings, not only yeast, but also bacteria with the capacity to transform sugars into a series of compounds like ethyl alcohol or ethanol.[138] Along this chain of conversion from sucrose-to-ethanol, producers in the Philippines have implemented innovations that increase the volume of alcohol in the *tuba* prior to distillation from the 6-8% v/v obtained by the traditional method employed in the colonial period to perhaps 10-12% v/v by means of inoculation.[139]

Distillation is a process that requires skills distinct from those used to collect the *tuba*, so the trade of master distiller is distinguished from that of the *tuberos* or *mananang-got*. The "rustic stills" that Comyn mentioned differed markedly from the metal stills and alembics (*alquitara*) of Arab origin that were used in Europe. The Asian-type still, which was utilized not only in the Philippines but also in nations like Japan, consisted of a hollow wooden trunk on which a metal vat was placed with a small clay oven below. It is clear that the stills described in the archipelago in the colonial period have varied over time, though photograph 5 shows a typical still from the town of Infanta in Pangasinán province (Luzon, the Philippines) that was used to distill aguardiente made from the nipa palm (*Nypa fruticans*).[140] Antonio de Morga's description from 1609 is especially useful here:

> What [people in the Philippines] drink is a wine made from the buds of coconut and nipa palm trees, which exist in abundance and are raised and cultivated as in vineyards, though with [less] work and labors. Once gathered from the palms, the *tuba* is distilled, to greater or lesser strengths, in stills with small ovens and instruments and made into aguardiente. As clear as water, but strong and dry, it is consumed on all the islands.[141]

Broadly, a typical distillation process requires four elements: an oven with a chimney, a cylindrical distilling tank, a connecting tube, and a condenser. The oven is made of clay with an opening in the upper part where the cylindrical tank is inserted with the *tuba* that is to be boiled, and a second orifice in the lower part for fuel. Once the tank is placed inside the oven a metal vat, usually of copper, is placed on top to receive and condense the vapors produced during distillation. Meanwhile, the exterior part is filled periodically with cold water. Of course, the tank has an outlet to expel the condensed vapor, an element usually made of bamboo. In technical terms, distillation is a process that consists in breaking down a homogeneous liquid mixture into its individual components.[142] The aim is to gather the spirits from the raw material, which gives rise to the name "spirit drink".

Photograph 5. Rustic Still for Making *Vino de Nipa*

Source: Infanta, Pangasinán (Luzón, the Philippines) Photograph by María Salomé Aurelio-Desoloc.

It is important to note that producing *vino de cocos* requires large amounts of *tuba*. In some present-day distilleries in the Philippines the ratio for obtaining just one liter of distillate can be as high as 8-10:1; that is, 8-10 liters of *tuba* for 1 liter of aguardiente, according to information provided by the *Mallari Distillery* in Tayabas.[143] The amount may be reduced depending on the amount of ethanol obtained during fermentation of the *tuba*. In her study, Priscila Chinte-Sánchez states that today 91 liters of *lambanog* can be produced from 570 liters of fermented *tuba*; that is, a ratio of 6 liters of *tuba* to 1 liter of distillate.[144] In the Philippines, the aforementioned traveler Jagor, who visited the Santa Cruz area in the Laguna de Bay region around 1875, observed that the *tuberos* had to extract 36 *cuartillos* of *tuba* to obtain 6 *cuartillos* of aguardiente, a ratio of 6:1, the same figure that Sánchez mentions.[145] This variation in productivity –both yesterday and today– depends on several factors: the more rustic the distillation process, as was certainly the case in colonial times, the greater the potential for shrinkage and waste. In contrast, a distillation method that utilizes modern materials, like stills made of stainless steel instead of hollow tree trunks and clay, and follows processes more strictly controlled, have a greater potential to optimize the raw material and achieve better yields.

Another point to take into account is that processes that involve double or triple distillation will considerably increase the amount of raw material required. On this topic, the Bolognese Ludovico de Varthema recorded, around 1505, that people in southern India cooked the sap of the palm trees and, after distilling it two or three times, obtained "a liquid (*aqua vita*)" that when simply smelled "alters men's brains".[146] In the 1580s, the Dutchman John Huyghen van Linschoten reported this practice in the same region, where natives distilled *tuba* or *sura*, calling it *fula* or *nipe* after the first distillation, and *uraca* after the second.[147] These data are very valuable for the history of distillation.

The average distillation time of *vino de cocos* in the Philippines today varies from 7 to 9 hours, depending on the amount of *tuba*. A master distiller can verify the quality of the drink by the amount and size of the bubbles the aguardiente produces when it is transferred from one container to another, just like master Mexican mezcal producers who utilize artisanal processes. A final aspect to emphasize in relation to the distillation of *vino de cocos* is productivity. A single palm tree in the Philippines can produce 1.5 liters of *tuba* per day, a figure comparable to findings from other countries in Southeast Asia, which report the following daily quantities for this activity: Malaysia, 1.49 liters; India, 1.59 liters; and Sri Lanka, 1.58 liters.[148]

Table 3 shows the estimated production of *lambanog* in the Laguna region, near Manila for the year 2008. Although these figures are over a decade old, the information is useful because it is based on a plantation of 875 coconut palms, distributed over 5 hectares, that can serve as the basis for calculating *vino de cocos* production on palm haciendas along the Pacific coast of New Spain.[149]

Table 3. Estimated Lambanog Production in Laguna, Philippines, as of 2008

Rubric	Amount
Number of palm trees	875
Daily amount of tuba per tree	1.5 liters
Total tuba collected daily	1,312.5 liters
Lambanog production every 5 days	1,151 liters
Annual lambanog production	84,046 liters

Source: Priscila Chinte-Sánchez, *Philippine fermented foods*, p. 150.

A Brief Overview of Tuba in the Philippines

Not all the *tuba* collected is destined for *vino de cocos* production, for this liquid is so sweet that some people consume it as a refreshing, even medicinal, drink as soon as it is brought down from the palm trees. A light fermentation of *tuba* can transform it into a drink with 2-4% of alcohol by volume, but it is also consumed as a beer-like beverage after adding bark from the mangrove trees (*Ceriops tangal*; *Rhizophora mucronata*) available around the archipelago that give it a reddish color but, above all, raise the alcohol volume (10-13% v/v). That bark is called *tungog* or *tangal*. On some islands in the Visayas –Leyte, for example– *tuba* may be stored for several months or even years, but then it is called *bahal* or *bahalina*, depending on how long it is aged.[150]

In the Philippines, *tuba* is part of a grand tradition of fermented drinks elaborated from diverse species of palm trees (Table 4), though the coconut and nipa palms stand out clearly as the most representative varieties; in fact, they share the characteristic that their raw materials have been used in distillation since pre-Hispanic times. *Vino de nipa*, as Spaniards in the Philippines called it, is elaborated mostly in zones near swamps, the tree's natural habitat, so its consumption is more circumscribed geographically than that of the wine made from *tuba* gathered from coconut trees. But the extraction processes are very similar, for the nipa palm's inflorescences must also be bent downward and cut very carefully, and the sap is collected and stored in small recipients. However, the *tuba* from the nipa palm ferments more rapidly than that of coconut palms and, once gathered, can reach 10-12% of alcohol by volume.[151] In his book on the Visaya Indians published in 1668, Father Alzina mentioned that the *tuba* from nipa palms "is not as sweet and flavorful as that of coconut palms because the soils where they grow are waterier and muddier", since those trees grow in marshy zones and other wetlands along riverbanks. While the technique used to extract sap is similar, the *tuberos* do not have to climb nipa palms because "almost all their fruit touches the ground or is in the water".[152] Regarding flavor, Alzina opined that: "this *vino de nipa*... is not as good, it seems, as that from coconut palms, nor as healthy as the other, according to those who have some experience with them".[153]

Table 4. Main Fermented Beverages from Palm Trees in the Philippines

Common Name	Scientific Name
Coco	*Cocos nucifera*
Nipa	*Nypa fruticans*
Buri	*Corypha elata*
Kaong	*Arenga saccharifera*
Oil palm	*Elaeis guineensis*
Palm yrah	*Borassus flabellifer*
Wild date palm	*Phoenix sylvestris*
Rafia	*Raphia hookeri*; *Raphia vinifera*
Kithul	*Caryota urens*

Source: Priscila Chinte-Sánchez, *Philippine fermented foods*, p. 150.

As an acute observer of the customs of the Visaya Indians, Father Alzina stated that they had "more [alcoholic] drinks than any other nation in the Universe".[154] Table 4 presents a list of the drinks elaborated from diverse palm species, but Alzina noted that similar juices were prepared from other raw materials, including drinks called *intus*, from sugarcane (*Saccharum officinarum*), *pangasi*, from rice (*Oryza sativa*), and *caravaran*, from honey.[155] Many of these still exist today. Though known by other names, they conserve a historical nexus from pre-Hispanic times: *tapuy* (*Oryza sativa*) and *basi* (*Saccharum officinarum*) are typical examples, but numerous other drinks with 10-15%

of alcohol by volume are made from various tropical fruits of American origin, like the pineapple (*Ananas comosus*), papaya (*Carica papaya*), guava (*Psidium guajava*), and anona (*Annona squamosa*).[156]

Consumption of *Tuba* and *Vino de Cocos* in the Philippines

Consumption of alcoholic beverages in the Philippines was associated with social occasions, evidenced in diverse fiestas, celebrations, and moments of merriment, but also with funeral settings. Visitors were welcomed with a glass of *tuba* or *vino de cocos*, and blood pacts were sealed with it as a sign of peace and friendship. The *Relazione del primo viaggio attorno al mondo*, by the Vicentine Antonio de Pigafetta –the chronicler of Fernando de Magallanes' voyage– is replete with allusions to *vino de cocos* in various presentations from one end of the Pacific islands to the other, from the Marianas to distinct regions of the Filipino archipelago. There we read that in March 1521 Samar, chief of the island of Homonhon in the Eastern Visayas, greeted Magallanes with fish, local fruits, coconuts, and a pitcher of *vino de cocos* "that they call *uraca*". Later in their journey, they met the king of a nearby island (Leyte?) who invited the captain and other Spaniards to a banquet where *vino de cocos* was a central element:

> He ordered that a plate with pork and a large pitcher of wine be brought. We drank a cup of wine with each bite; the wine left over the king would –sometimes– pour into a pitcher for his own use. His cup always appeared to be [full] and no one drank from it but he and I. Each time the king prepared to drink, he raised his hands together toward the sky and toward us; then, before drinking, extended his left fist toward me (at first, I thought he was about to punch me). Finally, he drank. When my turn came, I imitated him. Those gestures were immediately repeated by the others. The dinner came to an end with great pomp and numerous signs of friendship.[157]

Upon arriving in Cebu in the central Visayas, where he would meet his tragic fate, Magallanes had to sign a blood pact with the lord of that island, Humabon. On that occasion, the ritual consisted in drawing a little blood from the right arm of both signees and pouring it into a glass of wine from which both men then drank. Interestingly, this same ritual was repeated in 1565 with Miguel López de Legazpi on the island of Bohol, next to Cebu, when he signed a peace accord with a local chief named Sikatuna. Although the type of "wine" used to seal those pacts is not always specified, the context suggests it was *vino de cocos*.

The Spaniards who accompanied Legazpi soon became accustomed to drinking *vino de cocos*, as the captain mentioned in Cebu in 1565: "[the natives] also brought a large quantity of *vino de cocos* of which the Spaniards partook eagerly, saying it did not cause them to miss the wine of Castille".[158] However, when some of his crew – including a Mexican Indian named Juanes who was with Legazpi– were poisoned and died after drinking adulterated wine that a local woman sold to the Spaniards, the captain prohibited further consumption of the drink. Some of his men expressed resistance to the ban in no uncertain terms: "[despite] all this there were many, especially sailors, who said they preferred to die than to cease drinking [*vino de cocos*] [for] they could not work or sustain themselves without it".[159] The Indian woman who caused the intoxication suffered severe, exemplary punishment, as her body was drawn and quartered and then exhibited to the island's inhabitants as a warning of the fate that would befall anyone who harmed the newcomers.

Returning to Pigafetta, *vino de cocos* was practically the only alcoholic drink that the Vicentine adventurer mentioned during his travels through the Philippine islands; in fact, it was not until the expedition reached Palawan, in the extreme western region, that he observed inhabitants there making wine from distilled rice, "more abundant and better than *vino de cocos* ".[160] Spanish chronicles from the 17th century, both civil and ecclesiastical, confirm Pigafetta's earlier observations; for example, in his *Sucesos de las islas Filipinas*, Antonio de Morga narrated that:

> the meetings, weddings, and festivals of the natives of these islands are all about imbibing this [coconut] wine, days and nights without stopping, some in the circle singing, others drinking, so it is normal that they become quite drunk, though among them this vice is not [deemed] dishonorable nor a cause of infamy.[161]

This final feature of the Filipinos that Morga observed –that consuming *vino de cocos* was "normal" and did not cause conflicts within the community– was echoed by the Jesuit Father Pedro Chirino in the Visayas region around 1604:

> Celebrations of banquets [are] when they eat and drink to excess, much more drinking than eating [...] on occasions of illness, death, and mourning [but] also at betrothals, weddings, and sacrifices, as well as with guest and visitors. On all these occasions, no doors were closed to anyone who wished to drink with them [...] But we never see them so frenzied or crazed with drunkenness that they commit any kind of outrageous acts: indeed, they maintain normal conduct and treat one another with the same respect as always when drinking, appear rather joyful and conservative, and voice amusing sayings.[162]

Those natives, then, drank not only during festive times, but also at funerals. Nipa wine was not lacking on such occasions and was imbibed at weddings and cockfights, as well,[163] the latter a deeply-rooted tradition in the Philippines and across Southeast Asia.[164]

Illustration 5. *Lambanog* and *Tuba* in Contemporary Philippines

Lambanog from
Tayabas,Quezon
(Philippines)

Tuba from Bohol,
Central Visayas
(Philippines)

Source: Photographs by Paulina Machuca.

Clearly, tuba and lambanog occupy special places in Filipino culture. Tuba consumption is much more widespread because its elaboration does not require a complex process, as is the case of lambanog. The latter beverage has an important presence in Tayabas, Quezon, but is also produced in other regions on Luzon, such as Laguna, Batangas, Albay, Cagayan, Camarines Sur, La Unión, and Pangasinan.[165] Contrary to descriptions in colonial chronicles, today tuba distillation is not common in other areas of the Philippines, such as Visayas, where tuba stands out among the various fermented drinks consumed. It is precisely in Aklan, Western Visayas, that a short song dedicated to the children of tuberos describes how they live happily despite their condition of poverty. Compared to other, now industrialized, alcoholic drinks in the Philippines, *tuba* is seen as "the poor man's wine":

Song entitled "The children of the *tuberos*"[166]

Unga't Mananggiti	The children of the *tuberos*
Unga't mananggiti	We the children of the *tuberos*
malipayon bisan pobre.	Are happy though we are poor.
Mabilo! Mabilo!	Mabilo! Mabilo!

THE INTRODUCTION OF VINO DE COCOS INTO NEW SPAIN

No sooner did the coconut palm arrive on the shores of the Mar del Sur in New Spain than *vino de cocos* production began. This vertiginous development –the introduction of the technique for extracting and distilling *tuba*– was made possible by an inseparable binomial: the presence of coconut palms and the skill of the *indios chinos*. Without this human factor, neither *tuba* nor *vino de cocos* would have emerged in this new setting, for in other places in New Spain where coconut palms were cultivated –such as the modern-day zone around the Gulf of Mexico– but Filipinos were not present, the technique never developed.

The evidence available suggests that *vino de cocos* production began in New Spain in the final decade of the 16th century, with the earliest news coming from the province of Colima. While palm tree cultivation was underway by 1569 using the seeds that the sailor Álvaro de Mendaña had introduced from the Solomon Islands, it was not until 1598 that the first references to aguardiente production appear. While strolling the streets of Colima in 1586, admiring the surrounding vegetation, cotton fields, banana trees, and sapodillas, Friar Alonso Ponce noted the presence of numerous coconut palms, "a most beautiful and attractive tree".[167] Though he mentioned the benefits that people in

Colima obtained from this tree, he did not mention *tuba* production, instead emphasizing the tree's bounty as a source of food and drink noting, as well, that the shells were exported to Spain to be made into the *cocos chocolateros* so coveted by elites in New Spain and on the Iberian Peninsula:

> Those are very hot lands, like everything else born on the coast of the Mar del Sur [...] cotton, bananas, and sapodillas abound, and there are many coconut trees, most beautiful and attractive that grow as high as the palm, which it greatly resembles. When the coconut palm begins to bear fruit, after eight or nine years, it produces one cluster each month, each one with twenty or thirty coconuts or more, though not all prosper as [some] fall when still small leaving perhaps ten or twelve. They grow quite large and have a husk two fingers thick, smooth and green on the outside and full of fiber on the inside; under this husk there is a thin but hard, glassy shell that is white when the coconut is not yet ripe but turns black when it is [...] With that they make the coconut cups that are taken to Spain [to] serve as drinking vessels. Inside this shell, and adhered to it, there is a [layer] about a finger thick of very white, tasty flesh with a flavor like sweet hazelnuts or almonds; the rest is full of water, very thin and smooth, bland and very good to drink, [it] is consumed as the coconuts mature, until none is left when it becomes too hard. The shell has three holes in one end that look like a man's eyes and mouth, covered by the aforementioned white flesh. They are easy to split open.[168]

The *Relaciones geográficas*, written in the 1580s about Motines, Zacatula, and other places where distilling palm aguardiente would later be practiced, do not mention this activity, while the *Relación de la provincia de Motines* only notes in passing that the jurisdiction had "fruit trees" like plum, banana, magueys, pineapple, guava, avocado, zapote, mamey, and coconuts, among others.[169] The coconut tree did not merit special mention even though it was a foreigner among the area's exuberant vegetation. One could argue, then, that the final two decades of the 16th century were the key period for the process of introducing, cultivating, and acclimating the coconut palm that opened the way to the production of the distilled beverage by *indios chinos*.

Thus it was that when a resident of Colima named Cristóbal de Silva died in 1598, his properties were found to include not only a palm tree plantation in the locality of Popoyutla, near the coast in the jurisdiction of Colima, but also various kinds of gear for elaborating *vino de cocos*.[170] Moreover, in the year 1600 the colonial archives of Colima began to keep systematic records of the *vino de cocos* produced thanks to Filipino workers.

Harvesting *Tuba*: Distinct Materials, Same Procedure

How did the process of elaborating *vino de cocos* change when the technique was brought to New Spain? It is clear that the knowhow of the *indios chinos* had to be adapted to the natural resources available in the new environment, so the material culture employed to produce *arrach* in the archipelago was modified for local conditions. The details of the readaptation of the material culture for producing aguardiente from palm trees in Asian environs to New Spain are analyzed in the following lines. Before beginning, it is important to clarify that the sources available (some historical, others ethnographic) –once again, mainly from the colonial province of Colima– are quite limited.

There is a marked similarity between the Philippines and the colonial province of Colima regarding the methods used to extract and distill *tuba*. The first phase, called "harvesting", is performed following the same procedure, except that since big bamboo species did not exist on the coast of New Spain, sap was collected instead in small, gourd-like vessels called *tecomates* (*Crescentia*) –from the Náhuatl term *tecomatl*– that are widely distributed in coastal zones of Mexico and were used as jars and cups in pre-Hispanic times. It is possible, as well, that coconut husks were utilized for this purpose since both recipients are found in contexts where *vino de cocos* was produced and sold in the first two decades of the 17th century.[171] Another plant utilized to store *tuba* was *Lagenaria siceraria* (Illustration 6), somewhat larger than the gourds and still commonly used today by *tuberos* in Colima. As the 17th century advanced, pottery vessels came into use, for in 1664 the utensils belonging to Francisca Martha, a *china criolla* from Colima to whom we devote the following chapter, included 6 "pitchers where *tuba* was collected".[172] Those vessels were most likely pots where *tuba* was fermented, or perhaps the classic clay vessels (*porrones*) that *tuberos* in Colima were still using just a few years ago (Illustration 6).

Illustration 6. Materials Used in the Collection and Storage of *Tuba* in Colima

Porron made from clay for *tuba* gathering

Calabazo for *tuba* storage

Source: The Authors' Collection.

One feature that the Filipinos tried to transfer from the world of the Philippines was the installation of bridges among the palm trees to facilitate the work of gathering

Part I

tuba. Proof of this comes from a lease contract for coconut palms in the Caxitlán Valley, jurisdiction of Colima, dated 1605, which stipulated that the lessee had to keep the trees clean, "and not cut steps into them, but [utilize] wooden ladders and *bridges*". This evokes the long, thick bamboo shafts in the Philippines shown in Photograph 2, though people in Colima would have used locally available wood. That contract further established that at the end of the two-year lease, the lessee had to leave "an oven made to produce wine":

> In the Caxitlán Valley, jurisdiction of the villa of Colima, on the 9th day of the month of June of the year 1605, Francisco Rodríguez de Iniesta, a resident of this jurisdiction, and Juan Martín Parrales, also a resident, [both] known to me, appeared before me, a public scribe, stating that they had accorded and agreed that said Francisco Rodríguez would lease a hacienda with houses and coconut trees that he has in this valley, which abuts the hacienda of Antonio de Contreras Fiallo and forms part of another hacienda of Pedro Moreno, and another with the hacienda of Diego Morán, neighbors, for the time and space of two years that shall run and be counted from today's date [...] for two hundred and seventy *pesos de oro común* in *reales* paid as follows: one hundred and seventy pesos that said Francisco Rodríguez confirms he has received from said Juan Martín Parrales for this effect, and the rest which [the latter] shall begin to pay from the first of the year in parts every four months [and] from this day said Juan Martín Parrales is bound to keep said coconut trees clean and well cared for and *[is prohibited from] cutting steps in them but must utilize wooden ladders and bridges, and at the end of said two years must leave an oven for the production of wine* made of two large vats of fifteen pounds that shall be paid for by said [lacuna] Parrales but not for this reason [lacuna] is he obliged to leave suitable houses to live in or enter his coast; and if due to cutting steps, [the presence of cattle], the failure to provide water, or [committing] any negligence that causes the loss of some coconut palms, said Juan Martín Parrales shall pay for them according to their fair value.[173]

We cannot know whether building bridges among the coconut palms was the norm or, perhaps, the exception. It is also hard to imagine how *bridges*, though they would have facilitated harvesting the *tuba*, could have been incorporated into this experience in New Spain, for while the Philippines had a special variety of bamboo suitable for this purpose for it was very long and could support a man's weight, it would have been very difficult to find a substitute type of wood with similar characteristics in the Mar del Sur.

What materials were utilized to distill *vino de cocos*? The inventory of Francisca Martha's belongings –the aforementioned *china criolla*– provides part of the answer:

- 85 palm trees of all ages
- 1 oven for cooking wine with two old vats and their barrel
- 5 Castilian *botijas*
- 6 vessels (*cántaros*) into which the *tuba* is poured
- 2 full *botijas* of wine

The items that stand out are the oven for cooking wine, metal vats, and barrel, actually a hollow tree trunk. As we have commented, the vessels into which "*tuba* was poured" (*cántaros*) could refer either to those used to collect the sap or the recipients where it was left to ferment before distillation. As we saw earlier, *tuberos* in the Philippines used vessels made of bamboo, but also Chinese-made jugs to ferment *tuba*. Other important elements in the inventory are the clay vessels called *botijas peruleras* (jars of approximately 16 liters) which were used during the commercialization of aguardiente, as we will see in the next chapter.

Part I

Distillation of *Vino de Cocos* in New Spain

Was the distillation technique introduced into the area of the Mar del Sur the same as the one in the Philippines, or was it modified when transferred to this side of the Pacific Ocean? Thanks to Friar Antonio Tello's description of *vino de cocos* in his *Crónica miscelánea*, written around 1652, we know that the same Filipino technique functioned in Colima:

> [...] the raceme of fruit that the palm produces is tied very tightly with a few cords, using many loops, and then cut little-by-little, once in the morning and again in the afternoon, with a gourd or cup hung from it into which the water, that they call *tuba*, [falls], a most flavorful drink when consumed as it flows out, sweet and tasty; it is then poured into vessels to ferment a little, and is distilled in stills [to turn it into] wine; when removed carefully it is very strong like aguardiente from Castille.[174]

Tello used the word "stills" but later explained that they were "some hollow poles as thick as a man", topped by a copper vat full of water that "they [stir] as it heats up, and in the middle of the hollow [there is] a fitted round board with a spout coming out from one side, which is where it is distilled".[175]

It is extraordinarily interesting that, even today, people in the southern area of the state of Jalisco use a still quite similar to the one Tello described in the 17th century, a finding that corroborates the Asian influence on mezcal production in Mexico (Illustration 7).[176] Indeed, that still from Jalisco is analogous to the one used in the Filipino province of Infanta to produce nipa wine. The hollow wooden trunk is made from the monkey-ear tree (*parota*, *Enterolobium cyclocarpum*), while shoots of agave plants form the spout (*cañuto*) through which the distillate flowed, as can be seen in Zapotitlán de Vadillo, Jalisco.

Illustration 7. Filipino-Style Still for Mezcal Production (Zapotitlán de Vadillo, Jalisco, Mexico)

Source: Photograph by Paulina Machuca

On Stills and Alembics

Was an Arab-type alembic used to distill *vino de cocos*? The distillation technique of Arab origin that involved stills

Part I

and alembics diffused into Europe in Medieval times, so it is certainly plausible that it could have been introduced into the New World with the arrival of the Spanish on the American continent; however, the sources are silent on this point so it is difficult to determine precisely where and when the first metal stills appeared in New Spain for the specific purpose of elaborating alcoholic drinks. In contrast to the Filipino still, the main feature of the Arab apparatus was a two-part structure made entirely of metal: a boiler below where the fermented juice was heated, and an upper vessel that captured the vapor produced, which cooled as it flowed through a coil placed in a recipient full of cold water. As the vapor cooled, the condensed liquid was channeled into the final recipient (Illustration 8). In addition to elaborating alcoholic drinks, those stills were used to produce perfumes and medicines.

Illustration 8. Arab-style still made of copper.

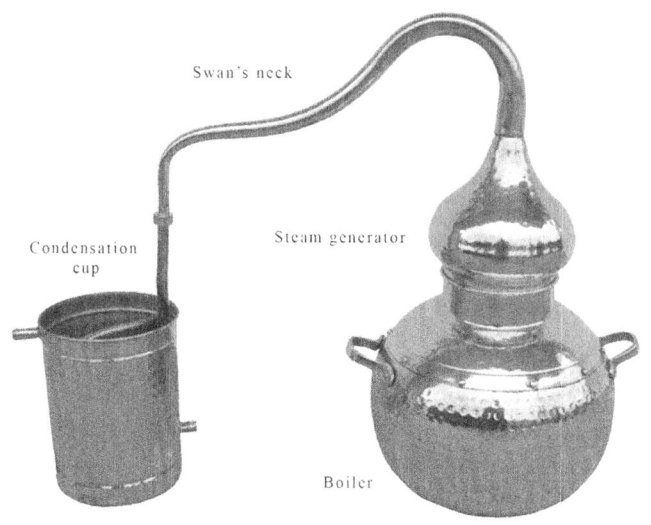

Source: Public Domain.

The fact that the Spanish called the Asian stills used to produce *vino de cocos* "alembics" or *alquitaras* when, in reality, those terms referred to the procedures involved, has generated confusion between the two techniques. Friar Antonio Tello used the word "alembic" when describing the procedure for elaborating *vino de cocos*, though it is clear that he referred to a Filipino-type still. In a similar case, the term *alquitara* was used: after the death of Cristóbal de Silva in Colima in 1598, his belongings on a palm hacienda in Popoyutla –near the port of Salagua (Manzanillo)– were found to include an old *alquitara*, two old pots (*peroles*) and a skillet, a spit, [another] small pot, and an axe;[177] clearly a typical set of utensils used to produce *vino de cocos*. The context of that document strongly suggests that, once again, the still was of the Filipino type.[178]

The Arab-style alembic seems to have been used in northern New Spain around the mid-17th century, concretely in Santa María de las Parras, to distill mezcal and an aguardiente called *orujo*. The estate of Captain Domingo de la Fuente, elaborated after his death in 1648, contained "a large, lidded vat to make mezcal wine";[179] in other words, a boiler with its cover. The historian Sergio Corona affirms that "there is no doubt that mezcal preceded *orujo* aguardiente in the history of distillation in Nueva Vizcaya", and that this phenomenon was due, in his view, to the influence of the Andalusians in that zone:

> In Nueva Vizcaya, as in other parts of Spanish America, experiments by the European population to obtain alcoholic drinks by distillation began practically with the discovery of [that] territory and the onset of colonization in the 16th century. Without doubt, the same stimulus that would later spur harvesters to establish their vineyards –money encouraged many Spaniards to try to produce distilled drinks to reap the economic benefits at a time when grapes were still rare or non-existent. This was possible because the distillation of alcoholic substances was known in Europe, especially Andalucía, from the Middle Ages, and many Spanish colonists knew the basic principles of the technique.[180]

Part I

Beyond the case of Parras, research on distillation with metal stills in New Spain is a pending topic that clearly merits study. It was not until the second half of the 18th century that documents from the Vice-Royalty on the uses and purchase-sale of copper stills began to abound, though it is clear that those devices were not used exclusively to produce aguardientes, but also to obtain aromatic essences.[181] A curious case from 1786 involved Juan María Roche, a Castilian newcomer in Mexico City who solicited a license from the *juez de bebidas prohibidas* (judge of banned drinks) at the time to use an alembic to extract scented waters, essences, quintessences for perfumes, and vinegar. His request was denied, however, because "the judge did not understand" that the apparatus was not going to be used to produce aguardiente. Later, Roche obtained authorization from the Viceroy himself.[182]

Brief Notes on *Tuba* in Colima

As in the Philippines, in Colima *tuba* was used not only as a raw material to produce *vino de cocos* but was also consumed as an alcoholic drink after being allowed to ferment for a few days to reach a volume of alcohol around 4-6%, just as occurred in the archipelago. There are no indications that mangrove tree roots or bark were added to accelerate fermentation, though this was a common practice in the Philippines. At some moment of the 19th century, or perhaps the early 20th, *tuba*'s destiny took another path, one quite distinct from its consumption as an alcoholic drink. Around that time, it began to be transformed into the drink we know today, a refreshing, even medicinal, beverage that came to be called *tuba compuesta* (compound tuba). This drink is similar to Spanish punches and sangrias because it acquires a reddish hue when mixed with pomegranate or strawberry and because pieces of seasonal fruits are often added.[183] We can also think of *pulque curado*, which includes all kinds of fruits. This type of drink, clearly invented in Colima, is not known in the Philippines, so here we must recognize transcultural processes that, despite a shared origin, are transformed over time in accordance with the needs and tastes of each locality.

Mathieu de Fossey, a French traveler who passed through Colima around 1857, observed the thousands of coconut palms that adorned the city's outskirts and broader surrounding area. When writing about *tuba*, a drink he compared to pulque, he expressed amazement for the agility of the boys and men who climbed the steps cut into the trunks of coconut palms: "they run up the trees, and from the tops of the palms that envelop them, balancing a hundred feet off the ground, intone plaintive songs known in the region by the name *valonas*".[184] Not to be outdone, *tuberos* in Colima also sang to the coconut palms and the *tuba* harvest just like their counterparts in the Philippines:

Song Entitled "The Tubero" (Colima)[185]

Yo soy del mero Colima	I'm from the heart of Colima
Lugar de palmas de coco	Place of coconut palms
De donde bajan la *tuba*	Where *tuba* is gathered
Que ya la conocen pocos.	Now known only to a few
De su espiga las palmeras	From the shoots of palm trees
Producen *tuba* sabrosa	A tasty *tuba* is produced
Que los tuberos la bajan	That the *tuberos* harvest
Con destreza valerosa.	With brave dexterity.
La tradición en Colima	The tradition in Colima
A muchos les causa asombro	Causes amazement to many
Venden la *tuba* sabrosa	They sell the tasty *tuba*
Con burra de palma a al hombro.	From [vessels] on their shoulders
A mis hermosas palmeras	My beautiful palm trees
Las subo por escalones,	I climb step-by-step
Divisando los volcanes	Viewing the volcanoes
Y vaciando los porrones.	And emptying the vessels.

PART I

PRODUCTION ZONES OF VINO DE COCOS

The coastal landscape of New Spain along the Mar del Sur, the setting where *vino de cocos* production began in the century 17th, underwent a series of important changes as Spanish colonization advanced. The introduction of plants from Europe and Asia modified not only the vegetation of those littorals, but also of some regions further inland, a phenomenon that by the year 1600 was an inescapable reality. As Pierre Gourou affirms, landscapes are constructed: human facts are not conditioned by nature, though they do maintain a close relation to it.[186] Humans, persistent "landscape makers", move in space and modify their surroundings in accordance with social, political, economic, and cultural codes. The establishment of palm haciendas for *vino de cocos* production is a clear example of this.

The Pacific strip of New Spain is a zone that was transformed from a land of cacao cultivation in the first half of the 16th century to a region that housed extensive palm tree plantations dedicated to *aguardiente* production. Later, when that industry collapsed, other crops were introduced –sugarcane, cotton, bananas, mangos– to satisfy new commercial demands. That succession of landscapes largely followed changes –both internal and external– in the socioeconomic panorama of New Spain. As a region with geographic and historical conditions suitable for cultivating tropical plants of American and Asian origin, those landscapes facilitated the development of a series of new agroecological dynamics.

The introduction of tropical plants from Southeast Asia thanks to the Manila Galleon contributed significantly to the accelerated changes in landscapes around the Mar del Sur. While the coconut palm is the most representative example of this transformative process, it is not the only one. As happens when plants are disseminated from one place to another, they modify not only the physical space of the area they embrace, but also the cultural space of the society that adopts them. To illustrate this reality, in the lines that follow we explain the process of the insertion of the coconut palm into the existing cacao-producing haciendas, which emerged as the most suitable ecological niche for the new tree.

Between Sea and Mountains

Palm haciendas were established along the Pacific littoral of New Spain between the modern-day states of Colima and Guerrero, along the skirts of an extensive mountain range called the *Sierra Madre del Sur*. The valleys where those haciendas developed were trapped between the sea and the mountains. Beneath them flowed the tributaries of rivers and streams that bathed the major human settlements. In the stretch of land between Salagua and Acapulco, the two most important ports in the study zone, one observes the protuberance that generated this series of sierras that emerged through the conjugation of various tectonic domains, whose relief evidences a complex geological history that began in the Precambrian. The *Sierra Madre del Sur* is a product of the collision between the Cocos Plate and the North American plate, an event that occurred over a billion years ago.[187]

This mountain range runs along the coast of the Pacific Ocean at an almost constant altitude of 2,000 m.a.s.l. Numerous currents are born there that run down into the ocean, including the Balsas River,[188] which has borne this name since at least the 16th century, as Captain Nicolás de Cardona attested to around 1614-1615: "the river they call Çacatula is the Balsas [River] of New Spain that flows into the Mar del Sur".[189] It also has important deposits of gold, silver, lead, and iron, the principal minerals that attracted the Spanish to the region early in the 16th century, especially the area identified as Motines in the *Relación de Zacatula* in 1581: "in the sierra of Motín... there have been very large gold mines where great quantities of [that metal] have been extracted, and there is still [gold] today in those mines and in the rivers that flow down from those sierras to the sea, and it is extracted by the Indians".[190] Over time, mining fever dissipated and the region was opened up to other economic activities, including the exploitation of cacao and coconut trees.

Broadly speaking, we can identify two basic nuclei of coconut palm haciendas: the first situated in the *alcaldías mayores* of Colima and Motines (Map 3), the second in those of Zacatula and Acapulco (Map 4). These two demarcations shared important physical, economic, and sociocultural characteristics. Physically, they had warm-humid and sub-humid climates. Haciendas were established near fluvial currents, ideal terrain for cultivating coconut palms and distilling aguardiente. Economically, those coconut palm plantations (*haciendas de palmas de beneficio*) were inserted into orchards where Spaniards had carried out intensive cacao cultivation, so *Theobroma cacao* and *Cocos nucifera* emerged as a profitable binomial for those hacendados. In terms of sociocultural features, we find that numerous Asians (our *indios chinos*) settled there and soon became the main laborers on the emergent palm haciendas. Those two producing nuclei remained mutually independent and attended differentiated markets with distinct characteristics, as we explain in the following section.

The Colima-Motines Nucleus

The *alcaldía mayor* of Colima extended over a coastal plain bathed by three rivers, the Cihuatlán to the north, the Armería in the center, and the Coahuayana to the south. The terrain presents low mountains that in some places reach down to the coast. Elevations range from sea level to 4,000 m.a.s.l. at the imposing *Volcán de Fuego* (Volcano of Fire). The climate is warm and semi-arid, except in the high mountains.[191] Although the province of Colima –created in 1523 by Hernán Cortés and his troops– lay within the ecclesiastical jurisdiction of the Bishopric of Michoacán, a small indigenous settlement called Almoloyan pertained to the Archbishopric of Guadalajara.

The establishment of palm haciendas in this *alcaldía* can be traced along two main roads from the villa of Colima toward the coast: one along the Armería River that ran through Coquimatlán and Jala. At the foot of that sierra lay the Caxitlán Valley, an extensive plain dominated by palm forests, a landscape that can still be appreciated today. This valley, at an elevation of 100-200 m.a.s.l, was the zone of the greatest *vino de cocos* production in the colonial period. In the second half of the 17th century, the Nahualapa Valley, west of Coquimatlán, experienced a marked increase in palm aguardiente production as a result of the resurgence of some haciendas that moved from the coastal plain toward the outskirts of the villa across the Armería River. Some distillation of *vino de cocos* was carried out in the *pueblo de indios* called San Francisco de Almoloyan that neighbored the villa of Colima, though it was of less importance than that of the haciendas that stretched out to the coast.

The Coahuayana River divided the *alcaldía mayor* of Colima from Motines and bathed the towns of Ixtlahuacán, Chiamila, and Zinacamitlán, where important palm haciendas also developed (Map 3). The *alcaldía mayor* of Motines had three important localities: Maquilí, Coalcomán, and the Alima Valley, the latter situated at the boundary with the province of Colima. As a result, the haciendas of many residents of Colima were actually located there. That *alcaldía* extended along the Pacific coast from the Coahuayana River to the Carrizal River, and inland to the mountain chain that separated it from the Tepalcatepec Basin. At the highest elevations (above 2,000 m.a.s.l.) the climate is cool, water is abundant, and the land is covered by forests. The climate in lower reaches, however, is warm and semi-arid. This demarcation was shared by the *alcaldes mayores* of Colima and Zacatula,

Part I

but in 1560 a separate jurisdiction was declared, centered on Coalcomán and, later, Maquilí. All the parishes in the zone pertained to the diocese of Michoacán.[192]

Map 3 shows the palm haciendas in the Colima-Motines nucleus. In the *alcaldía mayor* of Colima: the villa of Colima, Aguacatitlán, Tecuciapa, Xicotlán, Jala, Caxitlán, Nahualapa, and Zapotlanejo valley, and Coquimatlán, Tecolapa, Ixtlahuacán, Santa Ana Ecautlán, Popoyutla, Tepuxtitlán, and San Francisco de Almoloyan. In Motines: the Alima Valley, Achiotlán, Mexcala, Suchitzi, Zinacamitlán, Chiamila, Xolotlán, and Maquilí.

Map 3. Palm Haciendas in the Colima–Motines Nucleus

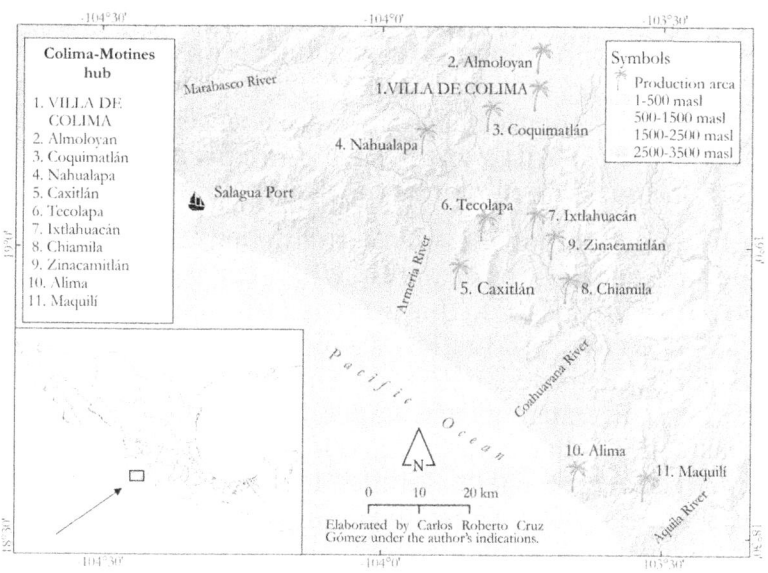

The Zacatula–Acapulco Nucleus

The *vino de cocos*-producing nucleus of Zacatula-Acapulco occupies a littoral plain at an elevation that begins at just 100 m.a.s.l. Today it is known as the *Costa Grande* region of the state of Guerrero. The width between valley and mountains ranges mostly from 5-10 km, but in some stretches narrows to less than 1 km. In other areas, in contrast, fluvial valleys extend a little over 20 km toward the sierra, where they reach their maximum altitude. The climate in the zone is warm and sub-humid with summer rains.[193]

The villa de la Concepción de Zacatula was founded in 1523 at a site where a shipyard had been established the year before. From 1524, that jurisdiction was represented by an *alcalde mayor* and extended from the Cachán River on the west to the mouth of the Coyuca River to the east. The Balsas River divided the province in two parts: the western area was known as Motines de Zacatula, while the eastern part was simply called Zacatula. In 1575, the *alcalde mayor* moved his residence from Zacatula to Tecpan, which explains why the economic nucleus of coconut palm haciendas in the 17th century was located in the latter town and San Miguel los Apuzagualcos –or Apasagualcos– a hacienda near Atoyac.[194] All towns in the region pertained to the ecclesiastical jurisdiction of the Bishopric of Michoacán.

Immediately outside Atoyac, this demarcation abutted the *alcaldía mayor* of Acapulco, where the fertile lands of Coyuca were located. This was the most important area of *vino de cocos* production in this nucleus. The *alcaldía mayor* of Acapulco, bathed by the Papagayo River and some smaller currents that emptied into lagoons along the coastal plain, had a hot, semi-arid climate, except in the forested zones at higher altitudes. In 1548, the *corregidor* of various localities[195] was raised to the rank of *alcalde mayor* of the port of Acapulco. Later, neighboring *encomiendas* were annexed. From 1570, with the onset of transpacific trade by the Manila Galleon, that port experienced growing dynamism, though concentrated at the time of the arrival and subsequent departure of the Galleon. Due to those circumstances, the *alcalde mayor* preferred to live in Acamalutla, Tixtla, Cuernavaca, or Mexico City for the rest of the year to avoid the intense heat. He was represented locally by a deputy (*teniente*) he appointed. It was also with the establishment of the transpacific route that the port gradually came to fill with a permanent population of negros, mulattos, and Filipinos, with only a few Spaniards.[196]

Around 1570, the *encomendero* García de Albornoz purchased some lands from the *pueblos de indios* in the zone where he built huts for his laborers and corrals for sheep, mules, and oxen. He set aside part of the plain to plant corn. By that time, more Spaniards were arriving, resulting in the creation of the haciendas of Santa Cruz, Nuestra Señora de Guía, Nuestra Señora del Buen Suceso, and San Diego, all situated between the Coyuca and Mitla lagoons, as well as the hacienda of San Miguel Apasagualcos.[197] This zone offered two important advantages: its proximity to the Coyuca River that emptied into the ocean, and two lagoons "where water was dammed [and] spread over the land to moisten it [...] the cacao orchards receive water from the river and lagoons [so they can] produce and be conserved".[198]

Map 4 shows the palm haciendas of the Zacatula-Acapulco nucleus. Most lay within the jurisdiction of the *alcaldía mayor* of Zacatula, though they also abutted the *alcaldía mayor* of Santos Reyes de Acapulco. Thanks to an inventory from the hacienda de San Pablo, in the Petatlán valley, we know that *vino de cocos* was produced there at least from the year 1609, when 80 *botijas* of the distillate were reported, together with some production utensils, such as vats.[199] Throughout the 17th century, *vino de cocos* production was registered on diverse haciendas, including those of San Pedro, San Juan de Tuxtepec, San Bartolomé Tuxtepec, San Luis, San Juan Bautista, Nuestra Señora del Buen Suceso, Nuestra Señora de la Concepción, San Miguel Apuzagualcos, and San Nicolás Tetitlán, as well as on ranches called Cayaco, Cacalutla, and –likely– San Jerónimo, San Francisco, and San José.[200]

Map 4. Palm Haciendas in the Zacatula–Acapulco Nucleus

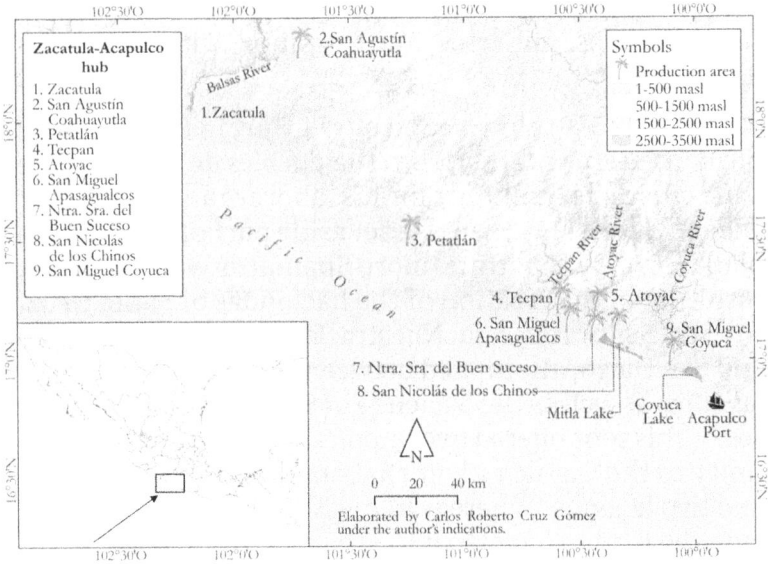

Changes in the Mar del Sur Landscape

In pre-Hispanic times, inhabitants of the coastal strip of the Mexican Pacific practiced the agricultural system called *milpa*, cultivating corn, chili peppers, beans, and squash. Some cotton, agaves, and cacao were grown, and salt and marine resources allowed local people to exchange the goods they produced with certain regions in central and western Mesoamerica. After the irruption of the Spanish, the ensuing dramatic reduction of native populations in coastal regions, and the scarcity of mineral deposits, drastic changes in land use allowed Europeans to remain in the region. One such use was cultivating cacao, a product that enjoyed high demand in New Spain and European markets in the second half of the 16th century. On this topic, we concur with Gerardo Sánchez Díaz, who affirms that the establishment of cacao plantations in the Mar del Sur in that century owed much to the collapse of the Zacatula shipyard and the unfruitful search for minerals near the coast.[201] While the *Theobroma cacao* L. plant is native to Central America, its apogee did not come about until the arrival of the Spanish. We are interested in examining those spaces where cacao exploitation flourished because it was precisely there that the coconut palm was inserted with such success in both the Colima-Motines and Zacatula-Acapulco nuclei.

Cacao cultivation in Colima, Motines, and Zacatula in the colonial period has been studied primarily by José Miguel Romero de Solís and Gerardo Sánchez Díaz, both of whom identify Manuel de Cáceres, originally from Extremadura, as the pioneer in cacao plantations in the Mar del Sur, beginning in 1528. In Lorenzo Lebrón de Quiñones' *Relación sumaria* we read that this crop reached its apogee in the mid-16th century when producers in Colima exploited 376,000 *casas de cacao* on their haciendas; that is, 752,000 trees.[202] According to Rolf Widmer, cacao haciendas in Coyuca emerged in the mid-16th century on the initiative of *encomenderos* established there.[203]

Why was cacao grown on the Pacific littoral? Because it was one of the most profitable native crops for Spaniards in that period, when it functioned not only as a food and raw material for making chocolate, but also as a means of exchange. We must keep in mind that in 17th-century Europe –indeed, still today– the three stimulating drinks that had the highest demand were chocolate, coffee, and tea,[204] so cacao exploitation served to satisfy both internal and external market demands.

It was in the final third of the 16th century that the coconut palm appeared in that landscape dominated by cacao plantations and haciendas. But why were those trees planted precisely there? For one simple reason: cacao plants need trees to protect them from the sun. In Náhuatl those trees were called *cacahuanantzin*, which means "the mother of cacao". In addition to a hot climate, *Theobroma cacao* requires "mother trees" to shade them from harsh solar rays. Suffice to recall the testimony of the *corregidor* Sebastián Macarro in 1580, who in his *Relación geográfica de Tancítaro* (Michoacán), wrote that the natives:

> harvest cacao [...] No kind of grass grows beneath [those trees] because the sun never shines on the ground where they are planted for [they] are most delicate: if they receive the sun's rays, or any frost, they are lost within an hour. So, when they plant them, they also plant other trees that grow tall and cover them with shade so the sun cannot reach them; because, as they say, they are covered and [the cacao] stays below. Hence, they call these trees, in the Mexican language, *ynances*, which means "mothers that raise those cacao plants (*cacahuatales*)".[205]

The "*Relación geográfica de la provincial de Motín*", written in 1580 by Juan Alcalde de Rueda, explains that those protector trees were essential for the survival of cacao:

> Hurricanes from the Mar del Sur occasionally strike this province with fierce winds from the Mar del Sur, sometimes with rain [...] sometimes without. They come with such force that they knock down very strong trees no matter how well rooted they may be. Their impact on cacao plantations [destroys] the foliage of the shade trees [...] leaving [those] trees exposed to the sun, causing great damage and destruction; though this occurs only once in a while.[206]

These references are fundamental for understanding, first, that the coconut palm came to replace native species of "mother trees" that sheltered the cacao, and second, the fact that they gained such quick acceptance: they performed a double function by supporting cacao cultivation and producing *tuba* that could be exploited to make *vino de cocos*. The *cacahuanantzin* (*Gliricidia sepium*) was a leguminous tree well-known in Mesoamerica for its medicinal properties. It was native to lowland areas in Mexico and dry regions of Central America. However, because the Spanish did not consider it a productive species, the coconut palm gradually displaced it. Without doubt, that phenomenon constituted one of the principal ecological changes that occurred along that coastal strip.

Colonial sources from the first half of the 17th century confirm the presence of the cacao-coconut dyad on Spanish haciendas in the *alcaldías mayores* of Colima, Motines, and Zacatula. This was a progressive phenomenon, so by the 1620s perhaps half of the cacao haciendas had added coconut palm plantations, as is evident in the cases of Colima and Motines (Table 5). From the decade of 1630 onward, almost 100% of the cacao haciendas reported in the *alcaldías* of Colima, Motines, and Zacatula had introduced coconut palms (Table 6).

Table 5. Residents of Colima Who Owned Cacao and Palm Haciendas in Colima–Motines (1622)

Owner	Place	Cacao	Palms
Juan de Aguilar Solórzano	Caxitlán	✔	
Alonso Álvarez de Espinosa	Caxitlán	✔	
Diego Arias Arellano	Alima	✔	
Rodrigo de Brizuela	Aguacatitlán	✔	✔
Jorge Carrillo de Guzmán	Caxitlán	✔	✔
Jorge Carrillo de Guzmán	Aguacatitlán	✔	✔
Juan Carrillo de Guzmán	Caxitlán	✔	✔
Andrés de Castilla Montemayor	Zapotlanejo		✔
García Dávalos Vergara	Alima	✔	
Pedro de Espinosa	Alima	✔	✔
Juan Fernández de Tene	Colima	✔	✔
Álvaro García de Grijalva	Caxitlán	✔	

Owner	Place	Cacao	Palms
Alonso García Nomparte	Caxitlán	✓	
Hernando Gómez Machorro	Suchitzi	✓	
Matías de Hoyo	Contla	✓	✓
Pedro López de Salazar	Maquilí	✓	✓
Diego Mejía de la Torre	Xicotlán	✓	
Juan Preciado	Caxitlán	✓	✓
Gaspar Ramírez Alarcón	Caxitlán	✓	✓
Gaspar Román	Caxitlán	✓	
Luis de Solórzano	Colima	✓	
Domingo Vela de Grijalva	Popoyutla	✓	

Source: AGI, México, N. 262 and N. 263; Juan Carlos Reyes Garza, *Por mandato de su Majestad. Inventario de bienes de las autoridades de Colima, 1622*, 2000.

Table 6. Cacao and Palm Haciendas in Colima, Motines, and Zacatula (1631 and 1649)

Year	1631		1649	
VILLA DE COLIMA	Cacao	Palms	Cacao	Palms
Valle de Aguacatitlán	✓	✓	✓	
Valle de Tecuciapa	✓	✓	✓	✓
Valle de Xicotlán	✓	✓	✓	✓
Valle de Jala	✓	✓	✓	✓
Valle de Caxitlán	✓	✓	✓	✓
Valle de Zapotlanejo	✓	✓	✓	✓
Popoyutla	✓	✓	✓	✓

Part I

Year	1631		1649	
Tepuxtitlán	✓	✓	✓	✓
SAN FCO. ALMOLOYAN	Cacao	Palms	Cacao	Palms
San Francisco	✓	✓	✓	✓
CHIAMILA	Cacao	Palms	Cacao	Palms
Valle de Alima	✓	✓	✓	✓
Achiotlán	✓	✓	✓	✓
Mexcala	✓	✓	✓	✓
Xuchitzi	✓	✓	✓	✓
MAQUILÍ	Cacao	Palms	Cacao	Palms
Maquilí	✓	✓	✓	✓
LOS APASAGUALCOS	Cacao	Palms	Cacao	Palms
The Apasagualcos	✓	✓	✓	✓
TECPAN	Cacao	Palms	Cacao	Palms
Tecpan	✓	✓	✓	✓

Sources: Ramón López Lara, *El Obispado de Michoacán en el siglo XVII. Informe inédito de beneficios, pueblos y lenguas*, 1973, pp. 109-118, 129-132; Francisco Arnaldo Issasy, *Demarcación y descripción de el Obispado de Michoacán y fundación de su Iglesia Cathedral* (1649), 1982, pp. 172-175.

This pairing of cacao trees with coconut palms thrived not only in New Spain, but also in the Philippines, though in the inverse order, as *Theobroma cacao* L. was introduced from America and incorporated into palm production units on the archipelago, a phenomenon that endures today (Photograph 6). In fact, many Filipinos now consider the cacao a native tree. It has received its certificate of naturalization and the memory of its origin has been erased. This cultural phenomenon is not exclusive to the Philippines, for the coconut palm has undergone a similar process: Colima is known as the "city of palm trees", *tuba* is its traditional drink, and the famous *cocadas* (sweets made from coconuts) are the typical candies *par excellence*.

Photograph 6. Cacao Tree Under the Shade of a Coconut Palm (Bohol, the Philippines)

Source: Barangay Ponong, Alburquerque, Bohol (Central Visayas, the Philippines). Photograph by Paulina Machuca.

Part I

But around the time that the cacao-coconut haciendas achieved a certain level of success in the Mar del Sur, events both internal and external brought about the collapse of the former. First, the Spanish Crown gave priority to the cacao produced in the Soconusco region and in South America, especially Guayaquil and Caracas.[207] Second, the delicate nature of this plant, which demanded all manner of care by those who cultivated it, gradually overcame growers' interest in pursuing this activity. Finally, cacao plantations continually suffered losses due to storms and cyclones. In 1612, Hernán Gómez Machorro, a resident of Colima, stated that "cacao trees are so delicate and sickly that when it is cold they freeze, when it rains they rot, [and] when it is dry they stop producing".[208] These circumstances, added to the competition with cacao from Soconusco and Chontalpa, and later South America, brought about a sharp decline in the cacao trade in the Colima-Motines nucleus in the 17th century, though it continued to be used locally as a means of exchange to pay the personal services of Indians.[209] To further complicate matters, Indian labor was becoming scarce, so many residents opted to shift their priority to coconut production. However, one specific event that accelerated this transition was the 1626 hurricane that devastated most of the cacao plantations in Colima, opened a more alluring horizon for coconut palm cultivation and, to some extent, marked a watershed in the trajectory of *vino de cocos*, as we discuss below.

Juan Carlos Reyes affirmed that by mere coincidence and the good fortune of people in Colima, coconut palm seeds had arrived in the province when cacao production was at its apogee, just in time for those plantations to reach full *tuba* production when the crisis struck cacao cultivation.[210] Sebastián de Vera, also a resident of Colima, expressed this in 1612: "though some residents of this coast have cacao plantations, their fruit and exploitation give but one harvest per year, [while] production of coconut palms and wine is year-round...".[211]

Tending cacao plantations required more work and entailed high costs for "cleaning, conducting water, and people to harvest",[212] as Rodrigo de Brizuela observed in 1622. Andrés de Castilla Montemayor noted, in contrast, that *vino de cocos* only needed "people and supplies".[213] Commenting on his cacao hacienda in 1622, Juan Carrillo de Guzmán remarked, "I have owned it and profited from its fruits since 1607; I have had yearly profits of 25 and 30 loads of cacao, although in two years [I harvested] 50 to 60 loads. Profits are not assured, for in some years it is worth 35 to 40 pesos, but in others its value may be greater or lesser, and the most common [price] is 25 to 30 pesos per load."[214] Also referring to cacao, Álvaro García de Grijalva noted that "profits aren't assured, for if the weather turns colder than usual, or the rains come before their time, a cacao [plantation] will not produce a profit, as occurred this year [when] the [cultivation] costs have been much greater than profits".[215]

Speaking of Colima in 1649, Issasy commented that "some cacao [is produced there] and much *vino de cocos* and some sugar mills that have been founded recently".[216] Referring to Maquilí, he observed that "there are three cacao plantation in the district, but they [produce] only a little, and some palms from which wine is made".[217] His comments on Chiamila included the following: "in this district there are… plantations that once had cacao, but now little is harvested on some, and vanillas are produced for chocolate and achiote. Today they are populated by coconut palms from which much wine and aguardiente are made and traded under license from the Viceroy and the Real Audiencia of Mexico".[218] Turning to the plantations in Caxitlán and Tecolapa, he stated that "there are eighteen coconut palm haciendas that each year produce four or five thousand *arrobas* of wine… corn and cotton are also grown there, [the latter] to make textiles. Some cacao and vanilla are harvested, as well as all manner of fruits of the land".[219] These accounts describe a situation quite similar to the fate of the cacao plantations in Compostela that suffered a marked decline in the early 17th century due to poor harvests and a scarcity of indigenous workers.[220] All these testimonies show clearly that around the mid-17th century cacao production in the province of Colima was collapsing, and that this opened the door to the dynamism of the coconut palms and their principal product: *vino de cocos*.

A history distinct from Colima's can be narrated for the Zacatula-Acapulco nucleus, where cacao cultivation continued with some success. In 1649 Petatlán, the residence of the *alcalde mayor* of Zacatula, had "good cacao plantations where some amounts of cacao and some of vanillas are harvested". In Tecpan, in the same year,

> corn, cotton, millet, and rice are harvested, much cacao, vanillas, tamarind, [and] coconuts are produced [and] wine is made from those palms on one or two haciendas of *chinos*; there are three haciendas with bovine cattle, five cacao plantations where harvests are abundant and wine is made, and corn and other seeds are planted, and many cattle are raised, and profits made from this each year.[221]

Thanks to the inventory from the cacao hacienda in San Juan Tuxtepec, jurisdiction of Zacatula, we know that there were 180 coconut palm haciendas there that produced small amounts of *vino de cocos*, proving that this vegetable binomial also predominated in that region.[222] In that production nucleus, cacao was a profitable activity until the late 18th century, when cotton was introduced successfully, eventually emerging as the primary crop. The coconut palm continued to generate some economic interest, but from the 18th century onward cultivation was oriented toward commercializing the fruit, especially copra, as occurred in the Colima-Motines nucleus as well.

Final Reflections

In this chapter we have analyzed the importance of *vino de cocos* and its raw material, *tuba*. We explained the process of elaborating *tuba* and some social aspects related to this drink. In the second section, we examined the movement of the technique of *vino de cocos* production to the coast of the Mar del Sur in New Spain and similarities and differences with respect to the Filipino archipelago. Part three described the places where coconut palm haciendas were established and identified two production nuclei: on the one hand, the *alcaldías mayores* of Colima and Motines, on the other, those of Zacatula and Acapulco. In ecological terms, the introduction of Cocos *nucifera* displaced other native species of trees, including one called "mother of the cacao" (*cacahuanantzin*).

In the 17th century, the coastal strip along the Pacific Ocean in New Spain witnessed the emergence of two new drinks, *tuba* and *vino de cocos*, that at the time competed with the so-called "drinks of the land" and even with wine from Castille. This phenomenon was made possible by the presence of *indios chinos* who successfully inserted themselves into the coconut palm haciendas that graced the landscape. This is the topic of the next chapter.

PART II
ACTORS OF THE FIRST GLOBALIZATION: A VIEW "FROM BELOW"

3. FRANCISCA MARTHA AND THE INDIOS CHINOS IN THE MAR DEL SUR

INTRODUCTION

In the decade of 1650, in the coastal valleys of the province of Colima, a peculiar figure entered the public scene, one that due to her unique nature deserves to be addressed in detail in this chapter: a *china criolla* named Francisca Martha, daughter of a Filipino father and an Indian mother who owned a palm hacienda where *vino de cocos* was produced. In contrast to the thousands of anonymous *chinos* who settled in New Spain during the first globalization, "minuscule lives" whose traces have gone virtually unnoticed, the case of Francisca Martha has left us some historical clues that make it possible to observe particularly interesting social phenomena, for she was a product of mestizaje between Asian migrants and the native population, a sector that struggled to integrate into a Colima society amply masculinized in the sector of *vino de cocos* production, but one that showed a certain aperture toward immigrants who arrived on the Manila Galleon, some of whom emerged as actors of great importance in the local economy thanks to their work as *vinateros* and producers of the drink distilled from the sap of palm trees.

While in chapter 4 we will analyze in detail the profiles of *vinateros* in Colima during the 17th century –all of them men– in this chapter we examine the trajectory of Francisca Martha and her relation to the palm haciendas where *vino de cocos* was elaborated. To contextualize her case, we begin by presenting some general features of the *indios chinos* in the province of Colima. We will not repeat what other authors have written, broadly, on Asian immigration in New Spain; for example, Tatiana Seijas, Déborah Oropeza, Matthew J. Furlong, Rubén Carrillo, and, more recently, Diego Javier Luis,[223] but shall focus on documents from archives in Colima that are especially helpful for contextualizing the presence of *indios chinos* –free and slaves– in this province where Francisca Martha developed.

BEING AN INDIO CHINO

Indio chino was a highly ambiguous term coined in New Spain to distinguish native Americans from Asians, so it must be seen as a unique construction of that time and place. This concept was not used on the Philippine islands, where other nomenclatures existed to designate the different ethnic groups that coexisted on the archipelago, beginning with the natives, generally known as "Filipino Indians" (*indios filipinos*) or *naturales de Filipinas* ("native Filipinos"). Where greater precision was required, people were identified by their place or region of origin, as *tagalos*, *visayas*, *cagayanes*, *zambales*, or *negritos*, among many others. People who came from China were called *sangleyes* or *champanes*, in reference to a kind of boat that was widely used in that nation.[224]

In New Spain, the concept of *indio chino* encompassed virtually all people from Asia, so it is very difficult to determine the real place of origin of different individuals.[225] This conundrum becomes even more complex when we read documents like the last will and testament of don Juan

Part II

de la Cruz, dated in Colima in 1717, which stated that he was a "native of Sengayan in the Philippines",[226] although Sengayam is actually a locality in Indonesia. In that case, the Philippines was not the place of origin but, rather, the site where he embarked. However, from the context of the documents consulted and based on the cultural baggage that many of those individuals carried to the places where they settled, it is feasible to affirm that the vast majority did, in fact, come from the Philippines followed, in order of importance, by nations and spaces like southern China, Borneo, Indonesia, New Guinea, Sri Lanka, and Portuguese India (Map 5). Japan occupied a special space because, although they were also Asians, in most cases the "Japanese" were distinguished from *indios chinos*.[227]

Map 5. Origins of the *Indios Chinos* Who Settled in New Spain

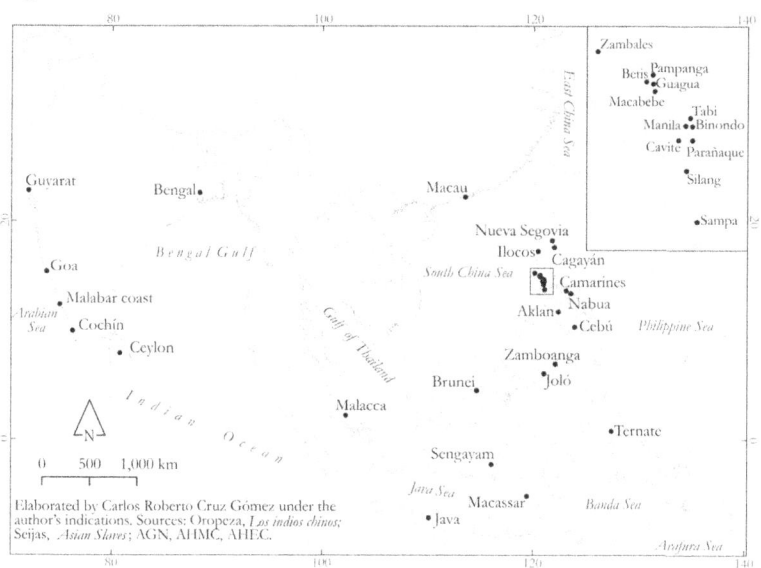

In the case of Fujian, we cannot forget that a close commercial relation existed with the Filipino archipelago, exemplified by the fact that around 1603 some 20,000 *sangleyes* lived in the Parian of Manila. Thus, it is not farfetched to think that many of them sailed on the Galleon to New Spain.[228] The presence of slaves from Bengal, Cochin, the Malabar Coast, Goa, and the region of Gujarat in the Portuguese *Estado da Índia* can be explained by the union of the Two Crowns in the period between 1580 and 1640, and by the dynamics of the Portuguese in the slave trade of both Asians and Africans.[229] Another group of *indios chinos* came from places that maintained political and commercial relations –and, hence, a certain human mobility– with the Philippines, as in the case of Terrenate, Sengayan, Java, Macassar, and Malacca, in the modern day nations of Indonesia and Malaysia; Brunei on the island of Borneo; Papua New Guinea; and Ceylon, in what today is Sri Lanka.[230] This latter migration reflects the temporary presence of Spaniards in Terrenate in the 17th century, the commercial dynamics of the Portuguese, and the establishment, in 1602, of the Dutch East India Company (VOC), broadly based in Batavia, that conducted intense commercial activity in Southeast Asia. Historically, of course, this region had been a commercial space before the arrival of Europeans. In this regard, Antonio de Morga, the *oidor* (judge) of the Audiencia de Manila, recorded in his book, *Sucesos de las islas Filipinas*, that:

> Some Portuguese ships come to Manila each year with the strong winds of the monsoon from the Moluccas, Malacca, and India bearing merchandise: cloves, cinnamon, and pepper, and with black slaves and *cafres* [...] At the same time, the *vendavales* bring some smaller boats with natives from the island of Borneo, who return with the first breezes, and enter by the river of Manila. From their boats they sell all they bring, finely-woven *petates*, some slaves for the natives [...] A few times boats come to Manila from Siam and Cambodia, bringing some *menjuí*, pepper, ivory, and sheets of cotton, rubies and poorly-worked, mounted sapphires, some slaves [...].[231]

Part II

As we read in this excerpt from Morga, Manila was a space of mercantile confluence *par excellence*, where trade in slaves from other nations was on the order of the day with participation not only by Europeans. It is interesting to observe that native Filipinos also purchased slaves, indicating that the system of servitude there clearly preceded the establishment of the Spanish colonial system.[232] It is important to emphasize that the *indios chinos* who came to New Spain represented, in reality, an ethnic melting pot whose origins were diluted in this ambiguous concept that only served to allow authorities in New Spain to group them in some emerging category and, in this way, assign them a place within the corporativist system that characterized the *Ancien Régime*.

In addition to the term *indio chino*, it is possible to locate –though in a much lower proportion– documents from New Spain that allude to *indios filipinos* ("Filipino Indians"), *naturales de Filipinas* ("native Filipinos"), or *chinos de Manila* ("*chinos* from Manila"). This finding opens two possibilities: that those people were actually and originally from the archipelago, or that Manila was the place where they set sail for New Spain, as we suggested above. In a very few cases the province in the Philippines where they came from is mentioned. The island of Luzon, in the north, is cited most often: Betis, Binondo, Cagayán, Camarines, Cavite, Guagua, Ilocos, Macabebe, Manila, Nabua, Nueva Segovia, Pampanga, Pangasinán, Parañaque, Silang, and Zambales. In the central region of Visayas documents identify Aklan and Cebu; while for Mindanao, in the south, Zamboanga and the neighboring Jolo Islands are mentioned (Map 5).

In some cases of *indios chinos*, the place of origin can be deduced from surnames, such as the appellative "Pampango". We know of a *vinatero* in Colima in 1603 named Bartolomé "Sampa", who may have come from that demarcation in the province of Batangas, south of Manila. Another *vinatero* in Colima, identified as Juan "Tabi", may have come from a town of that name in Luzon;[233] while, the *vinatero* Juan Bautista de Pantao, also in Colima, likely came from Pantau-Rugat, in Mindanao.[234] Matthew J. Furlong has suggested that numerous *indios chinos* came from the province of Pampanga, which neighbors Manila.[235] Kristyl Obispado mentions that some provinces near Manila were accessible for the recruitment of the native workforce.[236]

The Places Where *Indios Chinos* Settled in New Spain

Between 1565 and 1815, the port of Acapulco received between 10,000 and 20,000 *chinos*, according to estimates by Rubén Carrillo Martín, who studied the Asian presence in New Spain, with a focus on the city of Puebla de los Ángeles.[237] Carrillo revealed the discrepancies that exist among the figures presented by other authors who have addressed this topic. Edward Slack, for example, gave a number of 40,000 to 100,000 Asian immigrants; Floro Marcene proposed the figure of 60,000; Jonathan Israel calculated 48,000; Déborah Oropeza suggested there were around 10,000, and Tatiana Seijas indicated approximately 8,000.[238] It is not possible to determine the exact number simply because not all those individuals left behind any record of their arrival. Based on the records of the Caja Real de Hacienda (Royal Treasury) of Acapulco, Oropeza, for instance, determined that 3,377 *free chinos* and 3,776 Asian slaves entered New Spain, including a minority of slaves of African origin.[239] She recognizes that the number of people from the Philippines must have been around three times greater because other, illegal, entry points existed for people to reach the lands of New Spain; for example, the ports of La Navidad and Salagua. While the presence of *indios chinos* was accentuated in the coastal zone of the Mar del Sur and the capital of New Spain, we cannot ignore the fact that their dispersion spanned an area that today encompasses twelve states in Mexico; over one-third of the national territory: Mexico City, Colima,

PART II

Guerrero, Hidalgo, Jalisco, Michoacán, Oaxaca, Puebla, Tabasco, Tlaxcala, Veracruz, and Zacatecas (Map 6).[240]

Map 6. The Settlement of Indios Chinos in New Spain

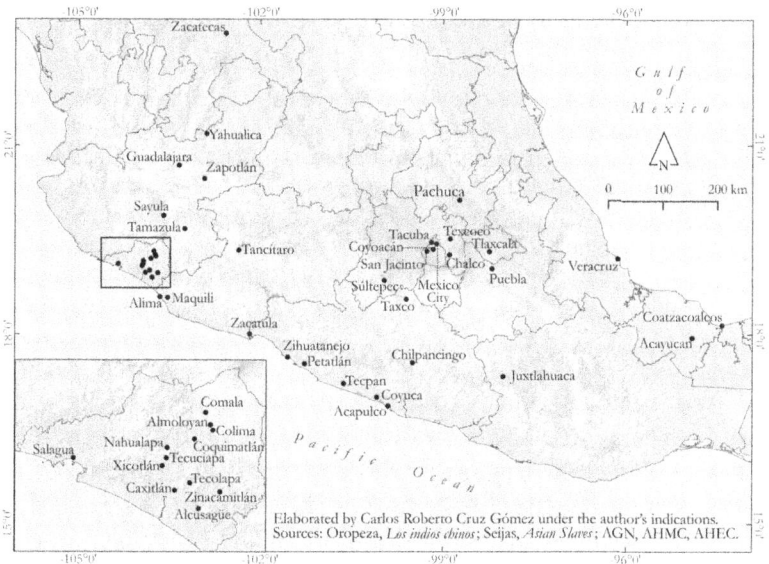

It is evident that the presence of *indios chinos* in Acapulco and the surrounding area can be explained by the dynamics of the Manila Galleon in that port, but the relation to the case of Colima is less clear or, at least, less well documented. We argue that the existence of numerous Asians in the *alcaldía mayor* of Colima reflects the fact that two ports there –La Navidad and Salagua– were points where people commonly disembarked illegally and merchandise was unloaded clandestinely when the Manila Galleon stopped for provisions on its route to Acapulco. Those were also the places where the *gentilhombre* descended with the Galleon's official message (*pliego oficial*) addressed to the Viceroy of New Spain, which was forwarded from there to Mexico City. The *gentilhombre* (from the French *gentilhomme*), was literally a man who was sent to the King with an important petition, or to provide news of some crucial event, like the conquest of a city square or the arrival of a fleet. It is thanks to files deposited in the Archivo Histórico del Municipio de Colima that we learned of the importance of this strategic stopover. In this regard, in 1612, the *cabildo* of the villa of Colima informed the Viceregal authorities that:

> When it is time and [people] expect the Galleons sent by order of His Majesty from the Philippine Islands to this New Spain, in said port of Salagua there are normal, continuous sentinels who upon perceiving them inform this villa so it can report to Mexico City with the petitions that are generally delivered to the people of said port who go to receive the Galleons, and take them the provisions and aid they need.[241]

In addition, thanks to notes in the diaries of Gregorio M. de Guijo, we learn that this practice continued well into the 17th century, and that Colima continued to be a strategic point for the arrival of the Galleon. As a result, from 1650 to 1655, the *gentilhombre* of the Manila Galleon disembarked in the port of Salagua systematically by the month of March. There, he would pick up a letter on the ship's condition issued by the *alcalde mayor* of Colima, and take it to Mexico City to inform the Viceroy of New Spain about happenings in the area.[242]

Both the practice of supplying the ship and the landing of the *gentilhombre* led to a third dynamic that resulted from the presence of the Galleon in the harbors of La Navidad and Salagua: the illegal disembarkment of men and merchandise to *tierra firme*. This was expressed in the *Estado político de Nueva España por los años de 1735* that, referring to the port of Colima, stated:

> where the *gentilhombre* disembarks from the Philippine Galleon [to deliver] the report that will be sent to inform the Viceroy [...] I can say with certainty that a merchant loaded with all manner of merchandise without paying any

duty to His Majesty [and] sell it along his way to Mexico, making the trip slowly as is convenient for him.[243]

With the same facility with which the *gentilhombre* left the ship to sell his wares once on land, surely some free *indios chinos* did the same. Unfortunately, those operations, carried out with the greatest possible stealth and discretion, have left only scant traces in the historical documentation and appear only in certain conjunctural moments; for example, cases of sailors who became ill and had to leave the Galleon before they planned to. This occurred in the case of Manuel Pérez, who disembarked in Salagua in 1580 hoping to be cured, but instead passed away in Tecolapa, a town near the coast of Colima.[244]

Another case involved Gaspar Pagés de Moncada, a scribe from a galleon called *Nuestra Señora de Atocha*. In 1625, he died in the villa of Colima from an illness he had contracted along the maritime route from Manila to Acapulco that forced him to leave the ship in the port of La Navidad.[245] These cases suggest that disembarkments by Asians before the Galleon reached the port of Acapulco, must have been more frequent than documents reflect in. For example, Domingo de la Cruz, a *chino* slave and native of Cebu, reported in 1678 that he had been sold to a ship's captain in the Philippines, who offloaded him in the port of Salagua and then sold him to a resident of Sayula, in Pueblos de Ávalos.[246]

This evidence leads us to think that the route of entry of numerous *indios chinos* to the western coast of New Spain ran through the ports of La Navidad and Salagua, though we do not deny that many must have reached this area from Acapulco or, perhaps, Mexico City, as occurred in the cases of some slaves and free Japanese in the 17th century.[247]

INDIOS CHINOS SLAVES IN COLIMA

Some recent historiography has paid special attention to the profile of the Asian slaves who arrived in New Spain on the Manila Galleon and settled in Acapulco and the surrounding area, as well as in Mexico City and Puebla de los Ángeles;[248] however, the case of Colima has been much less widely studied. Although in 1597 Felipe II prohibited the shipping of Asian slaves on the Galleon, we know that his order left loopholes that fostered a distinct reality, for certain personages –according to their hierarchy– were allowed to sail from Cavite to New Spain with a limited number of Asian servants. Those privileged figures included the governor of the Philippines, judges (*oidores*), treasury officials, wealthy merchants, and other "honored persons". Then, in 1620, that permission was extended to include certain passengers and sailors,[249] a concession that in some way incentivized a profitable trade for slaveowners who often traveled with more Asians than the law allowed and proceeded to sell them upon arriving in New Spain. The cost of a slave in Manila could range from 57 to 180 pesos, but in New Spain the price rose to a range of 200 to 450 pesos; hence the interest in participating in that business.[250]

Asian slaves came to New Spain in a period marked by a "chronic scarcity" of labor so, according to Jonathan Israel, "Filipino slaves constituted a complementary workforce".[251] Many of those slaves were concentrated in central New Spain, between Mexico City and Puebla, for they were sold in operations that took place in Acapulco, where traders like Simón López lived and dealt in slaves in Veracruz, Zacatecas, Guadalajara, and Mexico City.[252]

On the coast of the Mar del Sur, some Asian slaves worked on the cacao and coconut palm haciendas in the *alcaldías mayores* of Acapulco, Zacatula, Motines, and Colima,[253] but the case of the province of Colima stands out because most *chinos vinateros* there were freemen; a topic we explore in depth in the next chapter. It is revealing that

PART II

the purchase-sale letters we discovered for Colima from the 17th century do not present evidence that the few slaves there participated in work on the haciendas or in *vino de cocos* production (Table 7).

Table 7. Purchase and Sale of *Indios Chinos* Slaves in Colima (17th Century)

Year	Name	Value	Age	Owner	Purchaser
1620	Juan, "chino from the land of India"	450 pesos	22	Jerónimo Dávalos Vergara	Rodrigo de Brizuela
1620	Jerónimo	400 pesos	-	Juan Gutierre de Monroy	Diego Mejía de la Torre
1621	Antón	400 pesos	19	Pedro Blanco	Martín Alonso Enríquez
1622	Vicente	300 pesos	19	Alonso Álvarez de Espinosa	Diego de Novela
1622	Bartolomé, "native of Goa"	To be determined	24	Gregorio Fernández de Tene	-
1627	Ventura	250 pesos	-	Juan Bernal de Zúñiga	Juan de Sámano Quiñones
1628	Francisco	Sold at public auction			

Source: AHEC, Fondo Colonial, Protocolos de Escribanos, various files.

The seven cases presented in Table 7 show that some slaves had arrived from Portuguese India because the existing legislation prohibited enslavement of natives of the Philippines, who were considered vassals of the King. But, of course, there were exceptions: the Islamized *indios* of Mindanao taken prisoner in a "just war" were subject to slavery, so we cannot discard the possibility that some of them may have arrived on the Manila Galleon. Indeed, we have the case of Domingo de Urquiza, a public scribe in Querétaro who in 1625 claimed the return of Pedro, "a criollo from Manila" aged 29, for he was his "slave obtained from a just war" who had escaped to Nueva Galicia.[254] A law proclaimed by Felipe II in 1570, and ratified by Felipe III in 1620, provided support for de Urquiza's claim:

> The district of the Philippine Islands and its confines is adjacent to those of Mindanao, whose natives have rebelled, adopting the sect of Muhammad, and confederating with the enemies of this Crown have caused very great damage to our vassals, [so] to punish them an efficacious remedy seems to be to declare as slaves those taken prisoner in the war [...].[255]

It is not possible to verify the place of origin of all the *chinos* slaves cited in Table 7, but one interesting aspect is that some were associated with mining contexts, not with *vino de cocos* production. We can cite three examples. In 1621, Antón, "a rather black *indio chino*", with pierced ears, aged 19, was sold to Martín Alonso Enríquez –a resident of Colima– for 400 pesos. His owner was Pedro Blanco, from Pátzcuaro, who had acquired him from Martín de los Santos, a resident of Real de los Reyes de Ostotipaque.[256] It is not implausible that Antón was from Portuguese India due to the description of his "rather black" skin color.

In a second case, from 1622, Gregorio Fernández de Tene (also a resident of Colima) granted a power-of-attorney to Martín Fernández Partida, a public scribe at the Ostotipaque mines, to, in his name, sell Bartolomé, a native of Goa aged 24, at whatever price he could negotiate, as long as payment was in cash.[257] In that same year, Alonso Álvarez de Espinosa –also from Colima– sold a young slave named Vicente, aged 19, "from the Chinese nation", to Diego Novela, the priest of the *partido* of Maquilí in the Bishopric of Michoacán, for 300 pesos; Álvarez had bought Vicente from Melchor de Tornamira at the mines of Taxco.[258]

Could this mean there was a market for the purchase-sale of Asian slaves as mineworkers? Our attention was drawn to this because those operations mention not only the mines of Ostotipaque in Nueva Galicia, but also those of Taxco, near the port of Acapulco. On this topic, Déborah Oropeza emphasizes that some Asian slaves recently arrived in New Spain were bought by miners in Pachuca and Zacatecas,[259] so it is not unfounded to propose that, at some point, the idea existed to include Asian laborers in mining activity in New Spain. Tatiana Seijas, moreover, affirms that in 1638 a group of miners in Zacatecas, desperate for workers, suggested purchasing African slaves (*cafres*) from the Pacific route; that is, slaves were commercialized by the Portuguese through the Estado da India.[260]

Other examples of the purchase-sale of slaves in Colima are connected to the capital city of New Spain. In May 1620, the royal scribe, Jerónimo Dávalos Vergara, a resident of Mexico City, granted a power-of-attorney to his son, García Dávalos Vergara, and the *alcalde ordinario* of the villa of Colima, Domingo Vela de Grijalba, to, in his name, sell Juan, a 22-year-old *indio chino* slave from India who had a sign on his face that read "Ávalos".[261] Jerónimo Dávalos had bought Juan from Captain Diego González de Arcos, another resident of Mexico City.[262] In June 1620, Juan was sold to Captain Rodrigo de Brizuela, a resident of Colima, for 450 pesos.[263] In another case, on July 12, 1628, the sergeant major of the villa of Colima, Hernán Gómez Machorro, auctioned off a *chino* slave named Francisco, who had fled from his owner. Francisco had acquired a debt of 115 pesos in Colima. When Bernabé Osorio, a resident of Mexico City, paid that amount the *chino* was placed "on deposit" with him until his real owner might appear to claim him.[264] Since that was not a purchase-sale transaction, we cannot determine the price or how Francisco came to be in Colima.

Even the ecclesiastical authorities were involved in these transactions, for in 1627 the priest of the *partido* of Colima, Juan Bernal de Zúñiga, sold a Filipino named Ventura to the *alcalde mayor* in functions, Juan de Sámano Quiñones, for 250 pesos,²⁶⁵ a lower cost than in the previous examples. It appears he was a slave devoted to domestic service, as was the case, as well, of Jerónimo, a "black" slave from Cebu, who had been purchased by Diego de Monroy, a resident of Colima. Upon the latter's death, his son, Juan Gutierre de Monroy, inherited Jerónimo. Juan Gutierre later sold him –in 1620– for 400 pesos to the sitting *alcalde ordinario* of Colima, Diego Mejía de la Torre.²⁶⁶ It is interesting that, as a native of Cebu, Jerónimo was registered as "black", for this suggests that he may have been a member of the Aeta (*negrito*) ethnic group, according to the term coined by the Spanish in the Philippines.

Based on these data, we see that some Asian slaves in Colima were sold for the same price as negro slaves, around 400 pesos.²⁶⁷ Their average age was 21 years, so they were all from a young population sector. It is notable that although some were purchased in mining zones, upon their arrival in the villa of Colima they were employed mainly in domestic service.

FREE INDIOS CHINOS IN COLIMA

In contrast to the *chino* slave laborers on agricultural haciendas in Acapulco and the surrounding area, the *vinateros* of Colima were mostly freemen. The drifting of the Asian population between the two republics –*españoles* and *indios*– allowed them to create strong socioeconomic links in both spheres, but also fostered ambiguity in terms of their juridical category in a corporativist society that sometimes classified them on a par with native Indians, but at others grouped them with other castes. A first indication of the concern as to where this emerging population should be assigned arose in the early 17th century when, in March 1603, the *alcalde mayor* of Colima, Francisco Escudero de Figueroa, reported that the Viceroy Conde de Monterrey had ordered that "said [*indios chinos*] shall pay tribute, be censused, and be charged what the natives of this kingdom are accustomed to paying".[268] This command was directed toward those native and Asian Indians who worked in Spanish homes, haciendas, farms, ranches, and plantations, that lay outside the towns "of their nature" and, hence, had not been censused to determine their tribute status. A few years later, we find the case of Nicolás Rodríguez, who in 1608 approached the *alcalde mayor* of Colima, Juan de Rivera, to solicit the "privileges and ownership of properties and freedoms that [they] enjoy, and be exempt from tribute and personal service". De Rivera alleged that he was not an *indio chino* but, rather, a mestizo, son of an *encomendero* in the Philippines named Juan de Encinas and María de Agangay, a native of the archipelago.[269]

Thus it was that, like the local Indians, the free Asian population was forced to pay tribute, though it was exempt from paying the *alcabala* (sales tax) on any products it sold. However, since some Asians entered Acapulco in the category of slaves, while others were freemen, the question of *alcabala* payments also caused confusion among the Viceregal authorities who, in 1640, established that the registered, tributary *indios chinos*, like native Indians, were not obliged to pay *alcabalas*.[270]

The free *indios chinos* who settled in New Spain participated in distinct activities that Rubén Carrillo Martín has synthesized pertinently: barbers, silversmiths, artisans, muleteers, innkeepers, shopkeepers, bearers, merchants, diplomats, clergy, artists, soldiers, mill workers, and servants.[271] In Mexico City, Asian barbers stood out because they became strong rivals of Spaniards.[272] It was along the coasts that the work of free Asians was closely linked to agriculture, especially the cultivation of plants of Asian origin like the coconut palm and rice, but also native cacao. Others worked maritime activities, such as repairing ships, pearl fishing, and guarding coastlines. Regarding the latter, we can cite the example of the *indio chino* Luis Ortiz, who worked as a sentinel in the province of Colima. Ortiz lived in the town of Alcusagüe, near the coast. On one occasion in 1642, when he caught sight of a ship in the mouth of the Alima River –between Colima and Motines– he stated that Alonso García de Luarca, the deputy *alcalde mayor* of the Caxitlán Valley, had assigned him the post of sentinel there. When he made his statement, "he took the oath without an interpreter because he spoke the Spanish language though he is of the *chino* nation".[273]

It is difficult to establish with any precision the percentage of the Asian population in Colima because we have neither sequential data nor numerous censuses. But according to a census from 1619, in localities like the Caxitlán Valley –to which we will refer below due to the important number of palm trees cultivated there for *vino de cocos* production– one-fifth of the population was of Asian origin: "In this town [Caxitlán], there are 200 Indian residents, 50 married *chinos*, and 15 or 20 Spaniards".[274]

The traces that those *indios chinos* left in the baptismal records of the parish of San Felipe de Jesús in Colima are scattered and barely discernible. For the 1621-1680 period, we have only three baptisms out of a total of 3,523 christenings.[275] To these we can add some parents and godparents who were *chinos*. For this rubric, we found 11 mentions for the 1672-1698 period: six of parents and five of godparents, all males.[276] Though scant, these data are significant, for they allow us to extract some interesting conclusions. Clearly, we are dealing with a *chino* population that was almost exclusively masculine, for reasons we will elucidate when we examine the case of Francisca Martha.

We can see that the bonds of belonging to the Asian world were lost quite quickly through births in Colima and mestizaje –virtually obligatory– with native women, whether Indians, mulattos, or of some other caste. Those who conserved their identity as *chinos*, even in the late 17th century, were adult males very likely from the other shore of the Mar del Sur. Among those individuals one stands out: between 1681 and 1689, Francisco de la Cruz, a *chino*, was registered as a godfather on three occasions, surely a sign of some notoriety within that Asian community. This suggests that, even among exiles and re-composed collectivities, previous hierarchies were not forgotten. This tendency in ritual co-parenthood (*padrinazgo*) can be seen, as well, in Mexico City, where Rubén Carrillo noted that out of a sample of 170 *chinos* present in 78 baptismal records from 1637 to 1642, 51% of the godparents of children born to two *chino* parents were also *chinos*.[277] Here we have, of course, an indicator of the importance that this Asian community conferred to *compadrazgo* among countrymen.

It was very close to the town of Caxitlán, among palm trees and *vino de cocos*, that the story of Francisca Martha developed, a creole *china* (*china mestiza*) owner of a palm hacienda. Her case is exemplary because it represents, to a great degree, the biography of many of the free Filipinos who settled in the province of Colima, living among palm trees in a rural area, in co-existence with other *chinos* and devoted to distilling *tuba*. But her case is, at the same time, peculiar, for hers is the story of a woman of Asian origin who developed in a predominantly male activity and battled to survive in a highly-hierarchized society. Perhaps her case has not attracted footlights like those that have highlighted the famed *china poblana*, Catarina de San Juan, but at a more local level Francisca Martha can certainly compete for the title of the best documented history of a *china criolla* on the Mar del Sur coast.

THE PARADIGMATIC CASE OF FRANCISCA MARTHA[278]

The following lines are devoted to Francisca Martha, an *india china* of Filipino origin, born and raised among the palm trees of Colima and dedicated to *vino de cocos* production in the 17th century, a fundamental period for this economic activity. Insofar as possible, we attempt to answer these questions: what did it mean to be a Filipino woman in Colima in that century?, and to what degree is her specific case similar to, or different from, other experiences in that context? We cannot forget that one individual's trajectory can tell us not only a great deal about that person, but may also reveal, with even greater vigor, certain phenomena of the society to which she or he belonged and the environment in which she or he was immersed. The aim is not to study this woman for her own sake but, rather, to observe what her case may say about the behavior of the society and its nature, whether it was open or closed.

To begin, we must recognize and explain that we have only one documentary source on Francisca Martha; though quite brief, it is clearly of great value. This source contains the acts related to her death on a palm hacienda in the Tecuiciapa Valley, jurisdiction of Colima, in 1664.[279] The file, which consists of nine sheets printed on both sides, for a total of 17 pages, allows us to ascertain key aspects of Francisca Martha's life between 1652 and 1664, and even earlier. It has two sections, organized retrospectively. The first provides acts related to her death, in 1664: the official notification to the *alcalde mayor*, records of the investigation into the circumstances, an inventory of her properties, and declarations by her second husband, who believed that she had died intestate. The second part contains a will she dictated in 1652 while ill and, she believed, close to death. It seems this document had been kept secret, and this gives her story a rather unexpected twist.

Family and Socioethnic Setting

Francisca Martha was born in Colima, possibly around 1622.[280] All the papers refer to her as a *china*, and she identified herself as such. Thanks to the parish priest of the *partido* of Caxitlán and Tecolapa, jurisdiction of Colima, we know she was a *china criolla*[281] who had inherited her surname from her father, Juan Martín –also identified as a *chino*– while her mother, María Cornejo, was a native Indian from Colima. We know very little –in fact, almost nothing– about her parents, except that theirs was a legitimate marriage, and that they lived in the town of Nahualapa, just outside the villa of Colima.

Map 7. Palm haciendas in Colima (17th century)

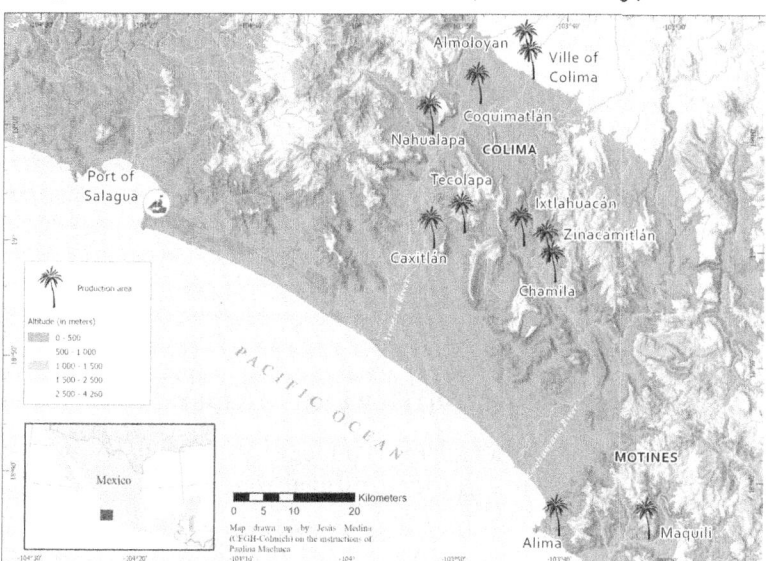

References to *china* women in New Spain are very scarce, and even more so for the colonial province of Colima. The vast majority of the Asian population that crossed the Pacific Ocean in the Manila Galleon were males whose presence revolved around working as sailors, carpenters, caulkers, or cabin boys: that is, trades that required considerable physical strength and, hence, were hardly going to be assigned to women. But this does not mean that no *china* women made that voyage; in fact, the female sector that arrived via Acapulco participated as slaves in domestic service for families of Spanish officials who returned from the archipelago.

The transport of female slaves aboard the Galleon was subject to severe restrictions. Due to sexual scandals on transpacific voyages involving officials who traveled with "small harems",[282] in 1605, the procurator of the Philippines, Hernando de los Ríos Coronel, petitioned that woman slaves be prohibited from embarking on those commercial voyages, a measure that Felipe III ratified in 1608.[283] We know, however, that his order was often ignored, for Tatiana Seijas recorded that of 598 slaves who crossed the Pacific Ocean in that period, 152 were women, one-fourth of the total.[284] Moreover, some women identified as *chinas* whose lives can be traced in contemporary documents, were actually *criollas* from New Spain; that is, daughters of *indios chinos* most of whom were married to native women.

Between Her Father and Her First Husband

Around 1642,[285] Francisca Martha legally married the *chino* Sebastián de la Cruz. In the nuptial agreement, her parents offered a not inconsiderable dowry (see Table 8) even for the Spanish universe —especially given her parents' status, a *chino* father and Indian mother. Asunción Lavrin tells us that indigenous women rarely afforded dowries comparable to those of the elites, and that this practice did not appear among the norms of the castes. Dowries were, after all, indicative of the position of the bride and her family.[286] What we can see in Francisca Martha's case is then, somewhat rare, for her parents –Juan Martín and María Cornejo– had clearly achieved a certain stability during their time in Nahualapa, the site of their hacienda –San Juan– which had 60 producing palm trees that they included in their daughter's dowry. The hacienda also had a house, three teams of oxen, six mules, and 12 horses, a modest herd kept to transport merchandise. In addition, the dowry included utensils for making *vino de cocos*, such as vats and ovens for distilling aguardiente, and some *botijas* of wine. But this opens a mystery: if her parents gave Francisca such a dowry in 1652, they must have had other assets. Sadly, we do not know what they were, or if Francisca inherited them later (which seems unlikely), or had siblings who would also have been heirs. Here, we can only accept that we have some faint twinklings among dark shadows.

Table 8. Properties of Francisca Martha and Sebastián de la Cruz (1652)

Dowry (from Francisca Martha's parents)	Goods provided by Sebastián de la Cruz	Goods acquired during their marriage
60 palm trees A house 15 botijas of wine 2 oven vats for cooking wine 3 teams of oxen 6 tame mules without harnesses 12 horses	5 draft mules 6 tame mares	Hacienda with 8 producing palm trees

Francisca's father, the *chino* Juan Martín, arrived in Colima on the Manila Galleon sometime between 1600 and 1630 when the greatest number of *indios chinos* was reported to have settled in that jurisdiction. As we saw above, parish registers say little about the births of children of Asian parents, as only scarce references exist. In 1631, a girl named María, daughter of Diego Correa and Isabel, a *china*, was baptized in the parish of Colima. The parish ledger where she was registered does not show her father's status, but he likely had some relation with the *bachiller* Diego Correa Gudiño, who is identified as the priest of the *partido* of Tecolapa (jurisdiction of Colima) and judge of the Spanish Inquisition in 1627.[287] In that same archive from the parish of Colima, a year before María's baptism, Agustín de Peralta, a *chino*, appeared as the godfather of a girl named Isabel, daughter of a female *negro* slave who worked in the household of Mariana de

Moscoso.[288] We found one other case of a godfather: in 1631, Gabriel, a negro boy son of Isabel, another female negro slave in service to Captain Gabriel de Trejo, was baptized and joined in spiritual kinship to a man identified only as "Gaspar chino".[289]

These few records are insufficient to reach any broad conclusions concerning the presence of *indios chinos* based on parish records in Colima. Marriages of recently-arrived *indio chino* men with Indian women were surely common, as occurred in the Zacatula-Acapulco production nucleus, where the founders of the *San Nicolás de los Chinos* neighborhood in Coyuca manifested that their community was populated thanks to "the Filipino Indians who come from Manila on the annual Galleon [...] many of whom settled and married Indians of other populations", thus increasing the number of inhabitants.[290] In 1619, Captain Sebastián de Pineda stated that "many of these natural Indians from the Philippine Islands who come as cabin boys are married on those islands, but as they are not known in New Spain they marry again".[291] It is also quite possible that concubinage was common in these cases.

Returning to Francisca Martha's father, we can follow some leads. Juan Martín dealt in cattle in 1635, for he sold eight tame male and female mules to Juan de San Pedro, a resident of Colima. His signature is affixed to the purchase/sale agreement (see Illustration 9), indicating not only his participation in cattle-breeding but also a certain level of acculturation. That activity would have complemented his income from his San Juan palm hacienda and other properties, notably the 60 producing trees and utensils for distillation.

Part II

Illustration 9. Signature of Juan Martín, a *Chino*, Father of Francisca Martha

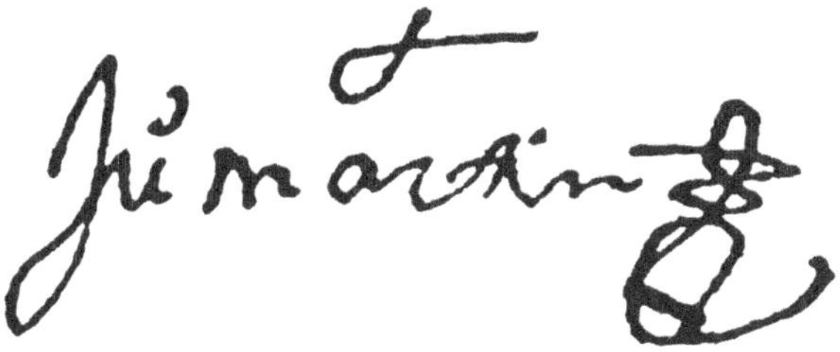

Source: AHMC, section B, caja 12, exp. 15.

The dowry that Francisca Martha's parents gave when she married Sebastián de la Cruz tells us that they were active in *vino de cocos* production,[292] an economic activity that allowed them to acquire properties, including their palm hacienda in the Tecuiciapa Valley. It is no accident that, as it was devoted to elaborating aguardiente, the hacienda sat precisely in the largest *vino de cocos* production zone in the province of Colima. There, around the decade of 1630, large and small haciendas of this kind produced some 8,000 *botijas* of *vino de cocos* annually, with the participation of Spaniards, Mestizos, and *chinos*. To give one example, the hacienda of the *chino* Martín Pano, in the same valley, had 100 trees that produced 365 *botijas* of *vino de cocos* per year, a rate of one *botija* per day.[293]

What is certain is that the binomial *indio chino/vino de cocos* functioned so well in the province of Colima in the 17th century that the work of Asians attained a high value –perhaps due to their scarcity– in the labor market by performing the trades of *vinatero* and "winemaking tradesmen" on palm haciendas. Those *indios chinos* had a trump card to play in that society because of its dependence on commerce in *vino de cocos* and, at first, on the traditional Filipino knowledge required to produce it.

We cannot determine if Francisca Martha's husband, Sebastián de la Cruz, was experienced in *vino de cocos* production, but we do know that after his marriage he purchased a piece of land with eight producing palm trees from an Indian in Tecuiciapa.²⁹⁴ The fact that De la Cruz brought five mules and six mares to the union suggests he was a muleteer or, perhaps, a small-scale cattle breeder, or both. It is not clear whether he worked the palms himself during their years of conjugal life, but whatever the case the activities of muleteering and *vino de cocos* production complemented each other quite well. A year before his death, perhaps from an illness that impeded the couple from working their lands themselves, Francisca Martha and Sebastián de la Cruz opted to lease both the San Juan hacienda and their property in Tecuiciapa to Matheo de Ocariz for two years –1651 to 1653– during a tragic phase for the couple, as we elucidate below.²⁹⁵

The Difficult Years

Sebastián de la Cruz died sometime between December 1651 and January 1652, but we have no information on the cause. Francisca Martha stated that he passed away "deprived of his senses" in Nahualapa.²⁹⁶ Three months after that event, which must have deeply afflicted the spirits of our *india china*, she fell ill and decided to dictate her will. Her properties –including those from her dowry and others acquired during her marriage– are listed in Table 8. At the moment she dictated her will, Francisca Martha had a close relationship with Magdalena de Arévalo, and worked in domestic service in her home. The amount she owed Magdalena –50 pesos "for all she has given me for clothes and other things"– leads us to assume that she had gone to live there after her husband's death, a fairly common arrangement for a widow left alone in that period. Her debt of 50 pesos was considerable for the time. It drew our attention because she became indebted during her years in domestic service. Her statement that it reflected "what she has given me for clothes and other things" confirms two elements that we often see in that epoch: first, that she was paid in kind, not cash; second, that wageworkers were subject to this kind of indebtedness, which is the central topic of the next chapter.

The evidence available suggests that Francisca Martha rented her palm trees to obtain income, then left the area in search of a family to protect her. Since Colima did not have women's shelters (*casas de recogimiento*) like the ones we know from other places in New Spain, well-known families often took women in under this modality, many, it was thought, because they needed to "correct their behavior". On this topic, Asunción Lavrin reminds us that the *casas de recogimiento* had a double objective: on the one hand, to shelter virtuous, unprotected women; on the other, "lost" women who needed correction so they would not continue to sin and "contaminate" other women.[297] In a society threatened by worldly menaces and the temptations of the flesh, in the words of Pilar Gonzalbo,[298] Francisca Martha may have chosen to take refuge in Magdalena de Arévalo's home instead of staying alone on the hacienda of San Juan in Tecuiciapa. At that time, Magdalena was also a widow since her husband, Jacinto Gutiérrez, a resident of Colima, had passed. The urban milieu offered safe haven to isolated women who shared their loneliness and, at times, their penury.

What illness led Francisca to dictate her will just three months after her husband's death? What was her purpose of living in Magdalena's house in the villa of Colima, when her hacienda was in the Tecuiciapa Valley? Was this due to the moral reasons just outlined or, perhaps, because commerce in *vino de cocos* was no longer sufficiently profitable? These and many other questions remain unanswered, including the key one of whether administering her hacienda would have required a man's presence?

The Second Marriage

At this juncture we must add another, even more essential, query, one almost philosophical in nature: was love an element of marriages in olden times? Of course, we cannot answer this, but we shall offer a derived response: that marriage may have been necessary in some cases, especially among the popular classes. This was true of Francisca's two marriages. At the time of her death, in 1664, a new figure appeared: her stepson Juan de la Cruz, a young "mulatto or mestizo" aged 23, son of Francisca's first husband. He was born around 1641, so he was only a year old –perhaps less– when his father wed Francisca. This suggests that if Sebastián de la Cruz married Francisca in 1642, he was a recent widower. His first wife may have been a black slave or Indian, for Juan is identified as both mulatto and mestizo. Among other reasons for re-marrying, de la Cruz may have needed a woman to help raise his newborn son.[299]

Though her life seemed to be fading in that agitated year of 1652, Francisca Martha surprises us once again, for we find that several seasons later she recovered her vigor, both economic and sentimental. After her period of mourning, followed by her illness, she remarried, this time with the mestizo, Miguel de Solís. Once again, we venture a hypothesis: this was the solution that allowed her to escape from her subaltern status in doña Magdalena's home, and return to her hacienda as the owner, supported by her husband. In this second phase of her life, she not only conserved, but actually expanded, her *vino de cocos* business, as a comparison of her properties in 1642-1652 and 1664 reveals (see Table 9).

Part II

Table 9. Comparison of Francisca Martha's Properties (1652–1664)

Properties during her marriage to the chino Sebastián de la Cruz (1642-1652)	Properties during her marriage to the mestizo Miguel de Solís (1664)
Dowry from her parents	• 3 draft mules with a saddle • 18 draft, tame horses
• 60 palm trees • A house • 15 botijas of wine • 2 oven vats for cooking wine • 3 teams of oxen • 6 tame mules without harnesses • 12 horses	• This hacienda with its lands, palm and fruit trees, including 85 palms of various ages, and a rustic dwelling • A foundation of sugarcane • An oven for cooking wine with 2 old vats and their barrel • 5 Castilian botijas • [6] earthenware vessels for tuba • 2 small botijas of wine
Contribution of Sebastián de la Cruz	• A vinatero named Juan Alonso who owes 41 pesos • A used shirt made of a coarse fabric (ruán), worn by the deceased
• 5 draft mules • 6 tame mares	• An old, green wool skirt • A new satin skirt with 5 silver and gold adornments
Properties acquired during the marriage	• A simple, rounded veil or cloth • A brass candlestick
Hacienda with 8 producing palm trees	• A small blanket • Some old, torn tablecloths

This inventory, presented upon her death in 1664, clearly shows that she continued to produce *vino de cocos*, for by that time she had accumulated 85 palm trees (more than the 60 from her parents dowry), an oven, vats, vessels, and jars. Most importantly, she had in her employ a *vinatero* named Juan Alonso (see Table 9). The fact that the inventory includes three draft mules suggests, moreover, that she commercialized the aguardiente she made, a common practice among producers.

The Popular Religiosity of an *India China*

Beyond the earthly world, it is very interesting to learn something of the religious aspect of Francisca Martha's life, as reflected in the stipulations listed in her will. She was a member of the chantry of *San Nicolás de Tolentino*, founded in the town of Ixtlahuacán. Upon her death, she asked to be mourned in the chantry of the Blessed Sacrament (*Cofradía del Santísimo Sacramento*), a particularly important chantry in the villa of Colima, together with that of the Souls of Purgatory (*Ánimas del Purgatorio*), since most members were Spaniards. She further requested that she be buried in the parish church of the villa of Colima, shrouded with the habit of St. Francis, accompanied by the priest of the villa with the cross held high, and with a funeral mass with her body present and offerings of bread and wax, "as is the custom", at least for people of a certain status. Finally, Francisca Martha insisted that prayers be said for the souls of her deceased loved ones: her husband Sebastián and her parents Juan Martín and María Cornejo. She asked that masses be celebrated for them, as well, and that alms be given from her possessions. In summary, those conditions mirrored, quite closely, those that members of the Spanish elite requested for their interments, reflecting the belief that because death was the final trance it had to be attended to with the greatest care. In death, it seems, the person's deepest aspirations were revealed.

Since studies of chantries in the colonial province of Colima are scarce,[300] we can only make some general observations on this topic, extracted from documentary sources. Table 10 shows that at least eight chantries existed, three centered in Indian towns where, doubtless, *indios chinos* resided: Caxitlán, Tecolapa, and Ixtlahuacán. Curiously, the only reference to the chantry of *San Nicolás de Tolentino* is in Francisca Martha's will, for no trace of it is found in other contemporary documents. We do know that in 1621 an altar was dedicated to San Nicolás in the Nuestra Señora

PART II

de la Merced convent in the villa of Colima, begging the question of how widely this saint was venerated in the region.[301]

Table 10. Chantries in the Province of Colima (17th Century)

Year of localization	Name of the chantry	Seat	Source
1605	Souls of Purgatory (Ánimas del Purgatorio)	Villa of Colima	AHMC, B-4, exp. 15, pos. 21
1621	Blessed Sacrament (Santísimo Sacramento)	Villa of Colima	AHMC, B-4, exp. 1, pos. 38
1621	Vera Cruz	Villa of Colima?	AHMC, B-4, exp. 1, pos. 38
1621	Our Lady of Solitude (Nuestra Señora de la Soledad)	Villa of Colima?	AHMC, B-27, exp. 32
1627	Our Lady of the Conception (Nuestra Señora de la Concepción)	Town of Caxitlán	AHMC, B-5, exp. 44
1627	Our Lady of the Rosary (Nuestra Señora del Rosario)	Towns of Tecolapa and Caxitlán	AHMC, B-5, exp. 44
1640	Name of Jesus (Nombre de Jesús)	Villa of Colima?	AHMC, B-25, exp. 24
1652	St. Nicholas of Tolentino (San Nicolás de Tolentino)	Town of Ixtlahuacán	AHMC, B-30, exp. 23

In 1701, Friar Joseph Sicardo mentioned that the Augustinians had introduced the devotion to San Nicolás de Tolentino into the Indies, and that by the early 18th century "it had grown so greatly that it is venerated throughout the Kingdom of New Spain [...] and it was rare not to see his image, even in Indian oratories".[302] While it is true that her will offers no evidence of Francisca Martha's devotion to *San Nicolás*, and we mention it here only because this chantry existed in Ixtlahuacán, it does raise the question if she may have been a member under her own name, or through her husband, or even her parents. Whatever the case, we can connect this saint to the Philippine archipelago through Friar Sicardo's report:

> The devotion to *San Nicolás* has existed on the Philippine islands since the temporal and spiritual conquests, due to the first Apostolic Augustine friars, who sowed the Faith on the Islands of that Archipelago, beginning their Evangelical preaching on the [island] of Cebu in the year 1565, and continuing for over a dozen years, with no other [missionaries], like those of the Sacred Religions [who] joined them later to help cultivate that new vineyard. And although some Temples were dedicated to *San Nicolás*, and Altars in the Convents and Parishes of that broad Province, devotion to that saint grew, especially in the City of Manila, with the [arrival] of our Discalced Friars in the year 1606.[303]

Clearly, the figure in our story who may have been familiar with this devotion on the Islands was Juan Martín, Francisca's father, not Francisca herself. What is interesting here is that, in addition to the chantry of *San Nicolás de Tolentino*, to which Indians and *indios chinos* may have belonged due to its existence in a *vino de cocos* production zone like Ixtlahuacán, Francisca Martha asked that upon her death she be named a member of a Spanish chantry: *las Ánimas del Purgatorio*. This fact is not so extraordinary when we consider that common people often sought to join that body as they their lives came to an end, if they could pay the required quota, for this was a way to ensure that others would pray for their souls.

Déborah Oropeza argues that one common feature of the *indios chinos* who settled in Mexico City in the colonial period was membership in chantries, mainly those of The Holy Christ (*el Santo Christo*) and the Most Holy Crucifix and Ritual Cleansing (*Santísimo Crucifijo y Lavatorio*), the

Part II

latter allegedly founded by the Asian community of the time:

> The *indios chinos* adapted to the religious life and organization of the Viceregal capital by forming part of at least two chantries: one, the "chantry and brotherhood of the *Santo Christo y Lavatorio*" (also mentioned as the *cofradía y hermandad del Santísimo Crucifijo y Lavatorio de Cristo*), supposedly founded by *chinos* with its seat in the convent of Santa Clara, which had an altar. The other was the guild chantry appended to the archconfraternity of the *Santísima Trinidad* in the church of the same advocation; *chino* barbers formed part of that *Cofradía y Hermandad del Santo Christo, de los Tres Gremios de Cirujanos, Barberos y Boticarios*...".[304]

The cases of Francisca Martha and the *indios chinos* in Mexico City led us to reflect on the processes of religious acculturation that this social group experienced, first in the Philippines and later in New Spain. Some had surely received the Christian doctrine from missionaries in the Philippine archipelago, so baptism, accompanied by the bestowing of Christian names, would have occurred on the Asian continent. Upon arriving in the Americas those Asians would have continued cultivating their local, but orthodox, religious practices. Some, like the *indio chino* Diego Juan de la Cruz, were accused before the Tribunal of the Spanish Inquisition of conducting practices deemed alien to Catholic norms. Born in Malacca, de la Cruz first went to Macao and later to Manila where he embarked for New Spain. There, he frequented Indian and mulatta sorceresses who offered him magic powders to attract women and become rich. It is interesting to observe that he had learned the Lord's Prayer and the *Ave María* in Malacca, a zone evangelized by the Portuguese from the early 16th century.[305] It is evident that, as a *china criolla*, Francisca Martha formed part of a generation of Asians and their descendants born during the period of colonial administration who, therefore, would have received indoctrination in the Catholic faith from a young age.

Francisca Martha's Death

Francisca Martha died in February 1664 on the San Juan palm hacienda in the Tecuiciapa Valley that her parents had bequeathed her. She would have been around 40 years old. The cause of her death was unknown. Witnesses simply stated that she died "of an illness that God had seen fit to send her". Pedro González, a resident of Sayula who often visited Francisca and her second husband, Miguel de Solís, said he only knew that "she died while ill in bed, and this witness saw her dead [body]". Her stepson, Juan de la Cruz, found her in the same condition. Together, Pedro and Juan claimed her body and took it for burial in the church in Nahualapa, where the Franciscan friar, Francisco de Nájera, preached to the faithful. One man who seems to have adopted a rather passive attitude toward Francisca's passing was her husband Miguel. According to declarations by the *alcalde mayor* of Colima, don Juan de Abárzuza, it seems that he did not participate in his wife's funeral. Perhaps this was because he too was sick in bed when notified of Francisca's death. One thing we do know is that on February 15, 1664, when the authorities (concretely, the *alcalde ordinario* of the villa of Colima, Joseph de Solórzano) arrived to interrogate him, Miguel declared that his wife had died intestate; that is, she had never written a will. Shortly afterwards, the *alcalde* conducted the inventory of the properties found in Francisca and Miguel's home. Miguel confirmed that "[they] were the properties that [she] had as her own". Perhaps this convinced *alcalde* Solórzano to leave those belongings on deposit with Miguel, instead of taking them to the general repository (*depositario general*), or leaving them with a "commissioner", as was often done. Miguel was "obliged to keep them on deposit and to hand each one over when so directed and, if not, to pay its value". The recent widower had enjoyed good fortune, for they had left all those possessions in his house, at least for the moment.

After the inventory was finalized, eleven days transpired before the *alcalde mayor*, Juan de Abárzuza, began his inquiry into the circumstances of Francisca Martha's death, but his investigation took only two days (February 26-27) and was witnessed by only three people: Juan de la Cruz (the stepson), Pedro González (the mestizo from Sayula), and a Spaniard named Diego Álvarez de Espinosa. They did not add any important details to those outlined above: that Francisca Martha had died on her hacienda in Tecuiciapa after suffering an illness, was buried in Nahualapa, and did not leave a will. It appeared at that juncture that Francisca Martha's case was closed, and all indications were that Miguel would inherit her properties, unless Francisca was found to have left some debts.

But an unexpected twist was in store for many of the people involved, for on March 13, 1664, a figure mentioned previously in this story appeared before the *alcalde mayor*: none other than the *bachiller* Diego Correa Gudiño, priest of the *partido* of Tecolapa and Caxitlán, and judge of the Holy Inquisition. Upon arriving in Colima, he stated:

> The news has come to me that Francisca Martha, *china criolla*, wife of Miguel de Solís in this jurisdiction, having died, certain judicial diligences have been issued by Your Mercy to verify her intestate status [but] in reality the aforementioned [dictated] her will before Juan Pedro –here present– on the twelfth of March, 1652, which I present in the original [...] so that I may be confirmed officially [...] as her executor and heir of her possessions, as is stipulated therein. I ask and supplicate that Y.M. deliver to me each and every one of the belongings left at the death of the aforementioned so I may [take possession] of them.[306]

To everyone's surprise –including her husband, the mestizo Miguel de Solís– Francisca Martha had not died intestate but had dictated her will many years earlier, when she believed that an illness would lead her to her death. The priest, Correa Gudiño, knew how to seize the moment.[307] The *alcalde mayor* recognized the will's authenticity and declared that its contents were to "be obeyed and fulfilled". With that, Correa was allowed to take all of Francisca's properties, not only as executor, but also as her universal heir.

Those acts were followed by the *alcalde mayor's* order to notify Miguel de Solís of the event. On March 14, 1664, the scribe Alfonso de Tovar Valenzuela read and notarized the definitive act for the recently widowed de Solís, who stated simply, "I have heard it". Could De Solís already have known of the will's existence? Or did Francisca hide that crucial decision from him throughout their years together? We will never know. What is certain, however, is that the story ended in a totally unexpected way, reminding us that in the world of social relations it is not always possible to make accurate predictions.

Table 11. Trajectory of Francisca Martha

Year	Event
c. 1622	Born in Colima.
1642	Married the chino Sebastián de la Cruz.
1651	Death of her husband, Sebastián de la Cruz.
1651	Leases her palm haciendas to Matheo de Ocariz.
1652	Dictates her will, naming Diego Correa Gudiño – priest of the partido of Caxitlán and Tecolapa– as executor and sole heir.
1658?	Second marriage, with the mestizo Miguel de Solís.
1664	Dies on her palm hacienda in Tecuiciapa.

Part II

Final Reflections

The story of the *india china* Francisca Martha brings us to reflect upon several broad themes. Clearly, she was a woman who lived between two worlds, each with its own characteristic features, not opposed, but complementary. On one side lay that of the Philippines, apparently transported to the reality of Colima with its palm tree-lined landscapes and *vino de cocos* production. Francisca never set foot in the Philippine archipelago, but she did learn something of its culture from her father and, possibly, her first husband, Sebastián: endogamy was not reserved for the nobility. On the other, we see her acting in a specific space of New Spain with many facets, including a colonial order that, while hierarchical, was not closed. Suffice to observe the social relations forged by our *china*: a second husband who was a mestizo, a mulatto stepson, service in the home of a Spanish family, and, above all, naming as her sole heir the priest of a *partido*.

This aperture did, however, have its limits, as in every corporativist society: it is better to live in community than in isolation; the corporations of the *Ancien Régime* were permanent, but individuals were transitory. The individual was deemed an imperfect being, for perfection could be achieved only in the bosom of a community, as António Manuel Hespanha reminds us.[308] This explains why, after the death of her first husband, Francisca Martha had no choice but to be "taken in" by a household so she would not be alone. Hence, she went to live in doña Magdalena's home for a short time before meeting, and marrying, her second spouse, the mestizo Miguel de Solís. Another possibility that may have emerged after her first husband's death is that, lacking a man's presence –especially one with experience in the wine-making trade– Francisca may have been unable to perform all the tasks required to operate her hacienda with its production of *vino de cocos*.

How did Francisca Martha achieve her insertion into Colima society? It seems that she was not rejected but, rather, integrated, perhaps largely because she shared certain first-order cultural codes, especially in the religious sphere, as she was a Catholic in the full extension of the term and, doubtless, yearned to form part of the elite. She knew how to knock on strategic doors, for we learn that her universal heir was a clergyman. But at this point we enter a zone of chiaroscuros due to the difficulty of penetrating more deeply into the life of an individual like Francisca Martha, to identify what relations, sentiments, and motivations might have emerged unexpectedly, and at key moments, to bring her into association with a figure like Diego Correa. Did that priest take advantage of our *india china*'s illness, when she was most vulnerable, to abscond with her few, but clearly interesting, possessions? Sadly, like so many other questions we have posited along our journey through Francisca Martha's life, this one shall also remain unanswered.

What we can demonstrate through Francisca Martha's case is that although she was a woman and an *india china*, she managed to weave a network of relations that spanned several levels. In general, we can affirm that hers was a case of the successful insertion of a *china* into 17th-century Colima society, one, we might say, that was open since a person's ethnic status or gender were not of critical importance, and she or he could, at least, thrive among the palm trees, as we shall show in the following chapter.

4. INDIOS CHINOS VINATEROS: RURAL CONNECTIONS ACROSS THE PACIFIC

> And so it is that among these Indians who come from the Philippine Islands there are many in New Spain who are dedicated to producing vino de cocos on the coast of the other Mar del Sur, which they make with a still as in the Philippines.
>
> —Captain Sebastián de Pineda, 1619

INTRODUCTION

In 1619, Captain Sebastián de Pineda, the *justicia mayor* of the port of Cavite in the Philippines, wrote a brief, but important, *relación* "on things regarding the Philippines", in which he expressed his point of view on the problems that plagued that Asian archipelago at the time.[309] A significant part of his narrative centers on the Filipino cabin boys who sailed from Manila and, upon arriving in Acapulco, dispersed across the territories of New Spain, never to return to their country of origin. As an example, Pineda cited the galleon *Espíritu Santo*, which had docked in Acapulco in 1618 with 75 cabin boys aboard but prepared to return to Manila a few weeks later with only five.[310] It is important to recall that of all the occupations on the Galleon, that of cabin boy was the most menial; perhaps that is why so many opted to desert and seek better opportunities in the expanses of New Spain.[311]

Captain Pineda, a fierce opponent of Filipino immigration to New Spain, argued that the harm this practice caused the Crown was manifested on at least two levels: the first was moral in nature, for it was said that most Filipinos who stayed were married men who remarried with women in New Spain, thus committing the crime of bigamy; the second reason was economic because, Pineda wrote, some Filipinos worked in *vino de cocos* production on haciendas along the Mar del Sur coast, thus encouraging consumption of that drink instead of wine from Castille, "because these people are inclined to drink [until they] become inebriated, and since [the drink] they make is distilled and as strong as firewater, they find it more appetizing than wine from Spain". As a distilled drink, *vino de cocos* had a much higher alcohol content than wine from Castille, so it enjoyed greater demand. To cement his argument, Pineda cited the case of the *vino de cocos* production that was underway in the province of Colima and Apasagualcos, as we noted in an earlier chapter. Finally, he suggested that the viceregal authorities should impede, at all costs, Filipino cabin boys from remaining in New Spain by imposing punishments like burning *botijas* of *vino de cocos* and cutting down palm groves:

> Those islands [the Philippines] are so short of natives that if His Majesty does not expressly indicate that no factories are to be erected there, no people will be left due to the events that have occurred on those islands over the past [eight] years, [including] the dead or captive among those who have stayed and those who reach New Spain as cabin boys on the galleons that come every year, [and] stay in New Spain. On the galleon *Espíritu Santo* that came last year, sixteen hundred and eighteen, there were seventy-five native cabin boys, and of those no more than five returned on that galleon, and if His Majesty does not [take measures] to remedy this it will surely continue every year and [...] the following things will ensue: first, grave offenses to our Lord because many of these natives from the Philippine islands

Part II

who come as cabin boys are married on those islands, but as they are unknown in New Spain, they marry again. [A second] great harm that is a disservice to His Majesty and the Royal Treasury is caused by natives from the Philippine islands who arrive as cabin boys and remain in New Spain. [If] not remedied in time, this will continue to damage these Kingdoms because many of those natives of the Philippine islands in New Spain have begun to produce *vino de cocos* on the coast of the other Mar del Sur, in stills as in the Philippines, and over time this will be part of the reason why the Indians of New Spain [cease to buy] wine from Castille and drink only [the wine] they make because they are prone to drink and drunkenness, and because the wine they make is distilled and as strong as firewater, it is more appetizing than wine from Spain, so every year your fleets will carry less [cargo] and it will be of less value. So great is the trade that goes on today on the coast of Navidad and in Apusabalcos, and throughout Colima, that they load more mule trains with this wine than with wine from Spain. And if applying the remedy sought herein is delayed, the same will happen as with the wines from Peru. But this can be prevented if all the natives from the Philippine islands are boarded and sent back, and the palms and *botijas* used to make this wine are burned, and the palms cut down with severe sanctions imposed on those who stay and return to making it.[312]

While Pineda's *relación* sheds light on the fate that awaited many of those Filipino cabin boys upon arriving in Acapulco, it also raises questions that, perhaps, not even the captain himself could answer. First, how many of those cabin boys would have known the "wine-making" trade? As we have explained, this was a highly-specialized occupation, and we must keep in mind that not all those cabin boys were necessarily Filipinos, for some may have been from other Asian nations. Second, it seems that by 1619, when this text was written, solidarity networks had already been forged among the Filipinos who participated in *vino de cocos* production, so the Asian crews recently arrived in Acapulco knew about the palm haciendas where their countrymen worked, and that knowledge would have facilitated their well-planned movements toward certain strategic places.[313] This migration to previously identified sites became more intense when they migrated in groups. Matthew J. Furlong confirmed that numerous *indios chinos* knew each other before boarding the Galleon, for he identified the Laguna de Bay region as a key site for recruiting laborers needed overseas. On this topic, he stated:

> The workers and administrators of eastern Laguna tied it to Manila and Cavite in several ways. First, it supplied laborers for the cortes in the montes of Laguna and Calilaya (Tayabas), including Mahayhay. Second, as a better-drained region, coconut palms grew well in Laguna, supplying vino de palma and coconut oil for royal storehouses. Its laborers brought lumber to Cavite, where some of they stayed as workers, providing a labor pool for intra-Asian and transpacific shipping.[314]

There are abundant cases of *indios chinos* who settled in New Spain and declared that they had known some of their Asian neighbors from the time they lived on the archipelago. In February 1608, Nicolás Rodríguez, an *indio chino* in Colima, appeared as a witness for his countryman, Francisco Perdomo, aged 40. On that occasion, he stated that "he had known [him] for over thirty years, in "China", and that [they were] raised because they are from a town in the Philippines".[315] This means that Francisco had known Nicolás since the age of 10 and suggests that they may have traveled to the province of Colima together, where they settled in the town of San José. The Pampanga region, another important source of emigrants to New Spain, offers another clear example of bonds of solidarity: just before his death in Zapotlán, Nueva Galicia, in 1618, Domingo de Villalobos, a merchant from Pampanga, named Alonso Gutiérrez, an *indio chino* from there, as his executor. Gutiérrez had lived in Zapotlán for some 20 years, and married an Indian *principal* from there.[316]

Part II

Sebastián de Pineda also revealed that when the Manila Galleon docked in Acapulco, Asians who had settled around the port came to recruit cabin boys to work in *vino de cocos* production: "when the Manila Galleon reaches the port of Acapulco, all the Indians who produce *vino de cocos* come and take away the natives who arrive as cabin boys, for this and other causes, almost none return to the Philippine islands".[317]

In the following sections, we will demonstrate clearly that the incorporation of Asians into palm haciendas (*haciendas de palmas de beneficio*) in the Colima-Motines production nucleus was a gradual process that began in the late 16th century, so by the early 17th century some were fully active in production and had been integrated, in distinct measure, into the local market system that was controlled by Spanish authorities and hacendados. Here, we would emphasize that the vast majority were free laborers who received a wage, and that their relations became increasingly complex as *vino de cocos* production approached its apogee.

We begin by defining the term *vinatero*, which appears in the *Diccionario de autoridades* of 1739 as "those who traffic with wine, or transport it from one place to another for sale".[318] This definition is broad and refers only to the commercial aspect, but in the provinces of Colima and Motines in the 17th century the term was used to identify individuals who made *vino de cocos*, so it is important to distinguish this sector from that of the merchants who sold wine from Castille. *Vinateros*, then, were men who produced *vino de cocos* on palm haciendas in return for wages. These three elements help us understand that a *vinatero* obtained a product (*vino de cocos*) in a certain setting (palm hacienda), under a contractual scheme (wage) that, as the reader will see, was flexible and varied.

As the 17th century advanced, the *vinateros*' work came to be regulated through contracts with standardized clauses, though over time diverse nuances appeared in specific cases. For this reason, we must analyze in detail distinct experiences. Labor relations in *vino de cocos* production were multiple and flexible; that is, certain mechanisms gave rise not only to traditional contractual relations, such as the so-called payments "in part" (*a partido*), paid advances (*enganches*), and debt peonage, but also to atypical forms, like debt transfers. In the next section, we outline five profiles of *vinateros* who were immersed in the world of *vino de cocos* production in the province of Colima to demonstrate, broadly, their degree of insertion and/or integration into Colima society.

The first type of *vinatero* refers to the pioneers in aguardiente production; that is, precursors of the drink who collaborated with Spaniards through mixed contracts that paid them some money but also *botijas* of wine for their work. The second type refers to *vinateros* who were trapped in systems of economic dependence, marked by greater subjection and labor vulnerability. The third characterizes *vinateros en route* toward economic emancipation since their working conditions allowed them a more equitable participation in *vino de cocos* production. A fourth type includes *vinateros* who were better integrated into the socioeconomic reality of their regions and, therefore, enjoyed a certain preeminence in the Ancien Régime. The final type, no less important than the others due to its unique features in New Spain, refers to the *alcaldes de chinos* (advocate of the *chinos*), legal figures with some judicial power who represented the guild of the *vinateros*.

THE EARLIEST VINATEROS: MIXED PAYMENT AS WAGE-WORKERS

What would that initial moment have been like, when *colimenses* (residents of Colima) witnessed the spectacle –if you will– of *chinos* climbing palm trees to extract *tuba*, the raw material of *vino de cocos*? Would such an inaugural event have occurred before the curious, amazed eyes of those who beheld the first *botijas* of *vino de cocos* elaborated in the warm lands of Colima? Might there have been a precursor, an enthusiastic pioneer who produced this alcoholic drink, soon to be emulated by others? There is one clue: on January 4th 1600, at the very turn of the century, Pedro Ruiz de Padilla complained to the *alcalde ordinario* of the villa of Colima, don Francisco de Cárdenas Fullana, that his neighbor, Francisco Rodríguez Machuca, had invaded his orchard near the Río Grande that traversed the villa and accompanied by a *chino* made some strange cuts in his coconut palms, as can be inferred from the records of the ensuing judicial process. Ruiz de Padilla accused the men of cutting "stairs" into the trunks with a machete so they could climb up, adding that they had "cut the trunks of a coconut tree to make wine from it". Clearly, this was a novel experience for the accuser, who was visibly concerned that his palms would dry up and wilt because the cuts would allow worms to penetrate, suck the sap, and render them incapable of producing fruit. Below, we transcribe a fragment from those records:

> Pedro Ruiz de Padilla, resident of this villa, appeared before me, Y. M., observing the solemnities of law [to] bring criminal charges against Francisco Rodríguez Machuca and an *indio chino* and other guilty parties, narrating the case of his complaint. Stating that the [defendants] without fear of God and with disdain for Royal Justice, yesterday, on the third day of this month, entered the orchard and lands I have in this villa near the Río Grande, which I own [having] bought [them] from Juan López Avecilla, as these [receipts] I present to Y. M. confirm, and cut into the trunk of a coconut tree to make wine from it, carving steps in said tree to its great detriment [for it] may dry up due to the entrance of worms through the cuts [that] suck its sap so it can no longer bear fruit [and] opening paths and trails through those plots of land. They have committed all manner of atrocious crimes that merit punishment and sanction. For this reason, I beseech and implore Y. M. to review the [receipts] and, having received information to support my allegations, order [the accused] to be apprehended and penalized so he cannot continue working on that tree, make wine from it, or cut fruits from the fruit

trees on those lands without my consent, and that the indio be punished. I implore for justice [to ensure] that whatever is necessary is done. [319]

Up to that moment, the only benefit that Ruiz de Padilla received from his palm trees was selling the fruit (coconuts), earning some 50 pesos annually, according to his declaration before the authorities.[320] By the early 17th century, mule trains leaving Colima for Mexico City loaded with cacao and salt had begun to include coconuts that were surely in demand in the capital of New Spain, not only as food but also for their shells, which were made into lavish cups with silver handles called cocos chocolateros, used to serve hot chocolate.[321]

However, the cutting of palm trunks to make vino de cocos that had so astonished Ruiz de Padilla soon ceased to be an anomaly. Francisco Rodríguez Machuca must have been one of the first men to show people in Colima how they could exploit their palms for wine production. On December 15th 1600, news reached Colima that aguardiente was also being produced in Caxitlán, one of the most fertile valleys for coconut palm plantations in the province. There, a judicial investigation had been opened due to a drunken melee involving Indians and chinos that broke out on the plantation of alférez Álvaro García de Grijalva while he was away. According to witnesses' statements, the brawl began when four chinos, Juan, Domingo, Agustín, and Francisco Hernández, entered the plantation and invited the overseer, Simón, an Indian from the nearby town of Xicotlán, and "a few female Indians" from the house, to drink vino de cocos. After a few cups (tecomates), they had all become quite drunk. News of a scuffle reached the ears of the plantation owner and led to the opening of a legal process that culminated with fines and exile for the chinos.[322]

It is probable that those pioneering vinateros received a mixed form of wages for their labors –part in money,

Part II

part in wine– as this was a normal procedure in the early years of *vino de cocos* production. Otherwise, they would not have been able to sell the drink to Indians in other towns, as the overseer Simón accused them of doing when he stated that "on Sundays and at fiestas there is much drunkenness caused by these *chinos* who sell wine, and this is very frequent". Because this file contains signatures in Baybayin, we will analyze it in depth in the following chapter.

Three years after the incident in the hacienda of *alférez* García de Grijalva, we learn of another judicial process, also in the Caxitlán Valley, this time involving not four but 15 Filipino *vinateros*. While the context is not very different, this one is much richer in information than the first case and allows us to analyze the kind of socioeconomic relations that were established between *vinateros* and their employers. The curtain opens on April 28, 1604, when Diego Martínez, the deputy of the *alguacil mayor* of Colima, accused several *vinateros* who worked on different palm haciendas owned by Spanish men and women, of working *a partido*, a term which meant that one part of their wages was paid in cash but the other in aguardiente, an arrangement that fostered illicit trade with Indians.[323]

Just a year before that charge was laid, on March 15, 1603, the *alcalde mayor* of Colima, Francisco Escudero de Figueroa, had prohibited palm hacienda owners from paying *vinateros a partido*, alleging that they either proceeded to sell the wine to Indians, or became inebriated by drinking it themselves, causing brawls and offenses to public morals. Clearly, his intent was not to impede aguardiente production, but only to regulate its commerce:

> It is well known that in this villa [Colima] there are many *chino* tradesmen who through accords with Spaniards work, each one in his trade [and are] paid half in cash, the other half in wine [which] they sell to Indians, negros, and mulattos. My Lord, from this time forward, I implore that they be paid only in cash and no longer be allowed to

sell [wine] by enforcing the ordinance that exists on this [matter].[324]

Proof that Escudero's command was not obeyed comes from an extensive judicial process that began with deputy Diego Martínez' accusation against Filipino *vinateros* in 1604, which sheds light on the labor dynamics that had been established by that time. All 15 of those *indios chinos vinateros* worked on palm haciendas in the Caxitlán Valley that were owned by Spaniards, some of whom held positions on the *ayuntamiento* of Colima. The average age of the *vinateros* was 27, so they belonged to the adult sector of the population, though they were quite young by the standards of our time, considering that *vinateros* today may work into their 70s.[325]

Most of the men testified that they "collaborated" with their Spanish employers, who had hired them under the *a partido* regimen, as Agustín Muñoz, one of *alférez* Álvaro García de Grijalva's *vinateros*, declared: "this witness knows that all payments are made *a partido* by the owners of the palms, half [is paid] in the wine they produce, as this witness has seen".[326] Juan Tabi, meanwhile, affirmed that "it's true that [they] are in league with their masters [in] *a partido* [payments] of wine which they take [and] sell for money and he does not sell it".[327] Juan Tabi and the other *vinateros* wanted to hide the fact that they sold the wine they received to Indians in order to avoid punishment, but their efforts were in vain for each one was fined 10 pesos, according to the sentence dictated by the *alcalde mayor*, Francisco Escudero de Figueroa (Table 12).

Table 12. *Indios Chinos Vinateros* in Colima (1604)

Vinatero	Employer	Age
Manuel González*	Diego de Monroy	30
Juan Tabi*	Diego de Monroy	34

Part II

Ventura Ortiz*	Joaquín Jiménez	33
Francisco Martín*	Alonso García Nomparte	26
Juan Gómez*	Antonio Carrillo	30
Andrés González*	Gaspar Ramírez (alcalde ordinario)	-
Francisco Perdomo	Gaspar Ramírez (alcalde ordinario)	30
Agustín	Magdalena Bote	-
Juan de Chávez*	Alonso Lorenzo	20
Pedro García*	Diego Morán	-
Juan Marcos*	Diego Morán	23
Agustín Muñoz	Álvaro García de Grijalba (alférez mayor) / Catalina Ruiz	27
Pedro Timban*	Álvaro García de Grijalba (alférez mayor) / Catalina Ruiz	20
Alonso Lorenzo*	Juan Fernández de Ocampo / Francisca de Carbajal	25
Bartolomé Sampa*	Juan Gutierre de Monroy	-

Source: AHMC, secc. B, caja 49, exp. 7. *Sentenced to pay 10 pesos.

Let us pause for a moment to analyze the *a partido* payment system that prevailed for at least the first years of aguardiente production in Colima, since this was a phenomenon similar to other work settings, such as vineyards in Peru and mines and pearl fisheries in New Spain. In the early 17th century, Indians in Peru, who were considered just as prone to drunkenness as those in New Spain, received wine as payment for their labor, so on May 26, 1609, Felipe III emitted a degree that ordered the Viceroy "to issue the strongest orders that their labor be paid in money", alleging that they "consume it all to satiate their appetite [and] leave [no money] to cover their nudity and that of their women and children".[328]

According to Eduardo Flores Clair, the *a partido* modality in mining consisted in the owners "granting, mainly to laborers, part of the mineral they extracted from the mines; in proportion to the mineral they brought out: for so much ore, so much *a partido*".[329] Another reference to this modality comes from the Jesuit Miguel del Barco, who described the organization of pearl fisheries in the seas of California:

> The equipper also provides the supplies necessary for the entire season, which usually lasts three months. He looks for the people he needs to work as divers. They are hired, some *a partido*, others for a wage. The equipper must pay the latter the amount accorded, but all the shell they collect is for [him]... in contrast, those who are paid *a partido* do not receive a wage, but divide the day's catch with [him], giving him half and keeping the other half for themselves.[330]

Here, del Barco points out that the *partido* consisted in half of the shell obtained, in contrast to the system in the mines, where the amount of ore given to the laborers varied according to the agreements reached with each mine owner. On this issue, Flores Clair insists that the *a partido* modality was essentially a practical measure because it was utilized by mine owners who were beginning their operations and had no clear idea of how much mineral they might extract or, perhaps, lacked sufficient capital to invest in wage workers.

This would explain why this system was implemented in the case of the *vinateros* of Colima, especially in the early years of *vino de cocos* production, when the hacienda owners were just beginning to determine the volume of alcohol they could obtain from their palm trees. The incentive of offering a wage plus an *a partido* payment may have reflected efforts to more firmly secure – "tie down" – their *vinateros*, for at that time only a few had the necessary *savoir faire* and, as Table 12 shows, they were distributed among a handful of Spaniards interested in this growing business.

Part II

Another aspect we cannot pass over is that the authorities were truly concerned about what the *vinateros* and mine workers might do with the products they received, since the *vino de cocos* could be distributed among the Indians, causing drunkenness, while in the case of minerals, they could be sold or bartered to obtain alcohol. This concern was expressed in a report written in 1770 by don Pedro Joseph de Leos on mines in Pachuca, Real del Monte, and Atotonilco:

> at the moment the worker receives the *partido* and whatever other iron, steel and mercury he can steal, he distributes it stupidly to middlemen (*rescatadores*), merchants, tavern owners, brokers and other vices; while his money lasts he never leaves the tavern or quits gambling and is easily given to killing others, sure of his impunity by fleeing to another mine.[331]

The *a partido* regimen seems to have endured well into the 17th century, for in 1647 Lic. Juan Fernández Nieto's hacienda in Xicotlán had six *chinos* working as *vinateros a partido*, indicating that this kind of contract did not disappear entirely with the consolidation of *vino de cocos* production.[332]

VINATEROS TRAPPED IN SYSTEMS OF DEPENDENCE

As the 17th century advanced in the Colima-Motines production nucleus, letters of service emerged as a way to hire *indios chinos vinateros*, a clear reflection of the growing demand for Filipino workers. Soon, being an *indio chino* became a synonym for *vinatero*, as a document from 1638 clarifies. It established that Juanillo, a native Indian winemaker from the town of Zinacamitlán, jurisdiction of the *alcaldía mayor* of Motines, climbs the palm trees of doña Catalina de Alarcón, wife of Captain Antonio Carrillo de Guzmán, "like a *chino*".[333] Being a *chino* and climbing palms to harvest *tuba* emerged as an indissoluble binomial. One may ask if this means that all the Asians who came to the province of Colima knew, *a priori*, the wine-making trade (rather doubtful) or if local society pushed them into it, boxing them into performing that work due to their ethnic and geographic origin.[334]

The demand for Filipino labor to produce *vino de cocos* surely fomented a practice that was by no means unknown in New Spain; namely, hiring *vinateros* by "hooking" them with an advance payment (*enganche*). We have the case of Juan Bautista de Pantao, "a native of the Philippine islands", who in 1632 was subject to an obligation to pay 82 pesos in *botijas* of *vino de cocos* to Pedro Andrade Saavedra, a resident of the Alima Valley, jurisdiction of Maquilí, as the following extract reveals:

> On the Achiotlán plantation in the Alima Valley, jurisdiction of Maquilí, on the seventh day of the month of February of the year one thousand six hundred and thirty-two, before me, the public scribe, and witnesses, Juan Bautista de Pantao appeared, a native of the Philippine islands, servant of Pedro Andrade Saavedra, a resident of this villa who I know and of whom I give faith, who confirmed that he owes and is bound to pay Pedro de Andrade eighty-two pesos *de oro común* because this was [the amount] the latter loaned him in *reales*, which he confirms having received freely. Regarding this, I waive the exception of monetary payment, the laws of delivery, and their proof as contained therein, which I am bound to pay in *botijas* of wine that belong to me as my share in the *a partido* arrangement that the undersigned grants me from his palms at the current price, fully and concretely at the moment of delivery, and I promise to never be absent from [his] house and palm trees until I finish paying said amount, and have no right to sell the wine [I receive] to another person, and if [I] am absent the undersigned can send a person to the place where this signee is with two pesos *de oro común* as wages for each day occupied in going, staying, and returning to find and bring back this signee, which wages he shall pay as principal, a promise that binds his person and properties, now and in the future, and in these terms he is subject to His Majesty's justices in any place, to whatever jurisdiction he may be subject, waiving his own [jurisdiction], the law *si convenerit*

de jurisditiones omnium juidicum, so he be compelled to pay as per the sentence passed in the case tried, renouncing his right, and so be it authorized and signed, before the witnesses Diego Arias and Diego Álvarez de Espinosa and Francisco Martín, Juan Bautista Pantao, before me, Clemente Hidalgo de Agüero, public scribe.[335]

Pantao's case shows how various procedures could be combined in one contract: an advance payment, or advanced sale of a product, a wage or *a partido* payment, and exclusive rights to the aguardiente produced. It is clear that Pedro Andrade, the owner of the Achiotlán plantation, paid the Filipino Pantao 82 pesos in advance in exchange for an anticipated purchase of the *vino de cocos* produced. But this can also be considered a form of entrapment since he paid for the Filipino's work in advance. Other clauses stipulated Andrade's exclusive rights to aguardiente production, and Pantao's promise not to abandon his work until his debt was paid. This presages another means of securing workers: debt peonage.

There are clearer cases. Up to now, we have argued that the *indios chinos vinateros* had free legal status, but in reality their condition as subjects of Spaniards who owned palm haciendas could derive in conditions quite similar to those of slavery. In other words, some laborers were bound to live and work in conditions of debt peonage, a practice that was likely very common, as suggested by the case of Sebastián Tumbaga, a *vinatero* hired by Bartolomé Bravo Lagunas. Tumbaga fled from Bravo's hacienda in August 1638, initiating a judicial process that ended with his imprisonment because he owed Bravo 41 pesos, six *tomines*. Tumbaga wrote this petition from his cell:

> Sebastián Tumbaga, *chino*, imprisoned in the public jail of this villa of Colima due to an accusation by Bartolomé Bravo, resident of this villa. I [appear] before Your Mercy to state that Bartolomé Bravo does not want me to return to work on his hacienda and pay him the amount I owe, nor to sell me to another place where they would pay for

me but, rather, only see me die of hunger here. So I beg for Your Mercy and implore you to order Bartolomé Bravo to sell me where they will pay for me or to give me food while I am jailed, for I am so poor that I have no means to support myself except my work, and I am very much in need...[336]

Two elements drew our attention to Tumbaga's case: first, the heading of the judicial process states that it involves a "*chino* who escaped from his master", although at no time is he identified as a slave; second, Tumbaga's insistence that Bartolomé Bravo "sell me where they will pay for me", as if this were a common practice in a society where a *vinatero's* skill set was highly-valued, for at that time wine-making was the most profitable economic activity in the province of Colima.

It is likely that Luis González, a resident of Colima who produced *vino de cocos*, paid Tumbaga's debt to Bartolomé Bravo because, in January 1640, he stated that he had made a deal with him for "a hundred and some pesos" to exploit a few palm trees, but denounced that he did not frequent his hacienda and had not paid his debt. Perhaps it was because Filipinos often fled from the haciendas that contracts imposed a penalty for escaping. We must recall that Bautista de Pantao's letter of obligation to the Spaniard Pedro Andrade Saavedra specified that if the Filipino left, the hacendado had the authority to send "someone to wherever the [signer] was", and charge two pesos in wages for each day that person spent searching for him. Nor can we forget that escapes and punishment were commonplace occurrences in other social sectors, especially among slaves and millworkers.

It is important to note that letters of service as a form of hiring appeared in times of Viceroy Martín Enríquez de Almansa (1568-1580), who systematically implemented a series of decrees in efforts to regulate indigenous labor in three modalities: voluntary service, debt servitude, and forced labor as punishment for committing a crime.[337]

In this regard, in 1609, an *indio chino* named Antón Pérez was earning a monthly wage of 3 pesos plus room and board in a mill in Querétaro. His letter of service had the same features as the one that *vinateros* signed; that is, the proprietor provided housing, food, and good treatment, but if the *indio chino* fled he would be hunted down and held responsible for the costs generated.[338] Who would have thought that as the 17th century advanced, those same *chinos* would be incorporated as workers in mills of this kind in central New Spain?[339]

A third experience in the sphere of labor relations of Filipinos on palm haciendas also appeared in Tumbaga's case. Finding himself unable to pay off the debt, his hope was that a third party would assume it in exchange for his services; that is, a negotiation would transfer his debt to a substitute master. It is difficult to determine if this practice was occasional, fortuitous, or atypical, or if it formed part of the daily life of those haciendas, but the debt transfer system was nothing new to the Filipinos, for the complex system of servitude that evolved on the archipelago from pre-Hispanic times included individuals called *tinubos* who were in debt to their masters who, eventually, could transfer that debt to a second master through an economic compensation.[340]

As early in the 17th century as the year 1604, when *vino de cocos* production had barely begun, Miguel de Vera,[341] a resident of Guadalajara, transferred to the *colimense*, Juan Gutierre de Monroy, the 57-peso debt of a *chino* named Nicolás Rodríguez. In their deal, Gutierre de Monroy agreed to pay De Vera that amount in exchange for Rodríguez' work as a *vinatero* on his palm hacienda in Aguacatitlán, at a monthly wage of 7 pesos for more or less eight months of work. Of course, the accord included the clause that Rodríguez would be penalized if he was absent or escaped. Finally, as part of the pact, Gutierre de Monroy promised to give Rodríguez housing and food and to cure his illnesses, but stipulated that "if he falls ill the wage shall not be paid".³⁴² It is interesting to see that offers like this one by the Spanish hacendado are not reported in other contracts, so one may ask if the room and board that Rodríguez received was part of a complementary payment to his fixed monthly wage, or was paid by the owner. This circumstance, in a period when specialized labor was still scarce and, hence, highly-valued, may also reflect the flexibility of that "wage market".

Another case involved Lorenzo de Aguilar, a "*chino* from Manila" who produced wine on the Zinacamitlán palm hacienda in the jurisdiction of Motines.³⁴³ Gregorio Fernández de Tene, a resident of Colima, once "heard that he was from Manila", and knew from other Filipinos that he was single and childless. De Aguilar likely reached Colima around 1644. Interestingly, people who knew this man also identified him as a "free *chino*", suggesting that in the mid-17th century the Asian population in New Spain still lived under an ambiguous juridical framework. Another intriguing aspect is how other people referred to Lorenzo de Aguilar. The overseer of the Zinacamitlán hacienda, the Spaniard Francisco de Castañeda, identified him as "a *vinatero a partido*". The only reference we have to de Aguilar's work names that hacienda, property of the scribe Clemente Hidalgo de Agüero who, with his overseer, paid the *vinatero's* wage in corn, clothes, or *reales*, following the practice used with others. Here is an inventory of Lorenzo de Aguilar's properties.³⁴⁴

- A new chest with key, inside, a cloth robe
- Some old underwear and other underwear of old cloth
- An old white soap
- An old doublet with black sleeves
- Some wool socks
- Two old white handcloths

Part II

- An old hat
- Two pairs of old shoes, one of cordovan, the other leather
- One new cotton [lacuna]
- Three old palm spoons
- A machete
- A digging stick
- One large chisel, and one small one, old
- One [lacuna] and a small axe, old
- Some loose papers
- An old broken box
- Two tame mares, one brown, one black
- Two female mules and one male
- A new house [...] with a wooden door and a lock with its key

In November 1654, De Aguilar fell sick and "was close to the end", but before he died, his countryman Juan de la Cruz suggested that he dictate his will. De Aguilar responded that "it was hardly necessary for his [meagre] possessions", after all, he would die single with no descendants. Perhaps that was why de la Cruz insisted: hoping he might receive some of de Lorenzo's material goods. In reality, it might have been worthwhile for him to dictate his will, when we consider that the inventory of his properties included a new house with a wooden door, lock, and key. His clothes and tools may have been old and worn, but they were his property and suggest that this immigrant enjoyed a certain level of material comfort for some years before his death.

In December of that year, Clemente Hidalgo de Agüero, Lorenzo's master, knocked on the door of the *alcalde mayor*, don Alonso de Aguilar Cervantes, to ask that Lorenzo's possessions be turned over to him to pay the deceased *vinatero*'s debt: 28 pesos from a total of 84 pesos "and all other things I gave him in *reales*, corn, clothes, and other necessities as is registered in my ledgers".[345] The witnesses that Clemente Hidalgo presented included the Spaniard Francisco de Castañeda, overseer of the hacienda of Zinacamitlán who, in February 1655, confirmed Lorenzo de Aguilar's debt and corroborated that he had received clothes and corn as wages. Castañeda also stated that a few days before dying, De Aguilar "told this witness that he did not want more clothes because he owed his master money and did not wish to owe him more".[346] Once again, the topic of debt peonage –or a similar modality– arises in this case of this *indio chino vinatero* who received wages in kind (corn, clothes) and, on occasion, a few *reales*. Regarding this issue, on June 20, 1567, Felipe II decreed the following:

> First, if an Indian is imprisoned for debt because he lacks the means to pay what he [owes], he is to be turned over to his creditor to serve him. You shall follow and obey the laws of these kingdoms as they refer to this and, in their observation and compliance, shall deliver said Indian to his creditor where he shall serve the time deemed necessary to repay the debt as it should be, and if said creditor does not wish to receive him, nor be served by him in payment of said debt, [then] he shall be ordered set free *but it is prohibited that he be sold to any other person in payment of the debt.*[347]

Other cases of indebtedness involving *chinos* on haciendas are recorded in a document called *Deudas de los chinos de la hacienda* ("Debts of *chinos* on the hacienda"), property of doña Catalina de Alarcón. Upon her death in 1638, her husband and executor, don Antonio Carrillo de Guzmán took possession of that ledger (Table 13).

Part II

Table 13. Debts of *Chinos* on the *Hacienda* of Zinacamitlán, Motines (1638–1639)

Name	Amount of the debt
Juan Bautista	39 pesos, 6 reales
Francisco	19 pesos, 3 reales
Agustín Pérez	44 pesos, 7 tomines
Alonso	10 pesos, 4 tomines (escaped)
García	71 pesos
Diego Pérez	87 pesos, 4 reales
Baltasar Francisco	18 pesos, 2 tomines

Source: AHMC, secc. B, caja 18, exp. 1.

By December 10, 1638, Diego Pérez had accumulated a large debt of 87 pesos, 4 *reales* with the hacendado, Antonio Carrillo de Guzmán. Records shows that Carrillo had paid a debt of 22 pesos, 4 *tomines* that this *indio chino* owed to Captain Pedro Gómez de Olvera; that is, Antonio Carrillo took on Pérez' debt in order to bring the *chino* to work for him "in the wine-making trade, or whatever he wishes". But Diego Pérez also owed Carrillo a mule, which meant that his debt had increased substantially.[348] Such a large economic burden was extremely difficult for an *indio chino* to pay off, especially considering that the average monthly wage for *vinateros* ranged from only 4 to 5 pesos. Around that time, Baltasar Francisco, another *indio chino* who worked on the same hacienda as Diego Pérez, owed Antonio Carrillo de Guzmán 14 pesos, but under distinct circumstances, for he had been hired as a *vinatero* at a wage of 4 pesos per month, but had received an advance payment of 18 pesos, which was being retained from his wages month-by-month.[349]

VINATEROS ON THE PATH TO ECONOMIC EMANCIPATION

The insertion of *indios chinos vinateros* into the palm haciendas permitted another type of labor relation, one perhaps more equitable than those outlined above. In this profile we find *vinateros* in more comfortable circumstances as they enjoyed some economic freedom. They could own haciendas and receive licenses to ride on horseback and brand their cattle. Far from encountering *vinateros* subjected to Spanish hacendados, we see in their experiences some phenomena of economic emancipation rarely observed among *vinateros* in general or in other non-Spanish groups of *colimense* society.

We begin with the case of Andrés Rosales, "a native of the Philippines" who in September 1618 signed a contract to produce *vino de cocos* with the then *alférez* and *alcalde* of the *Santa Hermandad*, don Jorge Carrillo de Guzmán. Via that accord, Rosales leased Carrillo 28 coconut palms in Tecolapa, near the Caxitlán Valley, so that the latter would produce *vino de cocos* with "one or two *vinateros*". In return, Rosales would obtain one-third of the profits at the end of the first two years of production. The terms further stipulated that Rosales would provide only the raw material, "without [performing any] work, or spending anything on [materials] needed to produce wine". That clause freed the Filipino from any formal labor relation with the *alférez*; in other words, he became a kind of capitalist partner in a kind of commercial society that they formed.

It is important to remember that *vino de cocos* production and distribution were still prohibited in 1618 since the council of the villa of Colima did not obtain its first license to freely trade aguardiente until 1627, as we discuss in detail in a later chapter. That ban weighed more heavily on Indians and *indios chinos* because of the moral and religious arguments that supported it. In the aforementioned document, we read that "the *alcaldes mayores* of this province have issued many commands that no *chino* or Indian can make *vino de cocos* from the palm trees and plantations because of the great damage done or that ensues". Rosales, then, was not breaking any laws, for he promised to lease his palms but would not participate in any way in *vino de cocos* production. It is surprising, however, that the accord between these men did not provide the identity of the *vinatero*, though in all likelihood it would have been a Filipino (perhaps Rosales himself?).

> [Andrés Rosales] has agreed and concerted with *alférez* Jorge Carrillo de Guzmán to give him these palms in partnership for a period of two years from [this] date so he can [hire] one or two *vinateros* and give me one-third [of the earnings], though I will not personally contribute any work or make any outlays necessary to produce wine. And said Jorge Carrillo de Guzmán shall pay those [tradesmen] their wage and sustenance [in exchange for] collecting the *tuba* and [obtaining] pots to cook the wine. For those expenses, he shall keep two-thirds of the income obtained from the wine produced. Said Jorge Carrillo de Guzmán accepts this accord and contract and is bound to observe and comply with its contents in this role, and he and Andrés Rosales signed it. Dated the fifth of September of the year one thousand six hundred and eighteen, witnessed by Juan Pérez de Espinosa, Pedro Sarmiento, and Juan Martín, *chino*.[350]

But after a few months, problems arose between *alférez* Carrillo and the Filipino Rosales. Perhaps due to an excellent yield from the 28 palm trees he had leased, Rosales complained to the *alcalde mayor*, Cristóbal Gutiérrez Flores, alleging that Jorge Carrillo de Carrillo had promised him half of the aguardiente produced, but that of the 70 *botijas* obtained up to that moment, he had received only 15, so he claimed he was owed 20 more, as well as "a vat, two empty *botijas*, and a lock that cost 4 pesos". Clearly, Rosales had leased not only his palms but also, perhaps, a hut or storehouse for tools, as it was common to find small buildings with locks on those palm haciendas.

In his defense, Jorge Carrillo presented the contract celebrated in September 1618, which established that Rosales would receive only one-third of the wine produced. Carrillo testified that in December 1618 they had reviewed the updated accounts, which showed a total production of 56 botijas of *vino de cocos*, of which he had given Rosales 15 and kept the other 41 for himself. He recognized that he owed Rosales three-and-a-half botijas, but nothing else. This episode ended with the parties "satisfied, content, and remunerated", for they both acknowledged the validity of the initial terms. Was Andrés Rosales trying to take advantage of the situation? Well, an element not mentioned in relation to him is that when he accused Jorge Carrillo of breach of contract, Rosales held the post of *alcalde de los chinos*, a legal figure that gave him some judicial power and fiscal attributions that, doubtless, strengthened his negotiating power. We will return to the topic of these *alcaldes* later in this chapter.

VINATEROS INTEGRATED INTO LOCAL SOCIETY

Another case of interest for this discussion features Nicolás Mananquel, who appears on the scene in 1618 as a debtor of Domingo de Villalobos, a Filipino merchant originally from Pampanga who lived in Zapotlán. Domingo de Villalobos had built a veritable network of clients across western New Spain based on commerce in luxury goods from China and other products "of the land". He had given Mananquel 10 pesos of salt to sell, and his list of debtors included at least four other *chinos*: Luis, Pedro Timbán, Juan Triana, and Francisco Matías.[351] After that date, Nicolás Mananquel's existence is shrouded in silence until he reappears in 1642, when the *alcalde mayor*, Cristóbal de Lugo y Montalvo, called the annual election of the *alcalde de los chinos* in Colima. Mananquel participated in that election but failed to garner the majority of votes. However, on April 8 of the following year (1643), he presented himself to the new *alcalde mayor*, Martín Esteban de Velasco, as "from the *chino* nation [and] a resident of this villa", to solicit the official registration of a branding iron for his mules and horses. How many animals? He did not say.[352] Who was this Filipino who emerged suddenly as a candidate to represent all the *chinos*, and then successfully applied for his own branding iron? This is not an easy question to answer, especially due to the silence of the sources. Might this personage have arrived and settled in Colima with substantial capital that allowed him to invest in the local economy? Over time, we learn that Nicolás Mananquel came to own a palm hacienda and had people working for him. Mananquel's case proves that opportunities for social ascent opened for certain *indios chinos vinateros*, including some women, like Francisca Martha, whom we discussed in detail in the previous chapter.

One final, but no less important, case of Filipino *vinateros* integrated into *colimense* society is that of Juan de la Cruz, "a native of Sengayan in the Philippines", who we mentioned in a previous chapter. His case is relevant not only because he left a will –however brief– but also because it is dated in the Caxitlán Valley in March 1717, a time when the *indio chino* population had decreased markedly and almost disappeared from contemporary records.[353] De la Cruz' parents were also from Sengayan, a town in Indonesia, though he stated that it was "in the Philippines". He married doña Magdalena de Carbajal, a *coyota*, and they had three children: Juan, Miguel, and Francisca, all of whom bore the surname de la Cruz, and were named as his universal heirs.

Juan de la Cruz' relation with *vino de cocos* is evidenced by "a few huts on that ranch with an oven for wines and six vessels for *tuba* and wine". Unfortunately, this document is severely damaged so we cannot ascertain if the ranch was in the Caxitlán Valley, though later it mentions a "small hacienda" that Juan apparently purchased from a man named Venegas, on which the census of the Virgen de Caxitlán (perhaps Nuestra Señora del Rosario?) charged a principal of 100 pesos. This may refer to the same property, in which case to the west it abutted the palm hacienda of *La Merced*; to the east, the Mogotal hill; to the south, the banks of a river (Río Grande of Colima); and to the north "a cliff/quarry". The fact that a river is mentioned is important because, as the reader will recall, a secure supply of water was necessary not only for irrigating the palm trees but also for distilling *vino de cocos*.

This *indio chino* from Sengayan, a Christian among Christians, manifested that his final wish was to be buried in the parish church of the villa of Colima, just like Francisca Martha. He asked to be interred "next to the font of holy water", an uncommon request for someone of the non-Spanish population.[354] We could find no trace of his wife and children, but it is clear that this is another case –perhaps the last one– of the successful sociocultural insertion of an Asian immigrant.

THE ALCALDES DE CHINOS

By the second decade of the 17th century, *vino de cocos* production was a vigorous activity in the Colima-Motines nucleus. The *vinateros*' trade was highly esteemed in the labor market, and distinct work relations had emerged between Asians and Spaniards, as we discussed in the previous pages. But another development awaited the *indios chinos*: the creation of a representative called the *alcalde de los chinos* (advocate of the *chinos*), an official position that carried judicial power and fiscal faculties.[355] This was a rather atypical phenomenon in New Spain, and one that emerged only where Filipinos worked in rural, agricultural contexts like the Colima-Motines and, as we will see below, the Zacatula-Acapulco nuclei.

For the case of Colima, we located records of five *alcaldes de chinos* for the years 1619, 1632, 1636, 1642, and 1651. In the first three cases, we learn only their names and the context in which they acted. Andrés Rosales was the *alcalde* in 1619. We mentioned him earlier, so the reader may remember that he forged a kind of partnership with the *alférez* of Colima at the time to produce *vino de cocos*.[356] The second note on an *alcalde de chinos* in Colima dates from 1632, when some *indios chinos* appeared before the *alcalde mayor* to solicit his ratification of their elected representative, "in accordance with the uses and customs that operate among us [*indios chinos*] to name an *alcalde ordinario* for us who will perform Your Mercy's diligences and services and collect tribute...".[357] On that occasion, the Asians elected Luis Ortiz, a married man whom they considered "reliable" (*seguro*).

The third reference is from 1636. It provides very little information, but does touch on one fundamental topic: the judicial attributions of the *alcalde de chinos*. It is difficult to determine the performance of these representatives of the Asian community as judges, but one judicial process in which Bartolomé Vázquez, the *alcalde de chinos* that year, participated, sheds some light on this issue. Bartolomé Vázquez was raised on a palm hacienda in Colima. On one occasion, he learned that a "furious, drunken" Indian had severely beaten a woman, causing a scandal and commotion among the hacienda's residents. Vázquez intervened in the dispute and was wounded by the infuriated Indian when he tried to stop his attacks. When interrogated by the *alcalde mayor*, Vázquez declared that he had intervened "because he was the *alcalde* [*de los chinos*]" and the Indian wanted to burn down the hacendado's house.[358]

Information on the representatives in 1642 and 1651 is richer, for we were able to find the official voting acts. In that period, these authorities were called "*alcaldes de los chinos, mulattos, indios laboríos* and free negros", so at some point in the 17th century this elected position evolved to include other castes, not only Asians, for by that time the palm haciendas had become multicultural spaces. To exemplify this, we can examine a command issued by the *alcalde mayor* of Colima in 1642, don Cristóbal de Lugo y Montalvo, which stipulated that "any and all negros and free mulattos, *chinos* and *indios laboríos* who work for Spaniards and walk freely outside the towns" must appear and pay tribute to His Majesty, or risk being punished with ten days in jail and six pesos.[359] It is evident that these were seen as groups that caused fiscal problems because they did not live in Indian towns but, rather, on palm haciendas and other Spanish ranches, so it is not farfetched to suggest that the "*alcalde de los chinos, mulattos and indios laboríos*" was deemed a figure who could resolve inconveniences among them.

Table 14. Voting for the *Alcalde de los Chinos, Mulattos, and Indios Laboríos* (1642)

The alcalde and other officials from the past year, one thousand six hundred and forty-one, are in conformity with the votes and [also] vote for the alcalde de los chinos and mulattos and indios laboríos for the coming year, one thousand six hundred and forty-two: 1. For Gaspar Hernández   IIIIIIIIII 2. For Agustín Pérez   IIII 3. For Nicolás Mananquel   IIII Gaspar Hernández received more votes due to the preference of all, so he shall occupy the post of alcalde this year with Juan Alonso serving as councilman and sheriff. In the villa of Colima, on the first day of the month of January of the year one thousand six hundred and forty-two, before me, General don Cristóbal de Lugo y Montalvo, alcalde mayor of this province and deputy of the Captain General for His Majesty [...] the chinos of this province exhibited this paper, in which they state that they have written their election of Gaspar Hernández for this current year and requested that I ratify it and deliver the staff of royal justice for the use of said office, and said Captain General alcalde mayor having seen it, he instructed me to approve it and the date of the election of Gaspar Hernández, whose oath was sworn and who swore before God and the Cross in conformity with the law, promising to use said office as he should and as he is obliged to do.

Source: AHMC, secc. B, caja 21, exp. 2.

The *alcalde* "and other officials" (a councilman and sheriff) from the previous year were present at the 1642 election (Table 14). Those posts could be filled by the same person in the case of elections for the councils of Indians. As with all ordinary elections, this one was held on the first of January. The result was ratified by the *alcalde mayor*, don Cristóbal de Lugo y Montalvo, who gave the *alcalde*-elect, Gaspar Hernández, his staff of justice.

The 1651 election (Table 15) had a similar format, as it was also held on the first of January to choose the *alcalde*, councilman, and *alguacil*. As in 1642, the latter two posts fell to the same man, Felipe Santiago. The *alcalde*-elect was a familiar face: Sebastián Tumbaga, who years earlier had faced judicial problems and been jailed. Despite that antecedent, during this election he was referred to as "a completely satisfactory person, married, with good accounts". Most of his opponents were of Asian origin, for we can recognize, at least, the names of Mananquel, Pano, Aguilar, and Sebastián de la Cruz; the latter, Francisca Martha's husband. There was, however, no mention of Agustín de la Paz or Hernando Donay.

It is true that although this *alcalde* represented several ethnic groups, the *indios chinos* controlled that office and, surely, the most strategic political relations with Spanish authorities. The prelude to the 1651 election makes this clear: "So say us, all the *indios chinos* of the Philippines". The *indios laboríos*, mulattos, and free negros are not mentioned until later, when the topic of tribute payments was broached. One difference between the 1642 and 1651 elections is that the presence of the *alcalde mayor* was not mentioned at the latter, though the event apparently proceeded without him and the document was taken to him later for validation.

Table 15. Election of the Alcalde de los Chinos, Indios Laboríos, Free Mulattos, and Free Negros (1651)

> So say us, all the indios chinos from the Philippines whose custom it is to name and elect the alcalde for the current year, six hundred and fifty-one, and other officials who shall be responsible for collecting His Majesty's royal tribute that we pay, as do the indios laborios, free mulattos, and free negros, for which we elect Sebastián Tumbaga as alcalde, raised as a chino who wishes to perform His Majesty's royal service, a person of complete satisfaction, married, who gives good accounts, and shall be aided in collecting by Felipe Santiago, as councilman and alguacil.
> We implore and supplicate Your Mercy in this [document] to order that the staffs be delivered, and swear before God and this Cross that this election [proceeded] without fraud, and sign it. Colima. January first of the year 1651.
> [Signees]
> 1. Nicolás Mananquel
> 2. Martín Pano
> 3. Sebastián de la Cruz
> 4. Agustín de la Paz
> 5. Hernando Donay
> 6. Lorenzo Aguilar

Source: AHMC, Fondo Sevilla del Río, caja 5, exp. 4, f. 8v.

It is important to emphasize that some communities of runaway slaves (*cimarrones*) in New Spain had their own representatives who defended their interests in the face of pressures exerted by Spanish authorities.[360] In Spanish America more broadly, there were *alcaldes de oficio* (advocates) for some guilds. Mexico City and Quito (Ecuador) had *alcaldes* for tailors, while the latter also had *alcaldes* for shoemakers. Constantino Bayle noted that the *alcaldes de oficio* were considered "representatives of guilds" and their members, who could "solicit conveniences and aspirations" in their name.[361] The position of *alcalde de los chinos* was also similar to the experience of some indigenous governments in Mexico City in the 16th and 17th centuries.

On this topic, Charles Gibson observed that the Mixtecs, Zapotecs, Tarascans, and Chichimecs all had their own sheriffs for tribute collection.[362]

Another surprising aspect is the similarity between these elections of *alcaldes de chinos* and those of *gobernadorcillos* in the Philippines. In his *Informe sobre el estado de las Islas Filipinas en 1842*, Sinibaldo de Mas y Sanz noted that several provinces were organized around the representation of leaders called *gobernadorcillos*, who acted as judges on palm production units and other plantations.[363] The mechanisms of election were as follows: first, three candidates were named by the headsman of each *barangay* (district).[364] Second, other posts, including those of *deputy* and *alguacil*, were elected; and, third, all voting was held on the first of January in the royal houses or local tribunals. All results, of course, were subject to ratification by the Spanish authorities. De Mas y Sanz' description of the elections of *gobernadorcillos* in the Philippines inevitably evokes the election of the *alcaldes de chinos* on palm production units in Colima.

Examples from both sides of the Pacific could easily be multiplied. What they reveal is a Spanish colonial system that was flexible and open, one that needed, at all times, to "incorporate" social groups with special characteristics. In the 15th century, the Iberian Peninsula was marked by the coexistence of Jews and Muslims, represented by a *rab mayor de la corte* and an *alcalde mayor de las aljamas de moros*, respectively, who, though situated in very different contexts, represented an *ancien régime* system that was much more open than one might imagine.[365]

By the second half of the 17th century, the figure of the *alcalde de los chinos* had disappeared from documents in Colima. Could this have been due to the decline of the Asian population and the collapse of *vino de cocos* production in that period? The answer is likely "yes", but we shall reserve these topics for a later chapter.

THE SILENT VINATEROS OF ZACATULA-ACAPULCO

Without question, the historical documents that reflect the importance of the Asian population in palm tree management are held mainly in archives in Colima. News of Asian immigrants in the *alcaldías mayores* of Zacatula and Acapulco, where *vino de cocos* was elaborated, though in much smaller quantities than in Colima is, however, scarce. In fact, the employment of Asian laborers there was distinct, as in Acapulco and the surrounding area *chinos* slaves, above all, participated actively in production.[366]

According to Matthew J. Furlong, *vino de cocos* production in that zone dated at least from 1609, when the distillate was being produced on a cacao hacienda. Elaboration of this alcoholic drink persisted throughout the 17th century, as production was registered on diverse haciendas, including those of San Pedro, San Juan de Tuxtepec, San Bartolomé Tuxtepec, San Luis, San Juan Bautista, Nuestra Señora del Buen Suceso, Nuestra Señora de la Conception, San Miguel Apusagualcos, and San Nicolás Tetitlán, and on ranches like Cayaco, Cacalutla, and, likely San Jerónimo, San Francisco, and San José.[367] Unfortunately, this list is only nominative, and we have no information on how *vino de cocos* production developed in this area –known today as the *Costa Grande* of Guerrero– or on the kinds of labor relations that existed between hacienda owners and their *chino* workers.

Significantly, the inventory of the Nuestra Señora del Buen Suceso hacienda in Coyuca mentions several *chino* servants who presumably participated in *tuba* and *vino de cocos* production, according to the materials mentioned in this document. In Table 16, we transcribe a fragment of that inventory.

PART II

Table 16. Chinos, *Tuba*, and *Vino de Cocos* on the *Hacienda* of Nuestra Señora del Buen Suceso in Coyuca (Fragment)

• Sebastián Moco, chino
• Domingo Moco, chino
• Francisco Bonita, chino
• Miguel Petition, chino
• Gonzalo Tullido, chino
• Antonia, china, wife of Sebastián Moco
• Two wooden buckets, one new the other old, used for tuba for wine
• Twenty-six botijas peruleras
• Plus four damaged botijas cascadas
• One empty Castille botijuela, normal size for Castille vessels
• Nineteen woven mats for drying cacao
• 40 gourds (tecomates) for extracting tuba, intact and damaged

Source: AGN, Tierras, vol. 3624, exp. 2, ff. 5-6.

That hacienda belonged to Pedro de Carrascosa, the *alguacil mayor* of the port of Acapulco, who also served as a guarantor (*fiador*) for the entry of Asian slaves into the port, especially from 1640 to 1660.[368] This explains the presence of numerous individuals in these circumstances. Though not identified as *vinateros* in the document, it is virtually certain that some plied the trade of extracting *tuba* for *vino de cocos* production, as is suggested by the kinds of utensils found on the hacienda. Another example comes from the cacao and palm hacienda of San Juan Tuxtepec, jurisdiction of Zacatula, where records for 1649 mention copper vats "for wine production", and a *chino* named Luis (aged 50) who surely administered the hacienda of 180 palm trees reported there.[369]

It may be that mulattos on the ranches of Alcholoa and Cacahuatepec also participated in producing this distillate.[370] This would suggest that –as occurred in Colima– this trade came to be practiced by other population sectors, apart from *chinos*. In this regard, it is revealing that a "mulatto de China" named Marcos de Ávila lived on the hacienda of San Juan Tuxtepec, for this suggests that mixed sectors of the population were in contact –directly or indirectly– with the production of this distillate.[371] The map of this region in Chapters 7 and 8 analyzes, as well, the zones where *vino de cocos* from this production nucleus was commercialized.

Another important finding is that some of the *chinos* who were subjects of debt peonage had the possibility to pay off part of their debt in *botijas* of *vino de cocos*.[372] This reveals another pattern similar to the one in Colima. Unfortunately, beyond these scattered data, there is a void in documentation from this area of the Pacific, so we cannot determine in any detail the role of Asians there and their relation to *vino de cocos*. This lies in stark contrast to the Colima-Motines production nucleus, where files –as we have reiterated– are more abundant. More information on the production of this distillate and its zones of commercialization will be presented in the chapters that follow.

Final Reflections

In these pages we have addressed three aspects related to the *indios chinos vinateros* who arrived in New Spain: their origin, destinations, and mechanisms of insertion into the workforce on palm haciendas in Colima. Although those immigrants settled in only a few localities, they show marked convergences that reveal the pattern of their role in *vino de cocos* production. One central point is the close, natural link between these immigrants and their native product –the coconut palm– and the traditional knowledge that opened the way for them toward a better, and faster, insertion into the society of New Spain. Without this *savoir faire*, it is probable that they would have faced a much more uncertain future.

Part II

The life trajectories presented herein reveal a notable fluidity of circumstances. In each place we find a veritable case study of work, for each labor relation was not only distinct but included diverse procedures: in part (*a partido*), advanced payments, formal contracts, and debt peonage. We are surprised to learn that the *chino* Andrés Rosales signed a production contract with *alférez* Jorge Carrillo de Guzmán, though it is no accident that, around that time, one of the principal merchants and "financial experts" in Guadalajara was a Japanese man named Juan de Páez.[373] In a universe with a sparse population that existed at the crossroads of four continents, behavior could not be guided by simple prejudices or attitudes forged elsewhere: that moment in Colima, with all its limitations, was but a fleeting instant, but one marked by a genuine acceptance of the "other", of strangers. Perhaps this was the case, as well, of the *Costa Grande*, in its own way, though our *vinateros* there had to negotiate their place with other social groups more diligently.

What happened to the *indios chinos vinateros* in the final years of the 17th century? On the one hand, Asian immigration to New Spain was suspended from the 1670s onward by the cautionary measures imposed to prevent forms of Asian slavery from entering the realm. On the other, *vino de cocos* production suffered a severe setback in the late 17th century when production and sales were prohibited, an imposition that surely discouraged the movement of more *indios chinos* toward the palm haciendas. The case of Juan de la Cruz, a native of Sengayan, sheds light on what may have happened to these *vinateros* in Colima. His will, dated in 1717, includes an interesting section on debt which suggests that he not only participated in producing and commercializing *vino de cocos*, but also other products, such as salt and corn.[374] This suggests that the economic activities of the *vinateros* had begun to be diversified during the 17th century due to the decadence of the palm distillate which, though it was still being produced, was a mere shadow of the thriving commerce that had marked the mid-17th century. In addition, by that time, they were not the only men who knew how to extract *tuba* and produce *vino de cocos*, for that secret, if it had ever existed, had been transmitted to Indians and sectors of the Mestizo population that quickly ceased to be simple consumers to become reliable *vinateros* themselves.

Our *indios chinos* virtually disappear from historical records in Colima in the early 18th century, though in the neighboring city of Guadalajara it is still possible to trace some *chinos* in the 1700s, especially those who married native women from Nueva Galicia.[375] It is highly likely that their migration was related to the opening of San Blas as a commercial port with direct connections to the Philippines, an event that occurred in the second half of the 18th century, but by that time *vino de cocos* production had ceased.

In the case of Acapulco and its surroundings, an emblematic event in the 18th century was the founding of the neighborhood (*barrio*) called San Nicolás Tolentino, San Nicolás Obispo, or San Nicolás de los chinos, which pertained to the doctrine of San Miguel Coyuca in the jurisdiction of Acapulco. A petition dated January 7, 1744, indicates that in representation of that neighborhood the *alcalde*, Pedro de Zúñiga, denounced an act of "dispossession and violence" against its lands at the hands of the administration of the hacienda of Nuestra Señora de la Concepción, a neighboring *barrio*:

> that *barrio* originated in ancient times when the Filipinos Indians who came from Manila on the annual Galleon neared their return [date] but left the port to seek refuge there for it was comfortable and not far away. And as many of them stayed on and married Indian women from other localities, it grew until today it is made up of a very large number of families and individuals, and is a formal [neighborhood] with its own chapel and corresponding adornments with houses, yards, gardens and plots of land where

they cultivate rice, corn, and cotton, and gather the fruits of their trees to whose good fortune they are subject.[376]

A description of the port of Acapulco in 1746, found in the *Theatro americano* by José Antonio de Villaseñor and Sánchez, indicates that 400 families of "*chinos*, mulattos and negros" lived there, [but] only eight families of Spaniards due to the hot-humid [climate] throughout the year.[377] In the neighboring town of Coyuca, Villaseñor recorded 120 *chino* families,[378] and noted the presence of, *chinos*, negros, mulattos, and three militia companies, at a time when the security of the coasts was being reinforced due to threats from abroad.[379]

Therefore, while it is true that Asian migration to New Spain declined significantly from the end of the 17th century due to laws that affected the transoceanic mobility of this social sector, what we observe in the first half of the 18th century is the full integration of those Asian *vinateros* who chose to live definitively in the lands of New Spain. Many of them left evidence of their *savoir faire* in extracting *tuba*, which is still consumed today in some localities along the coast, from Colima to Acapulco. Others passed into posterity by signing their names in Baybayin, the ancient Filipino alphabet, which constitutes a true documental rarity. This is the topic of the next chapter.

5. THE VINATEROS WHO SIGNED IN BAYBAYIN

INTRODUCTION

Another feature of some of the *indios chinos vinateros* that drew our attention was that they were able to sign their names, not only in Latin letters, but also in the characters of Baybayin, the ancient form of Filipino writing.[380] This chapter analyzes the trajectory of three Filipinos who signed in that modality. Curiously, their signatures were discovered on some of the few documents that still exist in this type of writing. Even more intriguing is the fact that they are held in the Archivo Histórico del Municipio de Colima, at a distance of over 13,000 kilometers from the Philippines, a clear case of the consequences of the planet's first globalization.[381] Those three Filipinos were not members of a privileged social stratum –far from it– nor travelers who penned remarkable narratives, nor collaborators in the organs of colonial administration who circulated under advantageous conditions. Quite to the contrary: they were most likely peasants hired to produce *vino de cocos* who labored alongside other servants on Spanish haciendas.

In the pages that follow, we will demonstrate how those signatures, affixed by Filipinos in Colima, form part of the historical episode marked by the broad mobilization and circulation of people, objects, and techniques spurred by transpacific commerce and its main protagonist, the Manila Galleon, which left profound tracks on both sides of the Pacific Ocean. We begin with a discussion of Baybayin and its historical context up to the arrival of the Spanish in the Philippines, then go on to examine the trajectories of the *vinateros* who signed in the Filipino alphabet and present some signatures in Latin characters of other *indios chinos*.

THE BAYBAYIN ALPHABET IN THE PHILIPPINES

The ancient Filipino writing system called Baybayin was used by various ethnolinguistic groups on the archipelago. The word Baybayin literally means "to spell"[382]. Upon arriving in the Philippines, the Spanish found vestiges of this writing only on materials used in house construction like bamboo trunks and tree leaves; that is, perishable materials that have made it difficult to conduct any in-depth study of that system before the 16th century.[383] The Jesuit Pedro Chirino, author of the *Relación de las islas Filipinas y de lo que en ellas han trabajado los padres de la Compañia de Jesús* (Rome, 1604), was among the first missionaries to remark on this ancient Filipino alphabet when he mentioned that the Visaya Indians

> wrote on stalks, or on palm leaves using an iron nib as a pen. Today they write not only in their letters, but also in ours, with a well-sharpened feather, on paper, as we do. They have learned our language, and pronunciation: and write it as well as we do, even better, for they are most skillful and learn things with great facility.[384]

A citation quite similar to Chirino's appears in the work of another Jesuit, the *Historia general sacro-profana, política y natural de las islas del Poniente llamadas Filipinas*, by Juan José Delgado, who in 1751 reiterated that "almost everyone in Visayas knows how to write in their characters",[385] and stated that the writing system was used with stalks, banana leaves, and other trees, from top to bottom and left to right, features seen among both Visayas and Tagalogs. Both William H. Scott and Christopher Miller emphasized the ability of the Filipinos to write in different directions, according to the material they used.[386]

But a significant change in Filipino writing occurred as the use of Baybayin was gradually superseded by the Latin alphabet. We know that this process was well underway by the 1660s, for yet another Jesuit, Francisco Colín, observed in his book, *Labor Evangélica*, that some Filipinos were so adept at writing Castilian that "they have earned positions as officials", such as scribes in accounting offices or secretaries in offices of colonial administration.[387] Pedro Chirino stated that Baybayin originated on the Island of Luzon, in the Tagalog region, and spread from there to other areas, including the Visayas. This hypothesis is open to debate, but there is a consensus that Baybayin is a single alphabet that presents diverse variants in its characters that reflect different writing styles and spatial and temporal contexts.[388]

Illustration 10 reproduces some regional variants published by Sinibaldo de Mas y Sanz in his *Informe sobre el Estado de las Islas Filipinas en 1842*. The left column shows how some characters were written in the provinces of Pangasinán, Ilocos, Batangas, Pampanga, Bulacán, and Tondo, with their equivalents in Spanish. The right column displays fragments of writing in Baybayin. A more recent work than Sanz' is by Miller, who recorded the diverse forms of this writing by region and epoch from the 1590s to the 20th century.[389]

VINO DE COCOS, THE PILGRIM BEVERAGE

Illustration 10. Variants of the Baybayin Alphabet According to Sinibaldo de Mas y Sanz (1842)[390]

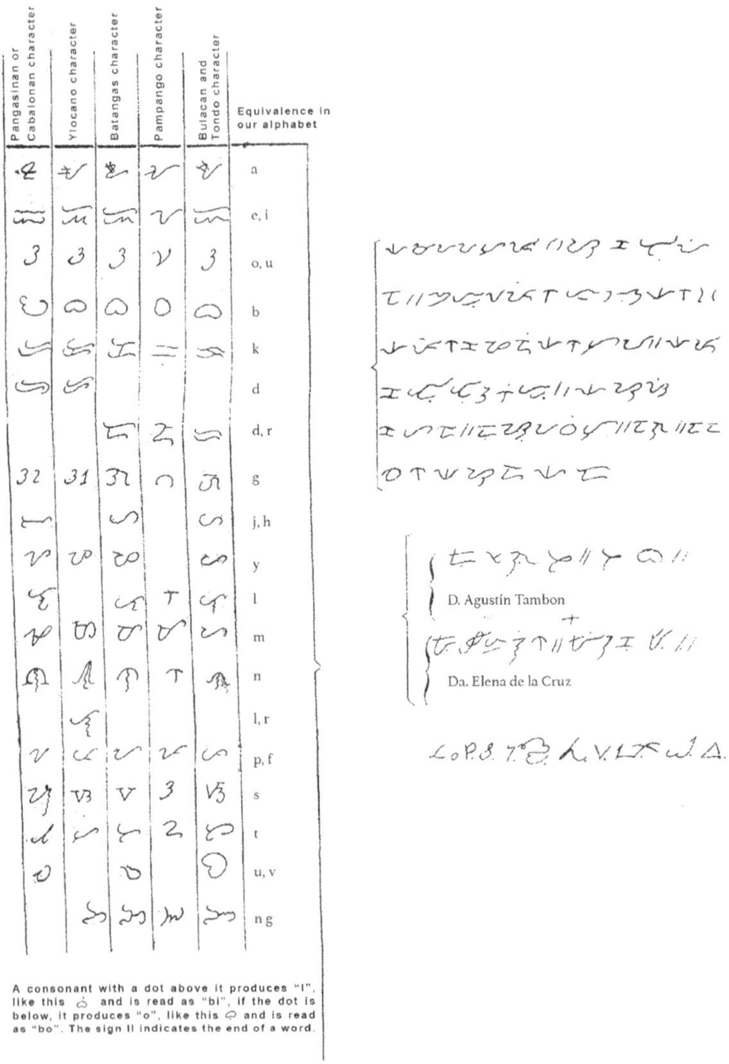

Source: Mas y Sanz, *Informe sobre el estado de las Islas Filipinas*, 1842.

Part II

Baybayin as an instrument of evangelization

One aspect that cannot be passed over is the link between evangelization and literacy. The year 1593 brought the publication of the *Doctrina christiana en lengua española y tagala* in Manila, the first book edited under colonial dominion where we find the Baybayin alphabet reproduced. Prayers like the Apostle´s Creed and *Ave María* were included as instruments of evangelization, following the pattern established in areas of Spanish America where catechisms and vocabularies in indigenous languages were elaborated in Latin characters.[391] In that year as well, a doctrine in Chinese was printed due to the growing numbers of *sangleys* that had settled around Manila.[392] Those works were translations of the doctrine by Cardenal Roberto Belarmino, a text that served as a model for religious instruction not only in the Philippines, but also in China and Japan.[393]

In contrast to the *Doctrina cristiana en letra y lengua china* (1593), written for new converts, other works, like *Shilu* by the Dominican Juan Cobo, were addressed to a non-Christian elite that sought information on this religion from the West.[394] This demonstrates the intense work carried out by missionaries in the Philippines after the arrival of the Spanish to the archipelago, not only with the numerous ethnolinguistic groups on those islands, but also with population sectors in Manila and its surrounding area, such as *sangleys* and Japanese, populations that were also targets of evangelization in their homelands. Apart from the aforementioned *Doctrina christiana en lengua española y tagala* (1593), other religious texts were printed in Baybayin, fomenting the policy that existed, at least during the first decades of colonization on the archipelago, of conserving local syllabaries. In 1621, for example, the *Doctrina cristiana* in the Ilocano language was printed in Manila by Father Francisco López, another book that utilized Baybayin characters.

Map 8. Records of Writing in Baybayin in Diverse Repositories Around the World

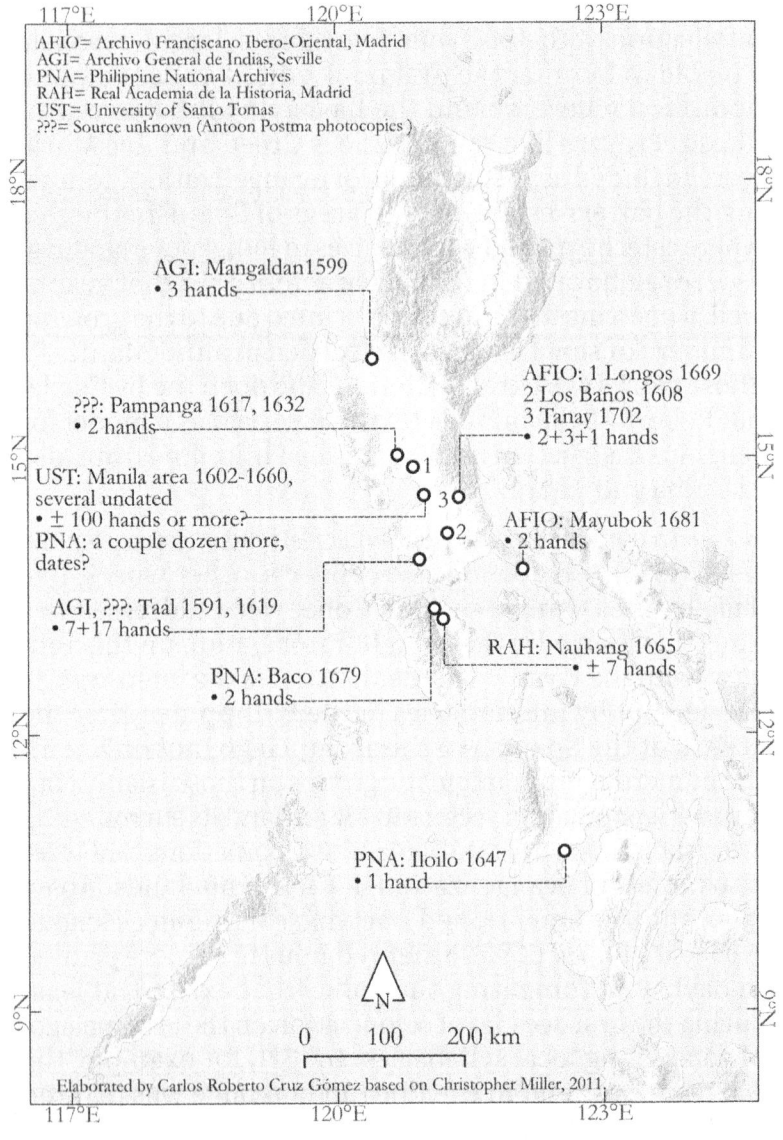

Part II

We know of other documents in Baybayin, varied in nature, held mainly in archives at the University of Santo Tomás in Manila, related to land sales around that capital. They have been analyzed by Ignacio Villamor, Alberto Santamaría, Christopher Miller, and Regalado Trota José, among others.[395] In the Archivo General de Indias (Seville, Spain) one can find signatures in this ancient Filipino alphabet on documents from 1591 and 1599 (Map 8), while a file conserved in the Real Academia de la Historia de Madrid contains the petition that the indigenous principality of Mindoro addressed to the then Archbishop of Manila, Miguel de Poblete, soliciting the presence of Jesuits there. That document is written in the local language, with Latin characters, but with signatures in Baybayin by some members.[396] Other texts with signatures of this kind are in the Archivo Franciscano Ibero-Oriental and the Archivo General de la Nación in Mexico City.[397]

The Baybayin language has 3 vowels (A, E-I, O-U) and 14 consonants (B, D, G, H, K, L, M, N, P, S, T, V, NG). There are no equivalents to J and CH.[398] Because the vowel "a" (ka, ga, ta, etc.) is implicit in all words in Baybayin, a diacritic mark (*kudlit* or *corlit*) is added above or below those syllables to mark the phonetic change to the vowels *e-i* or *o-u*; for example, to indicate *e-i*, a period/comma is written above the characters, while for *o-u* it is written below them.

VINO DE COCOS, THE PILGRIM BEVERAGE

Illustration 11. Baybayin Alphabet According to Pedro Chirino (1604)[399]

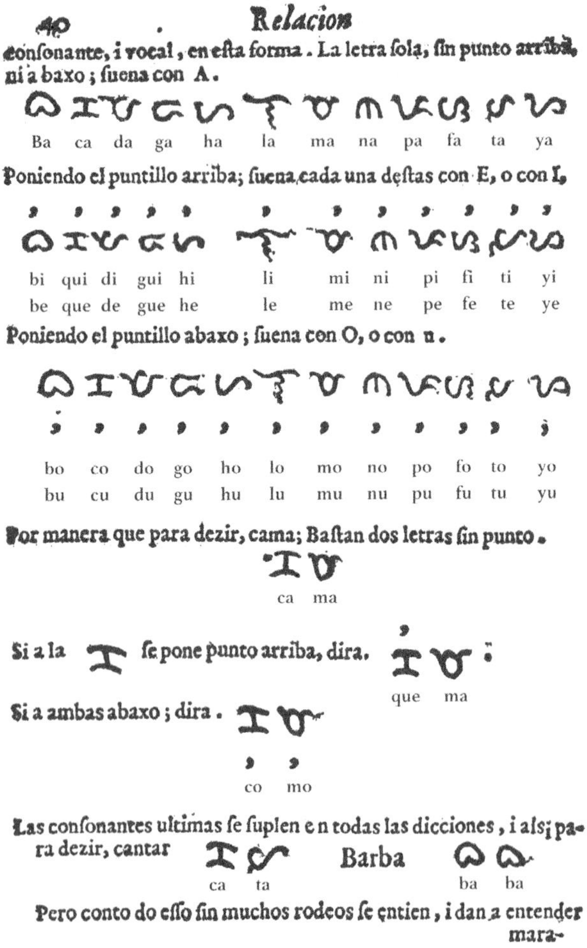

40   Relacion
Consonante, i vocal, en esta forma. La letra sola, sin punto arriba, ni a baxo; suena con A.

    Ba ca da ga ha   la   ma na pa fa ta   ya

Poniendo el puntillo arriba; suena cada una destas con E, o con I.

  bi qui di gui hi   li   mi ni pi fi ti   yi
  be que de gue he   le me ne pe fe te ye

Poniendo el puntillo abaxo; suena con O, o con u.

  bo co do go ho   lo mo no po fo to yo
  bu cu du gu hu   lu mu nu pu fu tu yu

Por manera que para dezir, cama; Bastan dos letras sin punto.

ca ma

Si a la ⊤ se pone punto arriba, dira,
que ma

Si a ambas abaxo; dira.

co mo

Las consonantes ultimas se suplen en todas las dicciones, i así para dezir, cantar   Barba
                  ca ta   ba ba

Pero conto do esso sin muchos rodeos se entien, i dan a entender mara-

Source: Pedro Chirino, *Relación de las islas Filipinas*, p. 40.

Given the context of the intense mobility and circulation of people across the Pacific Ocean, it is hardly surprising to learn that *indios chinos* left traces of their presence in the municipal archive of Colima. In the nearby city of Guadalajara, in the 1630s, an intriguing Japanese man, Luis de Encío, wrote his signature in Japanese characters on several notarial documents. That led Thomas Calvo to follow his tracks until he was able to identify him as an influential figure in Guadalajara society.[400] Later, thanks to the signatures that Calvo located, we learn that Encío had, in fact, attained the status of Samurai.[401] But there were also *indios chinos* from Portuguese India, like a slave from Cochin named Antón who lived in Mexico City and knew how to read and write in his native language, *Malayalam*.[402] Clearly, we are dealing with a cosmopolitan universe that reveals the consequences of the first globalization as people traveled with their cultural baggage, adapting to the structure of the Spanish Monarchy's widespread colonial system at each stop along the way, as in the case of our *vinateros* who signed in Baybayin.

THE VINATERO JUAN AND HIS SIGNATURE "IN CHINESE LANGUAGE" (1600)

The first document with a signature in Filipino characters is dated December 15, 1600. It appears in the records of a judicial process in Colima in which four Filipinos were accused of producing and selling *vino de cocos* to Indians. The authorities denounced that this had resulted in disputes, scandals, and "offenses against God".[403] The four Filipinos were Juan, aged 27; Francisco and Domingo, 30; and Agustín, 40. Only Juan, the youngest, knew how to sign his name, which he wrote in Baybayin characters (Illustration 12). He was likely born in 1573, two years after the founding of Manila by Miguel López de Legazpi. Without doubt, he grew up during the intense stage of the transformation of the socioeconomic life of the Philippine capital and its surrounding populations. Juan might have learned to sign his name in his family circle, as was the practice before the Spanish came. We have found during our research that some Filipinos of his age knew how to sign in Latin characters (as we will see at the end of this chapter) due to the influence of missionaries. This suggests that it is highly likely that Juan learned Baybayin in the family setting, as the ancient custom dictated. His participation in the judicial process, however, indicates that he also knew Spanish and had some familiarity with the workings of colonial administration. Now, if we assume that he began to write around primary school age –5 to 10 years– we corroborate that the Baybayin language was still in use many decades after the conquest of Luzon.

Illustration 12. Signature of Don Juan [de Chávez?]

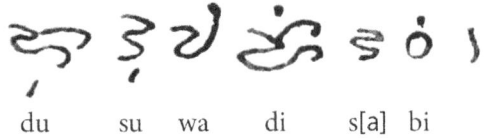

du   su   wa   di   s[a]   bi

Source: AHMC, Fondo Sevilla del Río, caja 5, exp. 4.

The document does not indicate Juan's place of origin, so it is difficult to say if the area where he was raised experienced extensive, or only limited, missionary activity. The Augustinians played a preponderant role in the Philippine archipelago during the first stage of evangelization, as it was the first order to establish a foothold after Legazpi's arrival, followed by the Franciscans (in 1578) and the Dominicans (in 1587). When the Jesuits arrived (in 1581), Juan would have been around 10. Could he have been part of the population nucleus alphabetized by the Company of Jesus? To date, historiography has paid little attention to the processes of alphabetization of local people in the Philippines after the arrival of the Spanish, though

Chirino's work (1604) seems to indicate that the Jesuit model focused special attention on converting children. In fact, the Company of Jesus built schools to initiate young people not only in the rudiments of the Catholic faith, but also in reading, writing, singing, and music. Women and indigenous principals were other groups targeted by the Jesuits' practices,[404] which must have been implemented in a more or less similar fashion by the other religious orders on the archipelago. The Jesuits, for example, founded the Colegio de San Gregorio in 1586 in New Spain to educate the children of indigenous principals.[405]

It is worthwhile to focus for a moment on one particularly revealing feature of Juan's signature: the fact that his name is preceded by the Spanish honorific "*don*", which was applied exclusively to members of the indigenous nobility in the Philippines (Illustration 12). Even the Spanish scribe recognized that detail by referring to him as "*don*" Juan. Though this may have seemed just a simple prefix, in reality it represented a significant identitary element in the structure of colonial administration in both the Philippines and New Spain. Here, it reveals the emergence of certain identitary traits of don Juan as a member of the indigenous Filipino nobility who sailed on the Manila Galleon and, through circumstances unknown, appeared as a modest *vino de cocos* producer in a town in Colima in the year 1600.

But "*don* Juan's" signature in Baybayin includes a second name; perhaps a surname, though it is difficult to determine because the scribe referred to him simply as "*don* Juan".[406] The problem in deciphering the surname lies in the fact that our reading of texts in Baybayin rests upon phonemes similar to, but not exactly the same as, those of Spanish. Moreover, we must consider regional variants: specialists like Jean-Paul G. Potet affirm that while Tagalogs and Pampangos used basically the same Baybayin alphabet, there were exceptions, like the letter "h", which does not exist in the latter.[407]

This difficulty in determining equivalences was likely one of the reasons that led the missionaries to abandon this alphabet and begin writing Philippine languages in Latin characters, just as occurred with the Mesoamerican languages of New Spain. The Franciscans on the Yucatán peninsula, for example, found a type of syllabic-logographic writing among the Maya that used symbols, visual elements –glyphs– through which it would have been difficult to convey the teachings of Christianity, so they opted to teach literacy in Latin characters.[408] As Marina Garone pointed out for the case of New Spain, "the complete conversion of the sounds of indigenous languages to the alphabetic system entailed problems with the phonological interpretation of local languages",[409] adding that the close link between orthography and pronunciation was a particularly important element for the missionaries who paid attention to even the finest details in the books written in diverse indigenous languages; in reality, an approach they inherited from Antonio de Nebrija, who considered letter and sound to be indissociable elements.[410] Missionaries in the Philippines like the Dominican Francisco Blancas de San José, in his *Memorial de la vida cristiana en lengua tagala* (1605), affirmed that Baybayin was impractical for evangelization because it lacked certain syllables equivalent to Spanish.[411]

Is it possible to discern "*don* Juan's" birthplace based on his signature? Potet recognized that while Baybayin has regional variants –for example, Tagalog *vs.* Visaya– both use basically the same alphabet.[412] Thus, it is challenging to try to link Juan's signature to a specific province because it presents similarities that could be attributed to one or more area; for example, the "d" in the word "*don*" is similar to the one registered in Batangas by Sinibaldo de Mas y Sanz, as illustration 10 shows. The function of the bar on the extreme right of the signature was to mark the end of the name, like a period, for as we observe in the writing forms found in Bulacán in 1652 (illustration 10), a double bar served to separate and finalize words. It is curious that in Juan's case we see only one bar, instead of two, which was the usual form.[413] The impossibility of identifying a specific region of origin in the Philippines by means of one signature also reflects the reality that, unlike printed letters, the exact form of handwritten letters varied with each individual's calligraphy.

Don Juan and His Work as a *Vinatero*

The other reality, don Juan's everyday life, reveals the evolution of his judicial process and the logics under which colonial administration functioned in its continuous adaptation to concrete situations and specific cases involving individuals from distinct universes. The narrative begins on December 15, 1600, just before Christmas, when the deputy *alcalde mayor* of Colima, Juan de Monroy, led an inspection in the Caxitlán Valley (see Map 9) because he had heard rumors that *indios chinos* were producing *vino de cocos* there, and Indians in the area were consuming it to get drunk. Those actions set off alarms among Colima's authorities because they had been informed that the distillate was circulating among both free Indians and *indios laboríos* in that valley and nearby towns. Deputy Monroy was sent to investigate a specific case: an episode of drunken carousing on December 11 on the plantation and in the house of don Álvaro García de Grijalva, the *alférez mayor* of the villa of Colima, a prestigious figure well known throughout the province.[414]

Map 9. The Caxitlán Valley (17th Century)

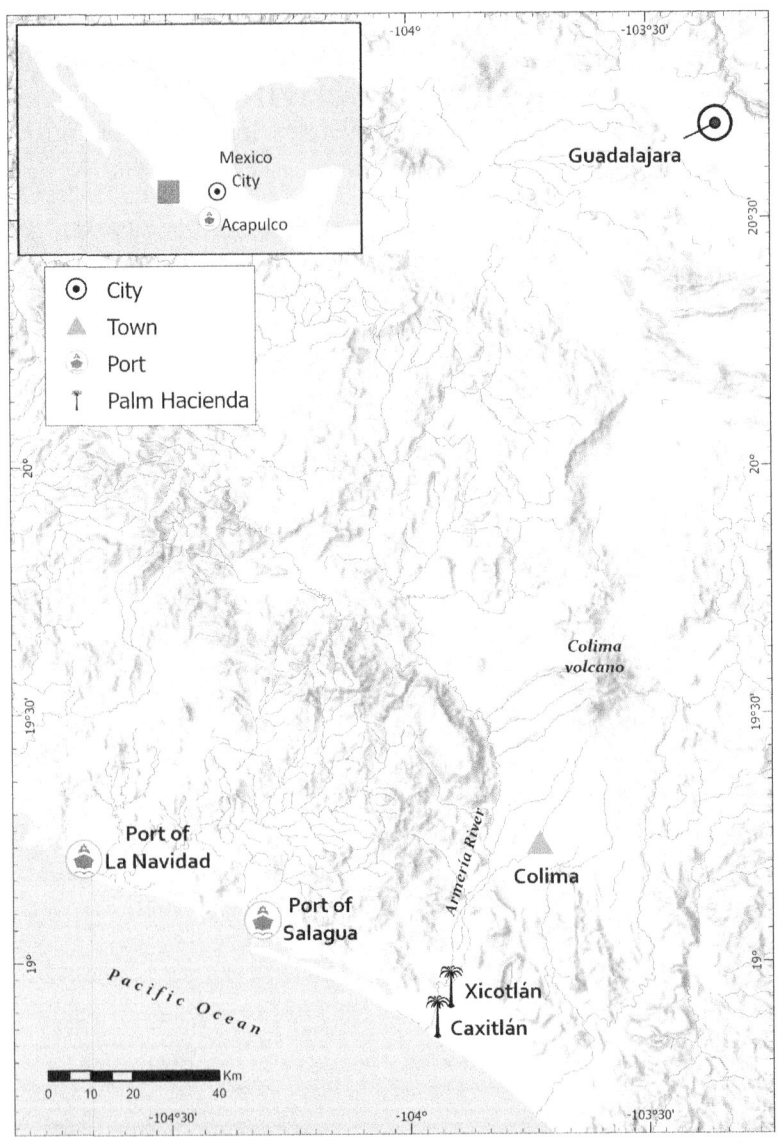

Source: elaborated by Jesús Medina (CEGH-Colmich) with information from the author.

Part II

One finding that stands out is the heterogeneity of the six witnesses who appear in the file: a Spaniard, a Náhuatl-speaking Indian, and four *chinos*, who co-existed on a daily basis on palm haciendas. All their testimonies coincided in that on an occasion when don Álvaro was away, a fiesta had taken place, attended by the hacienda's overseer, an Indian named Simón, servants (men and women) from the house, and Indians from neighboring towns like Xicotlán on the course of the Armería River (see Map 9). The troublemakers had been the four *chinos* –don Juan, Francisco Hernández, Agustín, and Domingo– especially the latter, for he had sent Simón to bring a *tecomate* (gourd) of *vino de cocos* from the nearby plantation of Ana de la Zarza, which everyone had drunk and become quite inebriated. The De la Zarza family had owned cacao plantations in the Caxitlán Valley since at least the late 16th century,[415] and we must recall that properties of that kind were precisely the sites where coconut palms were planted when they arrived from Asia. The fact that Domingo lived in doña Ana's house, while the others resided in places scattered across the valley, suggests that Filipinos tried to get together on their free days, perhaps due to affinity of origin, or to relive the custom of communal drinking that was a norm among diverse groups on the archipelago, as Chirino had noticed.[416]

Note how even the material culture of that time was immersed in the processes of transoceanic exchange, as *tecomates*[417] –gourds or vessels that in earlier times were used to store and serve drinks of the land– were now being filled with a distilled beverage whose production technique came from Asia. From that moment on, we observe that throughout the 17th century *tecomates* were used to serve *vino de cocos*. Like other Nahuatl loanwords, *tecomate* (i.e., gourd or recipient) was in common use in the Philippines: in his *magnum opus* on the Visaya Indians in 1668, the Jesuit Ignacio Alzina mentioned coconut shells "they call *tecumates* [that] serve as cups for drinking chocolate".[418]

Vino de Cocos, the Pilgrim Beverage

Who were the other *chinos* that accompanied don Juan and were also accused of selling *vino de cocos* to Indians? They were mature men for the time, as their ages ranged from 30 to 40 years. To a direct question posed by the deputy, Domingo replied that he was "an *indio chino* from Manila", while Agustín declared that he was from Parañaque (see Map 10), a Tagalog village in southern Manila. Unfortunately, the official did not ask don Juan or Francisco Hernández about their places of origin.

Map 10. The Island of Luzon (The Philippines)

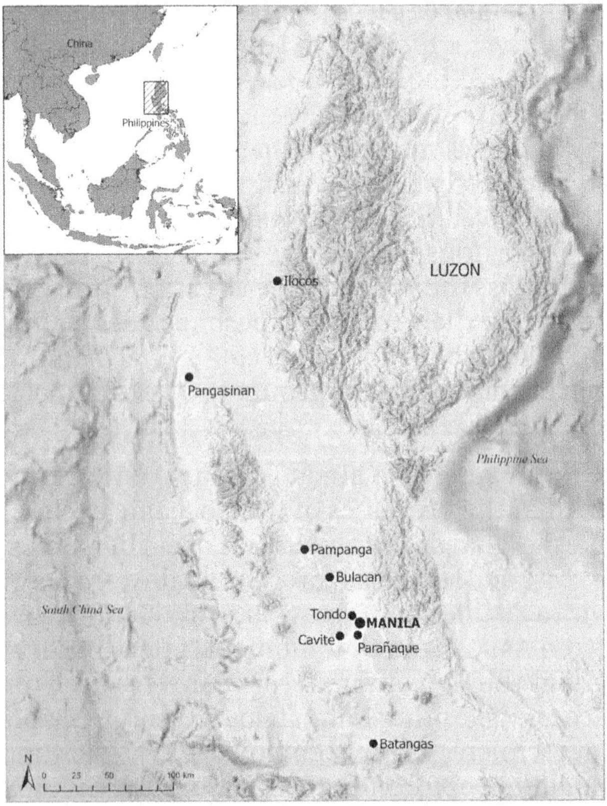

Source: elaborated by Marco Antonio Hernández A. (SIG-Colmich) with information from the author.

Part II

Although the other *chinos* did not know how to sign their names, we have some of their personal data: Agustín, aged 40 from Parañaque, said he was married in the Philippines but had left his wife six years earlier. Parañaque was an Indian town under the dominion of the Augustinians, the first missionary order to arrive in the archipelago, and the one that enjoyed the widest presence in towns near Manila. We do not know if Agustín had lived elsewhere before coming to Colima, but the fact that he was married set him apart from his countrymen, for at the end of the trial, in addition to being fined 15 pesos, he was ordered, in a maximum of 20 days, "to prepare to [return to] married life with his wife" in the Philippines. We cannot forget here that one important measure of Spanish colonial administration consisted in ensuring, whenever possible, that Spaniards were reunited with their families, either by returning them to the Iberian Peninsula, or sending their wives and children to the New World. Here we see this measure –reserved, at least in theory, to Spaniards– applied in the case of an *indio chino*. Had his sentence been carried out, Agustín would have had to go to Mexico City in custody and been held there with other men sentenced to the galleys and exile to the Philippines, awaiting the Manila Galleon to sail to Cavite.[419]

The sentences of the four *chinos*, therefore, culminated with pecuniary sanctions and other penalties because, in the view of the authorities, they had contravened the express ban on selling or distributing *vino de cocos* to Indians (see Table 17). Conjectures on the reasons for the differences in the sanctions imposed emphasize that Domingo, who received the largest fine (18 pesos) had sent the overseer, Simón, for the *vino de cocos* from don Álvaro García's house on that day of drunken revelry. Moreover, the interrogations brought to light a similar event that had occurred a few days earlier, in the house of a Spaniard named Juan Ramírez, when his servants had drunk aguardiente. Their night of debauchery ended with a fight in which Domingo allegedly wounded Juan, one of Ramírez' Indian ranch hands (*indios gañanes*). In his defense, Domingo affirmed that the man who struck Juan was actually a *chino* named Agustín, so Agustín was fined 15 pesos and sentenced to return to the Philippines.

Table 17. Sentences Imposed on the *Chinos Vinateros* (1600)

Name	Age	Sentence
Domingo	30 years	18 pesos and one year of exile from these plantations
Don Juan [de Chávez?]	27 years	15 pesos and one year of exile from an area 5 leagues around the Caxitlán Valley
Agustín	40 years	15 pesos and 20 days to prepare to return to married life with his wife
Francisco Hernández[420]	30 years	6 pesos

Source: AHMC, Fondo Sevilla del Río, caja 5, exp. 4.

Returning to our *chino* don Juan, who also received a fine of 15 pesos, we find that this was not the first brawl in which he had been involved, for on another occasion in the villa of Colima he was accused of injuring the mestizo Diego González in the face with the handle of his knife, and of seizing the sword the latter carried. Juan's defense was that he had acted in self-defense when González threatened to beat him. His status as a member of the Philippine nobility notwithstanding, don Juan behaved exactly like his countrymen, with no distinction. This was not the only case of an *indio chino* in Colima who, despite belonging to a colonial hierarchy distinct from that of the natives, behaved, *de facto*, as just one more of their kind. Thus it was that in 1608 the *chino* Nicolás Rodríguez solicited that the *alcalde mayor* of Colima exempt him from paying tribute and other services, alleging that he was actually an *indio chino* mestizo, son of a Spanish *encomendero* in the Philippines and a Filipino woman; hence, the accoutrements of his preeminence should be recognized.[421]

What do all these disputes reveal? That beyond the concrete case of drunken revelry in the *alférez* home, conflicts often broke out between this Asian sector of the population and other social groups, like Indians and mestizos. Clearly, don Juan had gained fame as a troublemaker, for he was asked directly: "why is it that wherever [you go], people get mixed up in drunkenness and quarrels?" Of these four Asians, the only one who was not mentioned in relation to brawls was Francisco Hernández, who was fined only 6 pesos, the smallest amount, and was not exiled. Hernández claimed that he was ill and thus unable to work and denied any involvement in producing or selling *vino de cocos* to Indians at that time. But he provided one clue by mentioning a third drunken episode, this one in the home of Ana de la Zarza, that also ended with an altercation between servants and the *chinos* that escalated because everyone was inebriated and armed with knives, clubs, or adzes. In the end, we learn that don Juan paid his 15 pesos with a garment that remained in the hands of the *depositario general*, since he did not have enough money to pay the fine.

TWO VINATERO SIGNERS AND AN INTERPRETER "IN CHINESE LANGUAGE" (1604)

The second document provides richer information for our analysis. It refers to a judicial process dated May 14, 1604, that involved fourteen Filipinos who worked producing *vino de cocos*.[422] Pedro Tinbán, Juan de Chávez, and Pedro García (through the latter's intermediation) signed that document in Baybayin, while fellow Filipinos like Agustín Muñoz, Francisco Pordomo, Juan Marcos García, and

Ventura Ortiz signed in Latin characters (see Table 18). This case involved over a dozen *indios chinos* who reflected three distinct realities characteristic of the archipelago at that time: (i) some men could sign in Castilian; (ii) others knew how to sign in the ancient Baybayin alphabet; and (iii) some could not sign their names. Especially noteworthy is the fact that almost half of those men had had some contact with writing, a finding that supports the Jesuit Chirino's narrative of the notable level of literacy in the Philippines.

The testimonies of two of those fourteen *chinos* are of particular interest because Pedro Tinbán and Juan de Chávez signed in Baybayin and the latter affixed a third signature, for he served as interpreter for his countryman, Pedro García. Though the personal data on the men are minimal, at least we learn their ages and the haciendas where they worked, while their testimonies revealed the involvement of civil and religious authorities in the incipient production of *vino de cocos*.

Tinbán, aged 20, worked on the plantation of the *alférez mayor*, García de Grijalva, whom we mentioned in the earlier case of the drunken revelry that occurred in his home in 1600. As with don Juan's signature, in Pedro's case we have a phonetic approximation to his name, with Pedro represented as "pi", "di", and Tinbán as "ti", "ba" (Illustration 13).

Illustration 13. Signature of Pedro Tinban

pi　　　di　　　ti　　　ba

Source: AHMC, Fondo Sevilla del Río, caja 5, exp. 4.

Part II

Juan de Chávez, also 20, produced *vino de cocos* on the hacienda of a clergyman named Alonso Lorenzo. This detail is important because it tells us that some ecclesiastical authorities in Colima were active in aguardiente production. Here, the phonetic approximation to his name was "su", "wa", "sa", "bi" (Illustration 14), likely reflecting the distinct pronunciation of the name "Juan" at that time compared to our modern form, and a phonetic variation that occurred between the 16th century and the first half of the 17th.[423]

Illustration 14. Signature of Juan de Chávez

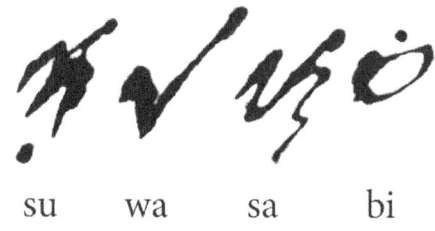

su   wa   sa   bi

Source: AHMC, Fondo Sevilla del Río, caja 5, exp. 4.

One especially important element here is that the testimonies identify him as a ladino *indio chino* who signed his name "in the Chinese language", according to a note written by the scribe, Jerónimo Dávalos Vergara. Dávalos' appreciation here concurs with what were known at that time as "China" and "the Chinese" in the Spanish American world in reference to the Asian continent and as a synonym for it. Dávalos did not say "Filipino language", choosing instead the adjective that his mental universe provided at that moment. Whatever the case, Juan de Chávez and Pedro Tinbán, who also reportedly signed in his "Chinese language", were certainly *indios chinos* and, hence, their writing must be considered as such.

Finally, Pedro García, the eldest of the three at 40, worked as a *vinatero* on Father Lorenzo's hacienda, but his case differed. Since he did not speak Spanish, his paisano, Juan de Chávez, served as his interpreter and signed in his name, which reads "pi", "di", plus the phrase "ba" "la" (we assume this means "in representation of"), followed by de Chávez' signature (Illustration 15). An additional detail regarding the *indio chino* Pedro was his ability to move beyond the confines of the province of Colima, for when asked about illicit *vino de cocos* production he defended himself by stating that he had been absent in Guadalajara, and so could not have been making aguardiente. We conjecture that Pedro had gone to the capital of the Reino de Nueva Galicia on the request of his master, the clergyman Lorenzo, for he was a servant who had earned his trust.

Illustration 15. Signature of Pedro García, Elaborated by Juan de Chávez

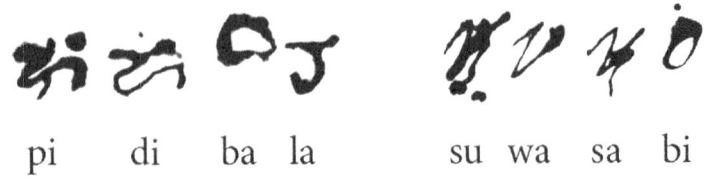

pi   di   ba   la   su   wa   sa   bi

Source: AHMC, Fondo Sevilla del Río, caja 5, exp. 4.

In addition to these *indio chino* signers, four other *chinos* who appeared in the judicial file also affixed their signatures, but in Latin characters: Juan Marcos García (aged 23), Agustín Muñoz (27), Francisco Pordomo (30), and Ventura Ortiz (33). Their signatures are shown in Table 18.

Part II

Thus, of those 14 *indios chinos*, half knew how to sign their names, whether in Filipino or Latin characters, a finding that raises the interesting question of the percentage of Filipinos who knew how to read and write before and after the arrival of the Spanish, and how many of them traveled to New Spain. In other words: is the percentage of Filipinos who signed their names in this sample from Colima representative of what had transpired in the archipelago? Were these itinerant Filipinos from more educated backgrounds than their countrymen? These are difficult questions to answer, but we do know that all our *indios chinos* were born after the Spanish arrived on the archipelago. Agustín, the eldest, would have been born in 1564, precisely the year in which the expedition led by Miguel López de Legazpi and Andrés de Urdaneta sailed to the Philippines from Puerto de La Navidad, reaching the island of Cebu in 1565. The fact that Manila was founded in 1571 means that all *vinateros* aged 33 or younger were born during the conquest period.

According to Chirino, it was common for men and women in the archipelago to know how to read and write before the arrival of the Spanish: "so gifted are all these islanders in reading and writing that there are no cases of men, much less of women, who do not read and write in the letters of the Island of Manila".[424] Note that he emphasized literacy among women, a tendency markedly distinct from the cases of the vast majority of women in the western world at that time, including the indigenous domains of New Spain.[425] William H. Scott, however, is more conservative than Chirino, for based on several files that he analyzed for the 1590-1620 period, he stated that not all members of the indigenous nobility knew how to sign their names.[426]

Beyond Chirino's affirmations in this regard, offering the reader a percentage of the Asians who could read and write in 17th-century Philippines is challenging, especially since the information available is so fragmentary. However, upon considering all the Asians in the files we have analyzed in this chapter (1600-1604) we have the following preliminary statistics: of 18 *indios chinos* who were asked to sign,[427] 39% (7 of 18) knew how to do so, without doubt a significant figure. Now, of those 7, almost half affixed their names in Filipino characters, while the other half used Latin. Furthermore, only one required an interpreter, so the rest were all "ladinos". Of course, knowing how to sign one's name does not necessarily mean that one can read and write, but affixing one's signature and signing documents reflects at least some knowledge of writing.

OTHER VINATEROS WHO SIGNED THEIR NAMES

It is now time to discuss the *vinateros* who signed in Latin, where two signatures stand out: those of the *vinatero* Francisco Pordomo in 1604, and Domingo de la Cruz, a slave in Guadalajara in 1678 (see Table 18). These signatures were more elaborate, elegant. Pordomo drew our attention due to the context, as he was a *vinatero* recently arrived from the Philippines where the evangelization process was still in its early stages. This suggests that he may have had the opportunity to receive instruction during the evangelization of the archipelago. Domingo de la Cruz' case is surprising, for he was a slave who belonged to Juan Sánchez Bañales (a resident of Guadalajara) who had been taken from his birthplace of Cebu to Manila at the age of six and later sold in New Spain to the captain of a ship that landed in Salagua. Though a slave, he somehow came to have knowledge of writing. Domingo was not a *vinatero* but his file seemed pertinent to our analysis. Regarding Juan de la Cruz, we know that he was a native of Manila who worked as a *vinatero* on the palm hacienda of the scribe Clemente Hidalgo de Agüero, in Zinacamitlán. He was 25 in 1654 when he signed as a witness to the death of another *indio chino*, Lorenzo de Aguilar.

Part II

Table 18. Signatures of Indios Chinos in Colima (17th Century)

Name	Signature	Source
Agustín Muñoz (1604)		AHMC, B-49, exp. 7, pos. 8
Francisco Pordomo (1604)		AHMC, B-49, exp. 7, pos. 8
Juan Marcos García (1604)		AHMC, B-49, exp. 7, pos. 8
Ventura Ortiz (1604)		AHMC, B-49, exp. 7, pos. 8
Andrés Rosales		AHMC, B-8, exp. 27
Sebastián Tumbaga		AHMC, caja B-15, exp. 15
Nicolás Mananquel		AHMC, caja B-23, exp. 1
Juan de la Cruz		AHMC, B-29, exp. 20
Juan Martín		AHMC, B-12, exp. 15
Domingo de la Cruz		ARAG, Ramo civil, caja 9, legajo 9, exp. 124
Juan de la Cruz (1717)		AHEC, caja 18, carpeta 12

The Filipinos who could sign their names, like Andrés Rosales in 1619, Sebastián Tumbaga in 1638, and Nicolás Mananquel in 1643, interested us as *indios chinos vinateros* who appeared not only in diverse judicial documents, but also in the records of elections of *alcaldes de chinos* in the mid-17th century, as we analyzed in the previous chapter. This combination of the ability to sign their names and the possibility of obtaining positions of representation in the colonial system cannot be fortuitous but, surely, is indicative of a certain status that those individuals had attained in the world of the palm haciendas.

Final Reflections

Far from the port of Acapulco and the activities of the Manila Galleon, in the province of Colima in New Spain we find a number of Filipino immigrants whose lives took diverse paths once they crossed the immensity of the Pacific Ocean during the world's first globalization. Those men moved among tropical landscapes of coconut palms, similar to those of the Filipino archipelago, but now heard voices speaking not only in Tagalog and Castilian, but also Náhuatl. They learned how to insert themselves into that receiving society by taking advantage of their knowledge of the traditional uses and handling of the coconut tree, especially for producing aguardiente.

Beyond our analysis of the lives of those pilgrims, an approach through global microhistory allowed us to explain other processes at the macro level that were developing, at the same time, on both sides of the Pacific, as the Spanish Monarchy experimented with, and extended, its models of alphabetization across varied native populations. The files examined reveal the type of globalized society that was emerging in that period, even in a marginal place like the Caxitlán Valley in the province of Colima: the use of distinct languages, authorities who recorded the use of a "Chinese language" that was actually Filipino, and the presence of interpreters for Náhuatl and Tagalog speakers in a document written in Spanish. All these manifestations occurred in the setting of a multiethnic society ensconced in the process of adapting to new times, where conflicts among Asians, Indians, and the mestizo sector became increasingly common. But this social complexity was found, as well, in the Philippines, where natives coexisted with other Asian groups. On this point, files conserved at the University of Santo Tomás in Manila eliminate any possibility of deception: cultural plurality is evident in documents that contain elements of Baybayin, the Roman alphabet and, as if that were not enough, characters in Chinese.[428]

In closing, we must recognize the importance of judicial archives as repositories of the memory of ordinary people, for we cannot forget that we owe the traces of Baybayin as an itinerant form of writing to the involvement of our *indios chinos* in legal processes that formed the backdrop to our detection of a lucrative trade that the Spanish learned to exploit, with *vino de cocos* and an ancient technique recently arrived from the other side of the Pacific Ocean as protagonists. Despite their modest lives, far from the spotlight, those Filipinos were able to adapt in a foreign society by putting their traditional knowledge into practice, and to affix their signatures to documents that, four centuries later, constitute remarkable traces of that first globalization.

6. INDIAN VINATEROS AND OTHER CASTES

> There is not a single nation in the discovered world that has not used some drink, fermented or distilled, to become inebriated.[429]
>
> —Conde de Tepa, 1781

INTRODUCTION

The introduction of the technique of distillation into New Spain in the 16th century brought significant cultural changes in the consumption habits of alcoholic drinks in Indian communities. The greatest transformation consisted in passing from fermented drinks with no more than 12% of alcohol by volume to beverages that, through the chemical process of distillation, could reach 50%. While it has been speculated in recent years that distillation was known in Mesoamerica –a topic discussed in the Epilogue to this book– what is certain is that there are no conclusive references in the early colonial sources that could allow this hypothesis to be corroborated. Even in the hypothetical case that distillation was practiced at some moment of pre-Hispanic history, it did not survive the passage of time, for at the time of the Spanish arrival only fermented drinks made from a variety of plants were consumed.

VINO DE COCOS, THE PILGRIM BEVERAGE

The question we seek to answer in this chapter is how the introduction of *vino de cocos* affected Indian towns, especially those located near palm haciendas. An initial observation is that a dual transition process emerged: from the ingestion of fermented drinks to distilled beverages, at the same time as the Indian population passed from being consumers to producers of *vino de cocos*, which entailed acquiring knowledge that, up to the 1630s, had remained, almost exclusively, in the hands of *indios chinos*.

The most abundant documentation for the development of this chapter comes from the archives in Colima, for references to the Zacatula-Acapulco nucleus are very scarce. The text is organized in three sections: in the first, we analyze the different types of fermented drinks that were elaborated along the coastal strip of the Mar del Sur where, by the late 16th century, the list of liquors that Indians consumed had grown as a result of the introduction of plants from Europe and Asia. In the second part, we examine *vino de cocos* consumption among Indians from the early 17th century onward, and the judicial repercussions of drunkenness in that sector. Third, we address the process through which Indians emerged as *vinateros* through their active participation on the palm haciendas.

THE MAR DEL SUR AND ITS ANCIENT ALCOHOLIC BEVERAGES

Ancient Mesoamerican societies had a long tradition of fermented drinks made from the natural resources available in each region. In his book, *Alcohol in Ancient Mexico*, a pioneering study in characterizing alcoholic drinks in pre-Hispanic Mexico, Henry J. Bruman examined the seven most representative drinks by area of specialization: *sahuaro, pitahaya, tesgüino, tuna-mezquite, pulque, mezcal-jocote,* and *balché*.[430] Regarding the zone that interests us, the coastal Pacific strip of New Spain, we learn that it was an area of *mezcal-jocote* production where Bruman ascertained that the predominant fermented drinks were made from maguey and plums (*Spondias* spp.). It is important to clarify that this did not refer to the distilled drink known today as "mezcal" but, rather, to the agave plant that in some places is called "mezcal" and is used to produce juice by cooking the heads of plants. Evidence from other provinces shows the presence of pulque and corn "wine", which coincides with information not only from early colonial sources but also from recent archeological studies. In Colima, for example, pre-Hispanic oven structures made of stone have been found in the form of shallow, circular excavations that have been interpreted as sites for cooking agave to produce liquor, a view supported by the presence of ceramic vessels with representations of agave plants.[431] Moreover, scientific analyses of pots called *tejuineras* excavated in residential areas of the Los Guachimontones archaeological zone in the Teuchitlán Valley (Jalisco) demonstrated the production of *tesgüino*, a corn-based drink mixed with other ingredients, in the Post-classic period (900 A.D.-1521 A.D.).[432]

The preparation of fermented drinks of Mesoamerican origin did not disappear with the arrival of the Spanish; in fact, it was enriched by the introduction of other plants, such as sugarcane. In 1612, the *ayuntamiento* of Colima reported that Indians there imbibed drinks fermented from maguey, plums, and corn, as well as sugarcane: "even before there was [*vino de cocos*], and after, those Indians made, and still make, wine for their boozing, from cane and maguey, plums and corn, and other [plants] they have in their homes and on their lands, that they make in great quantities at little cost".[433] Don Hernando de Alarcón Betancour, a sergeant-major on the town council of Colima, stated that the Indians elaborated drinks according to the season of the year: "In their towns and homes, those Indians have [plants] and make [drinks] according to their harvests of corn, plums, and cane… so for their fiestas and drinking they need look no further than to the products of their harvests...".[434]

The banana, a fruit introduced into New Spain in the early 16th century, was also used to prepare an alcoholic drink in Colima.[435] This is a significant finding when we consider that this fruit appeared in New Spain in the first half of the 16th century and very quickly was incorporated into indigenous diets.[436] We know that banana liquor was produced in 1716 in San Cristóbal Lachirioag, a town in the jurisdiction of Villa Alta, Oaxaca, where it was called *tepache de plátano* and was brewed together with *tepache de caña*.[437]

In the 1580s, when most of the *relaciones geográficas* were elaborated, there were reports of the presence of drinks made from corn and maguey in some provinces of Nueva Galicia and Michoacán. In the former territory "maguey wine", a drink made by cooking the heads of agave plants (*piñas*), was available in at least three places, Zapotitlán, Tuxcacuesco, and Ameca. According to the report, maguey plants were "exploited extensively" in the latter town. Referring to the effects of the liquor produced, the *alcalde mayor*, don Antonio de Leyva, wrote: "in general, all [Indians] are drunkards, waiting until they're drunk to avenge offenses, and reveling as they boast of their drunken misadventures".[438]

A broad review of the *relaciones geográficas* from the Bishopric of Michoacán around that decade reveals that other recently-introduced plants, like figs, were also used to produce liquor. Around that time, people in the town of Chilchota, "make wine from figs and cherries, and get drunk with it".[439] The *Relación de Querétaro* (an area that today lies outside the study zone but at that time was within the boundaries of that Bishopric) reported that "since figs cannot be carried comfortably, the Indians [leave them to dry] and, in time, they sell very well, and they make wine from them, with which they get drunk".[440] Clearly, the venerable Mesoamerican tradition of fermented drinks was soon complemented by new raw materials brought from the other side of the Atlantic.

Thus, corn, agave, and plums were accompanied by an ample list of introduced plants that came to be used as raw materials for elaborating new liquors for Indian communities, as was the case of the coconut palm. But the novelty did not end there, for by that time the technique of distillation had arrived via routes from Asia and Europe and been incorporated into this series of transformations, allowing a significant increase in the alcohol content of drinks and, hence, high levels of exaltation among consumers. The Colima-Motines nucleus and, though to a lesser extent, that of Zacatula-Acapulco, were the two main receiving areas of the tree (coconut palm), the technique (distillation), and the human ingenuity required (first the *indios chinos*, later, Indians).

In the ancient Bishopric of Michoacán, the *Relación de Sirándaro*, a place in the Hot Lands of the modern state of Guerrero, reported consumption of plum liquor: "they have many kinds of plums... that grow year-round, with which they make the wine they drink".[441] In 1579, the *corregidor* of Chilchota (Michoacán), don Pedro de Villela, affirmed that inhabitants there:

> drink corn and maguey wine, get drunk, and consider it honorable to [do so], not as something dishonorable. And in ancient times, children did not drink wine, and were not allowed to, [but now] Indians not yet four years old go around imbibing maguey wine into their bodies.[442]

This declaration by *corregidor* Villela leads us to reflect on another topic: the patterns of inebriety in Indian communities in the period after Spanish colonization. William B. Taylor has suggested that drunkenness in Indian towns in central Mexico became generalized after the Conquest, in contrast to earlier times when only a select sector of the population was allowed to consume alcohol.[443]

Thus, the arrival of *vino de cocos* coincided with a period marked by a loosening of the norms that governed the ingestion of alcoholic drinks in Indian towns. While at first, as Taylor suggests, consumption was restricted to people of high social rank with only sporadic "licenses" for the rest of the population to drink alcoholic beverages on festive occasions, by the second half of the 16th century the evident drunkenness among Indians had alarmed the colonial authorities. In fact, we can observe the impact of *vino de cocos* among Indians through a series of accusations and judicial processes.

THE ARRIVAL OF VINO DE COCOS IN INDIAN TOWNS

The process of the circulation of *vino de cocos* through Indian towns began immediately. The *indios chinos* had barely begun to distill the drink when Indians became aware of it and started to consume it. Soon, recurrent accusations by *alcaldes* and *alguaciles* surfaced, alleging drunkenness, crimes, and "offenses against God". Authorities kept a close eye on the sale of aguardiente to Indians, which from the early 17th century on was subject to sanctions. But *indios chinos*, Spanish merchants, and traders of all kinds took advantage of any opportunity to introduce *vino de cocos* into Indian towns (*repúblicas de indios*), selling it at varying prices or offering it in trade for corn and other supplies.

The first group that caught the authorities' attention were the *indios chinos*, a sector that quickly acquired ill repute. In the previous chapter, we cited the episode of drunkenness in December 1600 in the home and hacienda of *alférez* Álvaro García de Grijalva in the Caxitlán Valley. Here, we examine the background to that accusation. On that occasion, the deputy of the *alcalde mayor*, Juan de Monroy, learned that "the *indios chinos* who produce *vino de cocos* get the Indians in nearby towns and the *indios laboríos* drunk [...] causing great harm to residents".[444] In his testimony, Juan Ruiz de Rivera, a 50-year-old resident of the villa of Colima who often stayed in Caxitlán, blamed this on the Filipinos, alleging that:

> What we know is that very often [and] in many places one hears that those *chinos* have made many Indians drunk and make a custom of this, and that this has caused many injuries and brawls among drunken Indians [some] beat their women... this witness has treated many injured Indian men and women and [sees] that great harm and damage is done to residents of this Caxitlán Valley, constituting a terrible disservice.[445]

It appears that Ruiz de Rivera was the town doctor, and from that position denounced the *indios chinos* while describing the consequences for domestic violence that he attributed to drunkenness. For this reason, one of Francisco Escudero de Figueroa's first actions upon arriving in Colima as *alcalde mayor* was to prohibit the sale of *vino de cocos* to Indians. In fact, in a decree (*bando*) posted simultaneously in the town square of the villa and in the town of Ixtlahuacán (the administrative center [*cabecera*] of several localities with palm haciendas) ordered that "no Spaniard or *chino* or person of any other caste shall take from the haciendas and sites where said *vino de cocos* is made any amount to any Indian town in said province".[446] Disobeying this order brought a punishment of ten pesos for first-time Spanish offenders, ten pesos for a second transgression, and double that penalty plus a year of exile for a third incident. For *chinos*, Indians, mestizos, mulattos, and negros, the penalty was 100 lashes and a year of exile from the province. For all cases, the order stipulated that the *vino de cocos* was to be confiscated.[447] The fact that *alcalde* Escudero de Figueroa mentioned Spaniards and *chinos* first clearly foresees what we see in later documents: that control of the market lay in the hands of *indios chinos* and Spaniards.

It is highly significant that in the same year in which the *alcalde mayor* of Colima issued his decree, exactly the opposite occurred in the neighboring *alcaldía mayor* of Motines, as Indians there accused the *alcalde mayor* himself, Juan Velázquez de la Cueva, of selling palm aguardiente in their towns:

> Said Alcalde Mayor [Juan Velázquez de la Cueva] has had and keeps in his home, a tavern that sells *vino de cocos* openly to Indians, made [there] by two *indios chinos*, and sends it to be distributed in those towns at three pesos per *botija*, causing great offenses against God due to the drunkenness it provokes; and said Alcalde Mayor's wife receives the money from the wine sold, traded for profit, *because that wine has never been made in their towns*, but has caused terrible drunkenness, melees, and brawls among the Indians.[448]

This accusation resulted from a series of aggressions that the *alcalde* had committed against Indians in the Alima Valley in the jurisdiction of Motines, located a few leagues from the province of Colima on the coast of the Mar del Sur. Though references to the consumption of *vino de cocos* in this zone are scarce, it is clear that those two *chinos* found in the *alcalde* a staunch ally for commercializing "that wine". In this extract, we underscored the testimony of the Indians, which suggests that *vino de cocos* was a new drink: "*because that wine has never been made in their towns*". In organoleptic terms, imbibing a distilled drink compared to a fermented one would have been very attractive to consumers, as occurred in other moments with mezcal and sugarcane aguardiente (the aforementioned *chinguiritos*). In social terms, drinking aguardiente in excess excited people's spirits and could alter the mood of those who consumed it. This soon drew the attention of colonial authorities at various levels, who considered drunkenness among the Indians "the cause of all vices".[449] In this case, Indians in Alima voiced their opposition not only to the sale of *vino de cocos* but, especially, to the fact that it was knowingly being conducted, despite the announced prohibition, by an authority, the *alcalde mayor*, entrusted with protecting, not profiting from, Indian towns. Clearly, they wished to expose the greediness of Velázquez de la Cueva and his wife.

The Voracity of Spanish Merchants

By 1605, when sufficient time had transpired for people to learn about *vino de cocos* and appreciate its qualities as an alcoholic beverage, we find Spanish merchants commercializing it in Indian towns across the province of Colima. In the town of Coquimatlán in that year, for example, *vino de cocos* was sold to the Indians "measured by *calabacillo*". That incident was reported by Deputy Gaspar de Barahona, who took a *botija perulera* from the town to Captain Juan de Rivera, the *alcalde mayor* of Colima, as incontrovertible evidence of illegal sales of the drink.[450] Some merchants peddled *vino de cocos* door-to-door, offering it at a price of one *real* per *calabacillo* (small gourd), normally selling it with other wares, like cuts of meat.[451] It was quite common for merchants to sell products without the required license for, although it is true that colonial legislation regulated sales of articles in Indian towns, those measures generally met with little success.

To give one example, Spaniards like the merchant Martín Parrales carted their wares through several Indian towns in Colima, though they had no license to do so. Thus it was that in 1612 Rodrigo de Escobar, the *alguacil* of the judge-in-residence's commission, accused Parrales of selling *vino de cocos* to the Indians of the town of San José, "with false measures and no seal, trademark, or legal license".[452]

The circulation of illegal merchandise in Indian towns must have been a constant phenomenon, one that gave rise to the accusations of this activity that abound in the judicial archives of the time. Merchants like Martín Parrales simply went about their business in their own way, apparently quite willing to pay fines of a few pesos when some authority discovered them during their escapades. Perhaps for this reason Parrales was accused once again, this time in 1614, for illegally selling clothes to Indians, negros, and mulattos in the Caxitlán Valley, going from door-to-door to offer his wares.[453]

Another Spaniard who benefitted from the illegal trade of selling *vino de cocos* to Indians was Diego Rodríguez. His case reveals that, despite the passing of time, the same charges continued to be levelled for the same reasons. Unlike Parrales, Rodríguez had settled in the Indian town of Ixtlahuacán, living there since at least 1626. His business consisted in going from one Indian household to another offering a *tecomatillo* (small gourd) of *vino de cocos* at a cost of one *tomín*; taking advantage of those opportunities he also sold cuts of meat for another *tomín*. In 1628, however, news of his dealings reached the ears of the *alcalde mayor* of Colima, Juan de Silva y Mendoza. Among other Indians in Ixtlahuacán, he interrogated *the regidor*, Pero Martín. All those men coincided in confirming Rodríguez' illicit activities not only in that town, but also in nearby Indian communities like Ecautlán and Malacatlán.[454]

Control of the circulation of *vino de cocos* in Indian towns far from the villa of Colima and in localities that bordered on neighboring jurisdictions was virtually non-existent. Evidence seems to indicate that consumption of *vino de cocos* in Indian towns was a fact of life, as Indian governors and *alcaldes* negotiated with Spaniards and *indios chinos* to introduce the drink into their towns. As a result, the palm haciendas located near the boundary with the *alcaldía mayor* of Motines were of great concern to the *alcaldes mayores* of Colima, as were those established in towns like Ixtlahuacán, Malacatlán, Ecautlán, and Tamala in the district of San Salvador Chiamila.

PART II

Complicity of the *Alcaldes de Indios*

Much of the *vino de cocos* that circulated freely among the Indians did so thanks to the complicity of the *alcaldes* and *mandones* (leaders) of Indian towns who often operated as contacts between western society and the pre-Hispanic world. It is hardly surprising to learn that over the course of the 17th century complicity developed between Spanish merchants and Indian *alcaldes*, who were also often accused of drunkenness. The town of Zinacamitlán, in the jurisdiction of Motines, was the site of an inquiry in 1627 because the *alcalde*, Juan García, "even though he was serving as the *alcalde*", sold *vino de cocos* in a tavern in his home. According to witnesses' statements, drunken Indians paraded by his house causing public disorder. News of this reached the ears of Agustín de Alcalá, the deputy of the *alcalde mayor*. The disrepute into which *alcalde* García had fallen –vilified as "arrogant, shameless, and disobedient"– led him to be jailed in Maquilí (in the same jurisdiction) during a judicial process that lasted a few weeks. He denied all charges and was set free, but with the warning that if he were discovered selling *vino de cocos* again he would lose his trade.[455]

Accusations of drunkenness among Indians after consuming *vino de cocos* can also be traced to towns in the *guardianía* (religious jurisdiction) of San Francisco de Almoloyan, specifically in two towns: Coquimatlán and Quizalapa. In 1632, the *alcalde mayor* of Colima, Captain Juan González de Castro, reprimanded the *alcalde* of Coquimatlán for allowing consumption of *vino de cocos* in his community. The *alcalde* there, Juan Cruz, responded that there was no way he could apprehend traders from outside the town because most were mulatto "rascals" who did not respect his authority.[456] Some traders went door-to-door on horseback selling *vino de cocos* or bartering it for corn, especially at harvesttime.[457] Spanish, mestizo, and mulatto merchants well aware of the periods of abundance in Indian towns would barter their drink, then turn around and sell the grain they had received.

A scene that occurred near Coquimatlán, in the town of Quizalapa, allows us to perceive more clearly the complicity of the *alcaldes de indios* and Spanish traders in commerce involving *vino de cocos*. In mid-August 1643, Gregorio Fernández de Tene (a resident of the villa of Colima) appeared before the town's *alcalde*, Juan Martín, to request his help in having some Indians "raft" a few barrels of aguardiente to the far shore of the Río Grande, "which was rather swollen". It is not surprising that Fernández de Tene's first act upon realizing that he needed help was to approach the local *alcalde*, for it was well known that, as representatives of their community, they had not only the faculty to negotiate, but also the right to mobilize people in their towns. Bartolomé Francisco, another local Indian, affirmed that five raftsmen helped Gregorio Fernández de Tene transport his wine across the river, and that he paid the *alcalde* 4 *reales* for 7 loads. It is highly likely that those loads of wine were from the Tecuciapa Valley and were destined for the villa of Colima, passing through Coquimatlán.[458] But that event culminated with the mysterious death of one of the raftsmen, Martín Sebastián, who after finishing the job accompanied Fernández de Tene and his servants to Coquimatlán where "they drank and became inebriated". The next day, Sebastián's body was found in the river with numerous wounds to his head and chest, "apparently made by a knife", according to the dead man's widow, María Salomé.[459]

Some documents in the Archivo Histórico Municipal de Pátzcuaro indicate a similar panorama there, as we can see in the trial of an Indian named Pedro Pagua, from Nahuatzen, accused of selling *vino de cocos*.[460] In 1650, the *alcalde mayor* of Pátzcuaro issued a warning to all Indians, negros, and mulattos to not consume palm aguardiente, and ordered storekeepers to abstain from offering the drink to those groups.[461] Moreover, although consuming alcoholic drinks during religious celebrations was a common practice, in 1659 Pedro Priami, the *alcalde ordinario* of Pátzcuaro, imposed a one-week ban on the sale of *vino de cocos* from Palm Saturday to the last day of Easter Week.[462]

The Sale of Vino de Cocos in the Villa of Colima

Obtaining *vino de cocos* was easy for Indians living in the villa of Colima. In stores around the town square and the homes of some Spaniards, like the aforementioned merchant Juan Martín Parrales in 1605, a *cuartillo* of *vino de cocos* could be bought for one *real*.[463] Those traders had to be wary of the authorities because selling alcoholic drinks to Indians was always prohibited. In the case of Parrales, we find that he had two helpers in his home –one a young Spaniard, the other a mulatto– who served aguardiente and, despite the existing ban, sold *vino de cocos* clandestinely "from his own hands and those of his servants". He had a small coconut shell (*jícara*) reserved for his clients that he used to measure an amount that sold for one *real*. When news of this reached the *alguacil* of the villa, one of the authorities charged with keeping order and enforcing local ordinances, he took statements from witnesses that led him to infer that Parrales was abusing the Indians by serving them smaller portions of liquor than to the rest of the population. His measuring instruments –a *tecomatillo* and a coconut shell– also lacked the required official seal.[464]

Aside from homes, stores in the villa of Colima also sold *vino de cocos* to Indians illegally. Upon encountering two drunken Indians one day in July 1632 (Martín Sebastián and Pedro Elías from the towns of Comala and Coquimatlán, respectively) the *alguacil*, Pedro Moreno, had them jailed. When brought before the local judge, Baltasar Castelán, they confessed that "a young man" in the store of the merchant Bartolomé Bravo had sold them two *reales* of *vino de cocos*, with which they had become drunk and caused the scandal that ad led to their arrest.[465] It is likely that Sebastián and Elías were just passing through the villa since they are not identified as servants of a Spanish resident or as *indios naboríos*.

But Indians and other castes did not always have to buy *vino de cocos*, for on some occasions they received it as payment in kind for their work. This was demonstrated in 1664 in the sugar mill of one Juan de la Cruz, situated "two arquebus shots" from the villa of Colima. De la Cruz, who was not identified by caste, had set up the mill on his sugarcane fields near the hacienda of Pedro de Vitoria. A resident of Colima, de Vitoria complained that de la Cruz stole irrigation water from his plantations and waylaid his laborers "whether working or idle" "and paid their work with wine and *tuba*, which causes them to run off".[466]

TO "CLIMB LIKE A CHINO": A NEW TRADE

Up to this point, we have presented cases that show the Indians only as consumers of *vino de cocos*, since the production of aguardiente was in the hands of the Filipinos or *indios chinos* who possessed the required knowhow or *savoir faire*. Commercialization, as we have seen, was carried out mostly by Spaniards. By the mid-17th century, however, sufficient time had passed for the technique of distilling *tuba* to be transmitted to Indians and other castes as this *savoir faire* from the Asian world spread through simple observation on palm haciendas, where intense interaction took place among Filipinos, Indians, mestizos, and mulattos.

With the boom in *vino de cocos* consumption, the efforts of the *indios chinos vinateros* proved insufficient to satisfy demand for the drink, obliging hacendados to either search for specialized workers or train their own. The indigenous sector had the greatest potential for performing the tasks involved because some Indians were already working on nearby palm haciendas or on the numerous palm tree plantations that had been established on the outskirts of Indian towns. A document from 1638 is illuminating in this regard because it mentions that Juanillo, an Indian *vinatero* and native of the town of Zinacamitlán (jurisdiction of Motines), "*climbs palms like a chino*" on the plantation of doña Catalina de Alarcón, wife of Captain Antonio Carrillo de Guzmán.[467] "Climbing like chinos", then, was no longer a trade practiced exclusively by Filipinos, but one that had passed into the indigenous world.

It is important to recall that the coconut palm was incorporated quickly into the Mar del Sur coastal landscape, together with other introduced crops like bananas and sugarcane. Indian towns were not exempt from the impact of the ecological changes that occurred in the territory of New Spain from the onset of European colonization, as we discussed in an earlier chapter. As a plant that grows rapidly in conditions propitious for its development, the coconut palm also came to be cultivated in Indian towns, though it can be inferred from the documents examined that the Indians first went through a process of familiarization with, and appropriation of, palm tree cultivation, before beginning to produce aguardiente.

A statement by the *alcalde mayor* of Colima, Francisco Escudero de Figueroa, in 1603, gives an early indication that cultivated coconut palms existed in Indian towns at that time and were rented to Spaniards and Filipinos to produce *vino de cocos*.[468] However, when people wanted to occult the fact that Indians were involved in some stage of the chain of commercializing aguardiente, someone always emerged to deny that reality. This occurred in the case of Mateo de Sepúlveda, a resident of Colima who, in 1612, stated that palm trees were planted exclusively on lands inherited, or purchased, by Spaniards, "and the palms that are planted and produce [...] are not in ravines, on mountains, or in Indian towns".[469]

The question, then, is when and under what circumstances did the transfer of the knowhow for extracting *tuba* and elaborating *vino de cocos* pass from Filipinos to Indians? This clearly had occurred by the decade of 1630, when the official authorization to produce *vino de cocos* had incentivized the activity to such a degree that Filipino labor no longer sufficed to satisfy demand for the distilled drink. In the 1620s, *vino de cocos* production still depended on the *savoir faire* of the *indios chinos*, as don Pedro de Carvajal affirmed when he commented, in 1616, that he had been unable to exploit his palm trees "due to a lack of *chinos*". Carvajal's hacienda had produced *botijas* of *vino de cocos* since at least 1609, but production had ceased in 1611-1612, also due to "the lack of *chinos*" who could exploit the palm trees. Thus, we know that during the first two or three decades of the 17th century the art of distilling *vino de cocos* was the exclusive reserve of the Asian population.[470]

INDIAN VINATEROS IN COLIMA: A CASE STUDY

By the mid-17th century, there were around twenty Indian towns in the jurisdiction of Colima, organized in four *partidos*: the villa of Colima, the *guardianía* of San Francisco de Almoloyan, Tecolapa, and San Salvador Chiamila (Map 11). All four were Nahuatl-speaking communities whose populations had declined sharply in the early years of the Conquest. Due to the geography of the province of Colima, the towns were in three main regions: the slopes of the Volcano of Fire, intermountain valleys, and the coast.[471]

PART II

Map 11. Pueblos de Indios in Colima, 17th Century

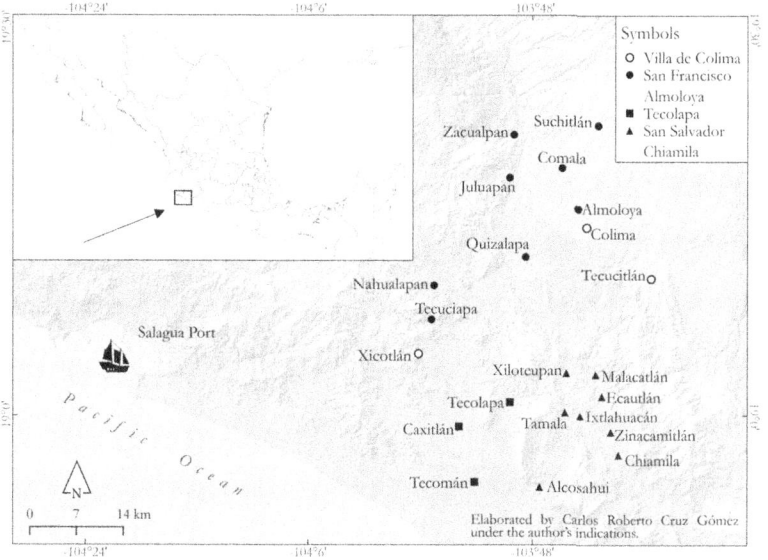

While, as we have seen, some *alcaldes de indios* participated in the *vino de cocos* trade, others vehemently rejected the insertion of "this evil" into their towns. Among the latter we find the *alcalde* of Ecautlán, Alonso Miguel, who in 1638 complained to the Viceregal authorities that the activities of *indios vinateros* and their sales of *vino de cocos*, were depopulating his town.[472] Documents that authorities in Indian towns sent to the *alcaldes mayores* began to reflect this reality as the Nahuatl language had incorporated the words *cocos* and *tuba* into its lexicon, as shown in the petition that the *alcalde* Alonso Miguel sent to the *alcalde mayor* of Colima in 1638 to denounce the mistreatment that his tributaries were suffering by being forced to extract large amounts of *tuba* (Illustration 16).

Vino de Cocos, the Pilgrim Beverage

Illustration 16. Document in Nahuatl from the Town of Ecautlán (1638)[473]

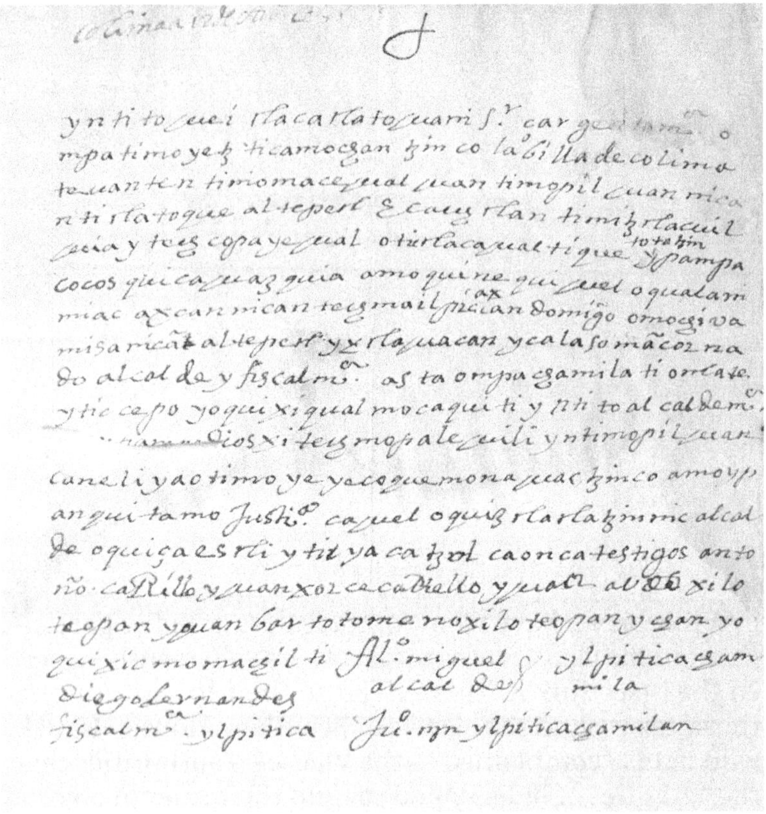

Source: AHMC, secc. B, caja 14, exp. 18.

The case registered in the town of Ecautlán, Colima, in 1638 provides clear evidence of this phenomenon, for the accusation by the *alcalde* Alonso Miguel denounced a whole series of abusive practices that were occurring on those palm production units; for example, a Spaniard named Juan de Santiago who owned a palm hacienda on the outskirts of Ecautlán had hired some Indians from the town to produce aguardiente. The document shows that at least eight Indians, all of them *vinateros*, were employed there to extract *tuba*.[474]

With the increase in demand for *vino de cocos* around that time, pressure on *vinateros* intensified since ever-greater amounts of *tuba* were required to distill the drink. Thus, Juan de Santiago and his overseer, a "fearsome" mulatto named Cristóbal, cruelly abused the Indian *vinateros* when they failed to produce the amounts expected. According to a declaration by Margarita María, wife of the Indian Juan Domingo, a *vinatero* who worked on the hacienda in Ecautlán, her husband arrived home one day with lash marks on his back because the mulatto Cristóbal had whipped him. Out of fear, Domingo fled to the Caxitlán Valley. Meanwhile, Catalina María complained that her husband, Pedro Simón, a *vinatero* on the same hacienda, had run away to parts unknown because Cristóbal had threatened him for not attending a cornfield (*milpa*). Her accusation confirms that palm production units were sites for other activities in addition to aguardiente production. Three other *vinateros* joined in denouncing the abuses committed on that hacienda in Ecautlán. Francisco Vela, Alonso Lázaro, and Francisco Bartolomé coincided in their testimonies that the mulatto Cristóbal had whipped them when he surprised them "adding water to the *tuba*"; that is, adulterating the product to complete the quota imposed.

Table 19 shows a total of 8 *vinateros* working on the Ecautlán hacienda who received a monthly wage of 4 pesos. Only Francisco Vela mentioned that he was paid 5 pesos, perhaps due to his skill or some other quality that allowed him to sell his product at a higher price than his mates. It is no accident that some *vinateros*, like Alonso Lázaro, received their wages in kind, being paid with clothes that the hacendado provided.[475] This practice, of course, allowed the hacendados to overvalue the merchandise they offered and thus cheat the Indians by paying them an uncertain value. Was this a thinly-disguised form of exploitation?

Table 19. Indios Vinateros on the Palm Hacienda of Ecautlán (1638)

Name	Status	Monthly wage
Juan Domingo	Native indio	4 pesos
Francisco Miguel	Native indio	4 pesos
Martín Lázaro	Native indio	4 pesos
Juan Agustín	Native indio	4 pesos
Melchor Pérez	Native indio	4 pesos
Francisco Vela	Native indio	5 pesos
Alonso Lázaro	Native indio	4 pesos
Francisco Bartolomé	Native indio	4 pesos

Source: AHMC, secc. B, caja 14, exp. 18.

The cases of the Indian *vinateros* who fled the Ecautlán hacienda begs the question of the kind of work relation that existed between hacendados and Indians in this economic activity. Was this an isolated case, or did it form part of a practice of systematic abuse in detriment of *vinateros*? In the previous chapter, we elucidated how the *indios chinos* fell into conditions of debt peonage and were by no means exempt from physical abuse when overseers demanded greater productivity. It would seem that the same types of abuse were practiced on the indigenous men who joined the workforce that produced *vino de cocos*.

Another incident was recorded in 1643, also in Ecautlán, when the *alcalde* Francisco Melchor accused the overseer of the Ocotlán hacienda, Francisco de Vargas Mariaca, of whipping him and other Indian nobles (*principales*) when they went to collect the *reales* they were obliged to pay as tribute in the home of the *chino* Sebastián Tumbaga. In his defense, the overseer alleged that the Indians were stealing *tuba* from Tumbaga, who had seen them climb palm trees illicitly to gather the liquid.[476]

Worker abuse affecting the native population can be observed in other settings as well; indeed, wherever there was high market demand for a product in which Indians constituted the main labor force. The mechanism was always more or less the same: the owner or hacendado, accompanied by his foremen and overseers, physically punished any worker who failed to fulfill production expectations that, not surprisingly, were usually higher than what the average laborer could provide. This type of ignominy was repeated well into the 18th century, as in the case Gaspar Martín, an Indian salt-worker from Tecomán who denounced that his hacendado, Antonio Viana:

> personally and with his servants and mulattos have been looking for me to whip me [...] [Acting] on his orders, one of his servants, a mulatto named Manuel Domingo, who supervised the saltworks, caught me, imprisoned me in a shack, tied me up, hung me from a pole, and gave me all manner of lashes, [until] seeing me so terribly wounded [he] let me rest, and then gave me more lashes, until blood ran down one leg.[477]

The similarities in these stories of the abuse suffered by Indian *vinateros* in Ecautlán in the 17th century and in saltworks in the 18th century reveals that, despite the distinct contexts, they were subject to long-established forms of harsh physical punishment, whether they worked producing *tuba* or extracting salt.

Risks of the Trade

Just as occurred in the Philippines, the *vinatero*'s trade in Colima was rife with inherent risks, especially precipitous falls from the towering palm trees. We know of one such incident in 1644 that affected Francisco Vázquez, an *indio tributario* who worked on a palm hacienda property of Blas de Mesina, a Spaniard who also worked as a storekeeper for the *alférez mayor* Juan Ochoa de Vitoria. One day while plying his trade, Vázquez fell from a tree and died before he could receive confession. Upon commencing his investigation, the *alcalde mayor* of Colima, Alonso de Aguilar Cervantes, ordered that Blas de Mesina be jailed, cover the costs of the judicial process, and pay 4 pesos for masses celebrated for "the soul of the deceased". *Alcalde* de Aguilar Cervantes argued that responsibility for the incident fell upon Mesina "because the Indian was in his service exploiting his palm trees [and that] occupation resulted in his death".[478] But the *alcalde's* actions infuriated Ochoa de Vitoria, whom several witnesses later saw enter the royal houses (*casas reales*) vociferating and shouting "who cares if that Indian died [for] all [Spanish residents] had Indians in their palms".[479] Ochoa de Vitoria seemed much more concerned for his storekeeper's absence from the town square than for the fate of Francisco Vázquez who had died from his fall. When all was said and done, as his words implied, tragedies like that could happen to anyone because everybody had Indians in their palm trees.

Four years earlier, in the town of Comala, the Indian Juan Martín had also died after falling from a palm tree, but the circumstances of that accident were distinct. According to Pedro Juan, the *alcalde de indios* of Comala, one Friday of San Andrés in 1640 Juan Martín was returning from the villa of Colima late at night and, while drunk, climbed a palm "in search of *tuba*".[480] Another Indian, Francisco Miguel testified that he "had heard that the night he fell from the coconut tree and died, he was returning from the villa drunk". Those trees were on lands belonging to the Indian town of Comala.[481]

VINATEROS OF OTHER CASTES

Finally, it is important to ask what occurred in terms of *tuba* harvesting in social sectors distinct from the indigenous one. It is surprising to learn that at such an early date as January 1604, a free negro named Marcos Melchor paid doña Juana de Solórzano 40 pesos annually to rent some "fields and coconut trees" in the Caxitlán Valley,[482] most likely to produce aguardiente. The fact that a negro had access to the means to enter into a rental arrangement of this nature indicates that the business of *vino de cocos* production had opened possibilities to other social strata, in addition to Spaniards and Filipinos. We do not know if Melchor hired a Filipino to make aguardiente, though at that date, so early in the 17th century, he likely did, for at that time the *vinatero*'s trade was not practiced by just anyone. Another case involved a mestizo, Miguel de Solís, who had a palm production unit on the outskirts of the town of Nahualapa around 1665. Thanks to a judicial process in which authorities in Colima investigated an Indian who had tried to "rape" a Spanish woman, we learn that this 30-year-old mestizo testified that the Indian was employed on his hacienda, where he performed the work of climbing palm trees.[483]

By the second half of the 17th century, therefore, a distinct panorama was emerging in the domain of *vino de cocos* production, as being a *vinatero* or "climbing like *chinos*" was no longer the exclusive reserve of Filipinos. The historical coexistence of *indios chinos*, Indians, mestizos, mulattos, and negros on palm haciendas over several decades had led to the technique for extracting *tuba* being transmitted among neighbors regardless of their social category. Though we know little about businesses run by Spanish women, it is clear that some also had *vinateros* on their haciendas as in the case of doña Polonia de San Pedro who, in 1654, had an Indian *vinatero* named Rafael working in her palm trees.[484]

One question that remains is to what degree Indians participated as "official *vinateros*" (*oficiales de hacer vino* or *maestros de hacer vino*); that is, actually distilling the *tuba*, not just extracting it. The documents reviewed clearly identify Indian *vinateros* only as men who harvested *tuba*, so they remain mute on their role in distillation. Was that activity still reserved for Filipinos? If that were the case, it would explain why elaborating the drink called *tuba* is still a traditional activity in Colima today while, in contrast, *vino de cocos* production virtually disappeared as the Filipino population in the area of Colima declined. But the reality is more complex than this, for we cannot lose sight of the fact that the Asian distillation technique was transferred to the mestizo and indigenous world through mezcal production, especially in the modern-day state of Jalisco, a topic that we explore in depth in the Epilogue of this book.

In the late 17th century, palm haciendas in Colima housed a true social mosaic. Although we can still identify some *indios chinos*, that sector was gradually being replaced by other castes. In other words, the exclusivity that Asians had enjoyed as *tuberos* and master *vinateros* in the first half of that century had been left behind. The social transfer of *tuba* harvesting and Filipino-style distillation to produce *vino de cocos* had passed to Spaniards, Indians, mestizos, and mulattos. The clearest example comes from the district of Caxitlán-Tecolapa, the site of the greatest dynamism in *vino de cocos* production during the first phase, and the abode of most of the Filipinos who settled in Colima. While in 1619 one-fifth of the population was made up of *chinos*,[485] the story changed for the decade of 1680. Thanks to the records of two censuses (one in 1681, the other in 1683) it is possible to analyze the social composition of the palm haciendas there (Table 20).

Of a total of 232 individuals listed as residents of haciendas in the 1681 census, 33.6% were Indians, 12.5% Spaniards, 5.6% *moriscos*, 3.4% mestizos, 2.6% *chinos*, 1.7% mulattos, and 1.7% negros. Unfortunately, the caste status of the rest of the population is not stated. The panorama in 1683 was similar: of 228 individuals employed on palm haciendas, 26.3% were Indians, 17.1% mulattos, 16.7% Spaniards, 13.1% mestizos, 6.6% moriscos, 2.2% chinos, 1.3% tresalbos, and 0.9% negros. As in the 1681 census, the caste status of the other residents is not cited, though we are inclined to think that the final sector referred to Indians.

Table 20. Census of the Palm Haciendas in Caxitlán, Colima (1681, 1683)

Caste	1681 census		1683 census	
	Total	Percentage	Total	Percentage
Spaniards	29	12.5%	38	16.7%
Indians	78	33.6%	60	26.3%
Negros	4	1.7%	2	0.9%
Chinos	6	2.6%	5	2.2%
Mestizos	8	3.4%	30	13.1%
Mulattos	4	1.7%	39	17.1%
Moriscos	13	5.6%	15	6.6%
Tresalbos	0	0%	3	1.3%
	Total	Percentage	Total	Percentage
Absent	0	0%	3	1.3%
Undetermined	90	38.9%	33	14.5%
Totals	232	100%	228	100%

Source: Alberto Carrillo, *Partidos y padrones del Obispado de Michoacán*, pp. 384-390.

Table 20 shows a predominance of the indigenous population on the haciendas, a finding that reflects a significant change from the first half of the 17th century when additional laborers came from *pueblos de indios* near the haciendas, but did not necessarily live on those properties, instead conserving their homes in their respective towns. As a result, palm haciendas in Colima at the turn of the century could produce *vino de cocos* without *indios chinos* since the tasks involved were being performed by other castes.

Of the 27 haciendas that were still operating in Caxitlán in 1681 only six employed a *chino*. In 1683, there were 24 haciendas but, once again, only six had a *chino*, but of these two were women who had married men of other castes who did not necessarily participate in aguardiente production. Some of the few Asians who remained belonged to the Triana family that lived on the hacienda of the widow María Ana Barroso. Others were dispersed on distinct palm production units: Pascual Juan on the hacienda of Matheo de la Torre, Martín Salinas and Alonso Martín on the property of doña Francisca de Figueroa, Agustín Ramírez on the hacienda of Miguel de Pedroza, and Catalina Marta, on lands belonging to Juan de San Pedro.

Another interesting fact involves the proprietors of those haciendas. While most were Spaniards, spaces had opened up to admit indios, mestizos, and mulattos in the circle of owners of palm production units. In 1681, the mestizo Moisés García owned the Aguacatitlán hacienda where 23 people lived, among them indios, mestizos, and mulattos. In the same year, another mestizo, Alonso Martín, had a hacienda in Aguacatitlán with 14 residents, including indios, mestizos, and mulattos, as well as one Spaniard who was likely under Martín's tutelage. Smaller production units belonged to the indio Juan Romero, Nicolás Monroy, a *morisco*, and Alonso García and Domingo Cedillo, two free mulattos. In 1683, other free mulattos appeared on the scene as hacienda owners: Lázaro de Victoria, Juan Hernández, and Domingo de Solórzano, in addition to García and Cedillo, who were registered two years earlier.

How are we to explain this increase in the number of mulattos and other castes who came to own palm haciendas in the late 17th century? One way to acquire these properties was to purchase a hacienda that carried some type of lien in the ecclesiastical census that had gone unpaid due to neglect or poor production. Selling patrimony of this kind meant that production would be reactivated in order to renew payment of the overdue debt (chantry), opportunities which, by that time, could be accessible to mulattos. In December 1691, Pablo de Espinoza, a free mulatto, acquired a hacienda in the Caxitlán Valley that had belonged to the scribe Clemente Hidalgo de Agüero. The property had been very productive throughout the mid-17th century but had declined markedly. In the year that Espinoza purchased it, the "hacienda was weak and deteriorated with no [manager] in the chantry to look after it". The property had 120 palm trees, fields, water, fruit trees, accesses, and exits; that is, all the features of an estate developed to produce aguardiente. However, it had been burdened by a debt of one thousand pesos that dated back to Hidalgo's death. Pablo de Espinoza bought the property for, precisely, one thousand pesos, promising to pay 5% of the purchase price on each 25th day of May; that is, 55 pesos.[486]

Unfortunately, information for the Zacatula-Acapulco production nucleus is scarce, so we cannot reconstruct the dynamics of *vino de cocos* production there for sectors apart from the *chinos*. Matthew J. Furlong suggests the possibility that some mulattos on ranches in Alcholoa and Cacahuatepec on the *Costa Grande* in the modern-day state of Guerrero, produced *vino de cocos* toward the end of the 17th century.[487] But long before that, in 1654, the inventory of the hacienda in San Juan Tuxtepec, where we know that *vino de cocos* was produced, revealed the presence of a "mulatto de China" named Marcos de Ávila, a finding which indicates that the mixed mestizo-Asian sectors of the population were in contact, directly or indirectly, with the elaboration of this distilled drink.[488]

Final reflections: *vinateros* or "master wine-makers"?

In this chapter we analyzed how, around the decade of 1630, a sector of Indians had ceased to be just consumers of *vino de cocos* to emerge as *vinateros*. But what exactly did the term *vinatero* mean? The reader will recall that in an earlier chapter we mentioned that *vinatero* was the generic term used to refer to individuals involved in elaborating *vino de cocos*. But this broad definition becomes problematic when we study Indians because it does not clarify the level of knowledge they acquired regarding the two fundamental phases of the technique of *vino de cocos* production; that is, first extracting and then distilling the *tuba*. Regarding the latter step, some documents mention the presence of "master wine-makers", possibly comparable to today's "master mezcal-makers" (*maestros mezcaleros*) who conserve a profound knowledge of the art of distillation. Could it be that some Indians mastered both phases of *vino de cocos* production, or did they participate only in *tuba* extraction and never come to distill the raw material themselves?

On the one hand, we were unable to find any documents that confirmed the presence of "master wine-makers" in the indigenous sector. In fact, it has been argued that one of the causes of the disappearance of *vino de cocos* in the 18th century was, precisely, that no Indians ever came to appropriate the distillation technique.[489] On the other, there are at least two indications –one of which has endured to the present– that Indians in western New Spain not only learned to distill *vino de cocos*, but actually transferred the technique to a distinct type of raw material –agave– and thus gave rise to the mezcal production.

In the earlier analysis of the composition of the haciendas in the Caxitlán Valley we mentioned the notably scarce presence of *indios chinos* in the 1680s that contrasted strongly to the abundant Indian, mestizo, mulatto, *morisco*, and *tresalbo* groups. Moreover, among the lists of hacienda owners we were able to identify two free mulattos, two mestizos, one Indian, and one free *morisco*.[490] Those findings allow us to venture the conclusion that the distillation technique was introduced among, and came to take root within, the non-Asian population. Now, the issue is why that distillation tradition eventually came to be consolidated in zones outside the two main *vino de cocos* production nuclei? Perhaps the answer is to be sought in the availability of raw materials, more than in the ability of certain individuals to perform one or the other of the two trades required.

PART III
THE PILGRIM BEVERAGE

7. PROHIBITION, APOGEE, AND DECLINE OF VINO DE COCOS

> A wine made from coconut palms [...] has been introduced into the provinces of Zacatula and Colima, so cheap and strong that Indians use it to such excess that it costs them their health and lives.
>
> —Viceroy Luis de Velasco, El Joven (1610)

INTRODUCTION

Up to the eve of the 17th century, the Crown had implemented a policy in New Spain to control and prohibit certain alcoholic beverages, those commonly called "drinks of the land" (*bebidas de la tierra*) to distinguish them from "wine of Castille". As noted previously, upon arriving in Mesoamerica, the Spanish encountered a wide variety of beverages elaborated mainly from corn and maguey, though the map of the diverse raw materials used in that activity included many other local plants. For that reason, in August 1529, the Empress ordered her Audiencias throughout the Indies to ban the use of "a root that [Indians] cultivate to add to said wine to strengthen it and enhance its flavor". Though neither the root nor the type of wine was specified, we can assume that she was referring to pulque and the ingredients that Indians in central Mexico traditionally added when preparing it.[491] The measure sought to prevent drunkenness among the Indians, who "while inebriated perform the ceremonies and sacrifices they used to do in olden times, and while so excited put their hands on others such that [...] many opprobrious carnal vices ensue".[492]

Later, on January 25, 1545, an order was ratified that prohibited Indians and Spaniards alike from producing "drinks of the land" and selling them, openly or clandestinely, "because [they] make them lose their senses and emit much howling and shouting, and in this state they [practice] idolatry".[493] That decree, reiterated throughout the 16th century, also banned the sale of wine from Castille to Indians, negros, and slaves. Dispositions of this kind reflected an ongoing concern over the consequences of drunkenness in non-Spanish sectors of the population that often ended in idolatry, especially in the early years of evangelization, or breaches of public morals.

The onset of *vino de cocos* production occurred in this context of prohibitions. In the final chapter, we address the ambiguous discourse of authorities in New Spain regarding the production and consumption of alcoholic drinks, but what we wish to analyze here are the four phases of *vino de cocos* production in the 17th century, from its emergence as a banned drink through its apogee, decline, and extinction. The first stage began in the year 1600, which brought the earliest news of the elaboration of this beverage in Colima, and ended in 1626 when a fierce hurricane destroyed broad swaths of cacao plantations and some palm trees. The production and sale of *vino de cocos* never received official authorization in that period; in fact, in 1612 the Real Audiencia of Mexico ordered that all palm trees in the jurisdictions of Colima and Motines be cut down to eliminate production of the drink. The second stage began in 1627 when, in the aftermath of the crisis caused by the hurricane, the Viceroy authorized the free

PART III

production and trade of *vino de cocos*. The third ran from 1670 to 1700, a period characterized by lights and shadows in the documentation available on this aguardiente, but where an interesting phenomenon emerged in the Colima-Motines production nucleus as the location of palm haciendas shifted from the coast inland at the same time as sales and transfers of haciendas increased in the coastal Caxitlán and Alima Valley. This sequence culminated in 1700-1724, when we see a clear decline in activities related to *vino de cocos*, accompanied by its prohibition decreed by Viceroy Marqués de Casafuerte.

THE PROHIBITED DRINK (1600-1626)

Around 1610, Viceroy Velasco received news that "a wine made from coconut palms" in the provinces of Colima and Zacatula was causing disturbances, and that the problem was so severe that in just one –unspecified– town some sixty taverns were measuring and selling it in abundance.[494] Velasco's ordinance prohibited consumption of *vino de cocos*, arguing that consuming it affected the health of Indians who, due to its low cost, were drinking it to excess. Second, he stated that sales of palm aguardiente were "interfering" with those of wine from Castille to the detriment of the royal finances. Third, Velasco was concerned that priests in local sacristies might replace Castilian sacramental wine with *vino de cocos* when celebrating mass.[495] For these reasons, he warned that severe punishment awaited those who committed the crimes of producing and selling *vino de cocos*, whether clandestinely or openly: a fine of one thousand Castilian ducats for Spaniards, one hundred lashes and exile for mestizos, negros, or mulattos, and fifty lashes while tied to a pole in the public square for Indians.[496]

The Colima-Motines production nucleus provides abundant evidence of *vino de cocos* production in the first decade of the 17th century. To cite two examples, in 1600, the alcalde ordinario of Colima, Diego Mejía de la Torre, was accused by a merchant from Mexico City, Mateo de Zárate, a distributor of wine from Castille, because "although making vino de cocos in this villa is prohibited", he blatantly violated the rules of his office by producing it in great quantities, thus contravening his functions as juez ordinario (first instance judge).[497] In addition, between 1603-1604 Indians in Motines charged that their alcalde mayor, Juan Velázquez de la Cueva, was operating a tavern in his home that sold vino de cocos to the Indians, causing "great drunkenness, disturbances, and brawls among [them]".[498]

One notable aspect of these two early references to the fabrication of this distilled beverage is that they implicated authorities of distinct rank. A key factor that spurred the emergence of vino de cocos and ensured its permanence and expansion throughout the 17th century was that from the outset the vested interests of proprietors associated with positions in local government or with Crown officials were involved. Proof of the growing economic interest in the drink is that in 1608 the Bishop of Michoacán ordered that residents of Colima were to pay their tithes (diezmos) in vino de cocos and salt, "which the people produce with their work and artifice".[499]

In the case of Zacatula, the earliest mention of vino de cocos production occurred in 1609, regarding a cacao hacienda on the Costa Grande.[500] Ten years later, in 1619, Captain Sebastián de Pineda reported that "trade is so great that at present there is [vino de cocos] on the coast of Navidad, in Apasabalcos and throughout Colima, [where] mule trains are loaded with this wine just as is done in Spain".[501] In this extract, Pineda refers to a large part of the coastal fringe of the Mar del Sur as a region where palm aguardiente was produced, including the Apasagualcos hacienda on the Costa Grande of the modern-day state of Guerrero.

Despite the prohibition decreed by Luis de Velasco El Joven in 1610, vino de cocos production continued. But the open disobedience of the *colimenses* spurred the Real Audiencia of Mexico to take action in 1612, when it announced that all palm trees in that province were to be felled to eliminate aguardiente production.[502] This resolution took residents by surprise and the town council reacted immediately by calling an assembly to appeal the order. The *cabildo* defended its posture with testimony from a dozen witnesses –all *colimenses*– who presented several convincing arguments against the massive toppling of palm trees, above all: that they were the villa's main source of sustenance, that they were not "wild, but cultivated" by conquistadores, that *vino de cocos* was healthy and medicinal, and that the measure would lead to the depopulation of the villa of Colima.

Armed with these justifications, the *cabildo* tried to convince the Audiencia that *vino de cocos* was the main economic base for people in Colima, alleging that "if the palms are felled, the widespread damage would be valued in over one hundred thousand Castilian ducats, because fifty out of every one hundred residents of this villa would lose over one thousand five hundred pesos".[503] These figures must be taken with a grain of salt for two reasons. First, the *colimenses* obviously had a personal stake in demonstrating the enormous economic importance of their palm trees, but the amount of 100,000 ducats (137,500 pesos) seems somewhat bloated. Second, even if half of the villa's residents were to lose 1,500 pesos each, the amount would only come to 75,000 pesos. This leads to the question of where that famous calculation of 100,000 ducats came from. Now, if we assume that there was, in reality, an investment of 100,000 ducats in palm trees, then in 1612 there would have been around 34,000 cultivated trees in the Colima-Motines production nucleus. If, however, we take the other –perhaps more credible– figure of 75,000 pesos, then the number of palm trees in the area would have been just over 18,000,[504] a figure still indicative of the vertiginous propagation of this tree along the west coast of New Spain.

According to the council's evidence, the entire economy of Colima in the early 17th century was permeated by the activity of the palm haciendas, as half of the inhabitants owned such plantations and the other half received indirect benefits, "because just as those who have such palms in their haciendas, those who do not exploit and [profit] from them".[505]

In the end, the Real Audiencia's order to cut down all palm trees in Colima was rescinded. In 1612, the council of Colima granted a power-of-attorney to Juan Nieto Dávalos, an attorney at the Audiencia, to represent it in its appeal of the ominous disposition, promising to pay him 1,000 pesos for his "work and solicitude".[506] Significantly, Nieto Dávalos had family in, and economic links to, Colima, as he was a nephew of Jerónimo Dávalos Vergara, who served as a scribe and the *alcalde ordinario* of the cabildo in the first decade of the 17th century.[507]

In 1614, the council granted Nieto Dávalos a second power-of-attorney, this one authorizing him to inform the Audiencia of Mexico that the villa of Colima had fallen into poverty due to "cataclysmic ruin" caused by fires. In its missive, the council pleaded that its coconut trees not be cut down.[508] Diverse economic interests were in play and the ability of Colima's governing council to negotiate the terms and conditions of *vino de cocos* production emerged clearly in the discussion that ensued.

First Lease Contracts for Haciendas

The argument that Colima's council presented in 1612 won the day and the order was suspended. Proof that, far from ceasing, palm tree exploitation continued for *vino de cocos* production, can be found in the earliest leasing agreements of palm haciendas in Colima. Notarial documents from

1613 to 1615 confirm that at least five leases were signed for properties in the Caxitlán Valley, accords that included other plants, as well, such as cacao and fruit trees. Those agreements stipulated the duration –one to two years– the amount to be paid, the conditions in which the hacienda was transferred, and the lessee's obligations.

In 1613, the *Huerta Vieja*, a property belonging to *alférez* Álvaro García de Grijalva, was leased to Pablo de Aguiar for one year at a cost of 17 loads of cacao. De Aguiar was obliged to maintain the hacienda clean, well-attended, and cultivated. Regarding the palm trees, he was bound to harvest them opportunely, both mature ones and those that would mature later,[509] a clause surely inserted to ensure that they would continue to produce sap (*tuba*) and that production would go on uninterrupted. That same year, two brothers, Juan and Jorge Carrillo de Guzmán, leased two palm haciendas, the first from Isabel de Villalobos, the second from Hernando de Solórzano, for a period of one year via payments of 60 and 100 pesos, respectively. One detail that stands out in the contract between Juan Carrillo and Hernando de Solórzano is the stipulation that if "the obligation and condition were to arise that before this period ends, *producing wine from those palms were prohibited*, the lessee shall pay the amount of the lease from the day of said [ban] to the end of that year.[510]

This shows that the owners of palm haciendas in Colima felt great uncertainty regarding the future of their palm trees in light of the dire threats issued by the Audiencia of Mexico, and that some, like Solórzano, tried to prepare for whatever resolution might come in order to avoid potential losses. Does this explain why the lease contracts were drawn up for only one or two years? Or were they of short duration because *vino de cocos* production was a particularly profitable activity? This second possibility cannot be ruled out, since we know that residents like Juan de Segovia made it clear, upon leasing his cacao hacienda, that he was renting only "the cacao bushes [but] reserved the palms for himself".[511]

Property Inventories from 1622: The Colima–Motines Nucleus

Vino de cocos producers in Colima did not seem overly concerned about the illegal nature of their activities; in fact, they made it public in official documents. In response to Felipe IV's order that obliged all authorities to declare their patrimony,[512] in 1622 a series of inventories was compiled of the properties of *colimenses*. In that year, their principal investments still centered on cacao plantations, but it is clear that palm aguardiente production was increasing, despite the fact that it was an illegal activity.

Table 20 shows around twenty palm haciendas established in the *alcaldías mayores* of Colima and Motines, property of *colimenses*. Unfortunately, the information is far from uniform, and of these 23 haciendas only three specify the number of palms, the value of each tree, annual *vino de cocos* production, and yearly profits. For the others, we see only the number of palm trees that were producing. The importance of the information provided by those three haciendas is that it allows us to estimate aguardiente production per palm tree. In this regard, Jorge Carrillo de Guzmán stated that he had "planted one hundred coconut palms, each one worth five pesos, that came to five hundred pesos [...] From the well-tended [trees] we can make two hundred botijas of wine each year, that are worth six hundred pesos".[513] Rodrigo de Brizuela declared that he had "one hundred and fifty palms, eighty of which give fruit, the others not yet; [each one] worth four pesos, coming to six hundred pesos. Annually, they produce one hundred and fifty botijas or arrobas of wine when production is good, at a value of three pesos per *arroba*;[514] in total, four hundred and fifty pesos.[515]

Part III

This information allowed us to estimate that producers extracted around 2 *arrobas* or *botijas* annually from one palm tree. The term *botija perulera* derives from the *perula trianera*, one of the recipients most often used in maritime trade between Spain and America in the 17th century, with roots in Andalusia for storing and transporting wine and oil.[516] Some authors suggest that the name *perulera* is due to the participation of Sevillian merchants in the Vice-Royalty of Peru, who were also known as *peruleros*.[517] Since no consensus exists as to the exact volume of the *botija perulera*, we use the common estimate of this recipient for wine and vinegar, which is around 16 liters.[518] Documents from Colima consistently use *arroba* and *botija perulera* interchangeably, so we will base our calculations on this premise.

According to the other property inventories, a "well-tended" palm tree in the stage of full production was worth up to 5 pesos, younger trees cost 4 pesos, and small ones or seedlings 3 pesos; thus, we can establish an average value of 4 pesos per tree. An *arroba* of *vino de cocos* was sold to the public for 3 pesos, while production costs were around 2 pesos, a figure based on tithe (*diezmo*) payments, an aspect we analyze in detail below. Using these criteria, in Table 21 we elaborated an annual estimate of *vino de cocos* production in the Colima-Motines nucleus for the year 1622 based on a figure of at least 5,844 palms in production that represented a total investment of 23,766 pesos, and that would have produced around 11,148 *botijas peruleras* of *vino de cocos*, equivalent to 178,368 liters.

Table 21. Annual *Vino de Cocos* Production in the Colima–Motines Nucleus (1622)[519]

Place	Proprietor	No. of palms	Value per tree (pesos)	Investment in palm trees (pesos)	Annual production (botijas)	Liters per year
Caxitlán	Juan de Aguilar Solórzano	254	4	1,016	508	8,128
Caxitlán	Alonso Álvarez de Espinosa	254	4	1,016	508	8,128
Alima	Diego Arias Arellano	254	4	1,016	508	8,128
Aguacatitlán?	Rodrigo de Brizuela	15	5	75	50	800
Aguacatitán	Rodrigo de Brizuela	80	4	600	150	2,400
Caxitlán	Jorge Carrillo de Guzmán	100	5	500	200	3,200
Aguacatitlán	Jorge Carrillo de Guzmán	80	3	240	160	2,560
Caxitlán	Juan Carrillo de Guzmán	500	4	2,000	1,000	16,000
Zapotlanejo	Andrés de Castilla Montemayor	325	3	975	100	1,600
Alima	García Dávalos Vergara	254	4	1,016	508	8,128
Alima	Pedro de Espinosa	300	4	1,200	600	9,600
Prov. Colima	Juan Fernández de Tene	400	4	1,600	800	12,800
Caxitlán	Álvaro García de Grijalva	254	4	1,016	508	8,128

Part III

Place	Proprietor	No. of palms	Value per tree (pesos)	Investment in palm trees (pesos)	Annual production (botijas)	Liters per year
Caxitlán	Alonso García Nomparte	254	4	1,016	508	8,128
Suchitzi	Hernando Gómez Machorro	254	4	1,016	508	8,128
Contla	Matías de Hoyo	400	5	2,000	800	12,800
Maquilí	Pedro López de Salazar	400	4	1,600	800	12,800
Xicotlán	Diego Mejía de la Torre	254	4	1,016	508	8,128
Caxitlán	Juan Preciado	50	4	200	100	1,600
Caxitlán	Gaspar Ramírez Alarcón	400	4	1,600	800	12,800
Caxitlán	Gaspar Román	254	4	1,016	508	8,128
Unknown	Luis de Solórzano	254	4	1,016	508	8,128
Popoyutla	Domingo Vela de Grijalva	254	4	1,016	508	8,128
	TOTALS	5 844	4	23,766	11,148	178,368

Source: estimates by the author with data from AGI, México, 262, nos. 2, 9, 19, 34, 50, 51, 59, 70, 90, 100, 108, 109, 112, 134, 165, 210, 227, 260, and 265; and AGI, México, 263, nos. 111 and 184.

Our calculations led us to examine the case of Andrés de Castilla Montemayor (Table 21), for it presents several challenges. He declared that he obtained only 100 botijas of *vino de cocos* from his 325 palm trees but, at the same time, stated that "some produce but others do not yet give fruit", and that "[production] in each year, with careful exploitation of the former and the latter [...] is one hundred botijas of wine".[520] Due to its exceptional nature, the case of Castilla Montemayor must be placed in parentheses.

The result, nevertheless, is tangible: at the macroeconomic level we can infer that in 1622 there were around 6,000 palm trees in the *alcaldías mayores* of Colima and Motines; clearly an *ad mínimum* figure compared to the 18,000 trees that presumably existed in 1612, the *ad maximum* figure. If we accept the validity of the first number, then annual *vino de cocos* production would have been around 191,360 liters. It is important to keep in mind that these results come from property inventories made in 1622 that represented some members of the Colima elite who had interests both there and in Motines. Nor can we forget that other haciendas existed, whose production would increase all these figures. Notarial documents from Colima in the first decades of the 17th century mention some cacao and palm haciendas but, unfortunately, the figures they provide are not systematic and, hence, are insufficient to establish productive relations for a corpus like the one analyzed above.[521] What those documents do reveal, however, is a pronounced dynamism in transactions involving aguardiente and purchase-sales of palm production units.

Two additional aspects that stand out in the property inventories from 1622 are the prices of palm trees and the maintenance costs that haciendas paid. Prices per tree ranged from 3 to 5 pesos, the lower value for recently planted palms or ones that were too immature to produce *tuba*. For this reason, Jorge Carrillo de Guzmán stated that his trees were worth 3 pesos each "[for] they are new and do not bear fruit".[522] It is important to clarify that the phrase "not bear fruit" does not refer to coconuts, but to the onset of sap production –*tuba*– as a raw material. As mentioned above, palm trees in production were valued at 4 to 5 pesos.

Part III

Costs and Maintenance of Palm Haciendas

We now turn our attention to the costs that hacendados incurred, which generally imply two rubrics: "people and supplies". *Vinateros* do not appear in the property inventories, but we know that each one was paid 4 to 5 pesos per month, depending on their performance.[523] Supplies included inputs like recipients and tools for cutting the inflorescences, containers for aguardiente, and utensils to assemble the rustic stills that *vinateros* used. If we consider the figures provided by Brizuela, Carrillo de Guzmán, and Castilla Montemayor, then the hacendados paid around one-third of their annual income to cover operating costs.

To obtain a more precise idea of the kinds of costs, we take as a reference two palm haciendas, that of the del Valle brothers in Colima in 1625-1626 (Table 22), and that of doña Catalina de Alarcón in 1639 (Table 23). Records for these two properties provide clear evidence of the specific costs of several activities, such as cleaning and maintenance, conducting irrigation water, provisions for workers, and utensils for aguardiente production. Since the documents are not from complete files but ones that are only fragmentary, it was not possible to extract the percentage of costs in relation to profits from aguardiente sales. Even so, these details on costs are valuable for our understanding of this rubric.

Table 22. Administration Costs on the Cacao and Palm Hacienda of the Del Valle Family (1625–1626)

Activity	Cost
1625	
Indians to clean the hacienda, open irrigation ditches, and "other labors"	20 *pesos*
Costs for the plantation house	30 *ps*

Activity	Cost
28 fanegas of corn for the sustenance of servants	56 ps
2 fanegas of beans	6 ps
Indios laboríos to irrigate, cultivate, and "other labors"	30 ps
One female Indian servant	18 ps
Meat, dishes, viscera for sustenance and provision	26 ps
Pumps, vessels (tecomates) for tuba, carrizo to fence the hacienda, and laborers	12 ps
TOTAL	198 ps
1626	
Indians to clean the plantation	10 pesos
14 fanegas of corn	28 ps
1 fanega of beans	3 ps
Indian fieldworkers	10 ps
Meat, salt, chili, viscera, and "necessary items"	10 ps
2 horses and 3 mares	20 ps
6 loads of cacao for tithes	15 ps
4 botijas of vino de cocos for tithes	10 ps
TOTAL	106 ps

Source: AHEC/Reyes, reg. 2154.

Table 23. Administration Costs on the Palm Hacienda of Doña Catalina de Alarcón (1639)

Activity	Cost
Plantation house and storehouse for grass and rope	5 ps
2 pesos to furnish the plantation house with rope	2 ps

Part III

Activity	Cost
Construction of a new oven and bowl, paid by Bartolomé Núñez	9 ps
Plus 6 tomines charged to dig a pit for the oven	6 ts
Paid to Francisco, indio, who has worked on the hacienda taking care of the house, irrigating the palms, and other necessary labors, at 4 pesos per month	48 ps
24 pesos to Luisa, india, per year of service, at 2 pesos per month, who fed the laborers and servants on the hacienda	24 ps
30 pesos to Baltasar, indio chino, who made wine on the hacienda from October 26, when doña Catalina fell ill and later died, to June 13, 1639	30 ps
Juanillo, indio who makes wine, paid from November 1 to today, working at a wage of four pesos per month, totaling 47 pesos	47 ps
21 pesos to Juan de Aguilera, a Spaniard who worked from November 1, 1638 to February 10, 3 months of work on the hacienda at a wage of 100 pesos per year	21 ps
Plus 6 pesos paid as tax (alcabala) on the rubrics of the hacienda, to the Sergeant Major and alcalde mayor of Colima, Félix Candela	6 ps
Plus 16 pesos paid to 8 indios who cleaned the palms and poured water into the canals, 8, and another 7, and other days less this amount, as all (eight) items in the ledgers of charges and expenses will show	16 ps
TOTAL	214 ps

Source: AHMC, secc. B, caja 18, exp. 1, f. 7-8v.

We will now situate the position of *vino de cocos* in relation to the brute figures on investments in Colima-Motines in 1622. While José F. de la Peña devoted some pages to the case of Colima based on property inventories from that year,[524] he did not take into account an element that we have added in Table 24; namely, aguardiente production and investments in coconut palms. That author meticulously reviewed elements like cacao, cattle, saltworks, and household items, but clearly gave only marginal importance to the palm haciendas, including their trees and the alcoholic drink produced there. De la Peña grouped the palms and other fruit trees together in his category "agriculture", though the latter are not worth mentioning here. After making the estimates outlined above, we discovered that *vino de cocos* production was the third-most important rubric in the economy of this nucleus, below only cacao production and cattle-raising. In fact, these three investments together represented almost 60% of the total; hence they constituted the three pillars of the region's economy.

Table 24. Distribution of Investments in Colima (1622)[525]

Investment	Pesos	Percentage
Cacao	161,870	39.97
Cattle	42,420	10.47
Vino de cocos	33,444	8.26
Slaves	28,045	6.92
Trousseau and kitchenware	27,390	6.76
Debts owed	24,924	6.15
Palm trees	**23,766**	**5.86**
Houses	20,910	5.16
Herds	9,095	2.24
Trades	9,087	2.24
Silver and jewels	6,633	1.63
Saltworks	4,660	1.15
Reales	4,500	1.11
Stables	4,146	1.02

Investment	Pesos	Percentage
Transactions	3,988	0.98
TOTAL	404,878	100

Source: modified from De la Peña, Oligarquía y propiedad, p. 69.

Property Inventories from 1622: The Zacatula–Acapulco Nucleus

In contrast to the wealth of information in the property inventories of *colimenses* that allowed us to establish the importance of coconut palms and their products in the local economy, the inventories from Zacatula and Acapulco present a very different panorama. First, those documents pertain to residents of Mexico City who did not live in Zacatula but only stayed there temporarily to occupy administrative positions, before returning to the capital of New Spain or moving on to another province to take up a position. Most of those men served as *alcaldes mayores* or officials in Acapulco. Second, because they had no firm attachment to the zone, we are not dealing with owners of cultivated lands but, rather, with authorities whose wealth was based on other kinds of property, such as homes in Mexico City, household items, clothes, jewels, and earnings from their administrative activities.

We found around ten inventories of those individuals for whom we are sure that coconut palms and their products –like aguardiente– did not figure among their economic interests, even though they lived in places on the Mar del Sur coast, like Zacatula or Acapulco. One of these men, an accountant named Gaspar Bello de Acuña, was the only one who mentioned among his properties a house in the port of Acapulco, a place he considered "so expensive and inclement", that it functioned as an inn for people from Mexico City who came on some commission, or even for soldiers who performed security functions and were related to people involved with the Manila Galleon. Some of those inventories, however, like those of Bello de Acuña and Lesmes Astudillo, reveal that they had *chino* slaves in their service, though no cases were related to work with palm trees, much less *vino de cocos* production.[526]

In his doctoral dissertation on the Asian population that settled in the *Costa Grande*, Furlong points out that overseers on the haciendas left only minimal records on *vino de cocos* production in the zone. However, some documents on chantries and litigations allowed him to confirm that *vino de cocos* was being produced on several haciendas around Petatlán between 1610 and 1660: San Pedro, San Juan de Tuxtepec, San Bartolomé Tuxtepec, San Luis, and San Juan Bautista. Later, we find that aguardiente was distilled on two haciendas in the area between the Coyuca and Mitla lagoons: Nuestra Señora del Buen Suceso (mentioned in the previous chapter) and Nuestra Señora de la Concepción.[527] Of course, the hacienda of San Miguel Apasagualcos, south of Atoyac, had appeared as a production unit since 1631, as we will show in Table 26, together with Tecpan and its surrounding area.

The Hurricane of 1626 in Colima: A Point of Inflection in Vino de Cocos Production

A meteorological phenomenon pushed *vino de cocos* out of its condition of illegality. While the evidence that *colimenses* presented in 1612 to defend their palm trees had calmed the attitude of the viceregal authorities, paradoxically, it would be a disaster that brought *vino de cocos* back as a focus of discussion. On October 29, 1626, a hurricane struck the province of Colima. According to contemporary testimonies, that violent storm ravaged the cacao plantations, literally crushing the trees to the ground. Owners of cacao haciendas, like Captain Juan Carrillo de Guzmán, suddenly found themselves in such dire economic straits that some contemplated abandoning the province and emigrating in search of new opportunities. In January 1627, Captain

Part III

Carrillo, grandson of one of the first conquistadores of New Spain (Jorge Carrillo), who had a long trajectory of administrative positions in local government in Colima, presented his credentials to the *alcalde ordinario*, don Pedro de Ceballos, where he admitted that he had

> fallen into poverty and need because of the hurricane, wind, and rainstorm that occurred in these parts on the twenty-ninth of October of the previous year. [In] the Caxitlán Valley of this jurisdiction I had a cacao plantation and fruit trees with which I honorably sustained my home and family, but [once] those trees were lost, destroyed, and rendered useless I was left in need.[528]

Captain Carrillo's goal was to receive an "urgent" grant from His Majesty because the son of a nobleman (*hijodalgo*) linked to an extraordinary history of merits and family service could not simply be left to his fate. He petitioned for a grant "of any kind". His desperation was shared by other *colimenses*, like Captain Rodrigo de Brizuela, who in the same year (1627) put the hacienda of doña María de Monroy –at the time away in the Reinos de Castilla– in the Aguacatitlán Valley up for lease or sale. However, no one came forward because "it had deteriorated after being razed by a great hurricane that knocked down and uprooted the cacao and coconut trees".[529] Some notarial documents from that period record suspensions of interest payments that haciendas owed.[530] As late as October 1644, the ravages of the hurricane continued to impact owners, like Juan Jiménez de Nava, who petitioned for authorization to abandon his cacao hacienda in the Caxitlán Valley,

> because said hacienda has deteriorated, having lost its cacao trees due to the hurricane that struck this villa, leaving everything ruined and lost, and though from that time to the present I have made efforts to clean it up and look after it, they have been to no avail, for each year in addition to producing little fruit, trees have been consumed, weakened, and lost, and the few that remain are so damaged as to be unproductive.[531]

At that time, a dispute arose between Jiménez de Nava and the bachiller Mateo Ruiz Montaño, priest and beneficiado of the villa of Colima, because the hacienda paid interest on a chantry endowed years earlier. What we seek to demonstrate with these examples is the economic impact that some colimenses suffered after the hurricane of 1626, for they confirm that the decade of 1630 brought the dying gasps of cacao cultivation in Colima. Indeed, in 1649, Dr. Francisco Arnaldo Issasy reported in his Demarcación y descripción de el Obispado de Michoacán y Fundación de su Iglesia Cathedral, that the population around Colima "has declined... since a great hurricane destroyed the cacao plantations".[532]

What happened in Motines, on the other side of the Coahuayana River? Although we have no evidence as to whether the hurricane struck there as forcefully as in Colima, it is clear that the neighboring jurisdiction also suffered decline, for we cannot forget that the cacao hacienda owners there were also colimenses who, facing the uncertainty of such a delicate crop, did not deem it worthwhile to maintain their risky investments. In fact, the Relación geográfica de Motín, by Diego Alcalde de Rueda (1580), was perhaps a bad omen of what was to happen a few decades later, for it narrates that "hurricanes tend to occur in this province with winds so violent from this Mar del Sur, sometimes with rain, sometimes without, that strike with such impetus that they knock down very powerful trees no matter how solidly rooted".[533]

Colima's council did not simply stand aside in the aftermath of this emergency, but immediately addressed the Viceroy of New Spain, Rodrigo Pacheco y Osorio, Marqués de Cerralvo (1624-1635), to inform him that because a cyclone had devastated the cacao haciendas, the area urgently needed his authorization to "freely" produce and distribute vino de cocos, the drink that up to then had only circulated illegally. The cabildo warned that this was the only measure that would allow the villa of Colima

Part III

to recover from the catastrophe. Representing residents there, Captain Domingo Vela de Grijalva reported the following to Viceroy Pacheco y Osorio:

> the past year of six hundred and twenty-six a hurricane so strong uprooted and knocked down all the cacao trees, coconut palms, fruit trees, and cane fields in those valleys, leaving them desolate [and] causing many residents to lose their haciendas with which they sustained themselves [...] finding themselves forced to start over, [many] have chosen to go to other provinces where they feel they will have better conditions.[534]

Meanwhile, Juan de Sámano Quiñones, the *alcalde mayor* of Colima at the time, warned the Viceroy of the risk that the villa could be depopulated if preventive measures were not taken, since most residents had begun to turn to other horizons for work, food, and sustenance. For this reason, he threatened to impose severe sanctions on people who tried to abandon the villa. Sámano reminded the Viceroy of Colima's importance "in His Majesty's service by guarding the coasts of the Mar del Sur", certainly a valid argument.[535]

This was not the first time that both residents and authorities had responded in this tone in the face of dire circumstances, for in 1612, threatened with the elimination of all their palm trees, they had presented the same arguments regarding the important role that the province of Colima played in defending the Pacific coasts and the severe repercussions that the colonial administration would suffer if the area were abandoned. But what could be done about the current crisis? Was there any solution for the desolate panorama of residents immersed in poverty by the hurricane, after the loss of their cacao haciendas? The answer was "yes", but the only escape valve at hand was *vino de cocos*.

APOGEE AND DECLINE OF VINO DE COCOS (1627-1670)

The council of Colima's petition was successful, as Marqués de Cerralvo granted a license –the first of many– on March 4, 1627, authorizing free commerce of *vino de cocos* for a period of ten years, though only within the Reino de Nueva España, thus excluding Nueva Galicia.[536] The Viceroy's concession must be seen in the context of the privileges that some cities in Spanish America enjoyed; for example, authorization to cultivate certain plants that the Crown normally prohibited.[537] It is important to mention that the licenses to produce *vino de cocos* granted by Viceroys in New Spain had a maximum duration of ten years and were subject to renewal.[538] The 1627 license was, in fact, granted provisionally, "until such time as said cacao haciendas [recover]" from the hurricane, but that never occurred.

Immediately after the viceregal announcement that authorized the free production and trade of *vino de cocos*, official figures on this activity began to flow, curiously, from the ecclesiastical domain. The most important data are from the *Minuta dellas doctrinas que hay en este Obispado de Mechoacan de 1631*, a document we have referred to previously, and one that allows us to locate the palm haciendas and learn the number of *arrobas* or *botijas peruleras* produced annually. Then, based on those figures, we can estimate other aspects, such as the number of palm trees, the volume produced in liters, and its value (Table 25).

The information provided by the Filipino Miguel Pano in 1631 is important because from 100 palm trees he obtained one *arroba* per day; that is, 58 liters of *vino de cocos* per tree per year. This testimony coincides with current *vino de cocos* (*lambanog*) production in the Philippines, where producers obtain around 55 liters of aguardiente per palm tree. Since we have no other record of the number of trees per *arroba* reported in the *Minuta de 1631*–aside from Pano's– we took the productivity achieved by that Filipino as a reference and then, based on the number of *arrobas* of *vino de cocos* produced on the haciendas,

PART III

proceeded to calculate the other rubrics that appear in the following lines.

The Colima-Motines nucleus (Table 25) reported the highest aguardiente production at 15,521 *arrobas* annually. The locality of Tecolapa, with almost 20 haciendas, produced 8,000 *arrobas* of *vino de cocos* per year, far above production in the villa of Colima, which was just 1,700 *arrobas*, and in San Francisco de Almoloyan (1,025). The highest production in Motines was reported in Chiamila –4,198 *arrobas*– followed by Maquilí with 598.

Table 25. Annual *Vino de Cocos* Production in the Colima–Motines Nucleus (1631)

Hacienda(s)	Palm trees	Liters distilled	Arrobas	Value*
COLIMA				
VILLA DE COLIMA				
Aguacatitlán Valley	150	4 800	300	900 pesos
Tecuciapa Valley	75	2 400	150	450 pesos
Xicotlán Valley	25	800	50	150 pesos
Jala Valley	5	160	10	30 pesos
Caxitlán Valley	500	16,000	1,000	3,000 pesos
Zapotlanejo Valley	100	3,200	200	600 pesos
TOTAL	855	27,360	1 700	5,100 pesos
SAN FRANCISCO DE ALMOLOYAN				
Tecuciapa (A)[539]	182.5	5,840	365	1,095 pesos
Tecuciapa (B)	330	10,560	660	1,80 pesos
TOTAL	515.5	16,400	1,025	3,075 pesos

VINO DE COCOS, THE PILGRIM BEVERAGE

Hacienda(s)	Palm trees	Liters distilled	Arrobas	Value*
TECOLAPA				
	4,000	128,000	8,000	24,000 pesos
TOTAL	4,000	128,000	8,000	24,000 pesos
LOS MOTINES				
CHIAMILA				
Chiamila	319.5	10,224	639	1,917 pesos
Tepuxtitlán	319.5	10,224	639	1,917 pesos
Chiamila	182.5	5,840	365	1,095 pesos
Chiamila	45.5	1,456	91	273 pesos
Chiquivetlán	182.5	5,840	365	1,095 pesos
Salahuacán, Alima Valley	547.5	17,520	1,095	3,285 pesos
Achiotlán	182.5	5,840	365	1,095 pesos
Mexcala	182.5	5,840	365	1,095 pesos
Xutzintzin	182.5	5,840	365	1,095 pesos
TOTAL	2 144.5	68,624	4 289	12,867 pesos
MAQUILÍ				
Maquilí	91.2	2 920	182.5	547.5 pesos
Maquilí	91.2	2 920	182.5	547.5 pesos
San José, Maquilí	53	1 696	106	318 pesos
Maquilí	63.5	2 032	127	381 pesos
TOTAL	298.9	9 568	598	1,794 pesos

Source: with information from the *Minuta de 1631*, in Ramón López Lara, *El Obispado de Michoacán*, pp. 109-118. The estimates of the number of palm trees, volumes in liters, and profits, are mine.

PART III

We can establish, then, that in the decade 1622-1631, *vino de cocos* production increased by around 30% in the Colima-Motines nucleus, from 11,148 to 15,612 *arrobas*. That was the maximum production peak in the short history of this drink. Without doubt, the Viceroy's authorization influenced this increase. The Zacatula-Acapulco production nucleus (Table 26), however, presents a distinct panorama, as the three palm haciendas in Tecpan produced only 210 *arrobas*, while the one in Los Apasagualcos, property "of a rich man", contributed 300. But the total from both sources falls far short of the figure for Maquilí, the least productive site in the former nucleus. It is notable that Zacatula continued to report a strong presence of cacao production, suggesting that aguardiente complemented that activity in the economy there, but never replaced it, as occurred in Colima.

Table 26. Annual Vino de Cocos Production in the Zacatula–Acapulco Nucleus (1631)

Hacienda(s)	Palm trees	Liters distilled	Arrobas	Value
Tecpan (three haciendas)	105	3 360	210	630
Los Apasagualcos	150	4 800	300	900
TOTAL	255	8 160	510	1 530

Source: with information from the *Minuta de 1631*, in Ramón López Lara, *El Obispado de Michoacán*, pp. 130-132. The estimates of the number of palm trees, volumes in liters, and profits, are mine.

The question now is how long did the increase in *vino de cocos* production last? The answer is only a very short time. The most immediate historical source after the *Minuta de 1631* is the *Demarcación y descripción de el Obispado de Mechoacán* (1649) by Arnaldo Issasy. Referring to trade and profits in the Colima-Motines nucleus, Issasy stated that the towns of Caxitlán and Tecolapa, jurisdiction of Colima, had "eighteen palm haciendas that [produce] four or five thousand *arrobas* of wine each year";[540] that is, barely one-third of what was obtained twenty years earlier. Regarding Chiamila and Maquilí in the jurisdiction of Motines, he reported "some palms from which wine is made" in the former, and "coconut palms from which much wine is made as aguardiente" for the latter.[541] Unfortunately, Issasy does not provide quantitative data on these two towns, so it is not possible to estimate production for Motines in the mid-17th century. However, another source –tithe payments–confirms a marked decline in this economic activity, as we show in the following section.

Vino de Cocos and Tithes

Tithes records from the Bishopric of Michoacán are another historical source that provide insights into *vino de cocos* production. Enrique Florescano and Lydia Espinosa published serial records from those documents in 1987. Listings of tithes in Colima, including the jurisdiction of Motines, in that documental corpus begin in 1630 and end in 1670. Sadly, we have no records for the first three decades of the 17th century or for all the intermediate years of that period (Table 27). The authors explain that the gaps correspond to the period when these jurisdictions were administered under a regimen of leases.

Around 1608, the Bishopric of Michoacán determined that one of the products in the Colima-Motines nucleus that should be subject to the tithe was *vino de cocos*. Responding to that order, in February 1608 the *ayuntamiento* of Colima commissioned Gaspar Ramírez Alarcón to go to the capital, Valladolid, in its representation to manifest its inconformity "[for] the villa should not have to pay this tithe and new imposition [ordered] by the council of Michoacán [that obliges] residents to pay [the tithe?] on the *vino de cocos* they produce from palms in this province, and on the salt that residents make with their work and artifice".[542] The Bishopric of Michoacán had issued a provision allowing *colimenses* to pay tithes in these two products from that year forward, but that measure triggered a reaction by residents and authorities alike. In April of that year the *ayuntamiento* granted Antonio Lorenzo a second power-of-attorney to represent it before all instances necessary to appeal the provision.[543] But by then the decision had been taken and the *colimenses* had to obey. By 1610 we find that they were paying tithes on the palm aguardiente produced in Colima and Motines.[544] Though documents from the early decades of the 17th century are scarce, we know from doña Elvira Gómez de Moscoso's will that in 1612 she paid fifteen bushels (*almudes*) of cacao and one *botija perulera* of *vino de cocos* from her plantation in the Contla Valley, jurisdiction of Colima.[545]

A decade later, tithe payments from Colima and Motines included six barrels of *vino de cocos* and products like cacao, *Cassia fistula* (a flowering tree), and salt.[546] In 1622, the tithe collection site in Colima-Motines was put up for auction and acquired by Gonzalo Díaz Betancour, a resident of Valladolid who, upon setting the prices of products, fixed that of *vino de cocos* at 5 pesos per *arroba*, citing the "risk and luck" he ran because "those goods might be worth more or less".[547] That price was extremely high considering that records from the 1630s indicate a value of 2 or 3 pesos per *arroba* that later fell to just 1.5 (Table 27). As Florescano and Espinosa affirmed in their work, any extra benefits that lessors might obtain were theirs to keep, so they could obtain profits as high as 25%,[548] depending on the specific circumstances of each product and, surely, their ability as tithe collectors (*diezmeros*).

Table 27. Tithes Paid on Vino de Cocos from Colima (17th Century)

Year	Boti-jas	Estimated annual aguardiente production	Unit price	Tithes paid on aguardiente	Total tithes	%
1638	591	5,910	2	1,255.87	2,950.37	42.56
1639	613	6,130	2	1,264.75	3,098.25	40.82
1659	1,384	13 840	-	-	2,622.50	52.77
1662	670	6,700	1.5	1,005	2,047.62	49.08
1664	616	6,160	1.5	912	1,362.87	66.91
1665	677	6,770	-	-	25	-
1666	593	5,930	1.5	875.50	1,411.38	62.03
1668	598	5,980	1.5	887	1,397.50	63.47
1669	439	4,390	1.5	651.50	1,094.75	59.51
1670	482	4,820	1.5	715	1,377.00	51.92

Source: Enrique Florescano and Lydia Espinosa, Fuentes para el estudio de la agricultura, vol. 1, p. 256; AHCM, Cabildo, secc. Administración pecuniaria, Colecturía, Diezmo, exp. 90, 91.

Tithe records from Colima in 1636 make it possible to estimate the value of *vino de cocos* production in comparison to other products. The first aspect that drew our attention was that the tithes paid on the distillate in that year far exceeded those of other articles: 1,416 pesos 5 *tomines* for *vino de cocos*, 962 pesos 4 *tomines* for cattle, 256 pesos 6 *tomines* for cacao, and 245 pesos 4 *tomines* for corn. In total, *vino de cocos* represented 46% of all tithes collected. Some large producers stand out, like Captain Rodrigo de Brizuela who reported two tithe payments made on 224 *botijas* of *vino de cocos* that totaled 549 pesos; that is, almost one-third of all the tithes paid for the concept of *vino de cocos*.[549]

For the year 1637, the value of the tithes paid on *vino de cocos* in Colima continued in the lead: 1,358 pesos 7 *tomines*; far above those paid on steers and colts (611 pesos 6 *tomines*), corn (303 pesos), cacao (81 pesos 2 *tomines*), mules (63 pesos), honey (50 pesos), cheeses (38 pesos 1 *tomín*), foals (22 pesos 4 *tomines*), rice (8 pesos), and beans (1 peso 4 *tomines*). [550] For the 1638-1670 period, we have only the figures provided by Florescano and Espinosa, with few details on other products (Table 27).

From 1636 to 1670, there was a certain stability, as the price per *botija* began at 2.5 pesos before decreasing to 1.5 pesos as the 17th century advanced, with a mean annual production of 5,000-6,000 *botijas*, except for the year 1659, when the total production reported doubled. This figure coincided with the suspension of the royal monopoly (*estanco*) on *vino de cocos* and mezcal in Guadalajara, an event that would have incentivized an increase in production in Colima. We will analyze the topic of the monopoly in detail in a later chapter, for the aspect we wish to address now is the place that *vino de cocos* occupied in the economy of Colima-Motines.

According to these tithe records, on average this drink accounted for 54% of all tithes paid, a clear indication of the importance of this activity in local investment. It is a pity that these records were interrupted in 1670 and that when they reappeared in 1692, *vino de cocos* no longer appeared on the list, having been superseded by products like sugar and *panocha* (unrefined sugar), native grains like corn and beans, and livestock. This leads us to think that between 1670 and 1690 *vino de cocos* production ceased to be profitable and vanished from the economic panorama of the jurisdictions of Colima-Motines, a phenomenon accompanied by the growth of the sugar industry and competition from other distilled drinks that were making inroads into the market for alcoholic beverages in New Spain, such as mezcal and sugarcane aguardiente.

One final question: how reliable may these figures for tithes be for reconstructing real *vino de cocos* production in Colima? Our attention was called to the fact that in the year 1622, 11,148 *botijas* were recorded, while the figure for 1631 was 15,612.[551] Curiously, however, the tithes for 1636 indicate a production of just under 6,000 *botijas*. Is it possible that production of this distillate plummeted so drastically in such a short time? Or, perhaps, did these tithe figures underestimate the real volume? We are inclined to favor the latter view because a key for understanding such a discrepancy comes from a ledger dated in 1637 that recorded all loads of *vino de cocos* transported from Colima to other areas of New Spain, a source to which we will return in the next chapter. There we find records of an estimated 10,074 *botijas*,[552] although the tithe records for that year indicate a production of just 6,560. If this situation was repeated throughout the 17th century, it would mean that tithe payments are underestimated by 35%, and this is likely true, as well, for other figures we have at hand.

Regarding tithes in Zacatula, we have records for only two widely-spaced years, but they indicate that *vino de cocos* was a product that paid tithes in that *partido*. In 1668, aguardiente represented 5.43% of all tithes, but in 1692 that figure shrank to just 2.13% (Table 28). Based on these two sources it is difficult to ponder a broader panorama, especially since we do not know whether in the 1630s, surely a period of *vino de cocos* production, the drink was subject to the tithe or came to be taxed much later. The tithes for 1655, for example, reported some *botijas* of *vino de cocos* that came from the Tetitlán hacienda in Tecpan.[553] What we do know is that, unlike in Colima, cacao continued to be the principal crop in Zacatula, not only in the 17th century but well into the 18th. This suggests that in this production nucleus, *vino de cocos* was, above all, a complementary economic activity, never one of high priority, as it was in Colima. Interestingly, we have tithe records from the Tecpan-Atoyac *partido*, two localities that pertained to the *alcaldía mayor* of Zacatula where *vino de cocos* was being produced around 1631. But those records make no reference to tithe payments on palm aguardiente, perhaps because the series does not begin until the 1720s.

Table 28. Tithes Paid on Vino de Cocos from Zacatula (17th Century)

Year	Barrels	Price per barrel	Liters	Arrobas	Tithes on aguardiente	Total tithes	%
1668	6	32	456	28.5	24	441.37	5.43
1692	22	9.50	1,672	104.5	26.12	1 224.37	2.13

Source: Florescano and Espinosa, *Fuentes para el estudio de la agricultura*, vol. 2, p. 458.

Another interesting inference that can be drawn from this series of tithes is the price of a *botija* of *vino de cocos*. In Colima, this decreased by 3 and 2 pesos in the first half of the 17th century, to 1.5 pesos after 1650. For Zacatula, the value was estimated not per *botija* but by barrel (approx. 76 liters/barrel), though two figures from that series are disconcerting: in 1668, the barrel was valued in five pesos, but by 1692 the price had fallen below one peso. Finally, it is paradoxical that the largest *vino de cocos* producing area –the Colima-Motines nucleus– did not report any production after 1690, but Zacatula registered 22 barrels in 1692, though in the following year aguardiente disappeared once again from the list of tithes. The scanty nature of the data available make it difficult to explain that phenomenon.

LIGHTS AND SHADOWS OF VINO DE COCOS (1670-1700)

Notarial documents mention two phenomena that occurred in the second half of the 17th century and impacted *vino de cocos* production: on the one hand, numerous sales and transfers of palm haciendas that, presumably, no longer generated sufficient profits to pay chantries; on the other, a geographic shift of those properties toward the environs of the villa of Colima, which coincided with the sales and transfers of haciendas in the Caxitlán and Alima Valley near the coast.

Transfers of Haciendas and Chantries

The Real Audiencia of Mexico's order of 1612 that dictated the massive hewing of all palm trees in Colima revealed the economic interests of the clergy –regular and secular– in *vino de cocos* production. On that occasion, Juan Polonte, a priest and witness to the evidence that *vino de cocos* producers presented in their defense, stated that the "palm haciendas" were burdened with 40,000 pesos in loans (*censuses*) related to the many chantries endowed by residents of Colima:

> Be it known that on the orchards and haciendas where said coconut palms are planted, in this jurisdiction as in the Alima Valley, a very large amount of pesos, that [as loans] total over 40,000 pesos, is imposed and charged for chantries served and prayed by the beneficiaries of this villa, and some priests who were ordained under their titles.[554]

According to Alberto Carrillo Cázares, in the 17th century chantries emerged as a way for priests who sought greater freedom in their religious functions to make a living, "though modest and limited".[555] Around 1650, however, the imposition of the loans for chantries and pious works that had burdened numerous palm haciendas for decades began to drown their owners in debt. For this reason, by the second half of the 17th century many plantation owners found they could no longer pay the interest charges. As is widely known, chantries were endowments in which a primary loan was made on a certain property at an annual charge of 5%, above all, for the sustenance of the head priest. Thus, the haciendas that individuals acquired often came with an established chantry that bound them to pay 5% to an ecclesiastical institution administered by a chantry (*cofradía*) or religious order. Paying a chantry during the bonanza of *vino de cocos* would not have caused any great inconvenience, but when production stagnated and ceased to be so profitable, plantation owners found themselves in such economic straits that many opted to abandon or sell their properties.

In 1654, Pedro de Cevallos, a priest in Colima appeared before the *alcalde ordinario* to certify the transfer[556] of a palm hacienda in the Caxitlán Valley that was burdened by a loan of 500 pesos, "because said hacienda is deteriorating every day [since] it does not have sufficient resources (*avíos*) and requires many outlays due to the difficulty in conducting water for irrigation". We see that this was not an opportune time to invest in palm haciendas, as this sale was announced for 30 days but no one showed interest, until Bernardo de Novela decided to buy it for 500 pesos that included the interest due on the chantry.[557]

In 1654, don Martín Esteban de Velasco, the *alcalde mayor* of Colima from 1643 to 1645, abandoned his hacienda in Aguacatitlán for the same reasons as Cevallos; that is, he could not maintain it, obtaining water was difficult, and he had acquired it with a pending debt for chantries that bound him to pay 115 pesos annually and tribute to three chantries: Santísimo Sacramento, Nuestra Señora del Rosario, and Ánimas del Purgatorio.[558] In both cases, the problems involving water drew our attention since both the Caxitlán and Aguacatitlán Valley were located near rivers. Had a drought that year altered the availability of this hydric resource? We do not know, but the sale was to be announced for 30 days to attract a buyer.

Finally, after the 24th announcement, on August 23, 1656, a mestizo named Alonso Martín offered a capital of 550 "*al quita*" (release), an amount far below what Captain Velasco owed. But as no other potential buyer came forth, usufruct rights to the hacienda in Aguacatitlán passed to Martín who could exploit "all the lands [and] water belonging to the hacienda that Captain Martín Esteban de Velasco possessed". We learn that Alonso later regretted his decision, for on January 18, 1657, the *mayordomo* of the Nuestra Señora del Rosario chantry petitioned the authorities in Colima to search for him and force him to keep his word, since "he has not deigned to come and sign the obligatory document of sale, though we have called on him and, through letters and people, urged him to come and fulfill the obligation of ensuring the hacienda", but he had gone into hiding, unwilling to appear. [559]

Similar cases occurred in the second half of the 17th century: in 1669, Santiago Rejón, a resident of Colima, petitioned to abandon his hacienda because he could no longer pay the 7.5 pesos in interest on a capital of 150 pesos, "because those lands are not convenient for me [...] I have paid without [cultivating] them for more than five years [though] when they were sold [I was told] they had sufficient water to produce, but they do not". In reality, Rejón made his request only after being notified, under threat of excommunication, that he was bound to pay 30 pesos in back interest because no payments had been made for four-and-a-half years.[560]

In contrast, the year 1679 seems to have been an especially rainy one because swollen rivers flooded some palm haciendas, like that of Francisco Ruiz Quintero, a *colimense* who petitioned to abandon 40 palm trees that belonged to the convent of Nuestra Señora de las Mercedes in the Contla Valley,[561] which he had worked for 18 years because, he affirmed, "today they are rendered useless by the floodings of the past year", leaving him unable to pay the annual interest of five pesos.[562] The acts with the description that Francisco Aguiar y Seixas presented in 1680 mention that Bartolomé Rodríguez' palm hacienda in Colima "was lost [...] this year for the river swept the palm plantation away".[563] This confirms just how vulnerable economic activities in Colima were to natural phenomena of this kind.

Thanks to the acts of the pastoral visits by Aguiar y Seixas in 1680, we know that the *partido* of San Salvador Chiamilan, Bishopric of Michoacán, still had some palm haciendas,[564] properties that belonged to don Joseph Beltrán, Captain Francisco Rodríguez, Mateo de Ahumada, doña María de Contreras, Lorenzo de Ventura, Sergeant-Major Pedro de Ventura Sáez, and Juan de Novela.[565] However, we have only scarce data on the number of trees there or the volume of aguardiente production. In fact, a succinct description of the activities of the Indians in those towns states that "[they] have no trades. Some are muleteers, some produce salt on their own, others for Spaniards".[566] This suggests that the Indians did not perform labors related to the palm haciendas.

Table 29. Chantries and Palm Haciendas in Colima–Motines (1680)

Names	Capital	Interest	Chantry
Haciendas with taxed chantries			
Pedro López de Herrera Catarina Botello	200 pesos	10 pesos	Priests of Colima
Álvaro de Herrera Isabel Ruiz	500 ps	25 ps	Priests of Colima
Clemente Hidalgo de Agüero	1,000 ps	50 ps	Priests of Colima
Melchora Fernández	400 ps	20 ps	Priests of Colima
Antonio de Ocampo	40 ps	2 ps	Vacant Council seat

Names	Capital	Interest	Chantry
Juan Carrillo de Guzmán	400 ps	20 ps	Vacant Council seat
Unknown	250 ps	12 ps 4 r	Vacant Council seat
TOTAL	2,790 ps	139 ps 4 r	
Haciendas without taxed chantries			
Captain Joseph Beltrán Captain Francisco Rodríguez Lorenzo Ventura Pedro de Ventura Sáez Mateo de Ahumada Juan de Novela			

Source: Alberto Carrillo, Michoacán en el otoño del siglo XVII, pp. 399-402, 422-427.

Another finding that allows us to confirm the decline and reduced profitability of aguardiente production is the low interest that was being paid on chantries in the late 17th century. In fact, notarial documents from the 18th century show that the foundations for pious works were no longer related to palm haciendas but, rather, to saltworks; indicating that this economic activity stood out above all others.

Unfortunately, the Descripción ordered by Aguiar y Seixas for the partido of Zacatula, signed by the deputy Diego Magdaleno de Liébana in 1683, contains scarce information, only a brief census of the villa and its residents. It says absolutely nothing about their properties and respective chantries, data that would shed light on the possible continuation of activities involving vino de cocos there.[567]

On the topic of religious orders in Colima, José Miguel Romero de Solís reported that two orders –San Juan de Dios (juaninos) and the convent of Nuestra Señora de la Merced (mercedarios)– established houses in Colima at that time and had economic interests that centered on haciendas.⁵⁶⁸ Although the regular clergy were prohibited from owning property, those two orders acquired patrimonial property through donations or by taxing chantries on certain properties, like haciendas. As time passed, however, and the relatives of the deceased could no longer pay, they often opted to leave their properties in the hands of the regular clergy who could then lease them or administer the lands themselves. It is precisely the latter scenario that was observed from the decade of 1650 onwards.

In 1668, the Mercedarians sold a hacienda with a burden in this area to Domingo de Solórzano, but he stated that the palm trees were transferred to him in poor condition, "barren, hilly, and lost". With time, Solórzano made some improvements, "with houses, an oven, cleaning [the trees] and [digging] ditches to irrigate those palms". But by 1675, he could no longer pay the interest (5 pesos annually on a capital of 300 pesos) and petitioned to abandon the hacienda and return it to the friars of the convent of Nuestra Señora de la Merced. This sparked a dispute between the two parties, as the Mercedarians alleged that they could not maintain the property and that Solórzano had an obligation to fulfill his commitment.⁵⁶⁹

To close the century, in 1697 we have the case of Pablo de Espinosa, a resident of the Caxitlán Valley who recognized that the palm hacienda he possessed there "is of no use to me whatsoever, and that [...] I have fallen behind and lost because [it] produced so little fruit and because to pay the interest I have been pawning [property] and drowning in debt".⁵⁷⁰ This may well have been so, when we consider that the loan on that property was one thousand pesos and he had to pay 50 pesos annually for the chantry that had been imposed for the mortal soul of don Clemente Hidalgo de Agüero, an important clerk in the scribes' office of the council of Colima in the first half of the 17th century.⁵⁷¹

Finally, in 1702, the commendator of the convent of Nuestra Señora de la Merced, Friar Juan de Garfias, put the loans of two abandoned haciendas up for sale, one in the Alima Valley, jurisdiction of Motines, "which had cacao and vanillas, that has been abandoned for many years and is lost, named Zapotlán [...] the other named San Juan del Monte [...] that had coconut palms".[572] Both properties were purchased for a census of 100 pesos by don Juan de Abárzuza, a *colimense* with interests in the *vino de cocos* trade, the same man who, in the 1690s, had petitioned the Real Audiencia of Mexico to grant permanent licenses for the free sale of aguardiente.[573]

What happened, meanwhile, in the *vino de cocos* production nucleus of Zacatula-Acapulco? One clear case was that of the hacienda de San Pablo in the Petatlán Valley, a property purchased between 1602 and 1609 by the priest Juan de Carvajal that included "a piece of [cacao] orchard and a few coconut palms". There were two *caballerías* of land on which rested a chantry of 2,800 pesos, without doubt an excessive amount. A cursory look in 1679 showed that the land "no longer had a house or dwelling, nor cacao trees [and] only one coconut palm with fruits can be seen [but they] could not be counted due to the height and thickness of the grass there". A witness valued the property in 800 pesos but it was only sold at that price with difficulty, constituting a great loss for the economy and the Church. A canon from Valladolid affirmed that due to the high interest on the chantry, for 45 years "no one has resided there nor [taken responsibility] for the [debt]". Is this situation comparable to the case of Colima, where it is clear that the dynamism of the haciendas that produced *vino de cocos* declined significantly in the second half of the 17th century?[574]

It seems that the situation in Tecpan did not evolve better than in Colima. In 1649, the aforementioned Issasy reported the presence of "palm coconuts from which wine is made on one or two haciendas of *chinos*",[575] but activity there seemed marginal compared to other plantations that were still profitable, such as the ones that harvested cacao. Earlier, we mentioned the hacienda of Nuestra

Señora del Buen Suceso as one where *vino de cocos* was produced. The property inventory made there in 1647 by the *alguacil* of Acapulco, Captain Pedro de Carrascosa, can serve as a reference, as it mentions "a large salon, two chambers and two storerooms, one for cacao, another for maintenance, five rooms where people live, a bowl where *tuba* is cooked, two wooden buckets for making wine from *tuba*, 40 *tecomates* for gathering *tuba*" [and] a vat from China...".[576] Clearly, the *tecomates*, a kind of gourd in which *tuba* was collected, were utilized to harvest sap from at least four dozen palms, so this was definitely a hacienda dedicated to *vino de cocos* production.

Movement of the Haciendas: From the Coast Inland

Another phenomenon observed in the evolution of palm haciendas in the second half of the 17th century, aside from the sales and transfers discussed above, was the movement of *vino de cocos* production toward the area north of the Armería River, closer to the villa of Colima. At that time, several palm production units were established around the Indian towns of Nahualapa, Coquimatlán, and Quizalapa at altitudes below 400 m.a.s.l., far from the coast.

It is important to mention that the Nahualapa Valley did not appear among the major *vino de cocos* production sites in the first half of the 17th century. The nearest places were Zapotlanejo, Xicotlán, Jala, and Tecuciapa. At a later date, Tecuciapa was integrated into Nahualapa, so the question arises as to whether this was a new producing region, strategically located near the villa of Colima. The tendency to move palm haciendas closer to that villa can be explained by the advantage of not having to ship aguardiente from Caxitlán and Alima.

A map from 1688 that Francisco Martínez de Moscoso of Colima presented with his petition to install a sugar mill (*trapiche*) shows that at least four palm haciendas existed within a league of the town of Nahualapa (Illustration 17).

Those properties belonged to Martínez Moscoso himself (in the center), a woman identified as "the widow of Anaya", Juan de la Cruz and Andrés Pérez, and Captain Brizuela, whose hacienda we mentioned earlier.[577] The location of these plantations confirms the importance of obtaining water from the nearby river to irrigate the palms and the proximity of the Royal road (*Camino Real*) that ran from the villa of Colima to Caxitlán, and from there to the saltworks in Cuyutlán on the coast. Thus, those haciendas were situated along the commercial route for *vino de cocos* and salt.

Illustration 17. Plan of the Palm Haciendas in the Nahualapa Valley (1688)

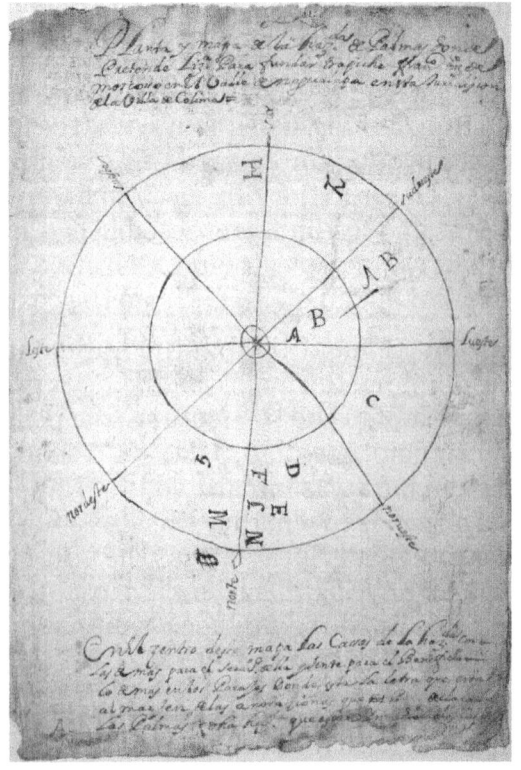

Source: AHMC, Fondo Sevilla del Río, Caja 5, exp. 9.

Part III

Description of the map: [578]

(A) The hacienda's palm trees, near the houses.

(B) Sites of two sugarcane fields a block from the house, and two *caballerías* of deforested land, partly cultivated, abutting a hill and the bank of a river that runs southward.

(C) Palm hacienda of Juan de la Cruz, neighboring that of Francisco Martínez de Moscoso.

(D) Hacienda of the widow of Anaya, neighboring that of Francisco Martínez.

(E) Hacienda of Andrés Pérez, neighboring those properties.

(F) Forest up to the margins of the *Camino Real* from the villa to Caxitlán.

(G) The same woodlands with barren lands that neighbor on that hacienda up to the letter that indicates it.

(H) Hacienda of Captain Nicolás de Brizuela that neighbors those lands.

(Y) Summit of the hill marking the boundaries of those lands with sugarcane fields.

(L) Town of Nahualapa, a league from that hacienda.

(M) Town of Coquimatlán, at two leagues distance.

(N) Town of Quezalapa, three leagues from that hacienda.

An examination of a purchase-sale contract from 1692 by the mestiza María Pano Carrillo –the first wife of Miguel Pano, an *indio chino vinatero*– in the Nahualapa Valley, shows an increase in the number of palm haciendas in that area.[579] Her hacienda, with 115 palms, which she later sold to Diego Pérez de Espinosa, had the following boundaries: the lower part with the palm hacienda that once belonged to Juan López de Ansa but was now owned by Juan Carrillo de Guzmán; the upper part with lands of the town of Nahualapa. The back area abutted the site of the sugar mill and palms belonging to Francisco Martínez de Moscoso, the man who presented the map and eventually received authorization to install the mill. María Pano sold the property with its cabins, sources of water, entrances and exits, and fruit trees. The will left by Captain Nicolás de Brizuela in October 1702, revealed that his properties included a hacienda with 400 palms in Nahualapa, "equipped with botijas and an oven".[580] Why was the Nahualapa Valley deemed more attractive than the Caxitlán Valley? The answer was its proximity to the villa of Colima, where most hacienda owners resided.

What happened to production in the Caxitlán Valley and the jurisdiction of Motines? We found some purchase-sale agreements from the late 17th century. In 1689, Joseph Vázquez, a resident of Caxitlán, agreed to pay Juan de Carvajal 240 pesos for 80 palms "to make *vino de cocos*" there.[581] In the same year, Lorenzo de Villa sold García Solano, another resident of Colima, a hacienda with 40 palms for *vino de cocos* production near the town of Zinacamitlán, jurisdiction of Motines, at a price of 20 *reales* per palm, for a total of 100 pesos.[582]

These two transactions suggest, first, that very few trees were involved and, second, that the price per tree had fallen from 4 pesos (the average in the first half of the 17th century) to just 20 *reales* (2.5 pesos). We identified another hacienda, this one in the will of doña María de Contreras in 1693 in which she bequeathed a property called Zapotlanejo with 500 palm trees, "some old, some new, but all in production for some time", and associated equipment: an oven, botijas, and gourds for *tuba*.[583] The fact that there were "new" palms suggests that interest in renewing plantations to produce *vino de cocos* persisted into the late 17th century.

We can cite other examples: in September 1691, Andrés de Mata sold a palm hacienda in the Caxitlán Valley to the priest Ambrosio de Loayza Trujillo for 200 pesos. That transaction included all entrances and exits, an oven for making wine, a barrel, two vats, six gourds, and two botijas *castellanas*; that is, all the inputs required to produce aguardiente. The purchase-sale contract states, as well, that the hacienda had 55 palm trees in production and 16 small palms. This shows that although this was a period of clear decline in *vino de cocos* production, some people were still willing to take a chance on this economic activity.[584]

PART III

In October of that year, doña Andrea Rosales transferred a hacienda with 80 palm trees and two *caballerías* of land to a scribe in Colima, Policarpo Alfonso de Tovar, on the "condition that within one year he plant two hundred more palms than those on the hacienda".[585] But it is a map that don Hilario Ceballos presented in 1720 that best evidences this venturesome spirit to plant more coconut palms.

Illustration 18. Plan of the House of Don Hilario Ceballos (1720)

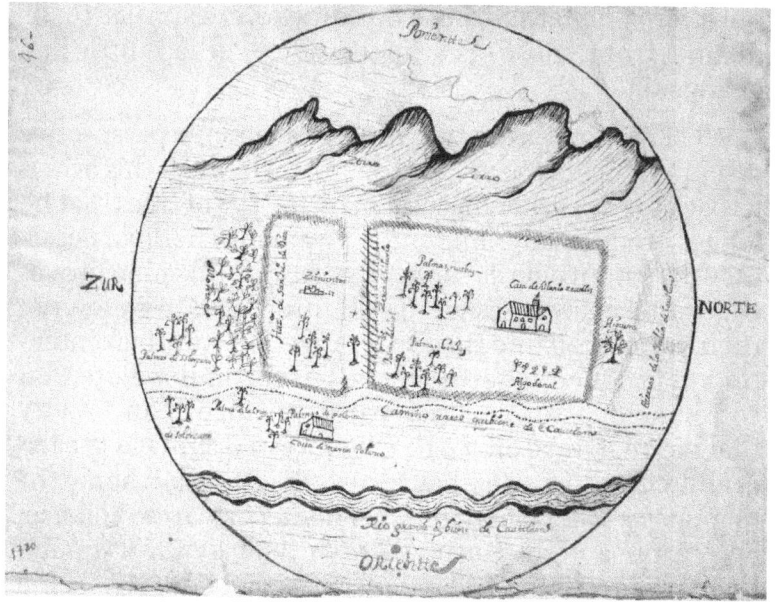

Source: AHMC, Fondo Sevilla del Río, caja 5, exp. 11.

This interesting illustration shows Ceballos' home with some palm trees and adjacent units. From an architectural perspective, Luis Gabriel Gómez Azpeitia emphasized that Ceballos' home was "finely expressed with great elegance", consisting of two floors and a tower that, the author surmises, may have been a mirador. It appears to be a solid house with walls of adobe or stone and a tile roof.

"The presence of three openings on the ground floor, like doors, leads us to think that there was probably a corridor around the property, or one that at least bounded one of its façades". The house drawn below, property of Marcos Polanco, is more modest, but has similar characteristics of construction. "Two openings on the ground floor also lead us to think of a perimeter corridor, which is not rare according to the oral tradition, that today refers to this type of rural construction as a 'hacienda house'".[586] The scarcity of visual representations of this kind in the 17th century, with landscapes of palm haciendas raises the question of whether those buildings were similar to, or distinct from, those of earlier decades. Perhaps little had changed.

What drew our attention from an economic perspective is the presence of "new" and "old" palm trees, as this brings us back to the earlier discussion on the age of trees that no longer produced the amount of raw material (*tuba*) necessary to sustain *vino de cocos* production. This map proves that some *colimenses* were still interested in renewing their palms well into the 18th century, but was their intention to produce aguardiente or sell coconuts? Note that cotton fields also appeared, early evidence of an activity that began to take off in the province of Colima in the 18th century. Note, as well, that around don Hilario's home the map shows other palm units, belonging to Marcos Polanco, Solórzano, and the Hospital de San Juan de Dios, though they were apparently abandoned. Gabriel Gómez Azpeitia suggests that Solórzano's trees belonged to Juan Manuel Solórzano –nickname, *el Chino*– who, he wrote, was a prosperous *vino de cocos* producer in the early 18th century.[587] Though we have been unable to find information on this man, he was certainly among the last palm aguardiente producers in Colima. If this map was indeed drawn in 1720, then we must recall that in 1724 the Viceroy ordered the eradication of all "drinks of the land" (*bebidas de la tierra*), including *vino de cocos*. Whatever the case, that was a period of sharp decline, and the Viceroy's ordinance just delivered the final blow to a once profitable activity that would soon collapse due to the circumstances we discuss in the following section.

THE EXTINCTION OF VINO DE COCOS (1700-1724)

To what can we attribute the stagnation and subsequent decline of *vino de cocos*? There is no simple answer because multiple factors were involved. We know that *vino de cocos* disappeared from contemporary documents early in the 18th century, for we no longer find references to master *vinateros*, hacendado producers, or commercializers. Apart from the cases mentioned above, one of the very few references after the year 1700 involved Felipe González de León, who in 1705 took four loads of *vino de cocos* to Zacatecas, where he offered the *botija* at a price of 18-20 *reales* (around 2.5 pesos), while a complete load was valued in 5 pesos.[588] Though later testimonies contain news of palm trees, they no longer mention *vino de cocos*. Clearly, the economy had shifted, as we will now elucidate.

Changes in the Agricultural Panorama

It is interesting to note that in the mid-17th century new crops were integrated into the palm haciendas. In the jurisdictions of Colima and Motines, and in that of Zacatula, we begin to see vanillas cultivated (*Vanilla planifolia* L.) for chocolate. As Henry Bruman insightfully pointed out, toward the end of the 16th century improved recipes for preparing hot chocolate began to appear with the incorporation of additives like sugar. This created new demand for vanilla for this purpose.[589] European markets imported vanilla from diverse production centers, such as Soconusco, Suchitepec, Veracruz, and Guatemala, so the plantations in Colima and Zacatula must be inscribed in that context. In fact, from 1667 to 1763, vanilla from Zacatula reported tithe payments amounting to 3,354 pesos, with a peak in 1695, when this plant represented 53% of total tithes for the year.[590]

Among the new crops incorporated into palm haciendas we also find sugarcane. A case in point is the Santa Ana hacienda in Aguacatitlán where witnesses in 1723 stated that it had "a few small palm trees", but had begun to cultivate sugarcane. Aguacatitlán had been characterized by *vino de cocos* production throughout the 17th century, but in the 18th it mirrored a process that was occurring on other haciendas in the zone as well.[591]

At some point, cultivation of *Cassia fistula* L. (golden shower) and achiote (*Bixa orellana* L.) also began in Colima with the objective of commercializing them in markets in New Spain, though that business seems to have been only ephemeral in the first half of the 17th century. We were able to detect the presence of these crops on three or four cacao and palm haciendas in 1622. *Cassia fistula* trees were valued at one peso and production was destined mainly for markets in Mexico City,[592] where a *botija* sold for 7 pesos.[593] In that year, tithes in the provinces of Colima and Motines were paid in cacao, *vino de cocos*, and *Cassia fistula*, demonstrating the importance that the latter product had achieved.[594] Achiote, which was also worth one peso per tree, was "exploited and profitable"[595] in the 1620s. In addition to reaching kitchens in New Spain, it must have been important for the colorants market. The only year in which tithes were charged on achiote was 1639.[596]

In the case of Zacatula, cacao continued to be a pillar of the economy, even after the turn of the 18th century. We must recall that Zacatula was not affected by the catastrophic hurricane that razed Colima in 1626, and that Mexico City, the area's principal market, continued to procure supplies from that region. The appearance of other crops, including rice, along the coastal strip of the Pacific Ocean thanks to the Manila Galleon, diversified agricultural activities in a nucleus where *vino de cocos* production never emerged as a main source of sustenance. By 1649, Tecpan had "corn, cotton and millet, and rice, much cacao, vanillas, tamarinds, coconuts grow...".[597] Déborah Oropeza emphasized the importance of the Asian population in introducing crops of Asian origin like rice and tamarind. As early as 1584, tamarind trees were seen in the yard of an *indio chino* named Juan Rodríguez on the outskirts of Acapulco, while around the same time, the hospital of Acapulco spent part of its budget to purchase foods like rice, cloves, and pepper because the cook was a *chino* named Gaspar who surely taught others how to incorporate these ingredients into their own dishes.[598]

What relation can we establish between the decline of *vino de cocos* and the onset of other agricultural activities? First, it is clear that Zacatula, a modest *vino de cocos* producer in the 17th century, never based its economy on that distillate, but relied on cacao and other crops, including vanilla. In reality, cacao cultivation was more profitable in Zacatula than Colima, in part because the latter was located over one hundred leagues from the capital of New Spain with the attendant difficulties and costs of transport, while Zacatula was closer and, having avoided the destruction of the 1626 hurricane, succeeded in maintaining this activity with no complications.

Colima, however, offered a distinct panorama: in addition to the distance from Mexico City –the main market for its cacao– and the crisis triggered by the hurricane, it apparently found an economic alternative in *vino de cocos* production since the largest markets for aguardiente were the mining zones in northern New Spain. In this sense, Colima held a clear advantage over Zacatula. But as other distilled drinks appeared and began to flood those markets, *vino de cocos* production ceased to be profitable, forcing the *colimenses* to find crops that could replace its palm trees. Those turned out to be sugarcane and cotton.

What happened to the palm trees in Colima-Motines and Zacatula-Acapulco? Indications are that production was reoriented toward coconut fruit, which was transported along the same trade routes as aguardiente. The decline of *vino de cocos* did not extinguish the palm haciendas; rather, they shifter their operations toward selling coconuts. In 1705 and subsequent years, muleteers from Colima transported loads of coconut to Zacatecas and Mexico City. In Zacatecas, a dozen coconuts sold for 6 *reales* (half a *real* per nut), while the cost in Mexico City ranged from 8 to 10 *reales*.[599] It is no accident that tithe records in Colima from 1725 to 1756 list 543 loads of coconuts valued at 1,321.75 pesos. This phenomenon was repeated in Zacatula between 1665 and 1724, though the number of loads was undetermined and the contribution to tithes was only 48 pesos.[600] Could it be that from early times Zacatula had oriented palm tree exploitation toward producing fruit, instead of *vino de cocos*, due to demand in Mexico City for coconut shells to elaborate *cocos chocolateros*? This is a possibility that must be explored.

Regarding the jurisdiction of Motines, Gerardo Sánchez affirms that a description of this zone from the final decade of the 18th century –a period quite distant from the one analyzed here– showed that the community of Maquilí:

> possessed, together with the saltworks at the mouth of the Aquila River, a little over 500 palm trees in production, while the community of Pómaro had some 2,000 palms, planted around the inlet of Maruata. However, the author of the report deplored the meager profits that the communal palm trees yielded due to the difficulties of the roads that [hindered] muleteers from taking the fruits to diverse markets in the center of the Vice-Royalty. In that period, the jurisdiction of Apatzingán reported palm trees associated with banana, orange, mamey, and tamarind plantations. In various towns, like San Juan Andacutiro, the Urecho Valley, and Santa Ana Amatlán, dried coconuts, *Cassia fistula*, and bananas came to constitute the main branch of regional trade.[601]

Part III

We end this section with the following reflection. The 18th century was characterized by broad changes in the patterns of consumers, a social phenomenon evidenced in the textile and food industries with protagonists that included natural resources like cotton and sugar. Luis Alonso Álvarez observed that, in the long term, those changes stimulated the appearance of massive demand due to the growth of profits and population, "that, in turn, will make artisanal products obsolete and unviable [but] a generalized change in technology essential [with] production on a scale characteristic of industrial processes".[602] Though Alonso Álvarez wrote these lines to exemplify the case of tobacco, can some kind of change in consumption patterns of *vino de cocos* be pondered? We believe the answer is 'yes': the emergence of other distilled drinks, elaborated with raw materials that were easier to access, would have accelerated the decline of palm aguardiente, as we argue in the following section.

The Entrance of Other Distilled Drinks

In addition to the diversification of crops in the Colima-Motines and Zacatula nuclei in the 17th century, distinct factors influenced the decline of *vino de cocos*. One was the appearance of other distilled drinks, like mezcal and sugarcane aguardiente. Mezcal debuted in Nueva Galicia in the first half of the 17th century, and its arrival was clearly related to the technique of distilling *vino de cocos*. By 1616, mezcal was being produced in the province of Ávalos and fabrication was underway in the sierra of Nayarit by 1621,[603] while by the 1630s, when the royal monopoly on *vino de cocos* and mezcal was imposed in Guadalajara, that drink was being produced in some abundance.

Production of sugarcane aguardiente –*chinguiritos*– was consolidated from the 17th century onward. José Jesús Hernández Palomo observed that in 1631 Marqués de Cerralvo issued an order prohibiting consumption of this drink,[604] and Teresa Lozano Armendares states that from the 1630s people had begun to elaborate distillates with the honey that flowed from sugarcane plants. For these reasons, ordinances in 1631, 1635, and 1699 repeated the prohibition on distilling the juices of the sugarcane and maguey plants, alleging that the drinks produced cause severe problems among the Indians.[605] That series of prohibitions indicates that, in reality, clandestine production continued, though the apogee of *chinguiritos* consumption did not come until the late 18th century when it could be sold legally, just as had occurred decades earlier with *vino de cocos*.

By the mid-17th century, wine and aguardiente produced in Santa María de las Parras were circulating freely in the mining zones of the north. Documents from Mazapil indicate that in addition to mezcal, other alcoholic drinks elaborated in northern New Spain were being commercialized in the center of the Vice-Royalty.[606] Since the 17th century, Parras had emerged as a key area of wine production (drinks called *caldos*), and in the following century it obtained tax exemptions (including from the *alcabalas*) from the Crown. The production of aguardiente made from pomace (*orujo*) in that zone emerged to satisfy a large part of the demand and came to be commercialized from Santa Fe in New Mexico to Mexico City.[607]

In summary, in the second half of the 17th century we find that the market for distilled drinks in New Spain had at least three competitors: *vino de cocos*, mezcal, and *chinguiritos*. All three shared certain key characteristics: as distillates, they reached levels of alcohol by volume above 30-40 degrees that made them more attractive than fermented drinks, and precisely because they were distilled they could be transported over long distances with no risk of spoilage. *Vino de cocos* was at a significant disadvantage compared to mezcal and *chinguiritos* due to the fact that gathering its raw material, *tuba*, was risky and much more difficult and required the highly-skilled, extremely demanding work of *tuberos*. Finally, the cultivation of coconut palm trees was limited geographically to isolated coastal zones or warm-humid lowlands. Agave, in contrast, had several species that could be used to produce mezcal, and they were distributed throughout New Spain. Arregui wrote that making mezcal only required cooking the agave shoots (today called *piñas* in Spanish) then pressing them to yield a most that was distilled in a rustic still (*alquitara*) to obtain a wine that is "clearer than water, stronger than aguardiente, and very flavorful".[608] But peasants did not have to climb trees twice day, 365 days a year, to ensure maximum yields, as was the case with *tuba*, where the additional risk of falling from towering palm trees made work unattractive. Gathering the raw material for *chinguiritos* presented no great difficulty either, as Teresa Lozano observed: "the few elements necessary for setting up a workshop, added to the speed of elaboration, and low prices at which it could be sold, made this commerce very attractive to anyone".[609]

Thus, with aging palm trees that may not have been replaced as a common practice in the 17th century, the entrance of other distilled drinks like mezcal and *chinguiritos*, and broader changes in the agricultural panorama, the palm haciendas experienced a serious decline over the final years of that century. But political factors also intervened, especially the 1724 decree by Viceroy Juan de Acuña y Bejarano, Marquis de Casafuerte, that prohibited all "drinks of the land", including *vino de cocos*.

Diverse colonial sources from the 18th-century attest to the disappearance of *vino de cocos* from the Colima landscape. In January 1744, don Juan de Montenegro, the *justicia mayor* and *capitán a guerra* for the jurisdiction of Colima, wrote that the main product traded in that demarcation at that time was salt, which benefitted Indians and Spaniards alike:

> trade and commerce of the *vino de cocos* that was produced in this jurisdiction on palm haciendas owned by Spaniards

and Indians have fallen into complete decadence, having been prohibited by the Duke of Alburquerque, Viceroy of this New Spain, [though it] contributed greatly to trade and contracts in this Republic as there are no species of metal here".[610]

In 1776, the *alcalde mayor*, Miguel José Pérez Ponce de León, mentioned that a few palm haciendas still existed on the coast of Colima, some cultivated to produce fruit for industry, but others continued to harvest *tuba*, thus demonstrating that this activity survived at least to the end of the colonial period, and revealing why *colimenses* maintain this tradition (Illustration 19). Ponce de León knew, however, that "when [distilled] *tuba* produces [a strong] aguardiente [...], in whose commerce residents participated freely, as today they do with *tuba* [...] the superior government prohibited production of that aguardiente [but] some continued to work despite that order".[611] This citation may be the final reference to *vino de cocos* production in Colima, because a *bando* issued by the *ayuntamiento* on January 6, 1773, "established and ordered that no *chinguiritos*, contraband *mistelas*, *tepaches*, *tubas*, mezcals or any other beverage of those prohibited in the repeated high orders of the superior government shall be allowed. Only the sale of legitimate wines from Spain shall be licensed".[612] Clearly, as far as the local authorities were concerned, *vino de cocos* had been forgotten.

Part III

Illustration 19. A Common Landscape in Colima with Coconut Palms (1802)

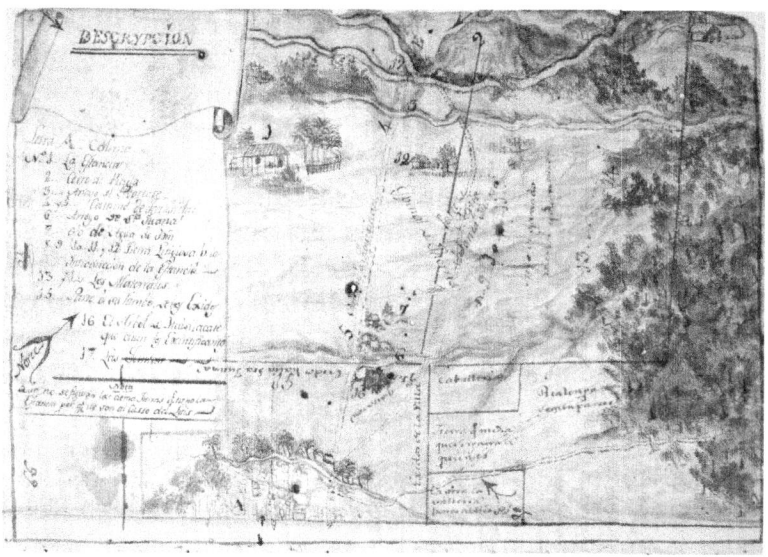

Source: AHMC, Fondo Sevilla del Río, caja 2, exp. 21. Original title: "Mapa del Litis de los terrenos de Santa Juana, Peregrino y la Estancia Vieja o del Pochote".

This underscores the importance of conducting detailed research on the production of distilled drinks in Colima in the 18th century, as that will allow us to better understand the phenomenon of the transfer of the technique of *vino de cocos* production to the elaboration of mezcal. By the early 19th century, the mezcals sold in the villa of Colima came from far off lands; namely, the zone known today as southern Jalisco. Customs (*aduanas*) ledgers from 1816 verify that this kind of aguardiente entered from Tuxcacuesco, Tonaya, Tapalpa, Sayula, and Xiquilpa, as well as Tequila.[613] Did no culture of mezcal production develop in Colima in the 18th century to replace that of *vino de cocos* when it fell into steep decline? Historical sources remain silent, but an in-depth study could shed light on this issue.

Regarding the other production nucleus –Zacatula-Acapulco– in 1744 towns around the port still celebrated the annual fair that marked the arrival of the Manila Galleon. That led José Antonio Villaseñor y Sánchez to write, in his *Theatro Americano*, that if the vessel were to fail to come to port for three or four years in a row, "without doubt, the population would desert [the site]". People there abandoned *vino de cocos* production and shifted to cultivating cotton, rice, corn, tobacco, and some fruits and vegetables, as well as raising species of cattle, large and small, but no activities related to the elaboration of aguardiente.[614] In the second half of the 18th century, the main economic activities in Zacatula were growing cotton, harvesting pearls, extracting salt, raising livestock, and commerce in local products and merchandise from Asia that arrived on the Galleon.[615] Neither *vino de cocos* nor cacao production appeared on that region's agricultural landscapes but, of course, taverns and brothels sold other distilled alcoholic drinks with the blessing of local priests.[616]

Final Reflections

In this chapter we have analyzed the four stages of production of *vino de cocos* in the nuclei of Colima-Motines and, in less detail, Zacatula-Acapulco. The more abundant information on the former made it more feasible to study historical processes and posit working hypotheses. It is clear that, despite the prohibition on *vino de cocos*, the drink continued to be produced in a considerable volume from the early 17th century to 1627, the year when a hurricane devastated economic activities in Colima and led the Viceroy to grant a provisional license that freed the production and distribution of palm aguardiente. In the decade of 1630, we observe the largest volumes of production in the Colima-Motines nucleus and, to a lesser extent, in Zacatula-Acapulco. But from that moment on, the sources for the latter area fall silent and it was only possible to determine

Part III

that *vino de cocos* production continued there based on tithe records from two years: 1668 and 1692.

In the case of the Colima-Motines nucleus, while we know that tithes on *vino de cocos* continued to be paid to the Bishopric of Michoacán until at least 1670, and that this product accounted for half of that concept, it is also true that in the second half of the 17th century the interest payments that burdened the palm haciendas began to drown their owners in debt, and abandonments and transfers began to multiply. The low profitability of those plantations may have been due, among other factors, to the age of palm trees planted early in the 17th century. Indeed, this may have been the reason why new palm plantations came to be concentrated in valleys closer to the villa of Colima, where hacendados had their residences, and numerous haciendas were established in the Nahualapa Valley, upriver on the Armería. In Colima, *vino de cocos* production developed as an economic buffer, a substitute activity that emerged after the nadir of cacao farming. For Zacatula, in contrast, it was never more than a complementary activity, as the economy there continued to depend on cacao. Where was the *vino de cocos* produced in these two nuclei commercialized? That is the topic of the next chapter.

8. COMMERCIAL ROUTES OF VINO DE COCOS

> Colima, with its palms and
> vino de cocos distilled there,
> has destroyed this province.
> —Priest of Arantzan, Michoacán (1680)

INTRODUCTION

During the colonial festivities of Easter Week in the main church of Pátzcuaro, Bishopric of Michoacán, the governor and officials of the *república de indios* gathered to celebrate Christ's Resurrection. As the religious ceremony came to an end amidst fireworks and music, the faithful moved to the Hospital de Nuestra Señora de la Salud, where women stewards (*mayordomas*) awaited with a rich banquet of "foods accompanied by abundant *vino de cocos* from Colima", as Felipe Castro Gutiérrez recorded.[617] We find ourselves in the full splendor of the 17th century when *vino de cocos* figured among the products subject to the tithe that *colimenses* had to pay in the city of Valladolid. At that time, as well, the clients of taverns in Mexico City and such faraway places as the mining districts in Nueva Galicia and Nueva Vizcaya also consumed *vino de cocos*. Clearly, the distribution circuits of this drink extended several hundred leagues beyond the palm haciendas.

What commercialization routes did *vino de cocos* follow upon leaving its production nuclei? For what periods can we trace that activity and discern how the element of time was related to wider economic contexts? These are the broad questions we address in this chapter.

AT THE GATES OF THE HACIENDA

Before describing how mules were loaded with *botijas* of *vino de cocos* in preparation for their journeys, we would like to pause for a moment at the gates of the hacienda of Zinacamitlán, in the production area of San Salvador Chiamila, jurisdiction of Motines. From the perspective of the *colimenses*, Zinacamitlán lay on the other side of the Coahuayana River, seven leagues from the villa. The hacienda there belonged to a resident of Colima named Antonio Carrillo de Guzmán. After his death, it was managed by his widow, doña Catalina de Alarcón. The property produced over 600 *botijas* of *vino de cocos* annually, but our interest centers on a ledger with records of aguardiente sales there from October 1638 to August 1639 that has been conserved. That ledger might seem to hold no special significance since it spans only nine months of transactions, but it is extremely valuable because it is the only known document of its kind,[618] and one that sheds direct light on such key aspects as the per *botija* cost of *vino de cocos* at the gates of the hacienda, transport costs to the villa, and the origins of some buyers (Table 30).

The hacienda was managed by Juan de Aguilera, a Spaniard who was paid 100 pesos per year, just over 8 pesos per month. He began to work there on November 1, 1638[619] and his arrival coincided with the earliest sales records, which are dated precisely from November 17 of that year to October 20, 1639. In that interval, the hacienda sold 248 *botijas*, which would project to total estimated sales of around 330 *botijas* annually, a reasonable approximation of the volume of *vino de cocos* that a hacienda in the

PART III

Colima-Motines nucleus could sell during the apogee of this aguardiente.

The cost per botija at the hacienda's gates was 2 pesos, but its value rose by 2 reales per botija when sold in the villa of Colima, some seven leagues distant. The only case in which botijas were sold for less than 2 pesos involved Martín Alonso, perhaps due to a prior agreement reached between the administrator and this client.

Table 30. Record of Vino de Cocos Production on the Hacienda of Zinacamitlán (1638–1639)

Date	Botijas	Buyer	Value (pesos)
17 November, 1638	17	Unknown	34
	2	Unknown	4
10 December, 1638	11	Unknown	22
	12	Francisco de Vargas	24
	13	Bartolomé Núñez	26
	6	A man from Agualulco	12
10 February, 1639	15	Agustín Ortiz	30
	10	Esteban Ordiales	20
25 March, 1639	19	Alonso de Vargas (Guadalajara)	38
2 April, 1639	6	Antonio Pinedas	12
	3	Gonzalo Rodríguez	6
29 April, 1639	21	Alonso de Estrada	42
	6	Cristóbal Fermín	12
	6	Diego Rodríguez	12

Date	Botijas	Buyer	Value (pesos)
1 June, 1639	16	Martín Alonso	30
2 July, 1639	21	Unknown	42
10 August, 1639	15	Diego Castañeda	30
	12	Antonio de Campos and Juan Higareda	24
	18	Esteban Ordiales and Gaspar Hernández	40
	7	Sold in Colima	15.75
	9	Pereda	20.25
	3	Cristóbal Fermín	6.75
TOTAL	248		502.75

Source: AHMC, secc. B, caja 18, exp. 1

Regarding the place of origin of the clients, only two are identified: Alonso de Vargas in Guadalajara, and "a man from Agualulco". We will discuss relations with the capital city of Jalisco in detail below, but let us stop for a moment in the town of Agualulco, province of Etzatlán, in the region of the Tequila volcano. Some early 17th-century notarial documents there report on commercial links between the townsfolk and the province of Colima, including sales of slaves and commerce in mules and *vino de cocos*, including transactions in which the drink served as a means of payment. The case of Bartolomé Chavarín, a resident of Agualulco, reveals the nature of the deals in which he acted as an intermediary with people in Guadalajara,[620] though the *vino de cocos* he acquired was commercialized not only there but also in the Ahuisculco-Tala-Agualulco-Etzatlán corridor, whence it could be sent on to the mines of Guachinango and Ostotipaque.[621]

Part III

From palm haciendas like the one in Zinacamitlán, botijas of *vino de cocos* were transported by mule to the villa of Colima and other provinces. The closest market for sales and distribution was that villa, though no real taverns existed there, only stores that sold it beside diverse wares. Obtaining *vino de cocos* in the villa was not difficult. In stores around the public square and the homes of some Spaniards, like the merchant Juan Martín Parrales in 1605, people could purchase a *cuartillo* of wine for one *real*.[622] Parrales had two helpers in his home who sold aguardiente, a young Spaniard and a mulatto who, despite the express prohibition on selling the drink, offered it clandestinely to Indians "from his hand and that of his servants". For those clients, Parrales used a small coconut gourd as a measuring cup. Testimonies by various witnesses regarding what went on in Parrales' home revealed that he cheated, not only by selling *vino de cocos* illegally to Indians, but also by serving an amount that was less than the *cuartillo* that he supposedly measured.[623]

In the periods when commercialization of *vino de cocos* was authorized, stores on the public square, like *La Vitoria* and one owned by Bartolomé Bravo Lagunas –the chief justice of Colima in 1639-1640– also sold the drink at one *real* per *cuartillo*, regardless of the client's caste, openly disregarding the ban on selling alcoholic drinks to Indians.[624] It is thanks to the judicial processes that followed upon accusations of these illegal practices that we can identify the locales in people's homes and stores in Colima where *vino de cocos* was sold. Those cases mention the recipients used to measure drinks, including gourds (*calabazos*) and *tecomates*, coconut shells, and white bowls "from Puebla".[625] The villa of Colima was not only a site where aguardiente from surrounding haciendas was collected and redistributed, but also a shipping point for transport to quite distinct destinations.

Table 31 shows the markets for *vino de cocos* in New Spain. In the 17th century, four regions maintained commercial relations with the province of Colima. We were able to reconstruct those circuits thanks to tax ledgers (*alcabalas*) that recorded the origins of the muleteers and traders who came to the province to buy salt, aguardiente, and other products.[626] These included, on the one hand, the Bishopric of Michoacán, the region called El Bajío, and Mexico City and, on the other, Nueva Galicia and northern New Spain. We have also taken into account Motines. Places where wine from Colima may have been taken, but that we could not confirm in the historical documents, appear in Italics.

Table 31. Market for *Vino de Cocos* in the Colima–Motines Nucleus (17th Century)

Mexico City, El Bajío, and surrounding area	Michoacán	Nueva Galicia	Northern mining districts
Mexico City	Acámbaro	Agualulco	Cuencamé
Celaya	Arantza	Aguascalientes	Durango
Guanajuato	Chilchota	Autlán	Guadiana
Irapuato	Churintzio	Cocula	Mazapil
León	Cuitseo	Guachinango	Nombre de Dios
Pachuca	Huaniqueo	Guadalajara	Río Grande
Puruándiro	Jacona	Hostotipaquillo	San José del Parral
Querétaro	Jiquilpan	Juchipila	Sombrerete
Salamanca	La Piedad	Los Ramos	Topia
Salvatierra	Maravatío	San Juan de los Lagos	
San Miguel el Grande	Pátzcuaro	Sayula	

Part III

Mexico City, El Bajío, and surrounding area	Michoacán	Nueva Galicia	Northern mining districts
Santa Ana Pacueco	San Juan Parangaricut	Tamazula	
Toluca	San Luis Potosí	Teocaltiche	
Valle de Santiago	Tangancícuaro	Tequila	
	Tarecuato	Tlajomulco	
	Taximaroa	Tlaltenango	
	Tepalcatepec	Tuxpan	
	Tingüindin	Villa de la Purificación	
	Tlazazalca	Zacatecas	
	Ucareo	Zapotlán	
	Valladolid		
	Zamora		
	Zinapécuaro		

Source: AHMC, secc. B, caja 28, exp. 20.

Based on the information in this Table, we elaborated a map of the places where *vino de cocos* from the Colima-Motines area was consumed (Map 12). To analyze these circuits in greater detail, we divided the sections into two routes: one encompassing Valladolid, El Bajío, and Mexico City, the other, Guadalajara and the northern mining zones.

Map 12. Places Where Vino de Cocos from the Colima-Motines Nucleus Was Consumed

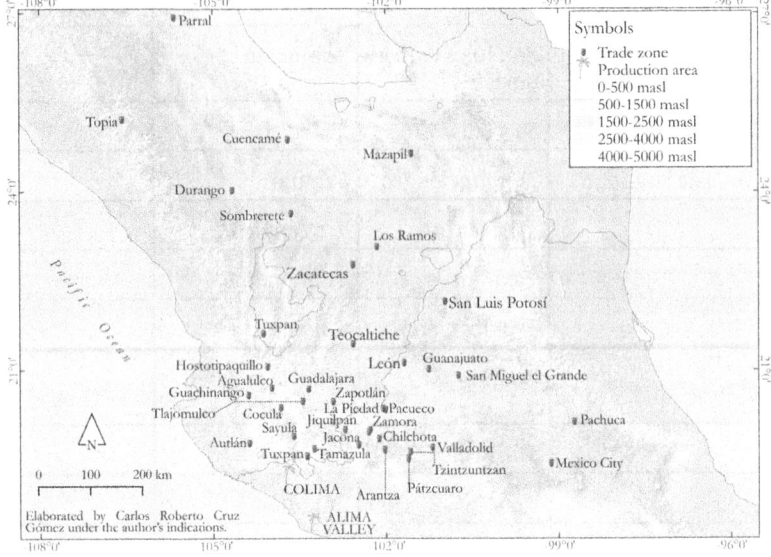

THE ROUTE TO VALLADOLID AND MEXICO CITY

Each place where vino de cocos was introduced and commercialized had its own logic: the route from Colima to Valladolid, seat of the Bishopric of Michoacán, reflected the obligation of people in the provinces of Colima-Motines to pay tithes since, as mentioned earlier, from 1638 to 1670 the tithes paid on this aguardiente constituted almost half of the total. From Valladolid, vino de cocos could be taken to Mexico City and sold in taverns with other alcoholic drinks. It was often transported by mule train with other goods, like salt and cacao.

Two routes connected the province of Colima to central New Spain: the northwestern path that wove through Tuxpan, Tamazula, Mazamitla, and on to Jiquilpan. There, travelers could choose the road to El Bajío via Zamora and La Piedad or turn toward Valladolid on the way to Mexico City. But vino de cocos could also travel directly from

PART III

Motines to Valladolid along the road that went through Coalcomán, Tepalcatepec, and other places in the Hot Lands to Pátzcuaro and from there to Valladolid. Juan Carlos Reyes wrote that the latter route had communicated the coast with the P'urhépecha seigneury of Tzintzuntzan from pre-Hispanic times.[627] From Valladolid, wine could be sent to Mexico City through Celaya and Querétaro, but if the final destinations were in the mining zones in the jurisdiction of the Bishopric of Michoacán, it went first to Guanajuato and then to San Luis Potosí.[628] Taximaroa and Toluca were other intermediate points between Valladolid and Mexico City.

Limitations on the Vino de Cocos Trade (1600–1627)

In the first three decades of the 17th century, *vino de cocos* traders in Colima faced a dilemma: while they were obliged to take their product to Valladolid to pay tithes, they had to proceed with great caution because, after all, it was an illegal drink banned by the Viceregal authorities. This predicament caused great confusion and tempted some *alcaldes mayores* and their aides at intermediate points along the way to take advantage of the situation by threatening to impose unjustified quotas on the traders or extorting *botijas* of wine. Episodes of this were especially common on the route from Jiquilpan to Pátzcuaro that passed through Chilchota and Tingüindín.

The case of Pátzcuaro is emblematic, not only because *vino de cocos* was well-received by people there, but also because local archives conserve records of some revealing judicial processes. More than any other town, Pátzcuaro was deemed "the city of Michoacán" or, at least, it began to call itself that around 1620, a clear reflection of its ancient status as the civic capital and episcopal seat in the earlier times of *Tata* Vasco. Sales of *vino de cocos* can be traced from at least that year, when Francisco de Cañedo Ordóñez, the deputy *alguacil* (*teniente-alguacil*), began an investigation into Juan Gabino, a *colimense* who was seen selling a barrel of *vino de cocos* "publicly, despite the prohibition". Gabino was a trader who circulated, offering his product to local merchants. When unsuccessful in selling all his wine on a certain day, he would retire to his room at a local inn and wait to try his luck the next day. Some witnesses stated that on the occasion in question Gabino had four loads of aguardiente –approximately 130 liters– though others said it was just one (perhaps 65 liters).[629] Whatever the case, this episode tells us that *colimenses* had been making efforts to open that market for some time, seeking to position their drink among people's preferences.

However, the harsh reality that their product was banned by local ordinances made sales difficult, as in the case of Pedro de Castañeda, a *vino de cocos* trader in Pátzcuaro who was accused of selling aguardiente.[630] What was sanctioned was not so much the *vino de cocos* itself but, rather, the illegal sale of "drinks of the land" to Indians because, it was argued, they caused drunkenness, disease, and death among the indigenous population, not to mention numerous offenses against God. Surely, more than one *colimense* spent time in jail in Pátzcuaro for this reason, but we know that this fate befell 25-year-old Juan Castelán, when his apparently thriving business collapsed. Castelán had been sent to Valladolid in 1627 by the priest in San Salvador Chiamila, don Gaspar Castelán –perhaps a relative?– to deliver some *botijas* of *vino de cocos* as his tithe payment to the Cathedral. Before fulfilling his task, however, Juan tried to sell the distillate but was denounced for participating in illegal trade and sentenced to jail by the deputy *alcalde mayor* of Pátzcuaro, Martín de Angulo.[631]

Problems arose not only during transport of the drink, but also in production areas. Even before the first license was granted in 1627, we have news of bad blood between the authorities in Motines and hacienda owners who lived in Colima but had their production units in the neighboring demarcation. In 1623, the *alcalde mayor* of Motines, Alonso

Part III

Muñoz, prohibited *colimenses* from producing *vino de cocos* in his jurisdiction because of the rampant drunkenness it caused among the Indians. People in Colima protested because many of them operated palm haciendas in the Alima Valley in the jurisdiction of Motines, and because *vino de cocos* was "[our] main source of sustenance [as we sell it] to traders who take it to the mines and areas where it is [used as) medicine, which is beneficial, and it aggrandizes New Spain and stuffs His Majesty's coffers with royal taxes [*alcabalas*]".[632] This shows that long before they obtained Viceregal authorization, some *colimenses* had been rehearsing their discourse on the medicinal properties of *vino de cocos* and the economic bounty it offered His Majesty's royal treasury.

Licenses for the Free Transit of Vino de Cocos (1627 Onward)

Light began to shine on the future of *vino de cocos* traders when, after the fierce hurricane ravaged the province of Colima in 1626, tumbling the few cacao trees still planted there, residents successfully negotiated a license with the Viceroy of New Spain, Rodrigo Pacheco y Osorio, to openly produce and commercialize their *vino de cocos* to mitigate the severe economic crisis that held the area in its grasp. The license clearly stipulated that "His Majesty's justices of government [shall not] impose any impediment or contradiction"[633] on traders. This was an enormous triumph for the *colimenses* because, for the first time, they did not have to hide their activities from anyone and *vino de cocos* production could finally emerge from the clandestine conditions in which it had been elaborated.

Thanks to the council of Colima's capacity to negotiate with the Viceregal authorities, several extensions were obtained: in 1627, 1637, 1644, 1653, 1664, 1668, 1671, 1675, 1683?, 1687, and 1691. It is not clear why the periods between one extension and the next varied so widely, as some were for ten years, others only eight, one for six, and some for just four.

Table 32. Licenses for the Free Production and Sale of Vino de Cocos (17th Century)

No.	Viceroy	Date	Duration
1	Marqués de Cerralvo	March 4, 1627	10 years
2	Marqués de Cadereyta	February 20, 1637	8 years
3	Conde de Salvatierra	December 15, 1644	10 years
4	Conde de Alba de Aliste	April 19, 1653	10 years
5	Marqués de Mancera	October 31, 1664	4 years
6	Marqués de Mancera	May 15, 1668	6 years
7	Marqués de Mancera	December 14, 1671	4 years
8	Payo Enríquez de Ribera	May 13, 1675	8 years
9	Conde de Paredes de Nava	1683?	4 years?
10	Conde de la Moncloa	August 25, 1687	4 years
11	Conde de Galve	May 10, 1691	8 years

Source: AGN, Ordenanzas, vol. 5, exp. 21; AGN, Indiferente Viceregal, caja 2949, exp. 52; AGN, Indiferente Viceregal, caja 6112, exp. 5.

Only a few years after the long-coveted license was granted in 1627, it occurred to an *alcalde ordinario* in Valladolid that *vino de cocos* should be sold only in two stores due to frequent scandals of drunkenness among the Indians who consumed it in excess. That *alcalde*, don García de Cisneros, deemed it convenient to restrict sales as a way to prevent inebriation or, at least, that was how he announced it in his edict. But the measure proved so harmful for traders in both Colima and Valladolid that one, Juan Sánchez Rendón, denounced the measure in Mexico City. In response, Pacheco y Osorio emitted an order in 1632 to clarify that "the [original] intent was not to establish a monopoly (*estanco*) for that wine but to allow it to be sold freely, as said order [mandated]".[634] The royal monopoly that the two stores sought to formalize failed, and the same *alcalde ordinario* in Valladolid, and the deputy of the *alcalde mayor* in 1632, Jerónimo Magdaleno de Mendoza, admitted that restrictions had been imposed on the sale of *vino de cocos* in the past, but had failed to achieve the goals for which they had supposedly been implemented:

> Efforts have been made to prevent drunkenness among the Indians, considering that it was caused by the *vino de cocos* sold in this villa, so orders were given to restrict sale to only two stores, but though this was enforced it was not the remedy because inebriation is caused, as well, by other wines, pulques, and concoctions, in consideration of which new licenses have been granted to some merchants to sell *vino de cocos* freely to Spaniards, [while] obeying the ordinances and orders issued by His Excellency.[635]

In that scenario, the council of Colima decided to issue copies of the licenses granted by the Viceroys for *vino de cocos* traders to carry with them to prevent local authorities from impeding their transit or demanding bribes in the form of *botijas* of aguardiente. Archives of the *ayuntamiento* of Pátzcuaro hold a copy of one such document from 1645. It states that the council of Colima informed authorities in Michoacán that *colimenses* bore licenses from the Viceroys of New Spain to cultivate palm trees and produce *vino de cocos* in the province of Maquilí, where many had their haciendas.[636]

Perhaps due to a lack of acumen in such dealings among *colimenses*, the 1627 license authorized palm aguardiente production exclusively in the province of Colima, not in the neighboring *alcaldía mayor* of Motines, where many hacendados actually resided. This set off disputes with *alcaldes mayores* in Motines, as the former sought to produce and sell their *vino de cocos*, while the latter impeded their efforts arguing that the license had been granted only to the jurisdiction of Colima. A case involving the decrees that banned *vino de cocos* in Michoacán arose in Pátzcuaro in January 1627, when the deputy of the *alcalde mayor*, Juan Luis de Aguirre, accused Agustín de Nava, a Spaniard, of selling *vino de cocos* to Indians in Tzintzuntzan, "resulting in terrible sins and offenses against God and great harm to the natives".[637] Nava's accomplices included another Spaniard, the son of the overseer of the Augustinian hacienda near the lake, and an Indian *alcalde* from the same jurisdiction, a clear illustration of the networks of favors that emerged around the sale of *vino de cocos*. Although in that year the Viceroy gave *colimenses* permission to freely sell their distillate, the ban on consumption in Indian communities was maintained.

When it came time to renew the license (in 1637), the jurisdiction of Motines was added, since

> in Viceroy Marqués de Cerralvo's first order, which granted said villa a ten-year license to make said wine, residents failed to clarify that their haciendas were in the jurisdiction of Maquilí [in Motines]: justices in the markets and towns through which they passed to sell wine harassed them, saying that the license did not apply in Maquilí. So, to avoid such inconveniences, I was asked to order that its terms be extended to include [said] jurisdiction of Maquilí, upon a solicitude by the residents of that villa, since most of their haciendas are located there.[638]

But even with those licenses in hand, traders faced constant difficulties in selling their *vino de cocos* in the Bishopric of Michoacán, for they were obliged to negotiate along the way with and, on occasion, denounce abuses by, local authorities who were determined to extract personal benefit. In the late 17th century, despite having full authorization, the *colimenses* still confronted obstacles. One, Juan de Abárzuza, commented that

> For over eighteen years, *alcaldes* have [insisted] they be given four pesos for each load, and have placed innumer-

able impediments that [we] have resisted. After paying the corresponding manifest and tax (*alcabala*); in Xiquilpa, Chilchota, and Tingüindín, Milord, the justices insist with force and vigor that a *botija* be given to each *alcalde mayor* through whose jurisdictions we normally pass... in consideration of this, Milord, all the residents of the villa implore Your Excellency to look upon us with merciful eyes and order that [our] *vino de cocos* be allowed to enter publicly in the Customs of this city [Mexico] paying the royal rights that pertain to His Majesty, and that this apply as well, Milord, in all other areas of Your Excellency's government.[639]

Did this problem affect *vino de cocos* exclusively? In reality, no, for pulque was subjected to similar conditions. José J. Hernández Palomo wrote that while pulque was not completely banned and that regulations governed its legal distribution, many *alcaldes mayores* in towns around Mexico City "unilaterally" set a tax of one *real* per load transported to the capital of the Viceroyalty. Despite official regulations prohibiting such measures, they remained in force for many years. The author also mentions that in 1633 the *corregidor* of Cuautepec demanded that Indians in the towns of Chimalhuacán, Atengo, San Agustín, and La Magdalena sell him pulque, which he would resell at double the price.[640]

The Sisa Tax on Vino de Cocos

Once the license was granted, *vino de cocos* became subject to taxation (*alcabala*) at its destinations. But it is interesting to note that, at least in 1633, it also had to pay a second tax, one called *sisa*, which was charged on consumer products. Some local governments, including the *ayuntamiento* of Mexico City, began to impose it in the final quarter of the 16th century to finance public works. According to Gerardo Sánchez, "control of the distribution [of *vino de cocos*] was effectuated through the so-called *sisa* branch, to which merchants contributed by paying a tax. Around 1670, perhaps 8 stores in Valladolid were selling *vino de cocos*, most of them managed by local merchants".[641]

A loose file in the Consulado branch of the Archivo General de la Nación contains a short list of 19 merchants who paid the *sisa* tax for the concept of *vino de cocos* sales in 1633. The rate was half a peso per botija. Those payments were likely made to the *ayuntamiento* of Valladolid, for the list includes merchants in the capital of Michoacán, such as Juan Sánchez Rendón, Baltazar Pereyra, and Pedro Moreno. There we learn that Pereyra commercialized spices in Valladolid in 1637,[642] while Moreno was the *corregidor* of the town of Charo in 1631 and operated a mule train that traded between Valladolid and Mexico City.[643] Juan Sánchez Rendón is the same man we mentioned above who presented the petition to Viceroy Pacheco y Osorio in 1632 to allow the sale of *vino de cocos* in other stores, apart from the two preferred by the *alcalde* of Valladolid. This suggests that aguardiente sales were a priority for him since he declared the largest number of botijas (Table 33). Considering the production figures from the Colima-Motines nuclei for those years (in the previous chapter), it appears that the Valladolid market represented 6% of the *vino de cocos*' producers' sales in those years.

A second record of the *sisa* branch, also from the *ayuntamiento* of Valladolid, but for 1670, shows that the volume of *vino de cocos* had decreased: the records for 1633 show 871 botijas entering the city from 19 merchants, but in 1670 the amount fell to just 110 botijas from 8 traders.[644] These figures mirror the decline in *vino de cocos* production analyzed previously.

Part III

Table 33. Sisa Tax on Vino de Cocos in Valladolid (1633)

Name	Botijas	Pesos
Jerónimo de Vega	77.5	38.75
Marcos Gómez	43.5	21.75
Domingo Ortiz	73	36.5
Baltasar Pereyra	77	38.5
Simón López	6	3
Juan de Salazar	72	36
Francisco Gudiño	45	22.5
Juan Sánchez Rendón	173	86.5
Martín de la Mesa	47.5	23.75
Francisco de Orozco	78	39
Thomas de Menchaca	18.5	9.25
Manuel López	14.5	7.25
Pedro Moreno	11.5	5.75
Pedro Navarrete	23	11.5
Salvador Duarte	36	18
Juan Molero	24	12
Jerónimo Pérez	12.5	6.25
Juan Alemán	7	3.5
Pedro Lorenzo Montero	32	16
TOTAL	871.5	435.75

Source: AGN, Indiferente virreinal (Consulado), caja 6390, exp. 12.

Here, it is relevant to reflect on Peter Bakewell's statement that sales of wine in general provided income not only to the direct producers and distributors in taverns, but also to *ayuntamientos*, especially through the *sisa* tax. He wrote that "it should not surprise us that since wine was a good source of profit for the authorities and private citizens, the prohibitions that affected its trade were rarely obeyed and enforced only sporadically".[645] Thus, whether in times of free trade in *vino de cocos*, or periods of prohibition, diverse local authorities persisted in their attempts to benefit from these sales.

Vino de Cocos in Mexico City

For the *colimenses*, trade with Mexico City can be traced back to the mid-16th century when they dispatched numerous loads of cacao and salt produced in the jurisdictions of Colima and Motines, so, their sales of *vino de cocos* in the capital of New Spain was not a particularly novel development on that commercial route. The new economic relations forged with the market sector for alcoholic drinks, however, were. In fact, in the late 16th century, well before trade in palm aguardiente burst onto the scene, some coconuts were being transported to Mexico City, likely to satisfy the demand for the food and drink derived from the fruit, and for the coveted husks used to elaborate *cocos chocolateros*.

An example of these transactions involved don Antonio Enríquez, the *alcalde mayor* of Colima in 1596-1597. After completing his time in office, Enríquez requested that a trip be organized to take 29 "thirds" (*tercios*) of cacao, "one-third" of salt, and "two-thirds" of coconuts to Mexico City.[646] It is interesting to note that Enríquez employed two *chino* servants, Alonso and Juan Jerónimo, and that his intermediary in Colima was Pedro Gómez Machorro, who had served as his deputy *justicia mayor*.[647] It is well-known that *alcaldes mayores* in Colima, ever eager to establish profitable businesses during and after their terms, took full advantage of the economic resources of their localities.

Part III

One of the earliest reports on shipments of *vino de cocos* to Mexico City dates from 1612, when the *colimense* Sebastián de Vera affirmed that "this witness has seen great quantities of said aguardiente sent by different people in this villa to others in Mexico City [...] in *botijas* because it is medicinal and approved".[648] It is important to point out that before the 1629 flood some 340 taverns were operating where,[649] without doubt, the preferred drink was pulque since consumers there were only beginning to become familiar with distilled drinks. After 1627, when the free production and commerce of *vino de cocos* was authorized, tavern owners began to solicit licenses to sell palm aguardiente, emphasizing the fact that producers in Colima had received the aforementioned authorizations. In 1650, Ambrosio García, a tavern owner in Mexico City, applied for a license to distribute *vino de cocos* from the villa of Colima.[650] In 1690, doña Leonor García, widow of Gabriel de Bustos, declared that she had a store near the San Jerónimo fountain where she sold wine and "wish to sell the wine and aguardiente called *de cocos* to sustain herself and an unmarried daughter". She therefore applied for a license "free of any impediment, in conformity with the general license conceded to the people of Colima".[651]

Due to the scarce documentation available, we were unable to determine the volume of sales of *vino de cocos* in taverns in Mexico City, but did ascertain that a *botija* of this distillate sold for just over 5 pesos; that is, double its value at the gates of the haciendas in Colima-Motines.[652] To this price we must add the final transaction cost between the wholesale buyer and tavern owner, both of whom had to make a profit when selling the wine to consumers.

THE ROUTE TO GUADALAJARA AND NORTHERN NEW SPAIN

Shortly after the activities associated with *vino de cocos* began in Colima, the city of Guadalajara emerged as one of the principal commercial destinations due to both its market for internal consumption and its connections to mining districts in northern New Spain. Some residents of that capital already knew *vino de cocos*: Dr. Santiago de Vera, who had served as Governor and Captain-General of the Philippines in the 1580s, drank it in Manila because he considered it healthful. Later, when he was named President of the Real Audiencia of Nueva Galicia, he discovered that the drink was produced in Colima and had several *botijas* sent to him, as one of his nephews wrote:

> This witness heard Dr. Sanctiago de Vera [sic] [...] say that he had lived in robust health for many years after drinking that aguardiente; and that he began to use it for his health and life while back in the Philippine Islands [...], that when he did not have it he felt great anxiety, and that God would reward anyone in Colima who had the goodwill to send him some bottles [to Guadalajara].[653]

Guadalajara, the capital city of the Reino of Nueva Galicia, was a nodal point on the transportation route of *vino de cocos* from Colima to the mining districts of northern New Spain. A particularly close relation between alcoholic drinks and mines had always existed, not only in New Spain but also in other places in Spanish America.[654] In the mines of Potosí in the early 17th century, for example, we find that the most widely-sold products included wine from Castille, *chicha*, and *coca*, three stimulants that helped mineworkers withstand the rigors of their work underground.[655] Wine from Castille (originally imported from Spain, but later produced in Chile) was sold in enormous quantities, though consumption depended on people's purchasing power, for it was more expensive than locally-produced alcoholic drinks. In the 1640s, the Audiencia of Guadalajara issued an edict in the city of Zacatecas which stated that "one of the principal and most necessary [aspects of] maintaining laborers is wine [but] whether from Castille or Parras it is costly; and it has become known through the experience and opinions of doctors that wines made from mezcal and coconuts are not only [innocuous], but actually useful and beneficial for workers, especially in mines.[656]

That decree was emitted during the time of the royal monopoly (*estanco*) on *vino de cocos* and mezcal in Guadalajara, a topic we discuss below. That proved to be a convenient time to promote consumption of both distilled drinks among mineworkers, a non-Spanish sector of the population. As Arturo Burciaga observed, "Mine owners magnified [the importance] of these two products, claiming they helped laborers resist their harsh workdays".[657]

A declaration by the *colimense* Gabriel Muñoz, in 1612, shows that *vino de cocos* was, indeed, being commercialized in San Luis Potosí, Los Ramos, Guadiana, and Topia.[658] In that same year, another *colimense*, Sebastián de Vera, confirmed Muñoz' observation, but added the city of Zacatecas.[659] To these sites we should add Pachuca, Guanajuato, and Parral, as well as other mining districts. While it may not be that all the *vino de cocos* marketed in mining areas was transported by *colimenses* themselves, what is certain is that all traders had to procure it in Colima, where they could also obtain loads of salt for mining operations. As Chantal Cramaussel has pointed out, although those places were located far from the principal cities of New Spain and accessible only over rough, treacherous roads, in times of mining bonanzas all manner of merchandise found its way there.[660]

After reaching Guadalajara, *vino de cocos* from Colima followed routes to northern New Spain through Nochistlán and Juchipila, especially from the second half of the 17th century with the opening of new extensions of the *Camino de Tierra Adentro* that led north and northwest. Leaving Zacatecas, where a deposit for *vino de cocos* and mezcal was inaugurated in the 1640s, the drink was taken to Sombrerete, Nombre de Dios, Guadiana, and Durango, and then to Parral or the mines of Topia, which reached their apogee in the late 1590s.[661] Another route ran through

San Juan de los Lagos between Guadalajara and mines in San Luis Potosí.

It is likely that some of the *vino de cocos* distributed in mining districts in central New Spain, like Guanajuato and Pachuca, also came from Valladolid where it was first taken as part of the tithe payments from Colima and Zacatula. Although references to sales of *vino de cocos* in the region of El Bajío are scarce, it is probable that it was taken there together with loads of salt. Records from León and San Miguel el Grande show that *vino de cocos* was also consumed there,[662] while the property inventory and list of debtors of Francisco Clemente Larios, a merchant in Colima in 1670, reveal that some of his clients for salt and *vino de cocos* traveled as far away as Santa Ana Pacueco.[663]

Remaining inside the Bishopric of Michoacán, but much farther north, the mines of San Luis Potosí were another market niche for *vino de cocos* and salt from Colima. We have already mentioned the importance of both products for mining activities, the former as a stimulant for laborers on their long working days, the latter utilized in the processes carried out to separate metal from ore. In 1655, Marcos de Abastua –who had served as an *alcabala* tax collector in San Luis Potosí for three years– complained that a resident merchant, Juan Enríquez, had evaded paying the *alcabala* tax on certain products, which was levied at a rate of 6 percent. In reality, Enríquez had been visited in his home by a muleteer named Josephe González on March 10, 1652, who sold him 33 loads of *vino de cocos*, 5 of salt, and 10 of sugar, for a total value of "over one 1,000 pesos",[664] which meant that he was obliged to pay over 60 pesos in taxes; however, he had paid only 43.

It is important to learn more about the principal figures involved in those long-distance transactions that involved journeys of over 500 km. The muleteer Josephe González, possibly from Colima, was "an agent of don Alonso Orejón", a figure who appeared around that time as the *alcalde mayor* of Colima.[665] The Juan Enríquez mentioned

Part III

above –as the *encomendero*, or intermediary, in San Luis Potosí for the official/merchant in Colima– is likely Juan Enríquez Delgado who, upon the creation of the council of the splendid new city of San Luis Potosí, held the position of *depositario general*.[666] From the profits obtained through his agents, Alonso Orejón ordered that money be sent to a man named Tiburcio de Urrea, in all probability the same merchant from Toledo that Louisa Schell registered in the 1630s as a cochineal trader in the Mixteca Baja (Oaxaca) region who sent products to his contact on the Iberian Peninsula, Miguel de Neve.[667] Urrea may have been the merchant who, behind the scenes, supported or managed the *alcalde mayor* Orejón. Evidence suggests that long-distance trade in *vino de cocos* and other products from Colima mobilized the cream of the merchant class and municipal –even royal– officials over broad expanses of western and northern –perhaps even central– New Spain, given that Urrea must have operated out of Mexico City.

Regarding Josephe González, we must clarify that he did not travel alone through the desert-like lands of Potosí, but was accompanied by a muleteer of unknown name, and that "they arrived together with an additional amount of wine".[668] We do not know if this muleteer sold his wine in that jurisdiction, or only passed through it, but we were able to confirm that at least six of the loads that he took to San Luis Potosí found their way to Mazapil, some 50 leagues distant.[669] It is noteworthy that the selling price of a load of *vino de cocos* in San Luis ranged from 4 to 4.50 pesos. Of course, González had no choice but to sell his merchandise, for returning home with it was not an option. In fact, once all his aguardiente was sold he proceeded to sell the barrels that had carried it.

This episode from the area of San Luis Potosí is representative of operations involving *vino de cocos* in the northern mining regions, where large amounts of the drink were needed due to its role as one of the "carburetors" that the "human engines" required in order to continue their labors of extracting and refining metals. Given *vino de cocos*'s high calorific power, much more moderate cost, and much greater energy supply compared to wine from Castille, trade in this beverage was profitable despite the high cost of transport by mule train to Mazapil, Zacatecas, Sombrerete, and Topia, or even lands' end in Parral, over 170 leagues from Colima (as the crow flies). As we learn from the bans imposed by local authorities in the latter mining district in 1639, *vino de cocos* was sold there together with mezcal; indeed, some merchants were accused of mixing the two drinks.[670]

Transport costs are a central element here, for mules could carry their loads for only a few leagues per day, before passing them to relay animals. On trips during the dry season, the animals ate corn at each stop along the way (as the reader will recall, the muleteer González reached San Luis in March). A second factor in this rubric was shrinkage. A man identified only as "fulano González" stated that of the 15-and-a-half loads of wine that he took to the mining district, 3 –nearly 20%!– were lost to shrinkage. While this is clearly a high percentage, the muleteers may have recovered part of it through their own wiles, for the effect of the human factor can never be underestimated in such cases. Another aspect that must be contemplated among the mechanisms of commercialization that operated across that immense geographic space, which fostered great flexibility, was that sales could be direct, as when the muleteer González operated as don Alonso Orejón's agent in San Luis Potosí, or indirect, through intermediaries like the trader Enríquez who acted as a middleman for his boss, Orejón, receiving a percentage of the selling price in return. In the end, those were traditional commercial operations, as Orejón would sell a portion of the product to Enríquez who would then commercialize it as best he could in the town.

Of course, the muleteers who transported loads of *vino de cocos* and other products to remote mining districts ran the risk of being assaulted on the way by bandits who might steal either their merchandise or the money from their sales, or both. One viable solution to this problem consisted in using *libranzas*; that is, letters of exchange that long-distance traders obtained at the point of sale in lieu of cash. This allowed them to travel home without cash but with a kind of a promissory note that they could exchange for the amount stipulated there. Trade in *vino de cocos* was sometimes conducted through this modality, as in the case of one Felipe González de León, who sold four loads of *vino de cocos* in Zacatecas but, fearing for the safety of the money on the return trip, negotiated with a merchant, Joseph Ramírez, in the villa of Zamora, Bishopric of Michoacán, a *libranza* in the amount of 220 pesos. Although that deal never materialized, González de León led other muleteers and companions to believe that he was heading back to Colima with no cash, only the *libranza* that he would later exchange. Zamora was not very close to Colima, but Ramírez went there occasionally with loads of salt.[671] We are inclined to think that these dynamics at the level of micro-financing were quite common in a world where the insecurity of the roads they had to travel forced traders and muleteers to implement measures of this kind.

One good indicator of the places to which *vino de cocos* was taken in the territory of Nueva Galicia in the 17th and 18th centuries was the creation of deposits (*asientos*) for this drink and mezcal. We mentioned previously that reports by *colimenses* suggest that mining zones were the places most often visited to sell this drink, and that they stretched through practically all three kingdoms: New Spain, Nueva Galicia, and Nueva Vizcaya.

In this regard, it is interesting to note that in 1640 in Zacatecas, an instruction was issued for the conservation and sustenance of the Barlovento Fleet (*Armada de Barlovento*). Efforts to obtain fiscal resources for this purpose involved establishing a monopoly on alcoholic drinks that included wine from Castille and Parras, *vino de* cocos, and mezcal because, as the document stated, wine was "a principal and necessary item for maintaining" the city. Moreover, *vino de cocos* and mezcal had been evaluated by physicians who recommended their consumption because "they are not harmful, but actually useful and beneficial for laborers, especially in mines".[672] When the *estanco de vino de cocos y mezcal* was imposed in Guadalajara in the first half of the 17th century, and later at other deposits for these drinks, *vino de cocos* was clearly being consumed widely in Nueva Galicia, as was mezcal, as we discuss below.

THE ROYAL MONOPOLY ON VINO DE COCOS AND MEZCAL IN GUADALAJARA

The apogee of *vino de cocos* production in Colima in the 1630s drew attention in the nearby city of Guadalajara, where the drink was marketed for local consumption and transported to the mining districts of central and northern New Spain. By that time, mezcal production had begun in Nueva Galicia. Mezcal and *vino de cocos* were two distilled drinks with a high alcohol content that made many fermented drinks far less attractive due to their low alcohol level by volume and/or spoilage during transport over long distances. Parallel to this sociocultural phenomenon, the capital of Nueva Galicia was always in need of revenue for hydraulic constructions and other public works, so authorities there soon came to look upon *vino de cocos* and mezcal as interesting sources of income that could help resolve that difficulty. It was in this context that Juan de Canseco y Quiñones, the President-Governor of the Real Audiencia of Guadalajara, decided to create the royal monopoly on *vino de cocos* and mezcal in 1637, as a means of financing projects to carry water to the city.[673]

In the words of Thomas Calvo, in the 17th century Guadalajara was a largely commercial city, surrounded by zones dedicated to agriculture and livestock-raising, with some mining activity. Thus, it was a strategic location for gathering and distributing all kinds of merchandise.[674] *Vino de cocos* was produced –formally and legally under licenses granted by the viceregal authorities– in the neighboring jurisdiction of Colima, while mezcal was elaborated in places in Nueva Galicia like the province of Ávalos and the Sierra of Nayarit (Guajimic, Guaynamota)[675] and, later, in the *corregimiento* of Tequila.

The first public auction of a two-year royal monopoly on *vino de cocos* and mezcal took place in 1637. Monopoly-holders (*estanqueros*) obtained a series of faculties that allowed them to control both drinks and prohibit anyone else from commercializing them in the jurisdiction subject to the monopoly without their consent.[676] The *cuartillo* was sold for 2 *reales*. Between 1637 and 1652, there were four *estanqueros*, all residents of Guadalajara: Francisco García Vidal in 1637; Sebastián Báez in 1640; the Japanese Luis de Encío in 1643; and Francisco Rubio in 1645. In 1650, Báez held the post for a second time. During those years, the cost of the monopoly at auction showed a downward trend, suggesting that the income obtained was not very high. García Vidal paid 2,800 pesos in 1637, but in 1640 Báez shelled out only 2,500 pesos to walk away with the monopoly.[677]

The *estanqueros* rarely paid the entire cost at the end of the auction but did so gradually, in installments. García Vidal's case is interesting because it opens a window on contemporary dynamics of handling money, as we see that it could be triangulated among the Real Audiencia, the *ayuntamiento* of Guadalajara, and private individuals. García paid the cost of the monopoly of 2,800 pesos in five installments; first paying 933 pesos, 3 *tomines* to Custodio de la Higuera, the designer of the plans for the aqueduct that would conduct water to the city. Those funds were destined to finance bridge construction.[678] The remaining payments were deposited with the *mayordomo* (official) of the Guadalajara council, as follows: 600 pesos in October

1638; 233 pesos, 3 tomines in January 1639; 400 pesos in June 1639; and 533 pesos in October 1639.[679]

All indications are that Sebastián Báez, the second monopoly-holder, liquidated the auction price of 2,500 pesos in one sole payment in 1640, one part with a bar of *quintada* silver, equivalent to 702 pesos, 1 tomín, the rest in pesos. Regarding Luis de Encío, known as "Luis, *el chino*" due to his Japanese origin, we are not sure how much he paid, but he did contribute 1,500 pesos from his rents to the construction of the royal palace and houses.[680] De Encío was a merchant of middling importance but he had contacts in the palace: without doubt the president at the time, the controversial Pedro Fernández de Baeza, was interested in securing a source of income that he would eventually be able to profit from.[681]

Thomas Calvo affirms that the main source of revenue for the city of Guadalajara in 1639-1641 was, precisely, this monopoly on sales of *vino de cocos* and mezcal.[682] We must note that the infrastructure to carry water to the city –the project that justified the monopoly– was not consolidated until the late 18th century, and that construction continued well into the 19th.[683] It is evident that from 1637 to 1651 returns from the *estanco* financed the construction of some bathrooms, "house, tub, and huts", installed half a league from Guadalajara, downslope in the Zalatitán ravine. Funds were also used to "hire a doctor, finish bridges and public works, and celebrate the fiestas of Corpus Christi and San Miguel", in addition to purchases of corn to feed the poor.[684]

Conflict with Producers in Colima

The creation of the royal monopoly promoted by Canseco y Quiñones was flawed from the outset, for it was not authorized by the Council of the Indies, an organism that was never notified of its instrumentation. To this irregular situation we can add a second serious inconvenience: the fact

Part III

that *vino de cocos* producers in Colima soundly opposed the *estanco* in Guadalajara, for the simple reason that they had negotiated licenses with the Viceroy and Real Audiencia of Mexico for the free production and commercialization of their aguardiente, and had paid the applicable taxes (*alcabala*) for successive authorizations since 1627. The creation of the *estanco* meant that the *colimenses* lost control of that trade –though not of production, which they maintained into the late 17th century– so they felt impelled to bring a lawsuit that would drag on into the decade of 1650.

Clearly, the *colimenses* were not going to sit idly by; in fact, as soon as they learned of the imposition of the royal monopoly in Guadalajara they protested with the support of their *alcalde mayor*, don Félix Candela, who emitted an order that prohibited trade in *vino de cocos* in Nueva Galicia. In November 1637, Candela determined that "no person, of any status whatsoever, shall depart for the city of Guadalajara with *vino de cocos* loaded on his mules, nor sell, deliver, or send [it] in any manner, until it is otherwise provided and ordered".[685]

In that setting, a ledger was created to record the loads of palm aguardiente that left Colima during a 45-day period from November 4 to December 18, 1637 (Table 34). Annotations there identify 26 *colimenses* with a total of 207 loads, indicating that an average of 4.6 loads per day left Colima for lands beyond. If this dynamic were maintained throughout the year, it would mean an average of 1,679 loads annually, not counting internal consumption. Seen from a different angle, if a load consisted of approximately six *botijas*, then the total would be 10,074 *botijas* per year. In monetary terms, this would mean that aguardiente sales put at least 20,000 pesos annually into producers' pockets, considering a value of 2 pesos per *botija* at the gates of the hacienda. Of course, these calculations are based on an estimate elaborated from the figures in that ledger.

Table 34. Loads of Vino de Cocos Sent from Colima to Other Provinces (1637)

Traders	Loads	Date
Juan de Campos	3	November 4
Diego Flores	6	November 4
Antonio Barradas	2	November 4
Cristóbal de Aguirre	10	November 5
José Durán	2	November 14
Joseph de Morales	9	November 15
Andrés de Mesa	11	November 17
Juan de Velasco	23	November 17
Cristóbal de Aguilar	2	November 21
Eligio de Carbajal	10	November 24
Trujillo	4	November 25
Martín de Solórzano	3	November 25
Juan Martín Manzano	6	November 26
Diego Sánchez	10	November 26
Gregorio Fernández de Tene	5	November 28
Diego López (free mulatto)	10	November 28
Alonso de Estrada	20	November 28
Bartolomé Chavarín	8	November 30
Lope de Cobián	8	December 4
Bartolomé de Molinedo	9	December 6
Mateo de Alfaro	15	December 6
Antonio Pinero	5	December 8
Rodrigo de Paneda	10	December 13

PART III

Traders	Loads	Date
Francisco Núñez	5	December 15
Juan Francisco (free mulatto)	5	December 18
Diego Flores	6	December 18
TOTAL	207	

Source: AHMC, secc. B, caja 14, exp. 3

Unfortunately, that document did not record the hometown of all the traders, information that would be valuable in determining the destinations of their aguardiente. One name that stands out on the list is Alonso de Estrada, who appears as a buyer of *vino de cocos* on the hacienda of Zinacamitlán that we analyzed earlier. He appears as both the largest buyer and the most important trader. This man may have been Captain Alonso de Estrada Altamirano, a cattle-breeder in Querétaro who owned land and conducted business in the region of La Barca, Lagos, Colimilla, Tlajomulco, Tala, and Tequila in Nueva Galicia.[686]

The accusation pursued by the *colimenses* brought to light a whole series of irregularities, especially during the government of Lic. Pedro Fernández de Baeza, President of the Audiencia of Nueva Galicia, whom Thomas Calvo considered a protagonist of some particularly notorious episodes in the history of that institution.[687] When alarms over poor administration sounded, Francisco Calderón Romero, a judge at the Audiencia of Mexico, was sent to investigate. Upon arriving in Nueva Galicia, Calderón asked to see the documents that accredited the legal creation of the royal monopoly on *vino de cocos* and mezcal, but was informed that "no such notice has been found".[688] At that moment, the council of Guadalajara, the main party affected by the controversy, entered the fray. In a session held on March 29, 1651, it declared that since this city has a lawsuit pending in this Real Audiencia involving the villa of Colima and commerce by merchants there who seek to suspend the *estanco* on *vino de cocos*, mezcal, and vinegar, and the *sisa* tax [and] because this business is of such great import, to better establish its defense in this dispute [we] appoint as [our] lawyer Lic. don Baltasar de Salinas y Molina who, with the aforementioned Martín de Pinedo, [shall] attend to this cause.[689]

Clearly, the *ayuntamiento* of Guadalajara was striving to justify the *estanco* due to its "great import" for the city, and had hired attorneys to defend its position. By that time (June 4, 1650), the *alcalde mayor* of Colima, don Luis de Caviedes, had issued an order that prohibited anyone, regardless of their status, from sending *vino de cocos* to Nueva Galicia, "until the Viceroy decrees the suspension of the *estanco de vino de cocos* in Guadalajara". His order stipulated a fine of 200 pesos for those who disobeyed.[690] Caviedes' inconformity, in representation of the entire *colimense* community, rested upon the fact that

> one Sebastián Báez, through influences, ruses, and favors that he has procured [and] availed himself of, holds the *estanco de vino de cocos* in the city of Guadalajara, where it is sold publicly at six-and-a-half pesos per *botija*, with merchants and other persons who desire it buying it at an extremely low price like 20 *reales* or even by barter; thus obliging the poor residents of this villa [Colima] to [sell] it at those prices [and] even to leave the barrels, among other inconveniences.[691]

As mentioned above, Báez was the monopoly-holder who won the auction at that time. Caviedes denounced that Báez' monopolist practices severely damaged producers in Colima, so he resolved to close the market to merchants in Guadalajara. It is clear that as long as control of the *vino de cocos* trade lay in Nueva Galicia, palm aguardiente producers in Colima would be at a clear disadvantage due to the severe constraints imposed on their ability to negotiate the price of the drink. If the cost of a botija at the gates of the hacienda was two pesos, and wine was sold in the villa of Colima at 2.25 pesos, then Báez was really filling his pockets, for he bought the drink in Guadalajara at almost the same price at which it was sold in Colima, without considering transport costs and taxes (*alcabalas*), then turned around to sell botijas at 6.5 pesos. This meant that he received 4 pesos for each botija sold under the *estanco*! Moreover, his profit rate of 300% was at a level that few products could attain in New Spain; for example, Chinese silk.

We can now understand the *colimenses'* reaction to Báez' unfair commercial practices, compounded by the accusation in *alcalde mayor* Caviedes' declaration that traders were often forced to leave their botijas on consignment. We can assume that when trade with the province of Colima was banned, Báez sought to procure *vino de cocos* clandestinely in the jurisdiction of Motines, through an individual of Portuguese origin.[692]

It was amidst this altercation that Lic. Calderón Romero arrived in Guadalajara. When he ended his visit, in 1652, he announced the suspension of the *estanco de vino de cocos y mezcal*. All the efforts by the *ayuntamiento* of Guadalajara to stave this off were in vain. Indeed, that decree, framed in the climate of corruption that enveloped the Audiencia of Nueva Galicia, was the prelude to governor Fernández de Baeza's divestiture in 1654, and his death a year later.[693] The suspension of the *estanco* that had led to the creation of a deposit in Zacatecas, impacted that center as well, as an ordinance that year banned the sale of *vino de cocos*, mezcal, and pulque under the argument that consumption of those drinks caused disease and death.[694] It was against this backdrop of irregularities and uncertainty that the first, brief, stage of the *estanco de vino de cocos y mezcal* in Guadalajara ended.

The Estanco Re-established: 1672

The suspension of the royal monopoly in the 1650s meant that the city of Guadalajara lost a key source of income to defray the costs of public works. In March 1671, don Fernando de Haro y Monterroso, fiscal of the Audiencia of Guadalajara, wrote in a letter that the ban on selling mezcal and *vino de cocos* to Indians generated many difficulties because they clandestinely produced other "noxious" drinks from corn and sugarcane, so it would be convenient for society as a whole to re-establish the *estanco* to prevent tragic incidents. The *Protomedicato* of New Spain intervened in favor of *vino de cocos* and mezcal by classifying them as "medicinal" drinks.[695] But those manifestations were simply the initial steps toward reopening the *estanco*, though this time legally with royal authorization.

In a decree of September 7, 1673, doña Mariana de Austria, the Queen Governor, authorized the re-establishment of the royal monopoly, clearly alluding to the goal of financing the project to bring water to Guadalajara. The *estanco* began to operate one year later.[696] From 1674 to 1701, it was auctioned to five monopolists, all residents of Guadalajara. The cost, however, bore no comparison to the previous stage, as the rights were auctioned for just 800 pesos. This time, the premises of the royal monopoly were as follows: (i) a maximum selling price of two *reales* per *cuartillo* (based on the terms of the last auction, to Sebastián Báez in 1650); (ii) that no one in the city or within eight leagues of its limits could sell *vino de cocos* or mezcal without the consent of the monopoly-holder; and (iii) all muleteers who transported the drinks to Zacatecas and San Luis Potosí (the most important destinations for this trade), and so traversed those eight leagues, had to declare their wares at sentry posts installed for that purpose in Sayula and Zapotlán, two obligatory stops *en route* from Colima to Nueva Galicia.[697] Of course, the entire apparatus of justice was alerted to monitor compliance with those stipulations through the services of *alcaldes*, *alguaciles*, and their deputies in the jurisdictions involved.

Table 35. Tithe Collectors for Vino de Cocos and Mezcal (1674–1701)

Years	Monopoly-holder	Cost paid at auction (pesos)	Annual payment, (pesos)
1674-1676	Miguel Thomas	1500	750
1676-1678	Francisco Palacios	1550	775
1678-1682	Francisco Palacios and Pedro Montero de Ledesma	3200	800
1682-1684	Joseph de Camarena	1600	800
1684-1686	Joseph de Camarena	1600	800
1686-1696	Joseph de Camarena	-	800
1696-1698	Lorenzo de Vargas	1400	700
1699-1701	Joseph de Camarena	1622	811

Source: AGI, Guadalajara, 15, R.1, N. 26.

Regarding the profile of the monopoly-holders, Miguel Thomas, who held the rights in 1674, was a chamber scribe who suffered an unfortunate fate, for he was jailed at the end of the second year for failure to pay the cost of his administration. Years later, his heirs would pay off part of his debt.[698] The role of Joseph de Camarena among the monopoly-holders in the last quarter of the 17th century also stood out. Since no other bidder for the *estanco* appeared after 1686, the end of his second period, he maintained control for another decade, until Lorenzo de Vargas posted the winning bid in 1696.

Another marked difference between the first and second stages of the royal monopoly, apart from its diminished value, was the destination of the income it produced. While at first, the *ayuntamiento* of Guadalajara enjoyed the benefits, by the end of the 17th century revenue was channeled into the coffers of the Reinos de Castilla. We cannot lose sight of the fact that the Queen Governor's decree of 1673 stipulated that the *estanco de vino de cocos y mezcal* was created to finance public works to bring water to Guadalajara, and that this was the posture, as well, of the *fiscal*, Fernando de Haro y Monterroso. In reality, however, only 779 pesos were destined to that project, paid by Miguel Thomas in 1674 from the income of his first year as the monopoly-holder. Pedro Montero de Ledesma would contribute by constructing a canal to carry water to the capital,[699] but in a decree dated July 27, 1682, the King ordered that all revenue from *vino de cocos* and mezcal sales in Guadalajara be remitted to the Royal Treasury in Mexico City and, from there, to the Reinos de Castilla.

Interestingly, the Royal Treasury's account books from the first half of the 17th century make no mention of *vino de cocos* or mezcal, perhaps because the *estanco* operated illegally at that time. But even later, after its legal re-establishment in 1672, those products are absent from the lists of goods registered.[700] Why was this? Could they have been included with some other merchandise? An exhaustive review of detailed lists and letters from the Royal Treasury (Tables 36, 37) eventually produced the following figures: between September 1680 and November 1699, 18,119 pesos, 2 *tomines*, and 4 *granos* were deposited in the treasury of the city of Guadalajara in several operations. Of that amount, 16,566 pesos, 5 *tomines*, and 4 *granos* were remitted to the treasury in Mexico City, in 13 parts, so in just two decades, over 90% of the income from the monopoly on *vino de cocos* and mezcal was forwarded to the Iberian Peninsula.

Part III

Table 36. Revenue to the Royal Treasury (Real Caja) of Guadalajara from the Estanco de Vino de Cocos y Mezcal (1680–1699)

Date	Amount entered (pesos)	Date	Amount entered (pesos)
September 2, 1680	1,400	January 13, 1689	800
October 26, 1680	1,000	December 22, 1689	800
November 4, 1680	200	April 23, 1691	800
January 27, 1681	200	February 4, 1692	800
February 25, 1681	550	April 20, 1693	500
June 4, 1681	250	December 5, 1693	300
February 27, 1682	300	December 24, 1693	500
October 29, 1682	700	November 3, 1694	1,100
February 9, 1683	266 ps 5 rs 4 gr	March 17, 1696	800
May 4, 1683	266 ps 5 ts 4 gr	August, 1697	466 ps 5 ts 4 gr
February 9, 1684	266 ps 5 ts 4 gr	September 30, 1697	800
June 23, 1684	533 ps 2 ts 8 gr	January 7, 1698	333 ps 2 ts 8 gr
November 7, 1684	266 ps 5 ts 4 gr	May 12, 1698	233 ps 2 ts 8 gr
April 22, 1686	800	September 15, 1698	233 ps 2 ts 8 gr
July 16, 1686	200	December 29, 1698	233 ps 2 ts 8 gr
February 20, 1687	600	October 8, 1699	540 ps 5 ts 4 gr
October 21, 1687	800	November 25, 1699	78 ps 5 ts

Date	Amount entered (pesos)	Date	Amount entered (pesos)
		TOTAL	18,119 pesos, 2 tomines, 4 granos

Source: AGI, Contaduría, 875.

Table 37. Revenue to the Royal Treasury (Real Caja) of Mexico City from Vino de Cocos and Mezcal Taxes (1683–1697)

Date	Amount entered (pesos)
May 28, 1683	5,433 ps, 2 ts, 8 gr
July 15, 1684	800
January 22, 1685	266 ps, 5 ts, 4 gr
August 16, 1686	1,000
March 2, 1688	1,400
November 19, 1689	800
January 18, 1690	800
April 30, 1691	800
December 5, 1692	800
April 28, 1693	500
December 27, 1693	800
May 9, 1696	1,900
November 28, 1697	1,266 ps, 5 ts, 4 gr
TOTAL	16,566 pesos, 5 tomines, 4 granos

Source: AGI, Contaduría, 875.

Part III

At various moments of the 18th century, in both New Spain and Nueva Galicia, monopolies on *vino de cocos* and mezcal were put up for auction. This has caused confusion among some authors who suggest that *vino de cocos* production continued well into the 18th century. A careful reading of the contents of those auctions, however, confirms that the monopolies simply kept the name "*vino de cocos* and mezcal" from the original events in Guadalajara in the 1630s when, in reality, the only distillate for which potential monopoly-holders were bidding was mezcal. To cite one example, on the initiative of don Ramón González Becerra, the judge of the Real Audiencia of Nueva Galicia and the judge of sales, assessments, and auctions there (*juez de ventas, avaluaciones y almonedas*), a decree was emitted on April 26, 1769, which declared that:

> As Your Mercy has been informed, the cit[ies] of Durango, villa de Llerena, Real and Minas de Sombrerete, Jerez and Fresnillo, Aguascalientes and the province of Juchipila, jurisdictions of Tlaxomulco, Caxititlán, Aguacatlán and Xala, Reales de Minas of San Sebastián and Hostotipac, Santa María de Tequepexpan, Guachinango and Mascota, villa de la Purificación, Ciudad de Nuestra Señora de los Zacatecas, Real de Bolaños and Mazapil, exist with no [revenue] from the monopolies on *vinos de coco* and mezcal, one of the branches that pertain to the Royal Treasury, and that if this were promoted in each [area] the increase would follow [and] be consistent, perhaps resulting in benefits in this regard.[701]

In that year, the *estanco de vino de cocos y mezcal* was put up for auction in villa de Llerena, Real, and Minas de Sombrerete. Although the announcement mentions palm aguardiente, in reality mezcal was the only drink subject to the measure.[702] Monopolies on mezcal, which carried the aggregate "*vino de cocos*" in their name simply through tradition, were also seen in the 18th century in places like the *corregimiento* of Tequila, Tepatitlán, and Zapotlán el Grande.[703] The main advantage of mezcal over *vino de cocos* was that it was produced in Nueva Galicia without the human and raw material costs involved in the latter. Moreover, it was easier to transport to Guadalajara and then distribute to mining districts in central and northern New Spain. In fact, the internal market of alcoholic drinks in Colima in the early 19th century received a substantial number of barrels of mezcal from Tuxcacuesco, Tonaya, Sayula, Tapalpa, Jiquilpan, and Tequila.[704]

But this meant that mezcal would bear the brunt of the social costs of the drunkenness caused by distilled drinks, to which all the evils of the Indians were attributed since those natives "live and die in ignorance of God" due to that drink. As the *alcalde mayor* of Colima, don Miguel José Pérez Ponce de León, narrated in 1776, it was the unbridled consumption of mezcal that caused the Indians of Zapotlán, a neighboring jurisdiction, to riot: "on Easter Thursday of the year seventy-four, a mob of plebes and Indians entered the church, extinguished the candles, disfigured the monument and closed the doors, among other grievous attacks".[705] As this shows, the moral load had passed from *vino de cocos* to mezcal, but that is another story.

VINO DE COCOS MARKETS IN ZACATULA-ACAPULCO

We have left the topic of *vino de cocos* markets in the Zacatula-Acapulco nucleus to the end. There is only scant evidence of the places where it was sold, for it seems that its market was restricted virtually to areas around the palm haciendas where it was produced. Only the wine sent as tithe payments to the Bishopric of Michoacán reached the market of Valladolid, though from there it may have been distributed to other places in New Spain. Information on this, however, is shadowy at best. All we know for certain is that in the second half of the 17th century –concretely in 1668 and 1692– aguardiente was transported to Valladolid, the seat of the Bishopric of Michoacán, as one of the products used to pay the tithe.[706] For this reason, it would have been sold along the route from Zacatula to Valladolid, in places like Churumuco, La Huacana, Santa Clara del Cobre, and Pátzcuaro. That road was a difficult one to transit, as we learn from the Relación de Zacatula: "the nearest town of Spaniards is the city of Valladolid, province of Michoacán; forty-seven leagues distant from this villa [...] long leagues of very rough terrain, roads with many curves, very difficult to walk because of deep ravines, boulders and poor trails; if the roads were not cleared every year, one could not take them.[707]

Furlong's research corroborates the conjecture that *vino de cocos* produced on the haciendas of Coyuca and the surrounding area was taken to two markets: one in the Hot Lands, where it was sold in Churumuco and Apatzingán in exchange for sugar and local textiles; the other around Valladolid and Pátzcuaro, where *vino de cocos*, cacao, and some vanillas were exchanged for wheat and other goods. It was, however, also transported from Coyuca to Ajuchitlán, a salt-producing region where laborers consumed enormous amounts of alcohol and tobacco. Likewise, indigenous merchants and elites from La Guaba, Zacatula, and Petatlán acquired *vino de cocos* from the hacienda of San Bartolomé, surely destined for sailors, stevedores, and merchants in Acapulco who absorbed most of the *vino de cocos* produced in the Zacatula-Acapulco nucleus.[708]

Map 13. Places Where Vino de Cocos from the Zacatula-Acapulco Nucleus Was Consumed

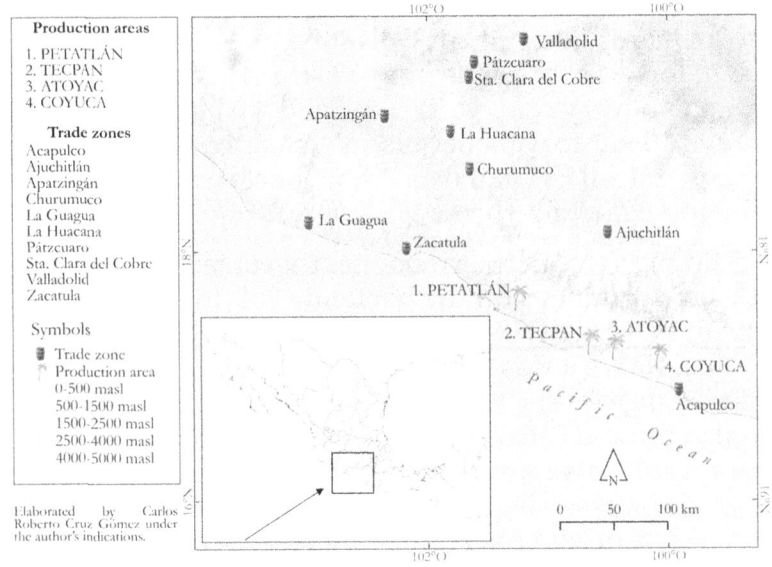

We cannot forget that, in contrast to what occurred in Colima, the production and commerce of this distillate in Acapulco and its surrounding was never officially licensed, a reality that, without doubt, impeded any broader distribution. Perhaps this trade restriction explains why vino de cocos from Colima became more well known than the aguardiente produced in this nucleus, because the Zacatula-Acapulco market was restricted to a more local circuit and did not reach other areas of New Spain? In both Pátzcuaro and the mining zones in central-north New Spain the place of origin of vino de cocos was clearly recognized in the name: the "wine Colima". This could have been a 17th-century equivalent to what we know today as a beverage's "designation of origin". We began this chapter with the serious accusation by the priest in Arantzan against vino de cocos producers in Colima who, in his view, had destroyed the town due to excessive drunkenness. In Zacatecas, vino

PART III

de cocos came to be known as "the drink they call Colima" ("*la bebida que llaman Colima*").⁷⁰⁹

It is, however, highly likely that *vino de cocos* from Zacatula-Acapulco reached taverns in Mexico City, whether along the Valladolid-Zitácuaro-Toluca-Mexico route or the well-traveled road between the port of Acapulco and the capital (see Map 14). The latter entailed a difficult journey over a particularly rough terrain crossed by mighty rivers with strong currents (like the Balsas), the precipitous ascent over, and descent from, the mountains of the Sierra Madre del Sur, and crossing from a zone with a hot climate to one where cold predominated.⁷¹⁰

Map 14. The Route from Acapulco to Mexico City (17th Century)

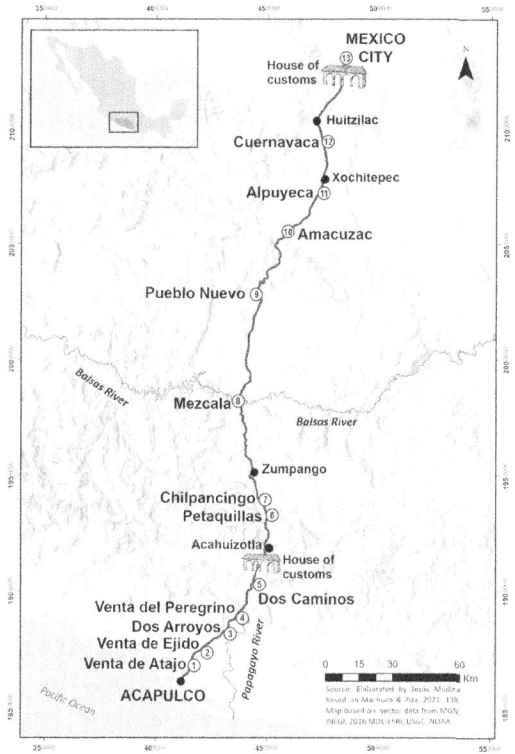

We cannot forget, either, that Mexico City received loads of cacao produced on haciendas in the jurisdiction of Zacatula, so merchants there may well have marketed cacao and aguardiente at the same time. It is also probable that the distillate produced there may have been sold in mining districts after it reached Valladolid, for it is well known that in colonial times a Tarascan commercial circuit began in Pátzcuaro, passed through Valladolid, and reached the mines of Guanajuato and even the city of Zacatecas, where Tarascan traders found markets, opportunities for sales, and stands where they could purchase merchandise and re-supply their stocks.[711]

Final reflections

In these pages we have addressed the topic of the commercialization of *vino de cocos*, following its movement from the gates of the palm haciendas along distinct trade routes. This drink was transported over long distances, a clear demonstration of the high demand it enjoyed in the market for alcoholic drinks. In places like Guadalajara, Valladolid, and Mexico City, the principal market consisted of people who consumed alcoholic drinks in taverns. *Vino de cocos* was attractive there because of its high alcohol content as a distilled beverage. Valladolid's position as the seat of the Bishopric of Michoacán and, hence, a site for tithe collection, meant that *vino de cocos* from both the Colima-Motines and Zacatula-Acapulco nuclei was taken there and then redistributed. Information on the mining districts in New Spain reveals a close relation with alcoholic drinks, for *vino de cocos* served as a stimulant for laborers during the arduous manual work of extracting ore. This explains why this drink reached places as remote as Parral.

But this panorama brings to the fore the question of why demand for *vino de cocos* declined in all those places where trade once enjoyed such marked success. Part of the answer lies in the emergence of other distilled drinks,

Part III

like mezcal and sugarcane aguardiente, which could be made at a much lower cost in both human labor and raw materials. In addition, production of those drinks was not limited to the coastal regions where palm trees grew. It soon became clear that mezcal could be distilled not only in zones near the coast but also in the sierra, depending on the variety of maguey native to each area. This meant that consumers could obtain distilled drinks with a similar alcohol content to that of Colima's *vino de cocos* close to urban areas and mining districts. As a result, consuming *vino de cocos* became less and less attractive. Finally, *vino de cocos* had to deal with prohibitionist policies at different times. This part of the story is the focus of the next chapter.

9. VINO DE COCOS AND PROHIBITIONIST POLICIES

> *For drunkards and pulque have existed since the Conquest.*
> —Anonymous vassal, New Spain, 1692

INTRODUCTION

On the afternoon of Sunday June 8, 1692, a mob of Indians, negros, and mulattos infuriated by the scarcity of corn for their sustenance, set fire to the palace and municipal government buildings in Mexico City amid shouts of *Death to the Viceroy!*, *Death to the corregidor!*, and *Long live pulque!* The celebrated author of New Spain, Carlos de Sigüenza and Góngora, witnessed the tumult and described in detail a terrifying scene in which thousands of rioters unleashed their fury against authorities in the capital. For many, the main cause of the uprising was pulque, the beverage *par excellence* of central Mexico from pre-Hispanic times that was sold in establishments called *pulquerías*. Reports by figures in government (*ayuntamiento*), the Cathedral, the University, and numerous ecclesiasts "considered pulque the concrete motive for the uprising".[712] Other observers, however, held that pulque was a pretext that officials used to occult the real cause, which was the absence of an adequate administration of public policies governing grains, for at that time supplies of corn, the staple of the pre-Hispanic diet and, later, of that of New Spain as well, had grown scarce.[713] On August 20, 1692, around two months after those events in the public square, a vassal in New Spain wrote an anonymous letter to the King to express his feelings. Among other things, he stated that the cause of the riot had nothing to do with alcohol, "for there have been drunkards and pulque since the Conquest".[714]

The 1692 uprising and denouncements of pulque provide good illustrations of the prohibitionist policy implemented in New Spain from the early Colonial period. While virtually all the decrees (*cédulas*), orders (*mandamientos*), and ordinances (*ordenanzas*) issued at distinct levels of government in attempts to slow or regulate the circulation of alcoholic drinks cited public morality and health as their principal arguments, they also mentioned economic inconveniences. Official discourses emphasized that drunkenness among Indians and other castes led people to "ignore God" and commit all manner of sins and crimes. At the same time, many "drinks of the land" were blamed for causing illnesses and deaths, especially when adulterated with substances that increased their alcohol content. A third argument that appears repeatedly in those bans stressed that the sale of local drinks harmed the King's interests by "interfering" in the collection of his *reales derechos*; that is, the tax that the Crown imposed on wine from Castille, but that was not applicable to locally-produced beverages.[715]

One thing, however, was very clear: when vested interests existed behind a certain drink that generated benefits for producers, middlemen, merchants, and authorities alike, all arguments could be reverted and, instead of being labeled "harmful", those beverages were presented as "medicinal", authorized by competent physicians. Broadly speaking, these were the limits within which the debate on prohibiting or authorizing fermented and

Part III

distilled drinks in New Spain developed, discussions that, of course, included *vino de cocos*.

Throughout its brief history, *vino de cocos* was a focus of debate between defenders and detractors. The former, including producers, merchants, and consumers of the distillate, argued that it was a healthful, medicinal drink that could cure almost any malady. The latter, mostly civil and ecclesiastical authorities at all levels, in contrast, viewed it as a threat not only to public morality and health, but also to the economic interests of vintners in Castille. As a result, *vino de cocos* was condemned for its dire effects and disorders of conscience among Indians and castes who committed crimes and offenses against God when they consumed it. So, while its defenders proclaimed it an effective remedy "for curing wounds and serious, difficult diseases",[716] in the words of a physician in Colima in 1612, on the opposing side, the parish priest of Arantza –a town in the Meseta Purépecha in the Bishopric of Michoacán– stated that "Colima has destroyed this province with its palms and the *vino de cocos* it distills"[717] because Indians, children and adults, women and men alike, had the "deeply-rooted vice" of drunkenness. Despite such diametrically opposed postures, this was an open society moved by vested interests on each side, fully capable of such flexibility in its discourses, so that when the occasion merited it two such disparate visions could be conciliated to allow a controversial product –like *vino de cocos*– to forge ahead.

Was this drink benign or malignant for the society of New Spain? The answer is 'both' at the same time, and the distinct perspectives just outlined lead us to reflect on the profound ambiguity that surrounded the issue of alcoholic drinks in New Spain more generally. Throughout the 17th century, authorities both civil and ecclesiastical maintained a dual discourse on *vino de cocos* consumption, repudiating it at certain times but defending it at others. As a result, the analysis of the precise context of these postures sheds light on each side's motivations, which transited through arguments based not only on public health and morality, but also on grace and clement justice. In the pages that follow, we analyze the fate of *vino de cocos* as it confronted viceregal policies.

THE PROHIBITION OF ALCOHOLIC BEVERAGES IN NEW SPAIN

In the western world, regulating consumption of wine dated back to Early Medieval legislation, conceived to ensure moderation in ingestion and prevent adulterations and the use of additives that could be harmful to human health. Óscar Cruz Barney explains that through the *Fuero Real* and the *Siete Partidas* authorities sought to impede imbibers from adding lime, salt, or other adulterating substances due to a serious concern "that wine causes men to ignore God and lose themselves"; hence, the need for temperance.[718]

Those ideas were carried to New Spain, where consumption of alcoholic drinks acquired other nuances, such as the paternalist posture of civil and ecclesiastical authorities regarding the Indians, who were considered childlike and, therefore, needed to be cared for and protected from their natural "inclinations" toward inebriety. That vision was the driving force behind laws created to prevent consumption of wine from Castille and pulque, the beverage (colloquially, *caldo*) that circulated most widely in central New Spain. The fear was that consumption of alcoholic drinks by Indians would lead them to return to their idolatrous ways, so the authorities soon became convinced that the nectar of the maguey plant, a vehicle for pre-Hispanic ceremonialism, had to be suppressed at all costs.

In his pioneering work on drunkenness in central New Spain and Oaxaca, William B. Taylor emphasized that both colonial officials and the clergy exaggerated the degree of inebriety among the Indians, whom they deemed infantile beings incapable of temperance. Spaniards drank, of course, but supposedly with moderation: "for Spaniards, grape wine was a symbol of civilization and Catholic tradition, and an essential cultural element of dining".[719] In the view of the Spanish, however, Indians drank uncontrollably and, worse yet, consumed concoctions made from plants and roots "of the land" that, even in the best cases, were linked to ancient ritual practices. Here we have two key elements that help us understand the attitude that the authorities assumed and expressed so clearly in Indian legislation: first, the lack of moderation among Indians and other castes who, due to their "natural inclination toward drunkenness", lacked sufficient self-control and, second, the high esteem in which a plant like the grape was held, to the detriment of maguey and "other local roots" that soon came to be identified with Mesoamerican ceremonial.

The First Prohibitions

The Empress, in Toledo in 1529, and the Prince, in 1545 in Valladolid, banned consumption of a "certain wine" –pulque– that the Indians strengthened by adding roots, "with which they become inebriated and when drunk perform the ceremonies and sacrifices they accustomed in ancient times", while also "losing their heads" and committing crimes and "nefarious carnal vices".[720] José J. Hernández Palomo explained that "white" pulque was allowed to circulate under very precise authorizations, but that adulterated forms fortified by adding "herbs" were banned.[721]

The 1545 law dealt with the concept of "drinks of the land" (*bebidas de la tierra*), a label applied to virtually all alcoholic drinks elaborated in New Spain to differentiate them from wines from Castile. That law prohibited "the production of wines of the land with roots, and their sale, whether publicly or clandestinely, due to the great harm they do to the Indians [who] lose their senses, emit much howling and shouting, and while in that state practice idolatry".[722] As the process of Spanish colonization advanced, the discourse on the "natural" drunkenness of Indians and the offenses to public morals they committed was accompanied by the economic damage that "drinks of the land" caused by competing with wines from Castille in detriment to the royal treasury. The arrival of Viceroy Luis de Velasco El Joven (1607-1611) marked a watershed in the production of local beverages, for one of his policies was to pursue and eradicate those drinks. In 1608, Velasco regimented pulque production and consumption, by strictly conditioning, though not completely prohibiting it.[723]

THE AMBIGUOUS DISCOURSE SURROUNDING VINO DE COCOS

On March 29, 1610, Viceroy Velasco emitted an ordinance that halted production of "a wine drink made from the coconuts of palm trees" that was elaborated in the provinces of Colima and Zacatula. Velasco was seriously troubled by information he received firsthand from the fiscal, Francisco de Leos, who notified him that the Indians became inebriated with this cheap, strong drink, which "costs them their health and lives". Moreover, *vino de cocos* circulated in such abundance that it could easily be mixed with wine from Castille "[blessed] to celebrate the ministries of the doctrine".[724] But the Viceroy's ban also had economic motivations, for the King had been losing revenue (*reales derechos*) since the drink was not subject to taxation. Thus, Velasco's prohibition presented three arguments: a concern for public morality, religious aspects, and criteria that were economic in nature:

> Don Luis de Velasco, Viceroy. Given that the Attorney don Francisco de Leos, His Majesty's fiscal in this Real Audiencia, has brought to my attention that a wine drink made from palm coconuts has been introduced into the provinces of Zacatula and Colima [and] is so abundant in the

Part III

towns that just one of them has sixty taverns where it is served and sold publicly [and] because it is so cheap and strong the natives [imbibe] it to such excess that it costs them their health and lives, and this impedes sales of wine from Castille in those provinces, causing great losses to His Majesty's royal revenue. Apart from these inconveniences, others occur in the sacristies of those towns where the Indians [in service] can mix *vino de cocos* with the wine from Castille that is [blessed] to celebrate the ministries of the doctrine. To remedy this, it would be convenient to prohibit *vino de cocos* under severe penalties. And, having seen that it is just to prevent the harm and inconveniences that can result from its production, I hereby prohibit and forbid, in general, any and all persons who are present, or reside, in those provinces, of any status or condition whatsoever, through their own actions or those of others, from making or producing *vino de cocos*, or selling said wine publicly or secretly for any effect, under the penalty of losing all the wine they are found to produce or sell and [paying a fine] of one thousand Castilian ducats, if a Spaniard, to be divided in thirds, tribunal, judge, and accusers, plus exile for two years from the area and place where this occurs, and from ten leagues around. In the case of mestizos, negros, or mulattos, in addition to losing their wine, they shall receive one hundred lashes in public and incur in the aforementioned penalty of exile. For Indians who produce or sell it, the vessels containing the wine shall be broken, and the drink spilled so they cannot benefit from it, and they shall be given fifty lashes while tied to a pole erected for this purpose in the square or market (*tianguis*) of the towns where this occurs. And I order that His Majesty's judges in those provinces, each one in his jurisdiction, be especially rigorous in the observance, compliance, and execution of this prohibition and announce it publicly so that all are so informed. Dated in Mexico on the twenty-ninth day of the month of March of the year one thousand six hundred and ten. Marqués de Salinas. By order of the Viceroy, Pedro de la Torre.[725]

The arguments that stand out in Viceroy Velasco's ordinance reiterate, to some extent, resolutions imposed on other drinks, like pulque and, later, *chinguiritos*.[726] According to the Viceroy, it was the low cost of *vino de cocos* that led to excessive consumption and its dire effects on the health of Indians and other castes. But he also held it responsible for reducing the King's revenue by "impeding" sales of wine from Castille, so he banned people of all castes from producing, selling, or benefitting in any way from *vino de cocos*, under threat of severe punishment.

Was Velasco's ordinance the first to ban *vino de cocos*? In reality, no. From the moment the drink was elaborated in the province of Colima, officials of the *ayuntamiento* and *alcaldes mayores* had issued warnings to curtail its circulation in Indian towns. It is interesting, however, to observe that their alerts did not seek to eradicate aguardiente, but only to remove the native population from the list of consumers.

Thus, from the early years of the 17th century, the *alcalde mayor* Francisco Escudero de Figueroa (1603-1605), upon discovering that both Spaniards and *indios chinos* were introducing *vino de cocos* into Indian towns, warned that he would sanction any Spaniard who failed to obey the order with a fine of ten pesos and exile from the villa of Colima, while the penalties for natives and *indios chinos* would be one hundred lashes.[727] Gaspar de Barahona, the deputy of the *alcalde mayor* Juan de Rivera (1605-1608), denounced that *vino de cocos* was being sold to Indians in the town of Coquimatlán, jurisdiction of Colima,[728] while the *alcalde mayor* Fernando de Hoyo y Azoca (1610-1612) condemned Juan Romo for selling *vino de cocos* and wine from Castille to Indians and "unscrupulous Spaniards".[729] Pedro de Palencia, the resident judge in Colima in 1612, sentenced the merchant Martín Parrales for selling *vino de coco* to Indians in the town of San José (Colima).[730] Clearly, the bans imposed on *vino de cocos* focused on Indians and "unscrupulous" individuals, but did not completely close the door to producing the drink, as long as it remained exclusively in the hands of Spaniards and their *indios chinos vinateros*. As the 17th century advanced, however, the ban was extended to mestizos, mulattos, and negros,

Part III

groups that lived under the watchful eye and suspicions of colonial authorities.

Despite Velasco's 1610 ordinance and the series of prohibitions imposed by some *alcaldes mayores* in the first decade of the 17th century in attempts to control consumption of aguardiente among the Indians, in practice *vino de cocos* continued to be produced and sold among the majority of Colima's inhabitants. Indeed, as the preceding chapter made clear, that was the period when long-distance trade in *vino de cocos* began, with the drink being transported from Colima to mining zones in northern New Spain and entering the markets for alcoholic beverages in places like Guadalajara, Valladolid, and Mexico City.

In Defense of *Vino de Cocos*

Reacting to the disobedience of Viceroy Velasco's order by residents of Colima, the Real Audiencia of Mexico decreed, in 1612, that all palm trees in the province of Colima exploited to produce *vino de cocos* were to be chopped down. This resolution took the entire population by surprise, but the town council reacted immediately by calling an assembly to organize and appeal the order. Its defense was based on the testimony of twelve witnesses –all residents of Colima– who articulated ten broad arguments to prevent the mass felling of trees because those plantations constituted the villa's principal economic activity:[731]

1. That the villa of Colima was one of the oldest in New Spain.
2. That the residents of Colima guarded the coasts and sighted enemy pirates.
3. That the residents of Colima provided supplies for the Manila Galleon.
4. That the palm trees were the villa's main source of sustenance.

5. That the palm trees were not "wild, but cultivated" by conquistadores.
6. That Indians did not get drunk on *vino de cocos* but on drinks made from other plants.
7. That *vino de cocos* was healthful and medicinal.
8. That products like oil, honey, and vinegar were also extracted from the palm trees.
9. That *vino de cocos* did not reduce consumption of wine from Castille.
10. That the villa of Colima would be depopulated if the trees were cut down.

The council's argument that hewing the palm trees would harm all residents began by emphasizing (i) that the villa of Colima was among the oldest in New Spain, and (ii) that the *colimenses* kept permanent guard against the threat of European pirates, were prepared to defend His Majesty's coasts, and provisioned the crews of the Manila Galleon for its voyages to Acapulco. How did these points relate to *vino de cocos*? Well, if the palm trees –that many voices described as the villa's "principal economic sustenance"– were hewn residents would have no choice but to abandon the province and look for better opportunities elsewhere, leaving the coast unguarded and vulnerable to attacks by pirates and the Galleon's crew members bereft of provisions. The council also showed its ingenuity by devising a posture that defended not only *vino de cocos* production, but also that of other derivatives of the coconut palm, such as water, copra, oil, milk, and sugar, which they identified as efficacious remedies for diseases that were difficult to treat, while emphasizing that because all *colimenses* had these substances at hand they did not need to travel long distances to obtain other kinds of cures. One protagonist of the defense of the trees was the villa's doctor, Martín Hernández, whose testimony included this view:

> through extensive experience this witness has found [*vino de cocos*] to be most healthful and medicinal [...]. It is commonly applied to cure lesions and severe, difficult diseases, as which experience has shown. Whether as a drink, a laboratory [preparation], or other remedies too numerous to mention, it has healed innumerable people [including] Indians in this province who have been cured with said aguardiente. And ingested as a drink it is very good and healthful, for it cuts phlegm [and] causes sweating against the stings of scorpions and other vermin.[732]

The medicinal properties that the surgeon Hernández attributed to *vino de cocos* were explained, as in all contemporary colonial documents, in terms of Galen's theory of the humors which, among other elements, sustained that the human body was constituted by four principal liquids –black bile, yellow bile, phlegm, and blood– such that the deficit or excess of any one was the cause of disease. In that period, several physicians of recognized prestige resided in the city of Guadalajara, including Enrique Tavares – said to be the first titled doctor to practice in the capital of Nueva Galicia– and Juan de Cárdenas. Both men recommended drinking *vino de cocos* to maintain good health, according to the *colimense* Sebastián de Vera, a nephew of don Santiago de Vera, governor and captain general of the Philippines and, later, governor of Nueva Galicia. Juan de Cárdenas treated don Santiago de Vera (an "old friend") in the early 17th century in Guadalajara.[733] His nephew affirmed that don Santiago often ordered *vino de cocos* from Colima because he had been drinking it since he lived in the Philippines, and only in this way could he maintain his "health and life".[734]

It is likely that Sebastián exaggerated Juan de Cárdenas' alleged recommendation to drink *vino de cocos*, for a review of his book, *Problemas y secretos maravillosos de las Indias*, authored in 1591, did not turn up any reference to the benefits of *vino de cocos*, even though two chapters of that work are devoted to discussing the properties and effects of chocolate. What his text does contain is his opinion on the characteristics of wine in general:

> As a hot [beverage], wine engenders many cold diseases; but be advised that it only has this effect [of causing cold diseases like grippe (*pasmo*), palsy, and *tortura de boca*] when given in excess, for it extinguishes natural heat and cannot be cooked or digested, so it engenders crude, phlegmatic excrements, and these are [the effects] that those illnesses engender.[735]

Cárdenas' explanation of the ingestion of wine in general thus also alluded to Galen's humors. Was *vino de cocos* a healthful drink or a harmful beverage? It is evident that the *colimenses* collected as much evidence as possible in favor of *vino de cocos* because nothing less than their palm plantations were at stake and, with them, a substantial portion of their economic income. But it is also true that a great deal was written on the medicinal properties of *vino de palmas*, not only in Colima but also in the Philippines, its place of origin. It is worthwhile to recover writings on this topic from the 16th and 17th centuries because in addition to their historical value they hold scientific interest that future studies could explore.

Dozens of pages were penned on the medicinal properties of *tuba*, *vino de cocos*, and other parts of the palm tree (Table 38). This tree represented a complete, highly useful system of traditional medicine in Southeast Asia and around the Indian Ocean that was later carried to the Mar del Sur of New Spain where *indios chinos* lived. One key affirmation in the *Provança* of 1612 was that the defense of the palm trees focused not only on exploitation of *tuba* and aguardiente, but also on the entire tree due to its usefulness in both medicine and daily life.[736] Colonial sources in Asia and America allow us to identify, in general, the activity of *Cocos nucifera* L. in three main systems:

digestive, renal, and respiratory.[737] Some observations by Father Francisco Ignacio Alzina in the Philippines summarize this affirmation quite well:

> Not only is the drink bountiful and healthful in daily experiences, as everyone knows, but is also a very good medicine, for it refreshes the blood, reduces inflammation of the liver, eliminates obstructions in the lungs, softens the abdomen and its blockages, and can be said to cure everything because many who could find no remedy for their difficult illnesses find themselves cured easily by drinking *tuba*.[738]

A recent scientific study determined that the *tuba* produced today in Colima has antimicrobial activity against E. coli, one of the most common bacteria that contaminates food and drinks worldwide, and that is found primarily in human waste. Moreover, *tuba* promotes proliferation of yeasts and acetic acid (BAA) and lactic acid bacteria (BAL), the latter considered probiotic microorganisms due to their health benefits. These findings show that the components of *tuba* improve the body's ability to use nutrients[739] and confirm the benefits attributed to the drink in past centuries.

Documents on the digestive system emphasize the use of coconut water and *tuba* to combat parasites and cure indigestion and diarrhea. Father Manuel Blanco said it was "an admirable medicine for those with phthisis".[740] Indeed, according to the *protomédico* Francisco Hernández, palm tree bark was very efficacious in controlling diarrhea, curing indigestion, and tonifying the stomach.[741]

Table 38. Medicinal Properties of the Coconut Palm and Its Derivatives

Product	Use
Vino de cocos	Beneficial for curing diseases of the urine and healing consumptives (Hernández, 1576). Efficacious with ground cloves for "chills", helps with buzzing in the ears and mange (De la Madre de Dios, 1611). Useful for refreshing the blood, reducing liver inflammation, eliminating lung obstructions, softening the stomach and its obstructions (Alzina, 1668 [Yepes, 1996]). Beneficial for those with phthisis and cures tuberculosis, gonorrhea, hernias, and maladies of the stomach (Blanco, 1837).
Tuba	Tuba with eggs relieves asthma and chest pain (De la Madre de Dios, 1611). Useful for reducing liver inflammation, curing urinary pain, eliminating pulmonary obstructions, and cleansing the stomach (Alzina, 1668 [Yepes, 1996]).
Water	Useful for curing fevers, tempering heat, curing and cleaning cataracts in the eyes, cleaning the cutis of women, correcting the blood, purging the stomach, cleaning the urinary tract, calming pain, relieving the chest, curing bilious fevers (Hernández, 1576). Beneficial for fevers and blood chambers (De la Madre de Dios, 1611) and for those with urinary problems (Alzina, 1668 [Yepes, 1996]). For curing tuberculosis, gonorrhea, hernias, and maladies of the stomach (Blanco, 1837).
Pulp	Multiplier effect on phlegmatic humors [and] aphrodisiac (Hernández, 1576).
Milk	Beneficial for purging the "chambers" or dysentery (Fernández de Oviedo, 1523). Taken with salt in the morning it aids in killing worms (Hernández, 1576).
Oil	Mild purgative of the stomach and intestines, useful for evacuating bilious and phlegmatic humors. Calms pains "caused by cold" and reduces scarring (Hernández, 1576). Useful in combatting cough, erysipelas, constipation, vomiting with blood, cataracts (De la Madre de Dios, 1611), and asthma (Alzina, 1668 [Yepes, 1996]).
Sugar	Beneficial for relieving grippe, easing the chest, strengthening the stomach and brain, aids in digestion (Hernández, 1576).

Part III

Product	Use
Shell	Beneficial for curing renal colic and expelling stones (Fernández de Oviedo, 1523). Relieves paralysis, strengthens the nerves (Hernández, 1576).
Bark	Efficacious in controlling diarrhea, curing indigestion and tonifying the stomach (Hernández, 1576).

In the renal system, *vino de cocos* was believed to have a beneficial effect on easing pain caused by kidney stones; that is, renal colic (nephrolithiasis). Thus, based on information he gathered from sources in Asia, Felipe II's *protomédico*, Francisco Hernández, stated in his *Historia de las plantas de Nueva España* that

> this kind of wine [de cocos], admirably benefits consumptives and is similarly effective for patients with urine and kidney problems. It is found only on the Philippine islands. Among the indigenous, or ourselves, who suffer from these diseases, the drink cleanses those parts and breaks up and expels the stones.[742]

Antonio de Pigafetta had observed the curative effect on the renal system in 1521. In his *Relazione del primo viaggio*, he narrated how inhabitants of the Ladrones or Mariana Islands never suffered kidney disease thanks to the availability of palm aguardiente. Drinking liquids from coconut shell gourds also came to be considered beneficial. In this regard, Fernández de Oviedo wrote that "those who suffer gallbladder pain and are accustomed to drinking from those cups say they have found a remedy for the disease [that] breaks up the stone they have and expels it through the urine".[743] The *protomédico* Hernández affirmed that those beautiful cups elaborated from coconut shells and adorned with gold and silver, "through I know not what virtues", gained fame for making drinks healthful and giving them the potential to relieve paralysis and strengthen the nerves.[744] Father Alzina was no less eloquent: "in addition to curiosity, they say that the water they drink for problems with stones is medicinal, and often administer the remedy in cups made from coconut shells".[745]

Vino de cocos could also be combined with other plants: when mixed with cloves it was useful in cases of "chills",[746] while mixed with tobacco leaves (Nicotiana tabacum L.) it functioned as a local analgesic, disinfectant, and anti-inflammatory substance. Father Manuel Blanco referred to this remedy:

> For hernias or fractures the Indians have the custom, after introducing the intestine, of applying a fresh tobacco leaf soaked in coconut aguardiente, and after heating it over a fire, placing a suitable cushion with a bandage on top: which is excellent medicine if the problem is recent, and I have seen some Indians cured in this way.[747]

The protomédico Hernández also noted that vino de cocos was harmful for "those who suffer obstructions, especially of the spleen, or dropsy".[748] The principal contraindication for vino de cocos was, of course, excessive consumption. In contrast, it was not recommended for people who suffered from dropsy; that is, the accumulation of water in muscle tissue. Father Blanco added that it was

> good for Indians and Europeans who are accustomed to it; but those who are not find the odor and flavor unpleasant, and it does terrible harm to the latter because in addition to accelerated aging, they begin to acquire irregular obesity, suffer sleep loss and lose their appetite and often die (many suddenly) of chest dropsy, or scurvy, or evacuations: others lose their intellectual faculties and become tremulous, or stupid with memory loss, or go insane. These terrible ravages are also caused by European wines and aguardientes, but they take longer.[749]

But now it is time to return to our starting point: the Provança. What happened to the order to chop down all the palm trees in Colima? Did the medicinal arguments offered in support of *vino de cocos* and other derivatives of the palm tree do the trick? Or did opinions opposed to distilled drinks like *vino de cocos* win the day? After elaborating its Provança, in 1612, Colima's town council granted a power-of-attorney to Juan Nieto Dávalos, a lawyer at the Real Audiencia of Mexico, to appeal the looming order in its name, promising to pay him one thousand pesos for his "work and petition".[750] This was a good first step to negotiations to defend the palm trees and *vino de cocos* production. What happened in the following months? It is highly likely that the Real Audiencia sent a commission to Colima to learn firsthand what was happening around aguardiente production, for in 1614 the council sent a second letter to the Audiencia through its lawyer, Juan Nieto Dávalos, to protest the annoyances caused by "some imposters" who, on the pretext of

> learning the affairs of the haciendas and ranches that operate in this province making *vino de cocos* [and] pretending to [act] against the ordinances, and Mesta y *matanzas*, measured the farms and visited them and other sites, fields, gardens, and homes of residents... for only one end and effect... in their own interest to hassle and annoy those residents for all they do is harm them and ruin this Republic.[751]

In the end, the Real Audiencia's order to cut down the trees was suspended. The *colimenses*' arguments, presented in their zeal to maintain control over local affairs, noted that people from outside wanted to benefit from the delicate situation they faced because of that order of the Real Audiencia of Mexico. For this reason, they warned authorities in the capital of any eventuality that might occur in relation to this matter. In the same letter, the council reported that the region was mired in poverty due to "extensive ruin" caused by fires. The Provança proved successful, as did the posture that the *colimenses* adopted to "obey but not comply" (*obedézcase pero no se cumpla*).[752] By that time, the coconut palm was deeply rooted in the zone and important economic and social interests had been created around it, as this episode shows.

The Censure of Vino de Cocos

To this point, we have discussed the many medicinal properties of *tuba* and *vino de cocos* according to sources in Asia and Spanish America. But what did *vino de cocos*' detractors say? On what did they base their justification for labeling it as harmful and pressuring to have it prohibited? We cannot fail to note that the controversy over the drink's harmful or beneficial properties for public health emerged on at least two fronts: the public health of Indians –mentioned earlier by Viceroy Velasco– and that of mineworkers. Regarding the latter, on January 10, 1646, the *corregidor* of Zacatecas, Pedro Sáenz Izquierdo, received a royal ordinance that ordered him to allow free transit of *vino de cocos* and mezcal. Like the *colimenses* mentioned above, he also applied the formula "obey but do not comply", for he considered those aguardientes "immensely harmful" for health, especially among mine laborers. According to his consultations with physicians and surgeons, those drinks damaged men's bodies because Zacatecas' climate was cold, but the drinks were very hot and affected "the natural heat of the extremes".[753] The following is a fragment of his opinion:

> Vino de cocos and mezcals [are] immensely harmful for the health of people of all statuses and castes in this city, whose climate has caused, and causes, severe diseases and widespread plagues, especially among native servants and mineworkers. In consultations with physicians and surgeons they agree that whenever said diseases have appeared their cause has been those wines, based on [the fact] that the climate is extremely cold, so the effects of [their] natural heat are felt in the extreme. They increase internal heat [and] violate and corrupt, causing diseases that do not occur in hot lands, because the natural heat dilates the extremes and [works] in the interior to eliminate this damage. [To] remedy this, the *corregidores* [and] their

antecessors have always banned them with severe punishments based on the prohibition imposed by the Lord visitors [of] this kingdom, especially don Diego de Medrano, in a decree of the past year of six hundred and twenty [that] allowed the sale of mezcals as a medication in pharmacies. And the causes [and] motives that existed to support said decree and the other acts of said *corregidores*, [and their] authorization are included in this royal provision to bring this to His Majesty's attention. And to [demonstrate] the damage that these wines cause, especially that of coconuts, and the effects they can have on a human body, they have been spilled on the ground [...] and small bags of chili seeds and lime to increase their strength have been found in the barrels that contain them.[754]

Corregidor Sáenz turned to the Hippocratic-Galenic theory to explain why distilled drinks so severely harmed the bodies of mineworkers, and stressed that *vino de cocos* was adulterated with chili seeds and lime, a measure also detected in other drinks elaborated in New Spain. A deposit for *vino de cocos* and mezcal had been established in Zacatecas only a few years earlier, after the creation of the royal monopoly in Guadalajara, so we cannot rule out the possibility that what lay behind the *corregidor's* posture were the vested interests of Castilian vintners[755] since *vino de cocos* was in high demand in that mining zone.[756]

In support of this affirmation, in 1640 an "Instruction" was issued to establish a concession (*asiento*) on alcoholic drinks in Zacatecas that included wine from Castille and Parras, *vino de cocos*, and mezcal. The measure was conceived to maintain and sustain the Barlovento Fleet by obtaining fiscal resources. We read in that "Instruction" that wine from Castille was "a principal, necessary sustenance" of the city, while *vino de cocos* and mezcal had been studied by physicians who recommended their consumption, for "not only [are they] not harmful, but actually useful and beneficial for the people who work, especially in mines".[757] It is clear, then, that economics played a significant role when it came to deciding when to prohibit and when to allow an alcoholic drink.

Perhaps the place that best evidenced the ambiguities and contradictions in the policies adopted on alcoholic drinks is the *estanco de vino de cocos y mezcal* imposed in Guadalajara in the 17th century. In the previous chapter we discussed the economic aspects related to that institution, but we now analyze the debates that centered on public health and economy, which were determining factors in its repeal and re-establishment.

In 1672, don Fernando Calderón y Romero, governor of Nueva Galicia, ordered the re-implementation of the *estanco de vino de cocos y mezcal* in Guadalajara. Calderón was the official "visitor" who, in the 1650s, had revealed the poor administration of the governor of Nueva Galicia, Pedro Fernández de Baeza, after which the *estanco* was suspended, in 1652. But now, as governor of Nueva Galicia, Calderón revived this royal monopoly to pay for public works in Guadalajara. To achieve his goal, he wrote "secret and separate papers" to the Bishop of Guadalajara, the prelates of the Orders of San Francisco and San Agustín, and the Society of Jesus, seeking their opinions on whether those drinks should be sold once again in the city. They all gave their approval.

The medical sector was not left out, as two physicians in the city were consulted, Juan de Vera and Simón de Oro. They opined, as well, that when consumed in moderation *vino de cocos* and mezcal, far from being harmful, were "intrinsically healthful and beneficial". They added that the Indians' practice of going into forests and ravines to elaborate their own drinks, far from any surveillance, caused grievous problems. But the key question was how to control inebriety and ensure temperance. Their view was that "this could be remedied through administration by persons of good conscience, and by providing [the drinks] to Indians in moderation or in the most convenient way".[758] They thus let it be known that they agreed with the *estanco*, provided it was administered by persons of "good conscience". It is important to mention here that, in 1641, Juan de Vera had been appointed physician for the Barlovento Fleet[759] and later, in the 1670s, had gone to reside in Guadalajara. Unfortunately, we have no additional information on Simón de Oro. Below, we transcribe a fragment of the viewpoint of physicians in Guadalajara on *vino de cocos* and mezcal:

> Most of the afflictions and pestilences the Indians suffer are caused by inebriety from the wines they make from diverse roots. The diligence of judges does not suffice to prevent this because with this goal in mind they go to ravines and forests. When consumed in moderation [the drink] they call *vino de cocos*, from Colima, is very healthful, as is mezcal, very medicinal and useful not only for Indians but also for other people of this Kingdom who drink it, as well as in religious communities. And drunkenness among the Indians is less harmful [when they drink] these wines from Colima than from those they make with pestilential roots and herbs, which they consume when [wine] from Colima is not available. Finally, we declare that *vino de cocos* from Colima and mezcal, consumed in moderation, are intrinsically healthful and beneficial, and that the inconveniences that led to the prohibition on their entry and trade in this city are due to excessive consumption, which could be remedied through administration by persons of good conscience and providing it to Indians in moderation or as is most convenient. This is our view in Guadalajara on March twenty-third of the year one thousand six hundred and seventy. Don Juan de Vera. Simón de Oro.[760]

This opinion sufficed for Calderón y Romero to secure the support of the Church and physicians to reintroduce sales of *vino de cocos* and mezcal in Guadalajara, based on two arguments; first, that when consumed temperately "it is not harmful, but actually very healthful"; and, second, that the earlier prohibition had caused great harm because the Indians could make other alcoholic drinks from sugarcane, corn, plums, or mesquite, "and to get drunk go to the forests, which has caused many contagious diseases, sudden deaths and, worse yet, all manner of grave sins".[761]

Thus, in a decree issued in Guadalajara on January 19, 1672, Calderón ordered that "*vino de cocos* can be sold publicly in taverns and stores for a period of four years [and] that license is to be issued to the residents of said town of Colima and its district, establishing settlements and rental agreements by the individuals who are to sell it".[762] On the conditions of the auction, they took the decade of 1650 as a reference; that is, when the *estanco* had ceased to operate in the city. Calderón added that "as is supported by declarations of the *protomedicato* of New Spain [and] the opinion of physicians of this city, not only is [*vino de cocos*] not harmful, but when consumed in moderation is very healthful and medicinal".[763]

That was not the only occasion when some authority or individual, desirous to demonstrate the medicinal qualities of *vino de cocos*, mentioned the support of the Protomedicato of New Spain. As John Tepaske observed, the Tribunal of the *Real Protomedicato de la Nueva España* was organized definitively in 1646, though similar bodies had existed earlier. Their functions included inspecting pharmacies and remedies and administering examinations to physicians and surgeons.[764] Unfortunately, the institution's records contain no reports of inspections of *vino de cocos*, but since numerous sources speak of this attribution it is highly likely that they occurred.[765]

Returning to Calderón, the urgency to demonstrate the medicinal properties of *vino de cocos* was driven more by the need to obtain resources to defray the costs of public works to carry water to Guadalajara –revenues that would come from the *estanco*– than any concern for the health of residents, especially Indians. In a decree of September 7, 1673, doña Mariana de Austria, the Queen Governor, authorized the re-establishment of the royal monopoly with the declared goal of conducting water to the city. The measure began to operate a year later.[766] But this time the move did not generate the results the city expected, for a large portion of the income was channeled to Spain, as we discussed in the previous chapter.

This episode does, however, reveal quite clearly that *vino de cocos* was deemed harmful when the goal was to benefit vested economic interests that opposed the drink, but was classified as "medicinal" and "healthful" when the aim was to capture resources for public works, or when the Crown perceived that its finances were being threatened. This situation was not, of course, exclusive to palm aguardiente. Juan Pedro Viqueira has pointed out that pulque faced a similar situation around 1663, when annual tax registers reported revenues of 40,000 pesos: "after discovering this unsuspected, potential source of income for the Royal Treasury, the Crown abandoned its longstanding opposition to pulque and began to discover its many virtues".[767]

CLEMENT JUSTICE AS A FORM OF POLITICAL NEGOTIATION

Without question, one of the main factors that led viceregal authorities to authorize free production and trade of *vino de cocos* was the devastation caused by the hurricane that ravaged the province of Colima in October 1626. In an earlier chapter we described the economic and geographic consequences of that resolution, so here we focus our analysis on how Colima's town council practiced politics by continually imploring clement justice to obtain the corresponding authorizations.

We must recall that, before 1626, *vino de cocos* circulated amidst ambiguity. But after the hurricane, and facing the state of emergency into which the storm had plunged Colima due to its widespread, devastating effects on agriculture, in the name of all *colimenses*, Domingo Vela de Grijalva informed Viceroy Rodrigo Pacheco y Osorio, Marqués de Cerralvo (1624-1635), that:

the past year of six hundred and twenty-six a hurricane struck which was so strong that it knocked over and uprooted all the cacao, palm, and fruit trees and sugarcane plantations in those valleys, leaving them desolated [and] divesting many residents of their haciendas with which they sustained themselves, and forced to start over, they chose to move to other provinces where it seemed they would obtain greater comforts.[768]

At the same time, Juan de Sámano Quiñones, then the *alcalde mayor* of Colima, warned the Viceroy of the risk that the villa of Colima could potentially be abandoned if preventive measures were not taken, since most residents had begun to look elsewhere for work, food, and sustenance. Indeed, due to the imminent risk of desertion, the *alcalde* himself had imposed severe penalties on anyone who attempted to abandon the villa. Sámano reminded the Viceroy of Colima's importance "in His Majesty's service in guarding the coasts of the Mar del Sur", an argument we cited earlier that was presented at similar conjunctures.[769]

The council's petition and the information provided by *alcalde* Sámano proved successful, as the Marqués de Cerralvo granted the first license on March 4, 1627, authorizing the free production and commerce of *vino de cocos* for a period of ten years. That measure was subsequently renewed in 1637, 1644, 1653, 1664, 1668, 1671, 1675, 1683?, 1687, and 1691, as we noted previously. Each time the *ayuntamiento* solicited an extension, it appealed to the Viceroy's clemency and mercy, leading Bartolomé Clavero to state that clemency was a doctrine not only religious, but also political. In each one of its petitions to renew the license, the *ayuntamiento* alluded to an earthquake, hurricane, or fire that had damaged the properties of *colimenses*, plunging them into misery. That was a recurrent, and highly successful, strategy in the 17th century, for the Viceroys granted the licenses each time.

Part III

It is important to emphasize that the province of Colima does, indeed, have a long history of fires, earthquakes, and hurricanes, with the most immediate records dating to the 16th century.[770] It was for this reason that council members organized a vote to choose a Patron Saint of "earthquakes and fires". The figure chosen was San Felipe de Jesús. Celebrations of this Saint began in 1668 and have been performed every year up to the present.[771] Similarly, veneration of an image of Our Lady of Mercy (*Nuestra Señora de la Merced*) had begun by the first half of the 18th century (if not earlier) because "[she] miraculously protects this villa and its jurisdiction from the eruptions of the Volcano of Fire since her church faces that Volcano which constantly spews fire from its mouth, though [only] ash has fallen upon said villa", as Juan de Montenegro, the superior judge of Colima, reported in 1744.[772]

Natural events of this kind occurred frequently, and local authorities became well-versed in taking advantage of them. The argument that supported their solicitude for the first license (the one granted in 1627) was that a hurricane had devastated the province, while the request for an extension in 1668 alluded to earthquakes. Around that time, Viceroy Antonio Sebastián de Toledo, Marqués de Mancera (1664-1673), was informed that the province had been left in ruins by constant earthquakes, so he authorized the extension: "in order to preserve the residents and repair the damage wrought".[773] It is important to note, however, that he granted an extension of only six years, not the ten that the *ayuntamiento* had requested.

Later, in representation of all *colimenses*, Juan de Abárzuza and Baltasar de la Vega appeared before Juan Garcés, judge of the Real Audiencia of Mexico, to inform him of the damage that the earthquakes of 1690 and 1691 had caused. His goal was to obtain another extension of the license to produce aguardiente. Captain de la Vega,

> resident of, and married in, the villa of Colima, sent to present myself at Your Excellency's feet with a power-of-at-

torney from the villa's residents to report the second earthquake that Our Lord sent on the day of Saint Gregory, March twelfth of this year, which due to its most terrible nature was believed to be the final judgment, for it lasted an entire Ave María [with] such force that it prostrated an ancient villa abundant in good fruits, knocking to the ground everything that had been rebuilt after the first earthquake, churches, homes, on February twenty-third of the year ninety, causing much extra work that cannot be done again [for it] destroyed sugarcane haciendas and mills, shattered structures and strewed the ground with sugars and honeys, for it struck during milling season. The second tremor that ensued [razed the] palm haciendas where medicinal *vino de cocos* is made. In many areas, entire harvests were lost, as plants were thrown to the ground and vessels broken, heavy losses that will be felt for many centuries, and tremors that continue day and night without fail.[774]

Abárzuza and de la Vega warned the viceregal authorities of the very real danger that the villa of Colima could be abandoned because:

> all residents are so terrified from what they have suffered that many want to leave their haciendas and roots and desert [the villa], afraid that no one will take the lead and the villa will be deserted [though] the elderly and those of reason have told them not to move anywhere until Your Excellency has been informed [...].[775]

Does this description bring something to mind? Without doubt, for it is almost a carbon copy of the panorama described after the hurricane of 1626, which also mentioned the risk that the province could be depopulated. After describing the desperate poverty and needs of Colima in detail, the petition implored the Viceroy to extend the license to produce *vino de cocos*, "so healthful and medicinal" as the *Protomedicato* of the Real Universidad has affirmed "so many times". That solicitude also underscored that the convents in the region received rent (*pie de altar*) from the palm haciendas which they used to pay tithes to the Holy Church, and that the clergy's chantries also depended on those properties.[776] It is hardly surprising to learn, then, that the license was conceded.

When the villa sought another renewal in 1699, residents commissioned Captain Baltasar de la Vega and the *bachiller* don Juan de Abárzuza to appeal to the Viceroy of New Spain, don José Sarmiento y Valladares (1696-1701). On that occasion, the arguments presented to implore the corresponding authorization were earthquakes, pirates, and even a fire. By that time, the *colimenses* were well aware of *vino de cocos*' importance in the economy of the province, for it was "the only natural fruit of the land".[777] De la Vega and Abárzuza argued before the Viceroy that it would be just to allow free trade in palm aguardiente, "because it [sustains] both pious and ecclesiastical causes and the royal goods and properties of the republic".[778] In this way, they urged the Viceroy to consider pious works because the products of their sales were used to maintain convents through tithe payments, chantries, and rents, while the King received "royal revenue" in the form of taxes (*alcabalas*) and customs duties. Banning *vino de cocos*, the men insisted, would have disastrous consequences, because the province would be left unprotected and invasions by enemy pirates would impact the entire kingdom,

> even more today when we weep for that port [Salagua] and the adversities it has suffered from the continuous [raids] along its coasts by pirates for five years. To which we must add the calamities caused by the repeated earthquakes that knock churches and homes to the ground, followed by broad damage, starvation and outbreaks of epidemics. Finally, on the tenth of April of last year, ninety-three, a voracious fire burned down twenty-six homes of families that had been rebuilt, consuming all the belongings and properties of the residents with huge losses, including the storehouses of merchants who suffered ravages and were left terribly destroyed and will remain so if Your Excellency does not grant the resource and faculty of selling those wines.[779]

However, on that occasion when De la Vega and Abárzuza appeared before the Viceroy to request that extension of the license something was awry. It appears that the pulque concessioners had begun to exert pressure to block the sale of *vino de cocos* in Mexico City, especially Captain Juan Domingo de la Rea who had held that concession since at least 1683[780] and was a person named in the *colimense's* suit.[781] Of course Captain de la Rea would come forth to pressure the authorities, for in the time he controlled the pulque monopoly –1683-1709– his profits amounted to 437,000 pesos —almost half a million![782]

What happened to the *colimenses'* petition? Unlike earlier Viceroys, Francisco Fernández de la Cueva, Duke of Albuquerque (1702-1710), rejected it, denying the license to produce and sell *vino de cocos*. We have been unable to find any licenses issued after 1691 and, though we have no written evidence of de la Cueva's rejection, thanks to don Juan de Montenegro, the superior judge and Captain of War in Colima in 1744, we know that "trade and commerce in the *vino de cocos* produced in the aforementioned jurisdiction has fallen into total decadence... having been prohibited by the Lord Duke of Albuquerque, who was Viceroy of this New Spain".[783] That decision put an end to 70 years of negotiations between *colimenses* and the Viceroys of New Spain to allow production and commerce of the *vino de cocos* made in Colima. In terms of political negotiations, the council of Colima knew how to take advantage of the adversities caused by natural phenomena to petition for the continuous renewal of its licenses, but their success, unfortunately, could not endure forever.

MARQUIS DE CASAFUERTE'S 1724 ORDINANCE: THE FINALE OF VINO DE COCOS?

On the Eve of Christmastime 1724, Marquis de Casafuerte lashed out against all the "drinks of the land" (*bebidas de la tierra*) produced up to that time in New Spain and issued an ordinance that definitively banned their elaboration, consumption, and commercialization under any circumstances. While numerous decrees prohibiting alcoholic drinks had been issued, this one was special. Written in a strong, exalted, even superlative tone, Casafuerte's order clearly reflected the context surrounding local drinks in all their dimensions: public morality and health, administration and profits, clientelist networks, and tolerance by civil and ecclesiastical authorities. In short, the order was elaborated with full knowledge of cause since two centuries had passed since the first decree that sought to regulate pulque was issued in 1529.

Regarding public morality and health, the order began by citing the weakness of "unworthy, soulless men" who, despite laws, royal decrees, ordinances, and other prohibitions, had introduced throughout the realm aguardientes made from maguey, sugarcane, honey, *cantincata*, *ololinque*, *mistelas contrahechas*, *vino de cocos*, the blood of rabbits (*sangres de conejo*), *binguíes*, tepaches, mezcal, *guarapo*, *bingarrote* (the ordinance mentions them in this order) and "many others" not cited.[784] Worse yet, in the Viceroy's view, was that not only servants and slaves participated in this "deplorable" experience, but also "many persons of quality and distinction" who, due to vice or the juicy profits that trade in alcoholic drinks generated, simply ignored the many interdictions that had been emitted.

Although his ordinance criticized the tolerance for "drinks of the land" that had existed in New Spain, the Marqués was careful not to mention religious institutions among the instances that benefitted directly from *vino de cocos* and mezcal production through tithes or endowed chantries. In fact, he praised the Church's noble efforts to curb circulation of those drinks: "to remedy [this] the enlightened Archbishops, Bishops and other ecclesiastical prelates in their dioceses have published censures [...] against all transgressors".

Suffice to recall, once again, the priest in the town of Arantza, in 1680, who so bitterly complained of the meagre results of his evangelical work among the Indians, for despite the zeal with which he taught the catechism and good customs, he had failed to lead them away from their deeply-rooted vices and errors, including drunkenness, which he considered the source of many evils. He said that the Indians, children and adults alike, got drunk on a daily basis "and first are drunks before being men". Worse yet, women participated in that abominable custom. He then pronounced his sentence: "Because of this, with its palms and the *vino de cocos* distilled there, Colima has destroyed this province". But he went even further in other declarations: "... and it is [*vino de cocos*] that conserves and sustains their villa and its residents, chapels, chantries and divine liturgy, with which they justify and petition for license to produce, distill, and commerce in this drink".[785]

The priest in Arantza had placed part of the problem on the discussion table; namely, that tithes and other ecclesiastical supports, like chantries, depended on the sale of those aguardientes. This made it clear that the Viceroy would require firm support from the Church for his decree to be obeyed. Here, we transcribe some of the order's key sentences:

> [Juan de Acuña, Marqués de Casafuerte] I have deemed it wise to issue the present pronouncement, ordering a band (*bando*) and edict to be published in the entire district of my government, and to be posted in the most public areas and notaries of this city and all places of this New Spain, so that all people being informed there is not the least pretext of ignorance for its transgression. To this end, I hereby order that no person, of any hierarchy, dignity, or elevation whatsoever, be they Gentlemen, soldiers, nobles, or plebeians, Spanish, Indian, mulatto, negro, mestizo, *lobo*, or *coyote*, or of any other status and condition, shall invent, produce, or introduce, or sell, or deal in, or commercialize, or use, or have in public or in secret, or in any other manner, any of the aforementioned prohibited drinks, or any others, of any nature, including those not mentioned by name,

Part III

and with no pretext of changing their names, or calling them by any other [...] with the only exception of those pure legitimate drinks (*caldos*) that are licit and licensed, because all those that are not [legitimate] I prohibit once again: *as I also prohibit [anyone] from seeking to turn to their advantage the frivolous excuse that they are licensed by written or spoken word, or tolerated by judges.*[786]

We emphasize the final lines of this brief transcription because, though it is not stated clearly, they refer to *vino de cocos*, a drink that circulated freely during the 17th century thanks to the licenses obtained, but was now banned despite being "licensed by written or spoken word". Was this ordinance of 1724 the cause of the disappearance of *vino de cocos*? The answer is no, for no evidence directly indicates that this decree was the end cause, given that the licenses that authorized the free production and circulation of *vino de cocos* ceased to be conceded in the late 1690s and, as we have argued in previous chapters, by that time *vino de cocos* had already entered a stage of decline.

What is true, however, is that the ordinance of 1724 quashed any possibility of reactivating *vino de cocos* production in the 18th century due to the Marqués' emphatic wording that closed all potential loopholes in the ban by labelling all those who failed to obey the edict as transgressors and delinquents, and warning judges at all levels that the slightest malfeasance would cost them their positions and send them into exile. This applied to even the lowest-level authorities, such as the *alguaciles* of *ayuntamientos* and *alcaldes de caminos*, officials responsible for guarding the entrances and exits to and from villas and cities and inspecting vehicles for illicit drinks. With this measure, the Viceroy sought to put an end to a period of supposed permissiveness, expecting "to achieve the desired goal [with] the extinction of such drinks [that are] the cause of innumerable sins and harm to the spiritual and temporal health of souls, as experience shows (with great pain for Catholics)".[787]

José J. Hernández Palomo suggests that the viceregal policies implemented to combat "drinks of the land" were due to an economic issue more than anything related to morality. While it is true that the Crown tried from the outset to curb drunkenness among Indians who consumed the spirits they made and so prevent scandals and social disorder, this author argues that by the early 18th century certain "recently created economic interests had to be defended", so persecuting "drinks of the land" was simply "a protective, supportive measure designed to increase fiscal income from pulque",[788] a drink that was fully regulated and filled royal coffers by generating huge profits. Operating behind the scenes, pulque concessioners in the viceregal capital were the figures who promoted the emission of these decrees against other alcoholic beverages.

It is a fact that *vino de cocos* production had declined markedly by the early 18th century, since by the end of that period we find only scarce references to this product. In his *Historia del Reino de Nueva Galicia* (1742), Matías de la Mota Padilla notes that coconut trees still abounded in the territory of Colima,

> from the bark of which poor people make beds or mats, as soft as if they were of wool; ropes like those made from hemp; from the inner shell they make very solid gourds, so black and smooth they seem to be made of black amber: these coconuts (some very large) are full of a very healthful, refreshing, delightful liquor; and they also make honey, wine, vinegar, and aguardiente; the pulp is very white and smooth to the taste, and with it they make many preserves, and also benefit by making butter and soap it.[789]

Similarly, don Juan de Montenegro, the superior judge of Colima in 1744, affirmed that *vino de cocos* production ceased once it was banned by the Viceroy, Duque de Albuquerque, even though the drink "aids greatly in the commerce and economy of this Republic, where no species of metal exist";[790] that is, in the absence of mining activity, the area was largely sustained by commerce in that aguardiente. Likewise, the description of the district of Colima in 1776-1777 by the then *alcalde mayor*, Miguel José Pérez Ponce de León, mentions numerous haciendas in the province and along the coast of the Mar del Sur where palm trees were cultivated for the coconut industry, from which people extracted a drink called *tuba*: "said *tuba* is a liquor from the [sap] of palm trees similar to how pulque is made from maguey".[791] Referring to *vino de cocos*, he recognized that the "superior government prohibited production of said aguardiente, though some make it despite that order".[792] This suggests that some people may still have been producing *vino de cocos* around that time.

It seems strange that after the *ayuntamiento* of Colima had so vehemently negotiated and petitioned for licenses throughout the 17th century, only a century later it had completely forgotten what was, in its time, the drink *par excellence* that had given the villa and province its identity, "the drink called Colima", as it was known in markets in New Spain. At a meeting in 1773, council members agreed "not to allow *chinguiritos*, *mistelas contrahechas*, *tepaches*, *tubas*, *mezcals*, or any other drink that had been banned in repeated edicts from the superior government, and only license sales of legitimate beverages (*caldos*) from Spain".[793] *Vino de cocos* does not even appear on that list, but only *tuba*, which at that time was consumed as a fermented drink, not as a distillate. *Vino de cocos*, it seems, had been buried in the past.

Final Reflections

We began this chapter by asking if *vino de cocos* was a healthful or harmful drink for the society of New Spain. To respond to that query, we analyzed the various postures of distinct actors involved at all levels, from Viceroys to governors, physicians, *alcaldes*, and residents, arriving at the conclusion that it was both at the same time. Producers argued that it was healthful because their economic interests centered on commerce in the drink. In the view of vintners in Castille and pulque producers in central New Spain, in contrast, it was harmful, for they constantly harped on the excesses and inebriety that *vino de cocos* caused and the problems of public health and morality that its consumption brought about.

Other visions, as we have seen, were more neutral and, hence, objective. Here we refer to the diverse descriptions of *tuba*, *vino de cocos*, and other products derived from palm trees in the Philippines and Spanish America that were written, not under duress or for the purpose of defending or condemning them. In those version we find a wealth of detailed information on the medicinal uses that different populations developed for *tuba*, *vino de cocos*, and other derivatives of the palm tree, including its nut, water, oil, milk, and sugar. An in-depth medical study might provide scientific responses that support this empirical knowledge, for, after all, diverse societies in the tropics have considered the coconut palm "the tree of life", and some still do today.

CONCLUSIONS

This book arose from two needs: on the one hand, to draw attention to the importance of Asian immigration to New Spain and its marked influence along the Pacific coast, and, on the other, to reinvigorate global history through views "from below" with "human dramas that bring history to life", to paraphrase Tonio Andrade in his focus on global microhistory.[794] Our research demonstrates that it is possible to analyze individual lives in global contexts, especially those in population sectors long marginalized by traditional, mainstream historiography. At the same time, we have examined the biocultural transfers of immigrants who arrived on the Manila Galleon and participated in *vino de cocos* production to reveal that the Galleon was not only the economic motor of the first globalization, but also a vehicle for cultural transfers on both sides of the Pacific.

Vino de Cocos, the Pilgrim Beverage. Filipino Knowledge, Colonial Encounters and the Forgotten Origins of Mezcal is guided by ten questions, the answers to which form the basis of its chapters. First, we discussed the problem of the biological revolution triggered by European expansion into America and Asia. The coconut palm (*Cocos nucifera* L.), a particularly important tropical tree due to its many benefits, arrived in coastal areas of Pacific New Spain, modified broad landscapes, and displaced some native palm species. Its success reflects not only the amenable geographic and climatic conditions it found there, but also the fact that its dissemination was accompanied by a contingent of thousands of Filipinos, possessors of millenarian knowledge of its uses and management.

Throughout the book we witnessed how the Filipino distillation technique was brought to palm haciendas in two nuclei of *vino de cocos* production: Colima-Motines and Zacatula-Acapulco. Without doubt, the province of Colima was where this economic activity played a crucial role thanks to the labor of, primarily, free *chinos*, though in Acapulco it was of only secondary importance, with the greater presence of enslaved *chinos*. This shows the heterogeneity of the Asian population in New Spain, a group whose global lives, in the words of Miles Ogborn,[795] had multiple destinies.

And this, precisely, leads us to another of the book's contributions: the discovery of signatures written in Baybayin characters by *vinateros* who settled in the province of Colima in the 17th century. We refer to a select number of documents at the global level that contain elements of that ancient Filipino alphabet and constitute an especially important contribution to the sociolinguistic history of the Filipino diaspora on the American continent. We analyzed the social phenomenon of the transfer of knowledges and techniques between the Philippines and Indians in Colima, which escalated so greatly that "*subir de chino*" –climbing palm trees like *chinos*– evolved into a trade that later came to be performed by Indians.

This book would not have been possible had we not incorporated the ethnographic research we conducted in the Philippines at various moments. Field interviews there brought answers to questions that documents could not, largely because *vino de cocos* production was abandoned in Colima in the 18th century, though it continues uninterrupted in the Philippines under the name *lambanog*. Under this premise, in the final part of the book, we examined in detail the phenomenon of *vino de cocos* production in New

Conclusions

Spain, analyzing the apogee of this drink and its demise over the course of a century, leading to its disappearance in the 18th century. We studied the success this distillate enjoyed in mining regions in northern New Spain and the ambiguous discourse that emerged over its properties, as it was denounced on some occasions for its "harmful" character but supported on others for its medicinal benefits. In the depths of these narratives we found economic interests, some that sought to block this commerce, others that strove to incentivize it. Of course, we also saw how the emergence of new distillates made from agave and sugarcane contributed to the nadir of *vino de cocos*.

The book concludes with an Epilogue which addresses a controversial topic that, due to its nature, seemed unavoidable; namely, the irruption of the first mezcals in Western New Spain, based on the production model of *vino de cocos* in Colima. Contrary to some current nationalist postures on the possible pre-Hispanic origin of mezcals, the evidence shows that this emblematic Mexican drink emerged in the 17th century, thanks to the adoption of the Asian-type still.

Finally, *Vino de Cocos, the pilgrim beverage* serves as a reminder that the immigrants who arrived on the Manila Galleon, those "*gente menuda*", also participated in forging global history. Theirs were global lives, for they learned how to recreate an alternate universe on the far shore of the Pacific, well beyond the will of the Spanish Crown. This book is thus an epitaph to their participation in the grand adventure that was the first globalization. We are grateful for the opportunity to be part of those lives. On certain evenings as we stroll along the palm-lined boardwalks in Colima, we see shadows of Francisca Martha that reach out their hands, reminding us that we too belong to this history.

EPILOGUE
MEZCAL: THE HEIR OF VINO DE COCOS?

At least a couple of decades ago, a debate –still open– began over the origin of one of the most emblematic drinks in contemporary Mexico: mezcal. The question posed at the center of discussion is whether this beverage is of pre-Hispanic origin or emerged in the colonial period after the arrival of Arab, Asian, or "Filipino" distillation techniques. Those who support the latter posture have posited, concretely, that mezcal is the heir of *vino de cocos*. In the context of these heated debates among academics and other specialists in the field, we feel it is now time to clarify our posture.[796]

Pre-Hispanic Distillation?

The idea that some Mesoamerican peoples distilled alcoholic drinks before the arrival of the Spanish, is not a recent one. As he trekked across western Mexico in the early 20th century visiting peoples like the Huichol societies of Nayarit, Carl Lumholtz observed the use of rudimentary stills, quite distinct from conventional Arab-style distillers made of copper, to elaborate a drink they called *tuchi*, produced from the sotol plant (*Dasylirion*). Taken aback, Lumholtz thought that those apparatuses were of pre-Hispanic origin, so he wrote: "[one] still finds among the Huichol of the mountains a *primitive* method of distillation that we are inclined to consider pre-Columbian [...] This distilling procedure is the most *primitive* one that we know of on the American continent".[797]

Many years later, this hypothesis was refuted by Henry J. Bruman, a geographer from Berkeley who wrote his doctoral thesis on alcoholic drinks in ancient Mexico. After passing through the same area in the 1930s,[798] Bruman debunked Lumholtz' view of a possible pre-Columbian distillation technique, arguing that the apparatuses he had seen were, in reality, Asian-type stills that had been introduced by the Filipinos who distilled *vino de cocos* in Colima in the 17th century. One of the key elements that allowed Bruman to suggest the Asian origin of those allegedly pre-Columbian stills was that the indigenous peoples used the term *tuba* to refer to the fermented product of sotol, which served as the raw material for their distillate. Moreover, he could find no Huichol words to designate any of the other processes and materials related to distillation, for all the terms he gathered were of Castillian origin. "The association of *tuba* with palm wine is of especial significance, since the word is used in this sense also in the Philippines, and related terms are found over a wide region among the islands of the southwest Pacific".[799] Bruman affirmed that the word *tuba* was also used among diverse peoples across western Mexico, as in Tequila, Tuxpan, Autlán, Tuxcacuesco, and Tolimán, to refer to the fermented product of agave heads that were cooked to produce mezcal, in a clear allusion to the influence of *vino de cocos* in the elaboration of both sotol and mezcal. To strengthen his case, Bruman drew a series of illustrations to explain, didactically, the distinct types of Asian stills, and compare them to those in use among the Huichol (see Map 15 for this comparison). In conclusion, he stated: "It no longer seems possible to consider the Huichol still a creation of independent Huichol genius.

We are compelled to assume, on linguistic, historical, and technological grounds, that the device was merely adapted from Filipino patterns".[800]

Bruman's research was echoed in a study developed much later by Daniel Zizumbo and Patricia Colunga. Through an approach based on ethnobotany and ethnohistory, these authors proposed that the origin of mezcals was to be found in the model used to distill *vino de cocos* in Colima, and that knowledge of stills of this kind had been disseminated across the Ayuquila-Armería River basin in western Mexico. They suggested that the apparatuses originally used to distill *vino de cocos* were later adapted to process the ferments obtained from cooked agave. In fact, they presented toponymic evidence from diverse places whose names are related to the word "mezcal", and recorded that in some areas of western Mexico the fermented must of agave is called "*tuba* de maguey", a finding that provides further proof of a relation between *vino de cocos* and mezcal.[801] In this vein, a team led by Ana Valenzuela supported the posture that favored an Asian influence in mezcal distillation in western Mexico, though they suggested that the model of the "Filipino still" proposed by Bruman and Zizumbo and Colunga was not the only one that existed. They hypothesized that the route of dissemination of this knowledge must have extended far beyond the hydrological basins posited by the latter authors, and commented that some mezcals in western Mexico used the same technique as the Huichol –or Asian-type– still and the *kabutogama chiki* of Japan.[802] More recently, Hyunhee Park analyzed the similarities among some stills of the "Mongol" type, used to produce *soju* (an emblematic drink of Korea) and some of the devices found in Mexico.[803] Her research supports the hypothesis of an Asian influence on the production of alcoholic drinks in Mexico.

The hypothesis of a possible pre-Hispanic distillation, however, persists and has gained momentum in recent years. In the 1990s, during an archaeological project on labor specialization among groups at the Xochitécatl-Cacaxtla site in the Formative period (800 B.C.-200 A.D.), Mari Carmen Serra Puche and Jesús Carlos Lazcano unearthed stone ovens similar to the ones utilized today to cook agave heads for the artisanal distillation of mezcal. Since then, they have proposed –in several publications– that mezcal was produced there using clay vessels that served as stills.[804]

To further complicate matters, two authors who originally defended the hypothesis of the origin of mezcals based on the production model of *vino de cocos* –Daniel Zizumbo and Patricia Colunga– recently proposed that pre-Hispanic distillation may have existed. Based on the hypothesis put forth in 1980 by J. Needham, these authors suggested the possibility that drinks containing ethanol were being elaborated in the modern state of Colima in the Early Formative period (1500-1000 B.C.) using a "Mesoamerican Capacha-type still".[805] Needham based his theory on a drawing by Isabel Kelly of a trifid vessel excavated in pre-Hispanic Colima, which led him to suggest that it had been utilized to distill alcohol, though he offered no supporting evidence[806] beyond citing John G. Bourke –and mentioning Lumholtz and Bruman– who in 1893 and 1894 published two articles on his hypothesis of "primitive" distillation among the Tarascans due to his discovery of some rudimentary apparatuses for mezcal production in the area around Lake Pátzcuaro. As evidence of "primitive distillation", Bourke argued that early colonial sources mention the word "distill", because in the *Recopilación de Leyes de Indias* (*Compilation of the Laws of the Indies*) he had found the phrase "the Indians of New Spain use a drink called pulque, which they distill from magueys, plants with many benefits due to their various effects", in a decree emitted by Charles V in 1529, only a few years after the arrival of the Spaniards.[807] However, the principal meaning of "distill" in that epoch was simply "to make a liquid flow or run drop-by-drop".[808] It is very common to find historical references to this meaning in documents from the 16th and 17th centuries, so the critique of sources, especially philological ones, is a fundamental element for emitting more robust conclusions.

In any case, Zizumbo and Colunga proposed that the origin and development of this still evolved from steamers and pots that were widely used in that period to allow groups to produce "a sumptuary product for ceremonial purposes, of great social and cultural importance". To demonstrate this, they conducted field experiments using replicas of those archaeological vessels. Among other results, they obtained an average alcohol content of 20.5% v/v, well above the maximum of 15% v/v that fermented drinks can reach. Cautiously, they concluded that *the possibility* of distillation existed, though they stopped short of stating, *de facto*, that it had been performed.[809]

The studies by Serra and Lazcano, on the one hand, and Zizumbo and Colunga, on the other, fanned the enthusiasm of some scholars, entrepreneurs, and producers in the industry of agave distillates in Mexico to present their mezcals in national and international forums as "ancestral drinks" and, as Serra and Lazcano affirmed, to discredit the fact that "we attribute a degree of development to pre-Hispanic cultures [that is] incompatible with the technologies of distillation and, in consequence, consider them incapable of creating a product with the refinement necessary to attain a high alcohol graduation".[810]

What is the basis of the hypothesis that the supporters of pre-Hispanic distillation favor? What is their strongest evidence? Anyone who is broadly familiar with the process of mezcal production today knows it consists of two fundamental stages: a) cooking the agave heads and fermenting the must; and b) distilling that raw material. Those who defend the thesis of pre-Hispanic distillation have substantiated, primarily, the first step; that is, the process of fermentation. The firmest support for their view comes from the discovery of stone ovens in archaeological sites around Mesoamerica that may have served to cook agave, an activity still visible today in some taverns that produce artisanal mezcal (Photograph 7).

Photograph 7. Cooked Agave Heads Recently Removed from the Oven (Ixcatlán, Oaxaca)

Source: photograph by Paulina Machuca.

Without doubt, cooking the heads of agave plants was a widespread practice in Mesoamerica, especially because magueys were a main source of carbohydrates for peoples there, an important complement to an alimentary system based on corn, beans, chili peppers, and squash. In fact, not so long ago, cooked agave was still a significant food source when harvests were poor.[811] Thus, it should come as no surprise that archaeologists show great interest in these ovens and other circular structures found from North to Central America.

Epilogue

The practice of cooking agaves is amply documented in Mesoamerica in both the archaeological record and historical literature from the 16th century, but this does not mean that distillation *per se* existed.[812] Archaeometric analyses have been unable to prove, scientifically, that the apparatuses presented as "pre-Hispanic stills" were utilized in distillation; indeed, doing so would be most challenging. The "Capacha-type" vessels that Zizumbo and Colunga used in their experiments were elaborated *in situ* and *ex profeso* for that purpose, while in the case of the Xochitécatl-Cacaxtla site, mezcal distillation was inferred from the similarity between the clay pots uncovered in that archaeological context and those used in mezcal production today in Oaxaca, Puebla, and Michoacán.[813] In their latest publication, Serra and Lazcano state that "mezcal, like alcohol, is a volatile element and its presence cannot be detected definitively in archaeological pots".[814] Hence, their principal support is the presence of cooked maguey and the fact that those archaeological vessels had been exposed to fire; that is, common, everyday elements of life in many Mesoamerican societies that in no way definitively indicate distillation processes.

Added to this uncertainty is the fact that at no point do early colonial sources mention any kind of pre-Hispanic apparatus that might have functioned as a distiller or still, the generic term for these devices. Why would such important historical sources as those by Friar Bernardino de Sahagún, Friar Toribio de Benavente Motolinía, and Francisco Cervantes de Salazar, among many others, have failed to mention concretely the consumption of distilled drinks and their processes of elaboration among Mesoamerican peoples? In other words, why did those chroniclers not describe the hypothetical "pre-Hispanic still", when early colonial sources from other areas of the Spanish Empire, like the Philippines, provide ample evidence of distillation practices among those islanders?[815]

In his account of Magellan's voyage to the Philippines, for example, Antonio Pigafetta mentions that in March, 1521, the chief of the island of Samar, in the Eastern Visayas, received the Europeans with fish, some local fruits, coconuts, and a pitcher of *vino de cocos*, "that they call *uraca*".[816] The term *uraca* comes from the Arab word *arak/'araq*, which means distillate. We know, as well, of other early European references that mention *tuba* distillation in India, for around 1505 the Bolognese traveler, Ludovico de Varthema, recorded how natives there heated palm tree sap over a fire and, through double and triple distillations, obtained "an *aqua vita*" that, with only a sniff, "alters a man's brain".[817] Likewise, the Dutch explorer John Huyghen van Linschoten reported, in the 1580s, that natives in southern India distilled *tuba* or *sura*, which they called *fula* or *nipe* after the first distillation, and *uraca* after the second.[818] Other diverse, specific sources like these describe the distillation of *vino de cocos*, but since we examined this topic in depth in the first two chapters, we will not repeat the evidence discussed there but, rather, return to the question of why early colonial sources in New Spain remain silent on the possibility of "pre-Hispanic distillation" when references to this activity in Southeast Asia abound in the 16th century? Moreover, why is there no Mesoamerican name for distillates derived from agave like those recorded for other drinks –like pulque– nor any detailed description of preparation techniques? Perhaps, simply because such drinks did not exist when the Spaniards arrived?

In 2019, the prestigious archaeologist and chemist, Patrick E. McGovern, published a study conceived to determine, definitively, whether or not pre-Hispanic distillation existed in western Mexico, utilizing an approach based on the discipline of biomolecular archaeology. His analysis centered on a double-chambered vessel and other utensils found in an excavation in Colima that dates to the Capacha phase (*ca*. 1500-1000 B.C.) and, presumably, had been used

Epilogue

to distill drinks,[819] a hypothesis that, as we have seen, was posited by Zizumbo and cols. in 2009.[820] It is important to mention that McGovern is the Director of the Biomolecular Archaeology Laboratory for Cuisine, Fermented Beverages, and Health at the Archaeology and Anthropology Museum of the University of Pennsylvania in Philadelphia with a long list of publications in this field. His study in Colima is part of a broader project on how the distillation technique that emerged in East Asia and the Middle East, was later adopted in Europe, and then taken to America; hence, the importance of his work. McGovern's conclusions are forceful:

> Needham's seemingly revolutionary hypothesis that the earliest distillation in the world began around 1500 B.C. in western Mexico has been tested and found wanting on all counts. The double-chambered jars, bowls, and miniature cups have not been found arranged in situ in the proposed arrangement as a "prehistoric agave still." The vessels are yet to be found in an occupational or industrial context. They occur only in tombs, and the decoration of the double-chambered jars suggests that they may be non-utilitarian and intended as burial goods. They show no carbon on the exteriors of their lower chambers, as would be expected if they had been used to boil a liquid over an open fire. Archaeobotanical remains of agave or other natural products of the Colima region are yet to be recovered inside the vessels or in their vicinity. Most telling, the lack of any firm chemical evidence, especially the total absence of the biomarkers tigogenin and hecogenin inside the lower chambers of the jars, seals the negative case against the hypothesis that agave or any other natural product of the region was distilled in the ancient vessels.[821]

Despite McGovern's results and the absence of historical evidence of the alleged pre-Hispanic distillation, some academic circles and social networks still assert that mezcal emerged as a drink long before the Spaniards arrived. Why is this? Perhaps Domingo García Garza provides one of the answers by proposing that the hypothesis of pre-Hispanic distillation may be anchored in the "invention of a tradition", paraphrasing Eric Hobsbawm:

> Everything suggests that this notion [of pre-Hispanic distillation] was influenced by a nationalist vision of culture which held that popular [beliefs], especially rural traditions, were direct reflections of the authenticity of the origins, irrefutable proof of the eternal existence of the nation. It was this vision that essentialized or naturalized a certain type of mezcal as an original product, one pure and immaculate.[822]

From a more critical stance, García argues that mezcal is a drink that emerged in the colonial period, at the point where the Filipino model of *vino de cocos* intersected with the later Spanish drink called *orujo*. He holds, moreover, that it is not an indigenous drink, but a *ranchero* or mestizo product, that today is associated with an artisanal drink that is linked to the cosmologies of pre-Columbian cultures solely as a marketing tool: "Producers and brand owners insist upon the supposed indigenous origin of mezcal [...] It seems that promoting it as 'artisanal' is good for business [so] it is registered in the same global classification that assigns ethnic identities to popular art".[823] In his book *La revolución mezcalera*, Garza goes further to suggest that the mezcal we know today –which he calls "fourth generation"– is a product of globalization and market demand that obliged producers to change it significantly by modifying and improving practices that were considered "traditional".[824]

Mezcal and the Model of *Vino de Cocos* from Colima

Are the postures that support pre-Hispanic distillation and Asian distillation in mezcal production incompatible? Some common ground may exist and, as Valenzuela wrote in a recent study, the two views may be more inclusive than exclusive.[825] If we assume that distilled drinks like mezcal had been produced at a specific moment of the pre-Hispanic period, then that knowledge would have allowed a much more rapid change toward the Asian distillation technique; after all, handling the cooked agave heads (*piñas*) that formed the raw material was a common, widespread art across Mesoamerica.

After evaluating all the evidence outlined above, our view is that the mezcals that emerged in western Mexico in the first half of the 17th century bore a marked influence of Asian distillation, following the model of *vino de cocos* from Colima. But even if pre-Hispanic distillation had occurred –though it has never been demonstrated– it would not have been related to the mezcals that appeared in colonial times, the forebears of the mezcals we know today. Regardless of whether or not some type of "pre-Hispanic still" existed, it is evident that what allowed the irruption, development, and evolution of *vino mezcal* –a name coined by the Spaniards– in the market of alcoholic drinks in New Spain and, hence, the answer as to why the colonial documents regarding the production, commerce, and consumption of this distillate in western New Spain can be traced back historically to the 17th century.

In Nueva Galicia, one of the earliest mentions of *vino mezcal* dates from 1616, when tithe collection in the Province of Ávalos was auctioned to Juan de Anguioçar[826] and Juan González de Apodaca Rubín, the latter the *alguacil mayor* of the court. They were ordered:

> to register and charge, as well, tithes on a wine [mezcal] that *was introduced only a few years ago*, made from plants called mezcal and maguey, *whose effects are not yet known*. That wine is beneficial, healthy, and of value, for at the lowest and most moderate price each *botija* is sold for six pesos in *reales* at wholesale, and at retail for two *reales* per *cuartillo*. Much talk is made of this wine in that tax district (*dezmería*) because many Spaniards produce it for consumption and sale, similar to how [wine] from Spain is made from grapes and sold at the prices mentioned above. Through this knowledge both Spaniards and Indians have

planted, and continue to plant, said mezcals and magueys on their ranches and lands, keeping all that belongs to them due to the well-known, great effect and benefit brought through the extensive commerce of said wine, reason for which Spaniards strive with great diligence to purchase these plants, one as much as the other, from the Indians, and those Indians do the same, extracting said wine for consumption and sale, [yet] *this genus is not formally registered for tithe payment due to the fact that it was introduced only a short time ago*.[827]

The arguments presented in this testimony are enlightening, for it states, repeatedly, that the introduction of *vino mezcal* into towns in Ávalos was a recent event that occurred around the year 1616, and that the measure of paying tithes on it was very likely based on the model of *vino de cocos* in Colima where, in the decade of 1610, that *diezmo* was imposed on the drink in the Bishopric of Michoacán, as we discussed in a previous chapter. Thus, the canon of the Cathedral of Guadalajara, who signed that document, Doctor Bartolomé de Arbide, ordered residents to "pay the tithe on said wine [mezcal] as it is paid on that of *cocos*", and threatened anyone who refused to pay the tithe to Juan de Anguioçar with excommunication. Canon Arbide acknowledged De Anguioçar's fear that some people might disobey this determination. In his words: "I feared that those Spaniards and Indians, and others who produce said wine, would raise some resistance, alleging that it is not the custom, or that those mezcals and magueys are wild plants". Clearly, the dilemma that emerged at that time centered on the use of wild plants to produce a drink that was only recently introduced or created and, hence, was "not of custom".

We also learn that the price of *botijas* and *cuartillos* of *vino mezcal* were the same as those charged for *vino de cocos*, a finding that strengthens the model of a distilled drink that followed upon an earlier one. Moreover, the fact that Spaniards bought agaves from the Indians to produce aguardiente echoes what occurred on the palm haciendas where *vino de cocos* was produced, where Spaniards controlled the palm trees or leased them to *indios chinos*. In contrast to the coconut palm, however, magueys were plants "of the land", deeply rooted in native culture, so in the ensuing years the Spanish were unable to impose their control on this incipient industry.

Our attention was also drawn to the fact that in 1630 some *chinos* in Mexico City were active in the purchase-sale of *vino de maguey*. A *chino* named Melchor de los Reyes, for example, mentioned that he had "produced *vino de maguey* that is called aguardiente for sale and profit, which he sells in all the towns and places in this New Spain", asserting that it was a medicinal drink.[828] At that time, the price of a *botija* of *vino de maguey* was 8 pesos,[829] higher than vino de cocos.[830] Even more revealing is the proposal that, in 1628, two Filipinos –Tomás López and Nicolás García– presented to the Real Protomedicato to obtain a royal monopoly on the production of aguardiente made from *aguardiente de pulque*, which used exactly the same method as *vino de cocos*, only replacing *tuba* with pulque as the raw material.[831] This demonstrates that Filipinos also had the opportunity to innovate in the binomial plant-technique by combining Mesoamerican agaves with the Asian distillation process in a relatively early epoch of the history of mezcal.

Finally, we return to the document from the province of Ávalos (1616) with a question because that source mentions that "many Spaniards produce [*vino mezcal*] for consumption and sale, similar to how [wine] from Spain is made from grapes". Could this fragment refer to *vino de orujo*? This is quite likely. We will take this opportunity to discuss the use of leather boots to ferment agave most, since hides were also utilized to ferment drinks in Europe. Thanks to an account from 1769 that described in detail how *vino mezcal* was produced in Nueva Galicia we learn how:

the maguey they call mezcal [was cut] and, after slicing off the branches (*pencas*), the heads are placed in a hot oven and covered with fire and red-hot stones, and maintained this way until they are cooked under the heat of the flames and removed, placed in wooden troughs [and] mashed with wooden mallets prepared for this purpose by fabricants, and when well mashed they are placed in a leather boot that is exposed to the sun, air, and cold, and when the boot reaches its point, the pure wine is extracted by stills with no concurrent mixing of any ingredient other than mezcal.[832]

It is still possible today to observe practices of this kind in artisanal taverns where leather from the hides of bulls serves as a container for the must that will be distilled later (Photograph 8). As the reader knows, bovine cattle did not arrive in New Spain until some moment of the 16th century, so it is highly likely that this step in the process of mezcal production was introduced sometime later, perhaps not until the 17th century.

Photograph 8. Fermentation of Agave Heads in Bull Hides (Ixcatlán, Oaxaca)

Source: Photograph by Paulina Machuca.

Epilogue

In addition to the auction that granted Anguioçar and González de Apodaca the right to collect tithes in the Province of Ávalos, another testimony to the elaboration of mezcal around that time was dated in 1619, when *vino mezcal* was being produced on a ranch owned by Francisco Ruiz Galindo, in the province of Amula, also in Nueva Galicia. In that year, Galindo paid his tithes with corn, cattle, and *vino mezcal*. Four *botijas* are registered, suggesting an annual production of perhaps 40 *botijas*, around 640 liters.[833] A more detailed review of this source for the following years could reveal additional sites where *vino mezcal* was made, and if Tuxcacuesco, Zapotitlán, and Tonaya, or other places where this drink is today a symbol of identity, also appeared on the map of tithe collection in Nueva Galicia in that period.

What other references to mezcals can we find in western New Spain? Well, in 1621, the oft-cited Domingo Lázaro de Arregui wrote that the sierra of Nayarit was an area that produced a "*vino* by [distillation] that is clearer than water, stronger than aguardiente and very flavorful".[834] Unfortunately, Arregui went no further and did not describe the process or the context in which that drink developed. Meanwhile, in the *corregimiento* of Tequila in New Spain, the cradle of this national drink *par excellence*, it is not until the mid-18th century that we detect real *vinomezcalera* (mezcal production) activity, for in the preceding decades people there made their living mainly by cultivating corn and sugarcane.[835]

Our search for colonial documents that allude to mezcal production in other areas of New Spain led us to visit two of the most important archives in Oaxaca: the Archivo Histórico Judicial del Estado de Oaxaca and the Archivo Histórico del Estado de Oaxaca. In the former, we corroborated that from the 16th century on there were numerous mentions of alcoholic drinks like pulque, tepache, and even beverages fermented from bananas, but that the word "mezcal", referring to the drink that interests us, did not appear recurrently until the 18th century.[836] In the second repository, we found a document from 1697 on a dispute between two merchants over the cost –80 pesos– of a barrel of aguardiente: the seller, Antonio de Urrutia, had sold the drink on credit to Francisco de Janderal, an *alférez* and trader in Oaxaca. The conflict began because the product was of poor quality. That file contains 63 folios, but not one clarifies if the drink was sugarcane aguardiente or *vino mezcal*, much less if it had been produced in Oaxaca or been introduced from some other place.[837]

Finally, we confirmed that in the decade of 1770 a proposal was made to create a royal monopoly on mezcal production in Oaxaca, similar to the one that had been imposed in Nueva Galicia, to finance a regiment on the coasts of the Mar del Sur with its seat in Acapulco, since a tax of four-and-a-half pesos per barrel was already being levied on sales of mezcal to repair the pier there. That measure was never ratified but is indicative of the importance that *vino mezcal* was acquiring in the region of Oaxaca.[838] Perhaps this explains why, in the early 19th century, we find descriptions of taverns, workers (at that time called *mezcalilleros*),[839] and commerce in this distillate.

Asian-Mexican Stills

Could it be that this two-sided debate over the alleged existence of pre-Hispanic distillation has led us to turn a blind eye to other relevant sociocultural phenomena, such as the adaptation and transformation of Asian stills in Mexico over time and in different regions? In their detailed studies, Valenzuela and cols. argue that at least two different types of Asian stills arrived in New Spain after the 1570s with the aperture of the transpacific route. Those two types (called "Mongol" and "Chinese"; in the 1940s, Henry J. Bruman identified the latter as the "Filipino still") did not endure simply "as is" but evolved over time and were modified and adapted according to the needs of each place.

Epilogue

This demonstrates, once again, that the phenomenon of cultural exchange is always dynamic and changing.[840] For this reason, Valenzuela and cols. called them "Asian-Mexican stills": While it is true that they originated overseas, their modification produced a genuine innovation that distinguished them as local artifacts (Map 15).[841]

Map 15. Asian–Mexican Stills and Their Distribution

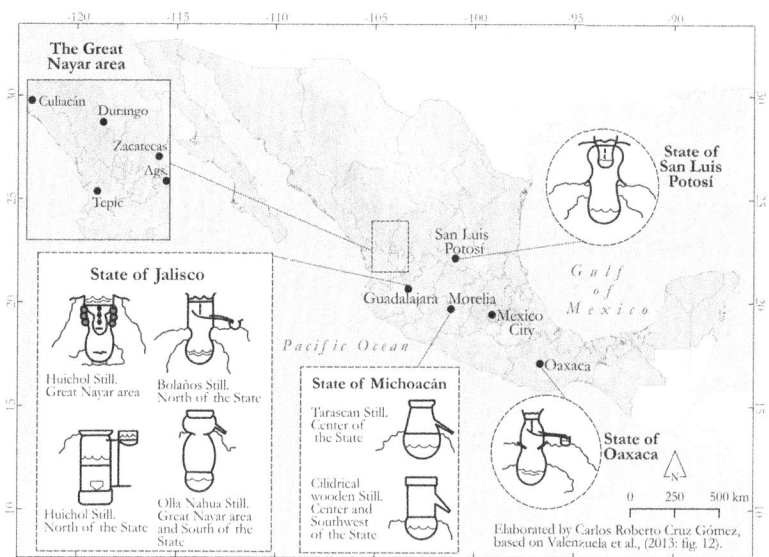

Mezcal: The Heir of *Vino de Cocos*?

We now return to the question posed at the beginning of this Epilogue: are mezcals the heirs of *vino de cocos*? We are convinced that this is, indeed, the case, though it may be more correct to say that they are the heirs of the Asian distillation technique, of which *vino de cocos* is but one modality. It was thanks to this technology that mezcal became known in the market of distilled drinks in New Spain; first, through the royal monopoly imposed on *vino de cocos* and mezcal and, later, independently. But for these same reasons, we consider mezcal a drink that is expressly associated with New Spain and then Mexico, for despite the external influence on its origins, it was in New Spain that it underwent a process of transformation, adaptation, and constant modification, according to the region of study. And while at first it was Asian stills who made it possible for mezcal to enter the market of alcoholic drinks, we cannot forget that around the mid-17th century Arab-style copper stills were being utilized in Santa María de las Parras to produce it, a fact that demonstrates the complexity of this phenomenon and the different routes it took.[842]

The diverse stills used by master *mezcaleros* in artisanal taverns today evidence a cultural phenomenon that has been produced over more than 400 years, and this is precisely wherein lies its importance. The fact that this history was nourished by external influences, far from decreasing its merit, is actually proof of how people in Mexico were capable of creating something new and transforming it into part of their identity. When all is said and done, agave is the biocultural axis around which this innovation has always revolved.[843]

The Resurgence of *Vino de Cocos* from Colima

On July 24, 2023, the engaging space that houses the Sociedad Cooperativa de Artesanías Pueblo Blanco, in Comala, Colima (Mexico), was the site of a singular event entitled *Vino de cocos y mezcal: la historia de un hermanamiento* ("*Vino de cocos* and Mezcal: the history of a brotherhood", see photograph 9). There, Jorge Velasco Rocha, a coffee producer from Colima with family ties to mezcal production, presented his *vino de cocos* (distilled from *tuba*) to the public, after several months of assays. After almost 300 years, a crowd of colimenses witnessed the rebirth of a drink that had given them an identity in the market

Epilogue

of alcoholic drinks in New Spain, where it was evoked as the *vino de cocos* "they call Colima".[844] Before the eyes of the many spectators, including mine, a large "Filipino" still that Jorge had designed and built was set up to demonstrate the complete process of elaborating *vino de cocos*. To our surprise, the brand name of that distillate of *tuba* was none other than "*La china mestiza*". The source of inspiration of this name was the story of our *india china*, Francisca Martha, born in Colima to a Filipino father and an Indian mother, who owned a hacienda where *vino de cocos* was produced in the mid-17th century, and whose life trajectory was explored in Chapter 3 of this book.

Photograph 9. Public Presentation of the *Vino de Cocos*, "La China Mestiza"

Source: photographs by Paulina Machuca and Edwin Mayoral (collage). Top: Jorge Velasco and Paulina Machuca; middle: Jorge Velasco in his tavern; bottom: Jorge Velasco with his bottles of *vino de cocos*.

Since that moment, Jorge Velasco has been striving to improve his *vino de cocos* and obtain the licenses required to commercialize his artisanal drink. On June 15, 2024, his tavern also called "*La china mestiza*" opened its doors in the town of Suchitlán, Comala, where distillates of *tuba* and agave are sold. Could this mark the rebirth of a long-forgotten tradition? Could *vino de cocos* be living a second phase in the history of Colima? Only time will tell.[845] What is paradoxical is that while the emergence of the first mezcals in western New Spain occurred thanks to the model of *vino de cocos*, today this equation has been inverted: in a certain sense it is due to the apogee of mezcals in the area around Zapotitlán de Vadillo, Jalisco, that *vino de cocos* is now the prodigal brother invited to the festival of distillates. After all, the so-called "Filipino" distillation technique survived in western Mexico thanks to mezcal, and this has allowed *vino de cocos* to be reborn and have a second chance.

A Final Point

Fernand Braudel has written that the 17th century witnessed the expansion of distilled drinks across the European continent: "in Europe the great novelty, the revolution, is the appearance of aguardiente and [drinks] made from grains; that is, alcohol. One could say that the 16th century attended their birth, the 17th saw their development, and the 18th lived their dissemination".[846] According to Braudel, nations in northern Europe, like Germany, the Low Countries, and northern France, were the earliest ones to produce and consume aguardientes, well ahead of Mediterranean countries. Due to increased demand, we find that the 17th century brought French cognac, armagnac, and calvados, as well as kornbrand, vodka, whisky, and gin, all of which appeared north of the commercial limit of grape wine.[847] This coincides with current, broad tendencies in the market of distilled beverages worldwide, for according to the evolutionary biologist Rob DeSalle and the paleoanthropologist Ian Tattersall, these included brandy, vodka, tequila/mezcal, whisky, gin, and rum/ cachaça.[848] In New Spain and Mexico, the 17th century attended the birth of distilled drinks, the 18th tended to their development, the 19th witnessed their dissemination, and the 20th and 21st brought their reinvention. But in today's epoch of globalization, one can find all these drinks on shelves virtually anywhere in the world.

ACKNOWLEDGMENTS

If I were to write a complete list of the people and institutions that made this book possible, it would be as long as the work itself. The names that deserve mention number in the hundreds, but editorial norms do not always allow this. To all those who do not appear, my sincere apologies. I would like to begin by thanking the Archivo Histórico del Municipio de Colima, my adoptive home for many years, which houses the largest documental collection on *indios chinos vinateros* in New Spain; especially José Miguel Romero de Solís, Rosy Alvarado Torres, José Luis Larios, and Patricia Sánchez Espinosa; to my dear friend Irma López from Centro INAH-Colima, for her generosity. Thanks to the Academia Mexicana de Ciencias and the Presidency of the Republic for granting me the Women's Fellowship (*Beca para la Mujer*) in Humanities in 2011 that allowed me to visit the Philippines for the first time; to Alejandro Solís at the Biblioteca Pública del Estado de Jalisco, to my friends in Zacatecas, always eager to notify me of findings on the *vino de cocos* that made its way to the mines of northern New Spain –Martín Escobedo, Thomas Hillerkuss, Tomás Dimas, and Arturo Burciaga– to all my colleagues and friends in various archives and academic institutions in Mexico City, Manila, Madrid, Seville, and Lisbon, who came to know me as "*La dama de los cocos*" (*Madame* Coconut) and generously sent valuable information; to Matthew Furlong and Déborah Oropeza for sharing their research on *indios chinos* in New Spain; and to Luis Alonso Álvarez, a key interlocutor in the final stages of the book. Special thanks to Noemí Obledo(+), a cherished researcher now in a better place; to El Colegio de Michoacán, especially my colleagues in the Laboratorio de Análisis y Diagnóstico del Patrimonio, and Isla Jiménez and Maricruz Piza, for sharing documents and conversing about this second edition; to Jorge Loyzaga, recognized architect and the best cultural promotor of relations between Mexico and the Philippines. Thanks, as well, to my "mezcologist" friends with whom I debated the origins of mezcals and their relation to vino de cocos: Pepe Hernández López, Diana Carrano, Edwin

Mayoral, Luis Nogales Echeverría, Domingo García Garza, Ana Valenzuela, and Nicolas Stevens. To Carlos Roberto Cruz Gómez, a special acknowledgment for elaborating the maps, as well as Jesús Medina Rodríguez and Marco Antonio Hernández; and to Alejandro Torres for his extraordinary aid with illustrations. To Esther Katz and Isaac Donoso for their generous reviews; and to Florencio Amezcua, Nico Mejía and Jorge Velasco Rocha for their love for Colima, our small homeland, our *"matria"* (motherland), in the words of don Luis González y González.

The Philippines became my second home thanks to the generosity of the Ateneo de Manila University where Fernando N. Zialcita and the team at the Ateneo Cultural Laboratory of Bohol (2012) and Aklan (2013) provided invaluable support during my ethnohistorical research. Siony, Bigs, Pinky, Alphae, Thea, Adrian, and Adel became true friends and guides who allowed me to gain detailed knowledge of the culture of Luzon and the Visayas. Ian Ocampo in Bohol, Joselito Mallari in Tayabas, and Alexander de Juan in Aklan shared their knowledge of the art of producing and distilling *tuba*. To the Cobato family and Mark Francis Francisco in Zamboanga, for allowing me to discover a part of Mindanao. To Tesz Millan, a Filipina, American and Creative woman, who made me part of her YouTube Channel.

To my parents, siblings, nieces, and nephews for following my new findings. My achievements are also yours; and to my husband, Thomas, my most critical reader and indulgent companion. I dedicate this book to him.

To don Leonardo Morán and Agustín, unforgettable *tuberos* in Colima, and to all the *tuberos* and *vinateros* of Mexico and the Philippines for preserving this centenarian tradition. May their knowledge endure for many more centuries.

Last, but not least, my eternal gratitude to Paul Kersey, who patiently translated this work over the course of several months, accommodating my constant last minute changes. My sincere thanks for his professionalism and friendship over these years.

Endnotes

1. Paulina Machuca, "Microhistoria global de una escritura peregrina: el alfabeto filipino baybayin en Colima de la Nueva España (1600-1604)", *Allpanchis*, no. 90, año XLIX, julio-diciembre 2022, pp. 85-121.
2. Paulina Machuca, "Medrar entre palmares: Francisca Martha, una 'india china' en el Colima del siglo XVII" in Thomas Calvo and Armando Hernández (coords.), *Medrar para sobrevivir. Individualidades presas en la fragua de la historia, siglos XVI-XVIX* (coords.), 2016, pp. 337-362. There, I included an annex with Francisca Martha's will. An abbreviated version of that text was published in French as Paulina Machuca, "Francisca Martha, une petite propriétaire de palmiers entre deux mondes: Philippines-Mexique, XVIIe siècle" in Sophie Dulucq et al. (coords.), *Au coeur des empires. Destins individuels et logiques impériales XVIe-XXIe siècle*, 2023, pp. 41-57.
3. Archivo Histórico del Municipio de Colima (hereinafter, AHMC), Fondo Sevilla del Río, caja 5, exp. 4.
4. As the reader will see below, tuba is a word of Malayan origin that refers to a drink made from palm tree sap.
5. AHMC, no. 178. Eigi Fuchigami, "Indios chinos en Colima, siglos XVI y XVII. Resumen rápido de los resultados de la investigación en el Archivo Municipal de Colima", n.d., 28 pp.
6. In 2000 Isolda Rendón Garduño elaborated the "Catálogo de los fondos del siglo XVII del Archivo Histórico del Municipio de Colima" as part of her B.A. thesis in Ethnohistory. Without that catalogue, it would have been very difficult to locate files related to the Asian population and vino de cocos production. I thank Isolda for her generosity and for introducing me to the complex world of 17th-century paleography in Colima.
7. Paulina Machuca, "Cabildo, negociación y vino de cocos: el caso de la villa de Colima en el siglo XVII", *Anuario de Estudios Americanos*, enero-junio 2009, vol. 66, no. 1, pp. 173-192; and Paulina Machuca, "El alcalde de los chinos en la provincia de Colima durante el siglo XVII: un sistema de representación en torno a un oficio", *Letras Históricas*, no. 1, otoño-invierno 2009, pp. 95-115.
8. Carlo Ginzburg, "Microhistoria: dos o tres cosas que sé de ella", *Manuscrits* 12, 1994, p. 33.
9. Arturo Giraldez, *The Age of Trade. The Manila Galleons and the Dawn of the Global Economy*, 2015, p. 2.
10. Tonio Andrade, "A Chinese Farmer, Two African Boys, and a Warlord: Toward a Global Microhistory", *Journal of World History*, vol. 21, no. 4, December, 2010, p. 574. His analysis is situated in Taiwan in 1661, in a connected world that allowed interaction among the Chinese, the Dutch, and African slaves.
11. Romain Bertrand and Guillaume Calafat, "Global microhistory: A case to follow", *Annales*, 73, no. 1, 2018, pp. 3-17; John-Paul Ghobrial, "Introduction: seeing the world like a microhistorian", *Past and Present*, supplement 14, 2019, pp. 1-22. For a recently published, useful synthesis of the future of global microhistory, see Jacques Revel and Antonella Romano, "Penser global?" in Jacques Revel and Antonella Romano (dirs.), *Penser global? Dix variations sur un thème*, 2024, pp. 7-39.
12. As Jacques Revel defines microhistory in his Preface to Giovanni Levi's, Le pouvoir au village: Jacques Revel, "L'histoire au ras de sol" in Giovanni Levi, *Le pouvoir au village. Histoire d'un exorciste dans le Piémont du XVIIe siècle*, 1989, pp. I-XXXIII.
13. Miles Ogborn, *Global lives. Britain and the world, 1550-1800*, 2008. For three fundamental texts that address the theme of Asian immigration to New Spain, see Tatiana Seijas, *Asian slaves in colonial Mexico. From Chinos to Indians*, 2014; Rubén Carrillo Martín, *Las gentes del Mar Sangley*, 2017; Déborah Oropeza, *La migración asiática en el virreinato de la Nueva España: un proceso de globalización (1565-1700)*, 2020; and Diego Javier Luis, *The first Asians in the Americas. A Transpacific History*, 2024. Oropeza calculates that from 1565 to 1700, between 7,500 and 20,000 "chinos" entered New Spain through the port of Acapulco (p. 330).
14. George Marcus, "Ethnography in/of the World System: The Emergence of Multi-Sited Ethnography", *Annual Review of Anthropology*, vol. 24, 1995, pp. 95-117.
15. As the men who extract tuba in the Philippines are called.

Vino de Cocos, the Pilgrim Beverage

16. An important support for my work was the Fellowship for Women in the Humanities (Beca para la Mujer en las Humanidades, 2011) from the Academia Mexicana de Ciencias and the Presidencia de la República. It allowed me to finance a one-month study period in Luzon and islands in the central Visayas in 2012. Later, I returned on two occasions: to Luzon and Western Visayas in 2013, and to Luzon and Mindanao in 2015.
17. Marcus elucidates six ways of constructing multi-sited ethnographies: "follow the People", "follow the Thing", "follow the Metaphor", follow the Plot, Story, or Allegory", "follow the Life or Biography", and "follow the Conflict". Cfr. Marcus, "Ethnography", pp. 105-113.
18. See the "Epilogue" of this book for information on the resurgence of vino de cocos in Colima in 2023.
19. Available on YouTube.
20. Alfred W. Crosby Jr., *The Columbian Exchange. Biological and cultural consequences of 1492*, 1972, p. 66.
21. Reyna María Pacheco Olvera, "El intercambio de plantas en la Nao de China y su impacto en México" in Janet Long Towell and Amalia Attolini Lecón (coords.), *Caminos y mercados de México*, 2010, pp. 593-607. The author describes the diverse methods that were used to protect plants during voyages: meaty species with seeds were conserved in ground sugar, while tubers like ginger were packed in dry sand.
22. Bronislaw Malinowski, "Prólogo" in Fernando Ortiz, *Contrapunteo cubano del tabaco y el azúcar*, 1973, p. 8.
23. The reader will notice that, starting with chapter 1, I will use the first-person plural, as in the original text.
24. We use the Victoria Yepes edition, *Historia natural de las islas bisayas del padre Alzina*, 1996, pp. 91-92.
25. Garcia da Orta, *Coloquios dos simples e drogas da India*, [1563] 1891, p. 235. A recent edition is by Rui Manuel Loureiro and Teresa Nobre de Carvalho, *Colóquios dos simples e drogas e coisas medicinais da Índia*, 2024.
26. Information from D. Granados Sánchez and G. F. López Ríos, "Manejo de la palma de coco (Cocos nucifera L.) en México", *Revista Chapingo*, vol. 8, no. 1, enero-junio 2002, pp. 39-48.
27. Bee F. Gunn et al., "Independent Origins of Cultivated Coconut (Cocos nucifera L.) in the Old World Tropics", Plos One, no. 6, vol. 6 (e21143), June, 2011, pp. 1-8.
28. Source: modified from the original (1883) by Alejandro Torres. Original: Hermann Zippel (botanist) and Carl Bollmann (engraver), Ausländische Kulturpflanzen in farbigen Wandtafeln mit erläuterndem Text ("Exotic cultivated plants on colorful wall panels with explanatory text"), Friedrich Vieweg & Sohn, Braunschweig, 1876-1899.
29. Cristóbal de Acosta, *Tractado de las drogas, y medicinas de las Indias Orientales, con sus plantas debuxadas al bivo por Christobal de Acosta, medico y cirujano que las vio ocularmente*, 1578, p. 99.
30. Francisco Hernández, *Obras completas. Historia Natural de Nueva España*, Vol. 1, 1959, p. 169. The author proposed that palm trees should be fertilized in winter with ash and manure, while in summer they only required water.
31. Information from Octavio Pérez Zamora, "Fertilización nitrogenada y potásica del cocotero en Colima", *Tierra Latinoamericana*, vol. 21, no. 3, julio-septiembre 2003, pp. 401-408.
32. Gunn et al., "Independent origins", pp. 5-6.
33. H. C. Harries, "The evolution, dissemination & classification of Cocos nucifera L.", *The Botanical Review*, vol. 44, no. 3, July-September, 1978, pp. 265-319.
34. Gunn et al., "Independent origins".
35. Ibid.
36. M. Foale, "An introduction to the coconut palm" in Pons Batugal et al., *Coconut Genetic Resources*, 2005, p. 1.
37. Ibid., p. 2.
38. We cannot forget that Ibn Battuta had described the benefits of this plant previously, in the 14th century, as the reader will see below.

Endnotes

39. Paul Teyssier, "Introduction" in Vasco de Gama, *La relation du premier voyage aux Indes (1497-1499)*, 1998, p. 16.
40. Vasco de Gama, *La relation du premier voyage aux Indes (1497-1499)*, 1998, pp. 45-57.
41. Vasco da Gama, *Roteiro da viagem em descobrimento da India pelo Cabo da Boa Esperança fez Dom Vasco da Gama em 1497*, 1838, p. 28.
42. Ibid., pp. 93-94.
43. Cited in H. C. Harries, "The Cape Verde region (1499 to 1549); the key to coconut culture in the Western hemisphere?", *Turrialba*, no. 3, 1977, p. 229.
44. Marco Polo, *Libro de las cosas maravillosas*, 2002, p. 140.
45. Ibn Battuta, *A través del Islam*, 2014, pp. 377-378.
46. Ludovico de Varthema, *Itinerario de Ludovico de Varthema Bolognese nello Egitto, nella Soria nella Arabia deserta, & felice, nella Persia, nella India, & nela Ethyopia. Le fede el vivere, & costumi delle prefate Provincie. Et al presente agiontoui alcune Isole novamente ritrovate*, 1535, fol. 50.
47. João de Barros, *Da Asia. Dos feitos, que os portuguezes fizeram no descubrimento, e conquista dos mares, e terras do Oriente*, [1563] 1777, pp. 309-311.
48. Orta, *Coloquios dos simples e drogas da India*, p. 235.
49. Francis Drake, *Récit des voyages (1577-1596)*, 2012, p. 22.
50. Acosta, *Tractado de las drogas*, p. 98.
51. Chau Ju-kua, *His work on the Chinese and Arabe trade in the twelfth and thirteenth centuries, entitles Chu-fan-chï*, 1911, p. 161.
52. Ludovico de Varthema, *Itinerario de Ludovico de Varthema*, fol. 50.
53. Victoria Yepes, *Historia natural de las islas bisayas*, p. 90.
54. William Dampier, *A new voyage round the world*, 1699, p. 295.
55. Manuel Blanco, *Flora de Filipinas. Según el sistema sexual de Linneo*, 1837, p. 717.
56. João de Barros, *Da Asia*, p. 310.
57. Orta, *Coloquios dos simples e drogas da India*, p. 235.
58. Juan González de Mendoza, *Historia de las cosas notables, ritos y costumbres, del Gran Reyno de la China, sabidas assi por los dichos libros de los mesmos Chinas, como por relación de los religiosos y otras personas que an estado en el dicho Reyno...* 1596, p. 323.
59. Victoria Yepes, *Historia natural de las islas bisayas*, p. 94.
60. William Dampier, *A new voyage round the world*, p. 294.
61. Ibn Battuta, *A través del Islam*, p. 378.
62. Sources: Ibn Battuta, *A través del Islam*, p. 378; Ludovico de Varthema, *Itinerario de Ludovico de Varthema*, pp. 50-51; Antonio Pigafetta, *Relazione del primo viaggio attorno al mondo*, 1999, pp. 204-211; João de Barros, *Da Asia*, pp. 309-311; Garcia da Orta, *Coloquios dos simples e drogas da India*, pp. 235-244; John Huyghen van Linschoten, *The voyage of John Huyghen van Linschoten to the East Indies. From the old translation of 1598*, 1885, pp. 43-51; Blas de la Madre de Dios, *El libro de las medicinas caseras de Fr. Blas de la Madre de Dios*. Manila, 1611, 1984; Victoria Yepes, *Historia natural de las islas bisayas*, pp. 90-108; William Dampier, *A new voyage round the world*, pp. 291-296; Ignacio Mercado, *Declaración de las virtudes de los árboles y plantas que están en este libro (Plantas medicinales de Filipinas)*, 2023, pp. 162-163; Manuel Blanco, *Flora de Filipinas*, pp. 716-722.
63. Ludovico de Varthema, *Itinerario de Ludovico de Varthema*, fol. 50 v.
64. Antonio Pigafetta, *Relazione del primo viaggio attorno al mondo*, 1999, p. 204.
65. Victoria Yepes, *Historia natural de las islas bisayas*, p. 96.
66. Garcia da Orta, *Coloquios dos simples e drogas da India*, p. 237.
67. Archivo General de Indias (hereinafter AGI), Filipinas, 25, R. 1, N. 6. According to Thomas Calvo, the galleon Santo Niño y Nuestra Señora de Guía, built in 1684, utilized 4,128 lots (gantas) of coconut oil, equivalent to 12,000 liters, perhaps to waterproof and lubricate the ship's cables; see Thomas Calvo, *Espacios, climas y aventuras: el galeón de Filipinas y la Fragata de las Marinas en el Pacífico occidental (1680-1700)*, 2016.
68. That is, to seal joints between the boards of ships to prevent water entering.

Vino de Cocos, the Pilgrim Beverage

69   Juan González de Mendoza, *Historia de las cosas notables*, pp. 323-324.
70   João de Barros, *Da Asia*, p. 311.
71   Victoria Yepes, *Historia natural de las islas bisayas*, p. 96; Mercado, *Declaración de las virtudes de los árboles*, p. 15.
72   Antonio Pigafetta, *Relazione del primo viaggio*, p. 204.
73   Manuel Blanco, *Flora de Filipinas*, p. 718.
74   Victoria Yepes, *Historia natural de las islas bisayas*, p. 96.
75   Ibid.
76   Bartolomé Leonardo de Argensola, *Conquista de las islas Malucas al rey Felipe III Nuestro Señor escrita por el Licenciado Bartolomé Leonardo de Argensola, capellán de la Magestad de la Emperatriz y Rector de Villahermosa*, Libro primero, 1609, f. 9.
77   With information from Fernando López-Ríos Fernández, cited in Guadalupe Pinzón Ríos, *Acciones y reacciones en los puertos del Mar del Sur. Desarrollo portuario del Pacífico novohispano a partir de sus políticas defensivas, 1713-1789*, 2012, pp. 295-309.
78   Ibn Battuta, *A través del Islam*, p. 377.
79   Titus Burckhardt, *La civilización hispano-árabe*, 2004, pp. 17-19.
80   "The question of the origin is obscure. Excellent authors have resolved it in different ways": Alphonse de Candolle, *Origine des plantes cultivées*, 1886, p. 347.
81   O. F. Cook, "History of the coconut palm in America", *Contributions from the United States Natural Herbarium*, no. 14, 1910, pp. 271-342. We know from Henry Bruman that his mentor, Carl O. Sauer, agreed with this view; see Henry J. Bruman, "Relations of Carl Sauer and Research in Latin America", *Geographical Review*, vol. 86, no. 3, July, 1996, pp. 370-376.
82   Gonzalo Fernández de Oviedo y Valdés, *Historia general y natural de las Indias, islas y Tierra firme del Mar Océano*, 1851, p. 335.
83   Víctor Manuel Patiño, *Plantas cultivadas y animales domésticos en América equinoccial. Plantas introducidas*, Vol. IV, 1963.
84   Fernández de Oviedo, *Historia General y Natural de las Indias*, p. 337. Emphasis added.
85   Ibid.
86   Pedro Mártir de Anglería, *Décadas del Nuevo Mundo, por Pedro Mártir de Anglería, Primer cronista de Indias, Tercera Década*, Libro X, 1964, p. 387. Víctor Manuel Patiño transcribed a fragment of this episode, though his version (which we have not seen) varies slightly, perhaps due to the translation from Latin.
87   Ibid, Vol. II, p. 530. Emphasis added.
88   Hugh C. Harries discusses the dissemination of the coconut tree by drift, and the time period and distances its seeds could have traveled without losing their capacity to germinate upon reaching their destination. See his article "The evolution", pp. 265-319. See also works by Henry Bruman: "Some observations on the early history of coconut in the New World", *Acta Americana*, vol. 2, no. 3, 1944, pp. 200-243, and "Early coconut culture in Western Mexico, *The Hispanic American Historical Review*, 25, 1945, pp. 301-314.
89   Cited in Henry Bruman, "Notes and comment: a further note on coconuts in Colima", *The Hispanic American Historical Review*, vol. 27, no. 3, August, 1947, pp. 572-573, p. 572. Bruman thanks a Mr. Conway for providing a photocopy of this letter. We have not been able to locate the original and do not know if it is held in some public documental archive. Emphasis added.
90   Ibid., p. 573.
91   Fray Alonso Ponce, "Relación breve y verdadera de algunas cosas de las muchas que sucedieron al padre fray Alonso Ponce en las provincias de la Nueva España, siendo comisario general de aquellas partes" in *Viajes de fray Alonso Ponce al occidente de México*, n.d., p. 113.
92   Patiño, *Plantas cultivadas*.
93   Henry Bruman, "Aboriginal drink areas in New Spain", 1940, p. 198.
94   Gunn et al., "Independent origins of cultivated coconut", p. 6.
95   Paulina Machuca et al., "Introducción y difusión temprana de recursos fitogenéticos en la región Balsas-Jalisco durante el siglo XVI: una perspectiva agro-histórica", *Geografía Agrícola. Estudios regionales de la agricultura mexicana*, no. 45, julio-diciembre 2010, pp. 77-96.

Endnotes

96   William Dampier, *A new voyage round the world*, p. 295.

97   Hugh C. Harries, "The Cape Verde region", pp. 227-231.

98   AGI, Patronato Real, 294, N. 2, chapter 27, n.d. Emphasis added.

99   Daniel Zizumbo Villarreal, "History of coconut (Cocos nucifera L.) in Mexico: 1539-1810", *Genetic Resources and Crop Evolution*, no. 43, 1996, pp. 505-515.

100 Álvaro Patiño de Ávila, "Descripción de la ciudad de Veracruz y su comarca" in René Acuña (ed.), *Relaciones geográficas del siglo XVI: Tlaxcala*, 1985, p. 321.

101 Felipe Sevilla del Río (ed.), *Provança de la villa de Colima en su defensa ante un mandamiento de la Real Audiencia de México, que ordenaba la tala total de los palmares colimenses. Año de 1612*, 1977, p. 68.

102 AHMC, 277, cited in José Miguel Romero de Solís, *Clérigos, encomenderos, mercaderes y arrieros en Colima de la Nueva España (1523-1600)*, 2008, p. 221.

103 Juan Alcalde de Rueda, "Relación de parte de la provincia de Motín que es en la costa de la Mar del Sur en esta Nueva España" in René Acuña (ed.), *Relaciones geográficas del siglo XVI: Michoacán*, 1987, p. 177.

104 AGI, Patronato, 259, R. 68, f. 2.

105 Gerardo Sánchez Díaz, *La costa de Michoacán. Economía y Sociedad en el siglo XVII*, 2001, p. 107.

106 Archivo Histórico del Estado de Colima (hereinafter, AHEC), Fondo colonial, caja 17, carpeta 4, f. 37.

107 Source: Felipe Sevilla del Río, *Provança*.

108 Felipe Sevilla del Río, *Provança*, p. 82.

109 *Ibid*, p. 59.

110 Referring to Friar Jerónimo Marin, an Augustinian who went on to China after participating in the evangelization of the Philippine Islands.

111 Felipe Sevilla del Río, *Provança*, p. 61. Emphasis added.

112 Adolfo Gómez Amador, "La presencia filipina en Colima y su aporte a la identidad regional" in Juan Carlos Reyes (ed.), *Memorias del Primer Foro de Arqueología, Antropología e Historia de Colima*, 2005.

113 *Ibid*.

114 *Ibid*.

115 Jerzy Rzedowsky, *Vegetación de México*, 1983, p. 350.

116 Terence D. Pennington and José Sarukhán, *Árboles tropicales de México*, 2005, pp. 61-62.

117 Archivo General de la Nación (hereinafter, AGN), Tierras, vol. 154, exp. 5, f. 152; cited in Déborah Oropeza, *La migración asiática*, p. 307.

118 For a deeper exploration of this topic, see Paulina Machuca, "La palma de coco: regalo de Filipinas a México (siglos XVI-XVII)" in Thomas Calvo and Paulina Machuca (eds.), *México y Filipinas. Culturas y memorias sobre el Pacífico*, 2016, pp. 321-340. On the suaderos, see Juan Carlos Reyes Garza, *La antigua provincia de Colima, siglos XVI al XVIII*, 1995, p. 160.

119 Francisco Hernández, *Obras completas*, p. 168.

120 Paulina Machuca, "De porcelanas chinas y otros menesteres. Cultura material de origen asiático en Colima, siglos XVI-XVII", *Relaciones Estudios de Historia y Sociedad*, vol. XXXIII, no. 131, verano, 2012, p. 78.

121 On this topic see Juan de Lara, "El coco de Vigo: el coco chocolatero de la Batalla de Rande, 1702", *Anales del Instituto de Investigaciones Estéticas*, vol. XVVI, no. 125, 2024, pp. 197-215.

122 Natalia González Heras, "Retazos americanos en las residencias madrileñas de los servidores virreinales", *Anales del Museo de América*, no. XXV, pp. 224-225.

123 "Per bonta de questo arboro quando gli Re hanno inimicitia l'un con l'altro, pur alcuna volta fanno la pace, ma tagliando l'un Re a l'altro di questi arbori mai in eterno non li saria dato pace"; Ludovico de Varthema, *Itinerario de Ludovico de Varthema*, fol. 51.

124 João de Barros, *Da Asia*, p. 311.

Vino de Cocos, the Pilgrim Beverage

125 Francisco López de Gómara, Historia de la conquista de México, 2003, p. 489. It is important to remember that, although his description is quite detailed, Gómara was never in the New World.

126 "They make fire, and very good ash for bleach. The trunk serves as wood, and the leaves for roofing. Cut it before it grows too much; and fatten the log. Gouge out the inside to gather [the liquid] and distill it, and that liquor is like syrup. If you cook it a bit, it turns into honey; if you purify it, it becomes sugar; if you cool it, it turn into vinegar, and if you add pulque (ocpatli), it becomes wine. They make preserves from the buds and tender leaves. When the sap from the shoots is roasted and hot it's squeezed over a fresh sore or wound to heal or close it. Juice from the small buds and roots, mixed with sap from wormwood (ajenjo) from the area, heals snake bites. Paper is made from the leaves of this plant [and] taken everywhere for sacrifices and artists. Sandals, mats, textiles for clothes, girths, halters, and harnesses are all made, and finally they make hemp and spin it. The thorns are so hard they can penetrate other wood, and so sharp they are used as needles to sew leather. For sewing, they remove the vein with the point or make a kind of awl. They cut [slaughtered animals] with these awls, or so I have heard on many occasions, because they don't break or lose their edge in the meat, and because they penetrate as far as is necessary without making a large hole."

127 Ludovico de Varthema, Itinerario de Ludovico de Varthema, fols. 50-51.

128 Marco Polo also mentioned tuba consumption in some tropical areas of Southeast Asia, as on the island of Sumatra whose inhabitants, he wrote, "have no wine, but make it from this [liquid]; they have many trees similar to palms, break their branches and water comes out of the breaks like that from grapes, and this liquor is white and red like wine. It is very perfect for drinking and exists in great quantities". Marco Polo, Libro de las cosas maravillosas, pp. 140-141.

129 Juan González de Mendoza, Historia de las cosas notables, p. 324.

130 Victoria Yepes, Historia natural de las islas Bisayas, p. 97.

131 Manuel Blanco, Flora de Filipinas, p. 719.

132 William H. Scott, Barangay. Sixteenth century Philippine culture and society, 2010, p. 236.

133 Fedor Jagor, Viajes por Filipinas, 1875, p. 61.

134 Tomás de Comyn, Estado de las Islas Filipinas en 1810, brevemente descrito por Tomás de Comyn, con permiso del Supremo Consejo de Indias, 1820, p. 87.

135 The pronunciation of tubâ in the Philippines stresses the final syllable. The word traveled to Mexico, but there stress is placed on the first syllable.

136 Tomás de Comyn, Estado de las islas Filipinas, p. 85.

137 Priscila Chinte-Sánchez, Philippine fermented foods. Principles and technology, 2008, p. 168.

138 For a deeper analysis of the fermentation of alcoholic drinks see the chapter by Anne Cristine Gschaedler et al., "Fermentación. Etapa clave en la elaboración del Tequila" in Ciencia y Tecnología del Tequila. Avances y Perspectivas, 2004, pp. 63-120.

139 Priscila Chinte-Sánchez, Philippine fermented foods, p. 158.

140 Information provided by my colleague and friend María Salomé Aurelio-Desoloc, who wrote her doctoral dissertation at the Ateneo de Manila University on nipa wine in Infanta, Pangasinán, the Philippines, entitled "Nipa lambanog: a product of Filipino ingenuity".

141 Antonio de Morga, Sucesos de las islas Filipinas, 2007, p. 225. Pedro Chirino, Relacion de las Islas Filipinas, i de lo que en ellas an trabaiado los padres de la Compañia de Iesus, 1604, p. 225.

142 Rogelio Prado explains this technically as follows: "Distillation utilizes a simple principle: creating intimate contact between the initial mixture (liquid) and a second phase (vapor) to achieve an effective transfer of mass between them. The two phases are later separated, so a distinct composition is made in each one. This principle has gone unchanged since its origin in ancient times down to our days"; see Rogelio Prado Ramírez, "Destilación" in Ciencia y Tecnología del Tequila. Avances y Perspectivas, 2004, pp. 123-170.

143 Information provided by Joselito Mallari of the Mallari Distillery in Tayabas, Quezon (Luzon, the Philippines) during our fieldwork in that area in April-May 2012.

144 Priscila Chinte-Sánchez, Philippine fermented foods, p. 170.

Endnotes

145 Fedor Jagor, *Viajes por Filipinas*, p. 61. It is likely that the ratio of 8-10:1 given to us at the Mallari Distillery reflected double or triple distillations, which gave some of their products over 50% alcohol by volume.

146 Ludovico de Varthema, *Itinerario de Ludovico de Varthema*, p. 50.

147 John Huyghen van Linschoten, *The voyage of John Huyghen van Linschoten to the East Indies*. From the old translation of 1598, 1885, p. 49.

148 Priscila Chinte-Sánchez, *Philippine fermented foods*, p. 172.

149 The Philippine Coconut Authority (PCA), an agency of the Department of Agriculture, reported that lambanog production has increased since 2014. However, due to cases of intoxication in some rural areas caused by high methanol content, added to the fact that this distillate is considered "the drink of the poor", it recognizes that lambanog does not boast a good reputation in the Philippines. This view has been mitigated by some recent international awards won by brands like Lakan, one of the most-renowned labels in the country. See: https://pca.gov.ph/index.php/10-news/283-the-philippine-vodka-lambanog-facts-misconceptions#:~:text=Lambanog%20is%20widely%20produced%20from,Luzon%2C%20 SOCCKSARGEN%20and%20CARAGA%20regions.

150 We have addressed the topic of tuba and its diverse consumption styles in the Philippines and Mexico in other works; see Paulina Machuca, "El arte de hacer tuba en México y Filipinas: una aproximación etnohistórica" in Angela Schottenhammer (coord.), *Tribute, trade, and smuggling: commercial, scientific and human interaction in the Middle Period and Early Modern World*, 2014, pp. 247-267; and Paulina Machuca, Hacer tuba en México y Filipinas: cuatro siglos de historia compartida, 2013. We have also taken information from Priscila Chinte-Sánchez' book, *Philippine fermented foods*, pp. 151-174.

151 Priscila Chinte-Sánchez, *Philippine fermented foods*, p. 152.

152 Victoria Yepes, *Historia natural de las islas Bisayas*, p. 105.

153 *Ibid.*, p. 106.

154 Victoria Yepes, *Una etnografía de los indios bisayas del padre Alzina*, 1996, p. 136.

155 *Ibid.*, pp. 136-137.

156 To learn more about fermented alcoholic drinks in the Philippines, see Chinte-Sánchez, *Philippine fermented foods*, pp. 175-213.

157 Antonio Pigafetta, *Primo viaggio*, p. 81.

158 Miguel López de Legazpi, "Expedición" in *Colección de documentos inéditos relativos al descubrimiento, conquista y organización de las antiguas posesiones españoles de ultramar: Segunda serie. De las Islas Filipinas*, vol. 3, II, Documento 39, 1887, fol. 110.

159 *Ibid*, fol. 208.

160 Antonio Pigafetta, *Primo viaggio*, p. 112.

161 Antonio de Morga, *Sucesos de las islas Filipinas*, p. 225.

162 Pedro Chirino, *Relacion de las Islas Filipinas*, pp. 78-79.

163 Comyn, *Estado de las Islas Filipinas en 1810*, p. 87.

164 Suffice to mention Clifford Geertz' magnificent study of cockfights in Bali, Indonesia, in his book *The Interpretation of Cultures*, especially "Deep play: notes on the Balinese cockfight", 2003, pp. 339-372.

165 Priscila Chinte-Sánchez, *Philippine fermented foods*, p. 170.

166 A popular song from Mabilo, a neighborhood in Kalibo, Aklan, Western Visayas, the Philippines. We thank Alexander de Juan, a professor at the Center for West Visayan Studies, University of the Philippines in the Visayas, for providing the lyrics of this song and the English translation.

167 Alonso Ponce, *Viajes de fray Alonso Ponce*, p. 113.

168 *Ibid.*, pp. 113-114.

169 Juan Alcalde de Rueda, "Relación de la provincia de Motín", p. 177. Emphasis added.

170 AHMC, secc. B, caja 1, exp. 5, f. 220.

171 AHMC, caja B-63, exp. 1; AHMC, caja B-57, exp. 7, pos. 3.

Vino de Cocos, the Pilgrim Beverage

172 AHMC, secc. B, caja 30, exp. 23.
173 AHEC, Fondo Colonial, caja 10, carpeta 4, N. 1313. Emphasis added.
174 Fray Antonio Tello, *Crónica miscelánea de la Sancta Provincia de Xalisco*... 1985, p. 381.
175 Ibid.
176 In the Epilogue, we discuss the relation between vino de cocos and the emergence of mezcal in Mexico.
177 AHMC, secc. B, caja 1, exp. 5, f. 220. Emphasis added.
178 The Diccionario de la Real Academia Española (1726) defines alquitara as "the same as alambique; though it is understood more commonly that the alquitara is made of lead or some other material and has a copper vat. The word in Arab is quatára, which, according to Diego de Urréa, means alambique, so in ancient times it was called alcatara, as is said in [that] place". Diccionario de la Real Academia Española, A, 1726, p. 243.
179 Sergio Antonio Corona Páez, *La vitivinicultura en el pueblo de Santa María de las Parras. Producción de vinos, vinagres y aguardientes bajo el paradigma andaluz (siglos XVII y XVIII)*, 2004, p. 157.
180 Ibid., pp. 135-136.
181 Fernand Braudel says that one fact is beyond doubt: "there were alambiques in the West before the 12th century, so it was possible to distill all kinds of alcoholic liquors. But for a long time only the apothecaries practiced the distillation of wine. Aguardiente, the result of the first distillation, and later ethyl alcohol [which] results from the second... were utilized as medications". It was not until the 16th century that aguardientes emerged from the domain of doctors and apothecaries and were transferred to the producers of alcoholic drinks. We discuss the topics of alambiques and distillation in the Epilogue of this book; Fernand Braudel, *Civilización material, economía y capitalismo. Siglos XV-XVIII. Las estructuras de lo cotidiano*, vol. 1, 1984, p. 201. Emphasis added.
182 AGN, General de parte, no. 51, vol. 67, f. 30.
183 Machuca, *Hacer tuba en México y Filipinas*.
184 Mathieu de Fossey, "Por los rumbos de Colima" in Servando Ortoll (comp.), *Por tierras de cocos y palmeras. Apuntes de viajeros a Colima, siglos XVIII a XX*, 1987, pp. 45-62.
185 Composer: José Leonardo Morán, a tubero from Colima.
186 Pierre Gourou, *Introducción a la Geografía humana*, 1979, pp. 11-15.
187 José R. Hernández Santana et al., "Regionalización morfoestructural de la Sierra Madre del Sur, México", *Investigaciones Geográficas*, no. 31, 1995, pp. 45-67.
188 With information from the portal of the INEGI, www.inegi.gob.mx.
189 Nicolás de Cardona, "Descripción de la costa de Colima. 1614-1615" in José Antonio Calderón Quijano (dir.), *Documentos para la Historia del Estado de Colima*, 1979, pp. 115-122.
190 Hernando de Vascones, "Relación de Zacatula" in René Acuña (ed.), *Relaciones geográficas del siglo XVI: Michoacán*, 1987, p. 459.
191 Peter Gerhard, *Geografía histórica de la Nueva España, 1519-1821*, 1986, pp. 79-84.
192 Ibid., pp. 198-200.
193 María Inés Mombelli Pierini, "La formación histórica del paisaje en el corredor Acapulco-Zihuatanejo", *Investigaciones geográficas. Boletín del Instituto de Geografía*, UNAM, no. 72, 2010, pp. 120-138.
194 All references in this paragraph are to Peter Gerhard, *Geografía histórica*, pp. 403-406, which mentions that a jurisdictional realignment occurred in 1649 that shifted the boundaries of Motines from the Cachán River toward the Carrizal River.
195 Pochotitlán, Ceutla, Suchitepec, and Xocutla.
196 All references in this paragraph are to Gerhard, *Geografía histórica*, pp. 39-42.
197 Rolf Widmer, *Conquista y despertar en las costas de la Mar del Sur (1521-1684)*, 1990, pp. 91-92.
198 Ibid., p. 91.
199 Archivo Histórico de la Casa de Morelos (hereinafter AHCM), Fondo diocesano, Justicia, Testamentos, Capellanías y Obras pías, caja 98.

Endnotes

200 This list of haciendas and ranches that produced vino de cocos is from Matthew J. Furlong, "Peasants, servants, and sojourners: itinerant Asians in colonial New Spain, 1571-1720", 2014, p. 480, although beyond the names of these towns there is no information on any aspects related to how the distillate was produced. We thank the author for allowing us to consult his doctoral dissertation.

201 Sánchez, *La costa de Michoacán*, pp. 84-85.

202 Lorenzo Lebrón de Quiñones, "Relación sumaria de la visita que hizo en Nueva España el Licenciado Lebrón de Quiñones a doscientos pueblos" in José Antonio Calderón Quijano (dir.), *Documentos para la Historia del Estado de Colima, siglos XVI-XIX*, 1979, pp. 62-64; Gerardo Sánchez Díaz, *Los cultivos tropicales en Michoacán. Época colonial y siglo XIX*, 2008, p. 39; José Miguel Romero, *Clérigos, encomenderos, mercaderes y arrieros*, pp. 192-219.

203 Widmer, *Conquista y despertar en las costas*, p. 91.

204 Fernand Braudel, *Civilización material, economía y capitalismo*, p. 207.

205 Sebastián Macarro, "Relación de Tancítaro" in René Acuña (ed.), *Relaciones geográficas del siglo XVI: Michoacán*, 1987, pp. 293-294.

206 Alcalde de Rueda, "Relación de parte de la provincia de Motín", p. 177.

207 For more on the decline of cacao, see Juan Carlos Reyes' text, *La antigua provincia de Colima*, p. 155.

208 Felipe Sevilla del Río, *Provança*, p. 46.

209 Juan Carlos Reyes Garza, *Por mandato de su Majestad*. p. VIII.

210 Ibid.

211 Felipe Sevilla del Río, *Provança*, p. 58.

212 AGI, México, 262, N. 34, f. 2.

213 AGI, México, 262, N. 59, f. 2.

214 AGI, México, 262, N. 50, f. 1.

215 AGI, México, 262, N. 108, f. 2.

216 Arnaldo Issasy, *Demarcación y descripción*, p. 127.

217 Ibid., p. 172.

218 Ibid., p. 172.

219 Ibid., p. 173.

220 Alonso de la Mota y Escobar, *Descripción geográfica de los reinos de Nueva Galicia, Nueva Vizcaya y Nuevo León*, 1993, p. 34.

221 Arnaldo Issasy, *Demarcación y descripción*, p. 174.

222 AGN, Tierras, vol. 104, exp. 6, f. 128.

223 Tatiana Seijas, *Asian Slaves in Colonial Mexico*; Déborah Oropeza, *La migración asiática en la Nueva España*; Matthew J. Furlong, "Peasants, Servants, and Sojourners". In addition to the exceptions cited in this and other chapters, Rubén Carrillo Martín's book, *Las gentes del Mar Sangley*, stands out for its analysis of the trajectories of some indios chinos in New Spain by demonstrating their heterogeneous profiles and diverse experiences; Diego Javier Luis, *The first Asians in the Americas. A Transpacific History*.

224 Diego Calderón y Serrano, judge of the Audiencia of Manila in 1678, explained the origin of the word "sangley" by alluding to the "those of the nation of China [who] are called sangleyes on these islands because [when] the Spanish first conquered these lands [and] the Chinese came from their provinces to this one for trade, the Spaniards asked how they were to recognize them, and they responded 'sianglay', which means 'traders who come'. That was the origin of calling them 'sangleies' [a] corruption of the Chinese language"; Archivo Histórico Nacional (hereinafter, AHN), Inquisición, 5348, exp. 3, f. 1 v. A list of Chinese words copied by Juan Bautista Muñoz in the late 18th century, defined the word "sangley" as "natives of China who come to trade in the Philippines"; Documentos varios relativos a Nueva España, Real Academia de la Historia de Madrid (hereinafter, RAHM), Colección Muñoz, Signatura 09-04853, A-118, tomo 73, fol. 340.

225 At that time, Jonathan Israel observed that the word "chino" existed in New Spain to refer to the child of an Indian woman and a cuarterón, but that it is not applicable in the 17th century;

Vino de Cocos, the Pilgrim Beverage

see Jonathan I. Israel, *Razas, clases sociales y vida política en el México colonial 1610-1670*, 1980, p. 82, note 51.

226 AHEC, secc. 2, caja 18, carpeta 12, f. 36. Our thanks to Irma López for sharing this file.
227 Cfr. Thomas Calvo, "Japoneses en Guadalajara: 'blancos de honor' durante el seiscientos mexicano", *Revista de Indias*, vol. XLIII, no. 172, 1983, pp. 531-547.
228 Juan Gil, *Los chinos en Manila. Siglos XVI y XVII*, 2011; Homer H. Dubs and Robert S. Smith, "Chinese in Mexico City in 1635", *The Far Eastern Quarterly*, vol. 1, No. 4, August, 1942, pp. 387-389.
229 Tatiana Seijas, "The Portuguese Slave Trade to Spanish Manila: 1580-1640", *Itinerario*, vol. XXXII, no. 1, 2008, pp. 19-38.
230 Here, we refer to Déborah Oropeza, "Los 'indios chinos' en la Nueva España: la inmigración de la Nao de China, 1565-1700", 2007, appendices 4, 5, and 6, pp. 254-295.
231 Antonio de Morga, *Sucesos de las islas Filipinas*, pp. 290-291.
232 On the system of servitude in the Philippines, see the work by William H. Scott, *Barangay*, pp. 127-146.
233 AHMC, secc. B, caja 49, exp. 7, pos. 8, f. 29 v. and 31.
234 AHMC, secc. B, caja 11, exp. 5.
235 Matthew J. Furlong, "Soldiers, Sailors, and Salesmen: Pampangan Service and Ethnicity in Colonial Mexico, 1591-1691" (26-30 October, 2010), XXIII Reunión de historiadores de México, Estados Unidos y Canadá, Querétaro. Historiography refers to the pampangos as the "Tlaxcaltecas of the Philippines" due to their support for the colonial administration and their activity as militias that served the Spanish.
236 She mentions the following places: Manila Bay, Pampanga, Pangasinán, Cagayán, Ilocos, Camarines, Tondo, Tayabas, Otón (Panay), Negros, Cebú, Leyte, Samar, Ybabao, Caraga (Mindanao), Mindoro, Calamianes, Mariveles, V Balayán, Bombón, Calilaya, Butuan, and Catanduanes. See Kristyl Obispado, "The Pacific sailors: global workers at and on the edge of the Spanish empire (1580-1640)", 2021, p. 62.
237 Rubén Carrillo Martín, "Asians to New Spain. Asian cultural and migratory flows in Mexico in the early stages of 'globalization' (1565-1816)", 2015.
238 Rubén Carrillo Martín, "Los 'chinos' de Nueva España: migración asiática en el México colonial", *Millars*, vol. XXXIX, no. 2, 2015, p. 22.
239 Déborah Oropeza, *La migración asiática*, p. 329.
240 Déborah Oropeza, "Los 'indios chinos' en la Nueva España", appendices 4, 5, 6, pp. 254-295.
241 Felipe Sevilla del Río, *Provança*, p. 26. We have modernized the orthography.
242 Gregorio M. de Guijo, *Diario (1648-1664)*, Vols. I, II, 1953.
243 RAHM, Colección Muñoz, Documentos varios relativos a Nueva España, Signatura 09-04853, A-118, tomo 73, fol. 340.
244 José Miguel Romero de Solís, *Conquistas e instituciones de gobierno en Colima de la Nueva España (1523-1600)*, 2007, p. 148.
245 Paulina Machuca, "De porcelanas chinas y otros menesteres", pp. 77-134.
246 Archivo Histórico de la Real Audiencia de Guadalajara (hereinafter, ARAG), Civil, caja 9, legajo 9, exp. 124.
247 See Thomas Calvo, "Japoneses en Guadalajara"; and Melba Falck Reyes and Héctor Palacios, *El japonés que conquistó Guadalajara. La historia de Juan de Páez en la Guadalajara del siglo XVII*, 2009.
248 Tatiana Seijas, *Asian Slaves in Colonial Mexico*; Déborah Oropeza, *La migración asiática*; Matthew J. Furlong, "Peasants, Servants, and Sojourners"; Rubén Carrillo Martín, "Asians to New Spain"; in the case of Diego Javier Luis, *The first Asians in the Americas* includes an analysis of Asian migration to places beyond New Spain, such as Guatemala, Oregon, and Lima.
249 Déborah Oropeza Keresey, "La esclavitud asiática en el virreinato de la Nueva España, 1565-1673", *Historia Mexicana*, vol. XLI, no. 1, julio-septiembre, 2011, pp. 5-57.
250 Ibid., p. 17.

Endnotes

251 Jonathan Israel, *Razas, clases sociales y vida política*, p. 83.
252 Déborah Oropeza, "La esclavitud asiática", p. 16.
253 Ibid., pp. 36-38.
254 ARAG, Civil, caja 449, exp. 20, progresivo 7400.
255 *Recopilación de Indias*, Libro VI, Título II, Ley XII.
256 AHEC, Fondo Colonial, Protocolos de Escribanos, caja 11, carpeta 2, f. 36-36v.
257 AHEC, Fondo Colonial, Protocolos de Escribanos, caja 11, carpeta 5, f. 122v-123.
258 AHEC, Fondo Colonial, Protocolos de Escribanos, caja 11, carpeta 5, f. 97-97v.
259 Déborah Oropeza, "La esclavitud asiática", p. 41.
260 Tatiana Seijas, *Asian slaves in colonial Mexico*, p. 102.
261 AHEC, Fondo Colonial, Protocolos de Escribanos, caja 11, carpeta 1, f. 43.
262 In 1624, Captain Arcos was sentenced to exile in the Philippines by the alcaldes of crime in the capital of the Vice-royalty; AGI, Filipinas, 5, N. 320. However, the Audiencia of Mexico suspended his sentence on the condition that he pay 2,000 ducats to royal officials in Mexico who, in turn, would remit the money to the receiver at the Consejo de Indias; AGI, Indiferente General, 451, L. A8, f. 182v-183.
263 AHEC, Fondo Colonial, Protocolos de Escribanos, caja 11, carpeta 1, f. 43v-44.
264 AHEC, Fondo Colonial, Protocolos de Escribanos, caja 12, carpeta 1, f. 47-47v.
265 AHEC, Fondo Colonial, Protocolos de Escribanos, caja 12, carpeta 2, f. 107-107v.
266 AHEC, Fondo Colonial, Protocolos de Escribanos, caja 11, carpeta 1, f. 45.
267 To give one example, we know of the sale of Luis, a negro slave, for 400 pesos in 1601 in the villa of Colima; AHEC, Fondo Colonial, Protocolos de Escribanos, caja 6, carpeta 3, f. 1.
268 AHMC, secc. B, caja 50, exp. 9, pos. 5, f. 22v.
269 AHMC, secc. B, caja 57, exp. 5, pos. 1. We have been unable to locate this encomendero.
270 AGN, Indios, vol. 13, exp. 112.
271 Rubén Carrillo Martín, "Los 'chinos' de Nueva España", p. 17.
272 Asian barbers emerged as strong rivals of their Spanish counterparts, to the extent that in 1635 the latter petitioned the Viceroy to limit the "excesses and inconveniences" that the chino barbers represented for the "Republic". After consulting with the city government, the council opted to reduce the number of Asian barbers to 12, and stipulated that they were to move to the suburbs to prevent "unfair" competition with the Spanish barbers in the city center; see Jonathan Israel, *Razas*, p. 83. Edward R. Slack, Jr. also analyzed the case of chino barbers in Mexico City in his article, "The Chinos in New Spain; A Corrective Lens for a Distorted Image", *Journal of World History*, no. 1, vol. 20, 2009, pp. 35-67. Other references to barbers in Mexico City are in AGN, General de Parte, vol. 8, exp. 66; AGN, General de Parte, vol. 14, exp. 50; AGN, Indios, vol. 10, exp. 249; AGN, Indios, vol. 15, exp. 29 y 86; AGN, Reales cédulas, vol. D18, exp. 27.
273 AHMC, secc. B, caja 22, exp. 4.
274 Alberto Carrillo Cázares, *Partidos y padrones of the Obispado de Michoacán (1680-1685)*, 1996, p. 381.
275 María Irma López Razgado and María del Carmen Ochoa Gutiérrez (coord.), Archivo Histórico Parroquial de San Felipe de Jesús, "El Beaterio". Libro de bautismos siglo XVII, t. I, 2021, pp. 12-13.
276 Ibid., p. 16. In reality, they were 6 fathers and 3 godfathers because Francisco de la Cruz is registered as the latter 3 times.
277 Rubén Carrillo Martín, "Los 'chinos' de Nueva España", p. 31.
278 An earlier version of this text was published as Paulina Machuca, "Medrar entre palmares", pp. 337-362. There, we annexed a copy of Francisca Martha's will. An abbreviated version in French was published as Paulina Machuca, "Francisca Martha, une petite propriétaire de palmiers entre deux mondes", pp. 41-57.
279 AHMC, secc. B, caja 30, exp. 23.

Vino de Cocos, the Pilgrim Beverage

280 The date is hypothetical: if she wed in 1642, the only suggested date available, she would have been around 20.
281 Bachiller Diego Correa Gudiño declared: "news came of the death of Francisca Martha, china criolla, wife of Miguel de Solís": AHMC, secc. B, caja 30, exp. 23, f. 5.
282 Tatiana Seijas, *Asian slaves in colonial Mexico*, p. 16.
283 Déborah Oropeza, *La migración asiática*, p. 147.
284 Tatiana Seijas, *Asian slaves in colonial Mexico*, pp. 15-16, 79.
285 In 1652, Francisca Martha declared: "perhaps some ten years, more or less, have passed since I wed Sebastián de la Cruz": AHMC, secc. B, caja 30, exp. 23, f. 6v.
286 Asunción Lavrin, "La mujer en la sociedad colonial hispanoamericana", *Historia de América Latina. América Latina colonial: población, sociedad y cultura*, vol. 4, 1990, pp. 109-137.
287 Archivo Histórico de la Parroquia de Beaterio (AHPB), Libro 1, carpeta 2, f. 3.
288 AHPB, Libro 1, carpeta 2, f. 2.
289 AHPB, Libro 1, carpeta 2, f. 4v.
290 AGN, Tierras, v. 3624, exp. 9, f. 2v-3.
291 AGI, Filipinas, 38, N. 12.
292 Paulina Machuca, "Cabildo, negociación y vino de cocos: el caso de la villa de Colima en el siglo xvii", *Anuario de Estudios Americanos*, vol. 66, no. 1 (enero-junio 2009): 173-192; Paulina Machuca, "El alcalde de los chinos".
293 Ramón López Lara, *El Obispado de Michoacán*, p. 175.
294 Francisca Martha mentioned that they bought a property with eight producing palm trees from an Indian of Tecuiciapa named Melchor Pérez. This indicates that this population sector participated in the dynamics of cultivating palm trees: AHMC, secc. B, caja 30, exp. 23, f. 8v.
295 It seems that Matheo de Ocariz was a Spaniard. This suggests that he also had to seek vinateros to produce aguardiente, as was common at that time.
296 On March 18, 1652, Francisca Martha stated: "my said husband died some three months ago in the town of Nahualapa, deprived of his senses": AHMC, secc. B, caja 30, exp. 23, f. 9.
297 Asunción Lavrin, "La mujer en la sociedad colonial", pp. 109-137.
298 Pilar Gonzalbo Aizpuru, *Vivir en Nueva España. Orden y desorden en la vida cotidiana*, 2009, p. 45.
299 AHMC, secc. B, caja 30, exp. 23, f. 3-4v.
300 An exception is the study by Irma López Razgado, "Dulce Nombre de Jesús: iglesia y cofradía de los mulatos y pardos en la villa de Colima, siglo XVIII", unpublished. We thank the author for sharing her text.
301 AHMC, secc. B, caja 4, exp. 1, pos. 43, f. 73-74.
302 Fray Joseph Sicardo, *Vida y Milagros del glorioso San Nicolás de Tolentino, religioso del orden de los ermitaños de nuestro padre San Agustín*, 1701, p. 282.
303 Fray Joseph Sicardo, *San Nicolás de Tolentino*, 292. We have modernized the orthography in the original edition.
304 Déborah Oropeza, "Los 'indios chinos'", pp. 144-145.
305 Déborah Oropeza discusses this figure in "Los 'indios chinos'", p. 145. The original document is in AGN, Inquisición, v. 372, exp. 20.
306 AHMC, secc. B, caja 30, exp. 23, f. 5.
307 Numerous complaints were recorded in the 16th-17th centuries, especially against doctrinaires who "diverted" inheritances from Indians, or from their religious order, in their favor.
308 António Manuel Hespanha, *Cultura jurídica europea: síntesis de un milenio*, 2002, p. 68.
309 AGI, Filipinas, 38, N. 12.
310 Thomas Calvo and Guillaume Gaudin published some biographical data on Sebastián de Pineda and the transcription commented on this relation in *Arar la Mar del Sur. Documentos sobre navegación y colonización de Filipinas (Siglos XVI-XVII)*, 2022, pp. 97-121.

Endnotes

311 The (Asian) native cabin boys received a wage of 48 pesos for their work aboard the Manila Galleon, far below that of any other trade, which was estimated at over 100 pesos; see Jean-Pierre Berthe and Thomas Calvo (eds.), *Administración e imperio. El peso de la monarquía hispana en sus Indias (1631-1648)*, 2011, p. 387.

312 AGI, Filipinas, 38, N. 12.

313 For a broader discussion of rural connections across the Pacific Ocean, see the work of James Gerber and Lei Guang, *Agriculture and rural connections in the Pacific, 1500-1900*, 2006.

314 Matthew J. Furlong, "Peasants, servants, and sojourners", p. 326.

315 AHMC, secc. B, caja 57, exp. 5, pos. 1, f. 2.

316 AGI, Contratación, 520, n. 2, f. 42 and ff. See also Matthew J. Furlong, "Soldiers, sailors, and salesmen", pp. 1-17.

317 AGI, Filipinas, 38, n. 12.

318 *Diccionario de autoridades* (1726-1739), vol. VI, Real Academia Española, www.rae.es.

319 A 17-page file that narrates the entire judicial process concerning possession of the palm tree plantation claimed by Pedro Ruiz de Padilla and Francisco Rodríguez Machuca. AHMC, secc. B, caja 44, exp. 8.

320 AHMC, secc. B, caja 44, exp. 8, f.

321 To cite one example, in August 1612, Gerónimo Dávalos Vergara sent around 60 loads (tercios) of large and small cacao, and one of coconuts "wrapped in hides" to Mexico City. The cargo was received by relatives there. AHEC, Fondo Colonial, caja 8, carpeta 9.

322 AHMC, Fondo Sevilla del Río, caja 5, exp. 4.

323 AHMC, secc. B, caja 49, exp. 7, pos. 8. It is feasible to think that some of the vinateros mentioned in this drunken brawl also appeared in another, perhaps Agustín, who worked for Magdalena Bote. According to Domingo's declaration in that document from 1600, Agustín was a "chino servant of Magdalena Bote" (AHMC, Fondo Sevilla del Río, caja 4, exp. 4, f. 3 f.). In this document from 1604, he reappears under the tutelage of the same person, indicating that he did not serve his sentence of exile to the Philippines, but continued working as a vinatero in Colima.

324 AHMC, secc. B, caja 50, exp. 9, pos. 5.

325 During our fieldwork with tuberos in Colima (Mexico) and the manananggot or mananguete in Central Visayas (the Philippines), we observed that the age range of the men who climbed the trees to collect sap (tuba) was 16-70, so this depended on each man's physical condition. It is certainly a broad age range for working in such an arduous trade.

326 AHMC, secc. B, caja 49, exp. 7; emphasis added.

327 *Ibid.*

328 *Diccionario de Gobierno y Legislación de Indias*, p. 342. Decree dated 26 May 1609. *Cedulario* tomo 16, fol. 254, n. 243.

329 Eduardo Flores Clair, "Minas y mineros: pago en especie y conflictos, 1790-1880", *Historias*, no. 13, abril-junio, 1986, pp. 51-57. Emphasis added.

330 Cited in Guadalupe Pinzón, "Desde tierra y hacia el horizonte marítimo. Una reflexión sobre la relevancia de los establecimientos portuarios del Pacífico novohispano", *México y la Cuenca del Pacífico*, año 17, no. 50, mayo, 2014, p. 80. Emphasis added.

331 AGN, Minería, vol. 148; cited in Silvana Elisa Cruz Domínguez, "Conflicto entre trabajadores y mineros del Real del Monte. Antecedentes, documentos y efectos", *Contribuciones desde Coatepec*, no. 23, julio-diciembre, 2012, p. 86. Emphasis added.

332 AHMC, secc. B, caja 27, exp. 8.

333 AHMC, secc. B, caja 18, exp. 1, f. 77 v.

334 To give one example, it is well known that when the Basques arrived in New Spain they showed a propensity to work in mining and metallurgy, perhaps due to their origin or their relations with these guilds.

335 AHMC, secc. B, caja 11, exp. 5.

336 AHMC, secc. B, caja 15, exp. 15. In Tagala, tumbaga means copper.

Vino de Cocos, the Pilgrim Beverage

337 For an interesting analysis of diverse letters of service in this context, see José Ignacio Urquiola Permisán, *Trabajadores de campo y ciudad. Las cartas de servicio como forma de contratación en Querétaro (1588-1609)*, 2001, especially p. 29.
338 Ibid., pp. 372-373.
339 Tatiana Seijas, *Asian slaves in colonial Mexico*, pp. 130-140.
340 William H. Scott, *Barangay*, p. 134.
341 Likely a bereaved relative of Santiago de Vera, then President of the Audiencia de Guadalajara and, earlier, governor of the Philippines. Could this chino have arrived with them?
342 AHEC, Fondo Colonial, Protocolos de Escribanos, caja 7, carpeta 5, ff. 3-4.
343 Most of the information on Lorenzo de Aguilar is from the file in AHMC, secc. B, caja 29, exp. 8.
344 AHMC, secc. B, caja 29, exp. 20.
345 AHMC, secc. B, caja 29, exp. 8.
346 AHMC, secc. B, caja 29, exp. 50.
347 Silvio Zavala, *Ordenanzas del trabajo, siglo XVI y XVII*, 1980, p. 140. Emphasis added.
348 AHMC, secc. B, caja 18, exp. 1, f. 74 f.
349 Ibid.
350 AHMC, secc. B, caja 8, exp. 27.
351 AGI, Contratación, 520, n. 2, R. 14, f. 32 and ff.
352 AHMC, secc. B, caja 23, exp. 1.
353 His will is in AHEC, secc. 2, caja 18, carpeta 12, ff. 36-40. We thank Irma López for sharing this reference.
354 It is interesting to note that in colonial Chile, some Indian wills reveal a predilection to be buried "beside a font of Holy Water", perhaps indicating a "desire for their bodies to be trod upon by all those who visit the church". See Julio Retama Ávila's book, *Testamentos de 'indios' en Chile colonial: 1564-1801*, 2000, p. 50.
355 In 2009, we published the article "El alcalde de los chinos", cited above. Since then, we have gathered the additional evidence presented here.
356 AHMC, secc. B, caja 8, exp. 27.
357 Eigi Fuchigami, "Indios chinos en Colima, siglos XVI y XVII", p. 22.
358 AHMC, caja B-13, exp. 15. It is interesting to note that this alcalde was a servant of Sebastián Gutiérrez on a palm hacienda in the Caxitlán Valley, jurisdiction of Colima.
359 AHMC, secc. B, caja 19, exp. 32.
360 Jane G. Landers and Barry M. Robinson, *Slaves, subjects and subversives*, 2006.
361 Constantino Bayle, *Los cabildos en la América española*, 1952, p. 174.
362 Charles Gibson, *Los aztecas bajo el dominio español*, 1996, p. 401.
363 Sinibaldo de Mas y Sanz, *Informe sobre el estado de las Islas Filipinas en 1842. Escrito por el autor del Aristodemo, del sistema musical de la lengua castellana etc.*, 1842.
364 These figures served like caciques in Indian towns of the Philippines. See Luis Alonso Álvarez, "Los señores del Barangay. La principalía indígena en las islas Filipinas, 1565-1789: viejas evidencias y nuevas hipótesis" in Margarita Menegus Bornemann and Rodolfo Aguirre Salvador (coords.), *El cacicazgo en Nueva España y Filipinas*, 2005, pp. 355-406.
365 For more information on this topic, see Ana Echevarría Arsuaga's article, "De cadí a alcalde mayor. La élite judicial mudéjar en el siglo XV", *Al-Qantara*, XXIV, no. 2, 2003, pp. 273-290.
366 Ibid., p. 93.
367 The list of the haciendas and ranches where vino de cocos was produced is from Matthew J. Furlong, "Peasants, servants, and sojourners", p. 480. Beyond the names of these localities, there is no information on aspects related to how the drink was produced.
368 Déborah Oropeza, "Los indios chinos en la Nueva España", p. 93.
369 AGN, Tierras, vol. 104, exp. 6, f. 127-128.

Endnotes

370 Matthew J. Furlong, "Peasants, servants, and sojourners", p. 480.
371 AGN, Tierras, vol. 104, exp. 6, f. 117 v.
372 Matthew J. Furlong, "Peasants, servants, and sojourners", pp. 479-480.
373 Calvo, "Japoneses en Guadalajara"; Falck and Palacios, *El japonés que conquistó Guadalajara*.
374 AHEC, secc. 2, caja 18, carpeta 12.
375 Jaime Olveda, "El puerto de La Navidad" in Jaime Olveda (coord.), *Relaciones intercoloniales. Nueva España y Filipinas*, 2017, pp. 121-123.
376 AGN, Tierras, v. 3624, exp. 9, f. 2v-3.
377 Joseph Antonio Villaseñor y Sánchez, *Theatro americano. Descripción general de los reynos y provincias de la Nueva-España, y sus jurisdicciones*, 1746, pp. 186-187.
378 Ibid., p. 189.
379 Ibid., p. 187. Maricruz Piza López' thesis, "Acapulco y sus alrededores: herencia filipina a partir del Galeón de Manila", 2019, is a good reference for situating the importance of the Asian population in this region.
380 This chapter was greatly enriched by comments from two specialists in Baybayin, Jean-Paul G. Potet and Christopher Miller, whom we thank for their generosity, suggestions, and careful reading of the first version, which was published in Paulina Machuca, "Microhistoria global de una escritura peregrina".
381 Due to the scarcity of documents in this alphabet, in 2014 the Philippines' National Archives declared all files written in Baybayin and conserved at the University of Santo Tomás in Manila (UST) a National Cultural Treasure, based on the criteria of rarity and importance for the nation's historical memory. The original documents and explanation of their importance can be consulted at **www.ust.edu.ph/the-baybayin-documents**. On the signatures found in these holdings, see also the pioneering work by Alberto Santamaría, "El 'Baybayin' en el Archivo de Santo Tomás. Algo de paleografía tagala", UNITAS, vol. XVI, no. 8, pp. 441-480; and, later, Christopher Miller, "Filipino Cultural Heritage in the UST Archives. Baybayin script in 17th-century land deeds", International Conference on the Heritage and History of the University of Santo Tomas, Universidad de Santo Tomás, Manila, 2011a; and Regalado Trota José, "Don Luis Castilla Offers to Sell Land in Manila (1629)" in Christina H. Lee and Ricardo Padrón (eds.), *The Spanish Pacific, 1521-1815*, 2020, pp. 91-113.
382 Domingo de los Santos, *Vocabulario de la lengua tagala. Primera y segunda parte*, 1794, p. 343.
383 William H. Scott states that Baybayin is one of a dozen forms of native writing from Southeast Asia whose origins can be traced to India. They share the feature that consonants have an implicit vowel "a", so they require special markers to represent other vowels, as we explain below; see William H. Scott, *Barangay*, p. 213. Christopher Miller provides evidence to support the thesis that Baybayin derives from an early variant of Bugis writing from Macassar which, in turn, descended from a variant of Devanagari, combined with a Kawi vowel system from Sumatra; see Christopher Miller, "Linguistic insights into the history of Philippine script: graphonomic structure, sociolinguistic variation, and contact phenomena", *Philippine Linguistics Conference*, University of the Philippines Diliman, Quezon City, 2011b.
384 Pedro Chirino, *Relación de las Islas Filipinas*, p. 41.
385 Juan José Delgado, *Historia general sacro-profana, política y natural de las islas del Poniente llamadas Filipinas*, [1751] (1892), p. 331.
386 William H. Scott, *Prehispanic Source Materials for the Study of Philippine History*, 1984, pp. 58-59; Miller, "Filipino Cultural Heritage in the UST Archives".
387 Francisco Colín, *Labor evangélica, ministerios apostólicos de los obreros de la Compañía de Jesús, fundación y progresos de su provincia en las islas Filipinas*, 1663, p. 54.
388 Santamaría, "El Baybayin", p. 472.
389 Miller, "Filipino Cultural Heritage in the UST Archives".
390 Modified slightly from the original to improve comprehension by Kennia Machuca Herrera and Alejandro Torres.
391 For a synthesis of documents written in Mesoamerican languages using the Roman alphabet, see Matthew Restall's article, "Heirs to the hieroglyphs: indigenous writing in colonial Mesoamerica, *The Americas*, vol. 54, no. 2, October, 1997, pp. 239-267.

392 Jorge Mojarro, "Los primeros libros impresos en Filipinas (1593-1607)", *Hispania sacra*, vol. LXXII, no. 145, enero-junio, 2020, p. 233.

393 Benigno Albarrán González, "La primera traducción de la Doctrina cristiana del Cardenal Belarmino al ilocano (Filipinas)", *Livius*, no. 12, 1998, p. 10.

394 José Antonio Cervera, "A cultural bridge between East and West in the Sixteenth Century: Juan Cobo and his book Shilu" in Florina H. Capistrano-Baker and Meha Priyadarshini (eds), *Transpacific engagements. Trade, translation, and visual culture of entangled empires (1565-1898)*, 2020, pp. 77-89.

395 The original files can be consulted at https://www.ust.edu.ph/the-baybayin-documents.

396 Jean-Paul G. Potet, "La pétition tagale: Caming manga alipin (1665)", *Cahiers de Linguistique. Asie Orientale*, vol. 16, no. 1, Juin, 1987, pp. 109-157; Jean-Paul G. Potet, *Tagalog linguistics and miscellanies*, 2013, pp. 99-156.

397 We thank Marlon James Sales, a professor at the University of the Philippines, for sharing his discovery of the signature in Baybayin dated 1584, found in the Archivo General de la Nación de México. His analysis of that signature will be published soon.

398 Ignacio Villamor, *La antigua escritura filipina*, 1922, pp. 11-12.

399 Modified slightly from the original to improve comprehension by Kennia Machuca Herrera.

400 Calvo, "Japoneses en Guadalajara".

401 Eikichi Hayashiya, "Preámbulo" in Melba Falck and Héctor Palacios, *El japonés que conquistó Guadalajara. La historia de Juan de Páez en la Guadalajara del siglo XVII*, 2009, pp. 15-17.

402 Déborah Oropeza, *La migración asiática*, p. 263.

403 AHMC, Fondo Sevilla del Río, caja 5, exp. 4.

404 Eduardo Descalzo Yuste, "La compañía de Jesús en Filipinas (1581-1768): realidad y representación", 2015, p. 392.

405 Matthew J. Furlong, "Peasants, servants, and sojourners", p. 610.

406 Jean-Paul G. Potet and Christopher Miller suggested that this surname could be read as "Di-Sa-Bi"; perhaps "de Chávez", in Spanish?

407 Jean-Paul G. Potet, *Baybayin. The Syllabic Alphabet of the Tagalogs*, 2014, p. 57.

408 Caroline Cunill, "La alfabetización de los mayas yucatecos y sus consecuencias sociales, 1545-1580", *Estudios de cultura maya*, vol. 31, 2008, p. 165.

409 Marina Garone Gravier, "Nuevos retratos para las viejas palabras. Libros novohispanos en lenguas indígenas", *Istor: revista de historia internacional*, año 8, no. 31, 2007, p. 103.

410 Ibid., p. 109.

411 William H. Scott, *Barangay*, p. 215.

412 Jean-Paul G. Potet, *Baybayin*, p. 58.

413 Christopher Miller told us that the script of the Manguianes, on the island of Mindoro, uses only one bar.

414 He bought the position of alférez mayor for 3,130 pesos in 1600 and held it for almost three decades: AGI, México, 177, N. 10.

415 José Miguel Romero de Solís, *Andariegos y pobladores. Nueva España y Nueva Galicia (siglo XVI)*, 2001, pp. 618-619.

416 Pedro Chirino, *Relación de las Islas Filipinas*, pp. 78-79.

417 From the Náhuatl tecomatl, an object used as a vessel or recipient for liquids, usually of the species Crescentia alata.

418 Victoria Yepes, *Historia natural de las islas bisayas*, p. 96.

419 Some sentences of exile to the Philippines appear in the AHMC, like those of eight Spaniards in 1616, after an attack on the alcalde ordinario, Diego González Conde, though we cannot be sure if they sailed to the Philippines to serve their sentence, AHMC, secc. B, caja 3, exp. 8.

420 The sentence erroneously mentions Francisco Sánchez, instead of the original name, Francisco Hernández.

421 AHMC, secc. B, caja 57, exp. 5, pos. 1.

Endnotes

422 AHMC, secc. B, caja 49, exp. 7, pos. 8, ff. 21-32 v.
423 Miller, "Filipino Cultural Heritage in the UST Archives".
424 Pedro Chirino, *Relación de las islas Filipinas*, p. 39.
425 Matthew Restall, "Heirs to the hieroglyphs", p. 245.
426 William H. Scott, *Barangay*, p. 210.
427 Here, we refer to the judicial processes involving indios chinos vinateros in 1600 and 1604 that correspond to the signatures in AHMC, secc. B, caja 49, exp. 7, pos. 8, and AHMC, Fondo Sevilla del Río, caja 5, exp. 4.
428 Trota, "Don Luis Castilla Offers to Sell Land in Manila (1629)", p. 95.
429 Memorial sobre las bebidas de la Nueva España, sus efectos, y sus gravámenes excesivos, Biblioteca Nacional de España (hereinafter, BNE), Mss. 19518, f. 1.
430 Henry J. Bruman, *Alcohol in Ancient Mexico*, 2000.
431 Daniel Zizumbo et al., "Archaeological Evidence of the Cultural Importance of Agave spp. in Pre-Hispanic Colima, Mexico", *Economic Botany*, vol. 63, no. 3, 2009, pp. 288-302.
432 Miguel Novillo, "Tinajas arqueológicas del sitio Los Guachimontones, sector Talleres, durante el Posclásico (900-1521 d.C.): una aproximación a su uso y funcionalidad", 2014.
433 Felipe Sevilla del Río, *Provança*, p. 27.
434 Ibid., p. 82.
435 Ibid., p. 47.
436 Paulina Machuca, "El arribo de plantas a las Indias Occidentales: el caso of the Balsas-Jalisco a través de las Relaciones geográficas del siglo XVI", *Relaciones, estudios de historia y sociedad*, vol. XXXIV, no. 136, otoño, 2013, pp. 73-114.
437 Archivo Histórico Judicial del Estado de Oaxaca (hereinafter, AHJEO), secc. Villa Alta, Penal, Bebidas alcohólicas, leg. 10, exp. 25.
438 "Relación de Ameca" in René Acuña (ed.), *Relaciones geográficas del siglo XVI: Nueva Galicia*, 1988, p. 32.
439 "Relación de Chilchotla", in René Acuña (ed.), *Relaciones geográficas del siglo XVI: Michoacán*, 1987, p. 109.
440 "Relación de Querétaro", in René Acuña (ed.), *Relaciones geográficas del siglo XVI: Michoacán*, 1987, p. 243.
441 "Relación de Sirándaro", in René Acuña (ed.), *Relaciones geográficas del siglo XVI: Michoacán*, 1987, p. 264.
442 "Relación de Chilchotla" in René Acuña (ed.), *Relaciones geográficas del siglo XVI: Michoacán*, 1987, p. 109.
443 William B. Taylor, *Embriaguez, homicidio y rebelión en las poblaciones coloniales mexicanas*, 1987, pp. 49-115.
444 AHMC, Fondo Sevilla del Río, caja 5, exp. 4, f. 1.
445 Ibid., f. 2f.
446 AHMC, secc. B, caja 49, exp. 7, f. 21.
447 Ibid., f. 21 and ff.
448 The original document is in AGN, Tierras, 2811, exp. 5. I used the transcription by Ernesto Lemoine Villicaña, "Relación de los capítulos que los naturales de los pueblos de Maquilí y Guacomán y Pómaro y lima y Chinacamitlán de los Motines de Colima y sus sujetos y estancias...", *Boletín del Archivo General de la Nación*, t. 1, no. 2, 1960, pp. 202-212, p. 210. The document is written in Náhuatl, accompanied by a brief transcription in Spanish. Emphasis added.
449 Taylor, *Embriaguez, homicidio y rebelión*, p. 68.
450 Situated on the outskirts of the Villa of Colima, Coquimatlán was surely a zone marked by widespread consumption of palm aguardiente; AHMC, secc. B, caja 54, exp. 12, pos. 3.
451 AHMC, secc. B, caja 57, exp. 7, pos. 3.
452 AHMC, secc. B, caja 63, exp. 1.

Vino de Cocos, the Pilgrim Beverage

453 AHMC, secc. B, caja 2, 3xp. 31.
454 AHMC, secc. B, caja 57, exp. 7, pos. 3.
455 AHMC, secc. B, caja 6, exp. 12.
456 AHMC, secc. B, caja 10, exp. 2.
457 Ibid.
458 On vino de cocos production in this zone, see the chapter on the palm haciendas.
459 AHMC, secc. B, caja 23, exp. 20.
460 Archivo Histórico del Ayuntamiento de Pátzcuaro (hereinafter AHAP), caja 9, carpeta 16. We thank Felipe Castro Gutiérrez for providing the documental references from this archive.
461 AHAP, caja 11, carpeta 5.
462 AHAP, caja 13, carpeta 4.
463 Equivalent to approximately 0.5 liters.
464 AHMC, secc. B, caja 63, exp. 1.
465 AHMC, secc. B, caja 10, exp. 5.
466 AHMC, secc. B, caja 30, exp. 18.
467 AHMC, secc. B, caja 18, exp. 1, f. 77v. Emphasis added.
468 AHMC, secc. B, caja 49, exp. 7, f. 21.
469 Felipe Sevilla del Río, *Provança*, p. 50.
470 AHCM, caja 98, exp. 22, f. 42 v.
471 Most of these towns were located near water and fertile land. In the early 16th century, they all produced corn, beans, cotton, and some native fruits, later incorporating some non-native tropical plants like bananas, sugarcane, and coconut palms. For an informative treatise on the pueblos de indios in Colima in colonial times, see Juan Carlos Reyes Garza, *Al pie del volcán. Los indios de Colima en el virreinato*, 2000.
472 AHMC, secc. B, caja 14, exp. 18. Ecautlán was one of the towns that, with Ixtlahuacán, Tamala, and Xiloteupan, supplied the priest in their district in San Salvador Chiamila with hens from Castille, eggs, corn, lard, and candles; see AHMC, secc. B, caja 29, exp. 9.
473 Petition written in Náhuatl by the alcalde of Ecautlán (1638), jurisdiction de Colima, who emphasized the word "cocos" in line six.
474 AHMC, secc. B, caja 14, exp. 18, f. 8v.
475 Ibid.
476 AHMC, secc. B, caja 24, exp. 36.
477 AHMC, caja 3, exp. 21.
478 AHMC, secc. B, caja 29, exp. 23.
479 Ibid.
480 Not to become more inebriated, but because the tuberos had to collect tuba in the afternoon or evening and then make the required incision and place the recipient correctly to collect tuba the following day.
481 AHMC, secc. B, caja 18, exp. 10.
482 AHMC, secc. B, caja 52, exp. 11, pos. 3.
483 AHMC, secc. B, caja 31, exp. 6. Could this have been the second husband of Francisca Martha –our china criolla– the protagonist of Chapter Three?
484 AHMC, secc. B, caja 29, exp. 32.
485 Alberto Carrillo, *Partidos y padrones del Obispado de Michoacán*, p. 381.
486 AHEC, Fondo colonial, caja 17, carpeta 4, f. 47.
487 Matthew J. Furlong, "Peasants, servants, and sojourners", p. 480.
488 AGN, Tierras, vol. 104, exp. 6, f. 117 v.
489 Adolfo Gómez Amador, for example, argues that "the large number of haciendas devoted to producing vino de cocos and their palm trees meant that chino laborers were insufficient, they

Endnotes

taught Indians and negros to prepare the palm to obtain tuba, but reserved for themselves the knowhow for elaborating the liquor" (emphasis added); see Gómez, "La presencia filipina en Colima".

490 Alberto Carrillo, *Partidos y padrones del Obispado de Michoacán*, pp. 384-386.
491 José Jesús Hernández Palomo, *El aguardiente de caña en México*, 1974, p. 22.
492 Alonso Zorita, *Leyes y ordenanzas de las Indias del Mar Océano*... libro 6, título 3, ley 4, 1974, p. 311.
493 For a succinct treatise on this topic, see Óscar Cruz Barney, "El vino y el derecho: la regulación jurídica de la producción, comercio y consumo del vino en México (1529-1888)", *Anuario Mexicano de Historia del Derecho*, no. 16, 2004, p. 175.
494 AGN, Ordenanzas, vol. 1, exp. 144, f. 130 v.
495 *Ibid.*
496 We analyze this ordinance in the final chapter of the book.
497 AHMC, secc. B, caja 20, exp. 1, pos. 22.
498 Ernesto Lemoine, "Relación de agravios", p. 210.
499 AHEC/Reyes, reg. 370.
500 Matthew J. Furlong, "Peasants, servants, and sojourners", p. 480.
501 AGI, Filipinas, 38, N. 12.
502 Felipe Sevilla del Río, *Provança*.
503 *Ibid.*, p. 28.
504 Taking as a reference the average cost of 4 pesos per palm tree, though this means disregarding the reference by Juan Carlos Reyes in La antigua provincia de Colima, p. 158, which states that "assuming that the palm trees had the same value as cacao trees [of] one peso per tree, this would mean the existence of at least 138,000 palms". In the early 17th century, fully mature palms cost 5 pesos, while "new" ones cost 3, and some very young ones, just 3 years old, could be worth only 2. AHEC/Reyes, regs. 927 and 1400.
505 Felipe Sevilla del Río, *Provança*, p. 28.
506 AHEC, Fondo colonial, caja 9, carpeta 1, f. 2.
507 AHEC/Reyes, regs. 705 and 1091.
508 AHEC, Fondo colonial, caja 9, carpeta 1, f. 2.
509 AHEC, Fondo colonial, caja 9, carpeta 7.
510 AHEC, Fondo colonial, caja 9, carpeta 5. Emphasis added.
511 *Ibid.*
512 Juan Carlos Reyes Garza elaborated a detailed paleographic study of these inventories in Por mandato de su Majestad. However, during our review of the original documents in the Archivo General de Indias, we found that they did not coincide with Reyes' classification due to an internal change in the numeration of the inventories. Here, we cite the references as they appear today in the AGI.
513 AGI, México, 262, N. 51, f. 1v.
514 It is important to note that owners gave the same value –3 pesos– for both the botija and the arroba.
515 AGI, México, 262, N. 34, f. 2.
516 Gabriel Escribano Cobo and Alfredo Mederos Martín, "Botijas en yacimientos arqueológicos subacuáticos de las Islas Canarias. Una fuente complementaria para el análisis del comercio canario-americano" in Francisco Morales Padrón (coord.), *XII Coloquio de Historia Canario-Americana*, vol. 1, 1998, pp. 539-568.
517 Carmen Mena García, "Nuevos datos sobre bastimentos y envases en armadas y flotas de la carrera", *Revista de Indias*, vol. LXIV, no. 231, 2004, p. 464.
518 *Ibid.* We thank Luis Alonso Álvarez for his suggestions on this topic.
519 Plantation owners used arroba and botija synonymously, each equivalent to approximately 16 liters. Rodrigo de Brizuela declared that only 80 of his 150 palms were in production, and

520 AGI, México, 262, N. 59, f. 1v.
521 The reader can consult, for example, AHEC/Reyes, regs. 407, 485, 512, 519, 638, among others.
522 AGI, México, 262, N. 59, f. 3.
523 AHMC, secc. B, caja 18, exp. 1, f. 74 v.
524 José F. de la Peña, Oligarquía y propiedad en Nueva España, 1550-1624, 1983, pp. 66-71.
525 We eliminated the rubric agrícolas from the original because it surely included not only palms but also Cassia fistula, achiote, and corn. We added the rows marked "Palms", where we calculated an average value of 4 pesos per tree, and those marked Vino de cocos.
526 The inventories are: Juan de Aguilar (AGI, México, 259, N. 4), Francisco de Montoya y Linares (AGI, México, 259, N. 134), Francisco López Muñiz (AGI, México, 259, N. 141), Alonso Sánchez Redondo (AGI, México, 259, N. 236), Juan Luis Aguirre (AGI, México, 260, N. 5), Lesmes Astudillo, (AGI, México, 260, N. 17), Gaspar Bello de Acuña (AGI, México, 260, N. 22), Simón Téllez de Trejo (AGI, México, 260, N. 198), Luis de Villegas y Jasso, (AGI, México, 260, N. 212), and Tobías Marín (AGI, México, 261, N. 123).
527 Matthew J. Furlong, "Peasants, servants, and sojourners", p. 480.
528 AHMC, secc. B, caja 6, exp. 38, f. 1v-2.
529 AHMC, secc. B, caja 7, exp. 11, f. 1 f.
530 AHEC/Reyes, regs. 2141, 2147 and 2238.
531 AHMC, secc. B, caja 22, exp. 1, f. 3 f.
532 Arnaldo Issasy, Descripción y demarcación, p. 126.
533 Juan Alcalde de Rueda, "Relación de la provincia de Motín", p. 157. Emphasis added.
534 AHMC, Fondo Sevilla del Río, caja 5, exp. 22.
535 Ibid.
536 Ibid.
537 Beatriz Rojas, "Repúblicas de españoles: Antiguo régimen y privilegios", Secuencia, no. 53, mayo-agosto 2002, p. 21.
538 The topic of licenses is discussed in a later chapter.
539 This hacienda belonged to the indio chino, Miguel Pano. Productivity was above average as he obtained over three arrobas annually per palm, when the average was 2. Could this reflect his greater mastery of the use and handling of coconut palms that he had learned in the Philippines?
540 Arnaldo Issasy, Demarcación y descripción, p. 173.
541 Ibid., p. 172.
542 AHEC/Reyes, reg. 370.
543 AHEC/Reyes, reg. 380.
544 AHEC/Reyes, regs. 565 and 666.
545 AHEC/Reyes, reg. 864.
546 AHEC/Reyes, reg. 1941.
547 AHEC/Reyes, reg. 1953.
548 Enrique Florescano and Lydia Espinosa, Apuntes para el estudio de la agricultura colonial, 1987, 2 vols.
549 AHCM, Cabildo, secc. Administración pecuniaria, Colecturía, Diezmo, exp. 90. We thank Isla Jiménez Pérez for sharing this document with us.
550 These are the accounts given by Diego Correa, priest of the partido of Tecolapa, who was the tithe administrator for the villa de Colima and its partido. Note that the rubric "colts" is repeated. The specific tithes were: Captain Rodrigo de Brizuela, 117 and one-third botijas (20 reales each /293 pesos 3 tomines); Antonio de Solórzano, 79 and two-thirds botijas (20 reales each/199 pesos 2 tomines); Joseph Durán, 20 botijas (18 reales each/45 pesos); Joseph de Labayen, 119 and three-quarters botijas (18 reales each/269 pesos 5 tomines); Joseph de

Endnotes

Viana, 100 and a half botijas (18 reales each, 232 pesos 3 tomines); Miguel de Castañeda, 51 botijas (18 reales each/121 pesos); Rodrigo de Brizuela, 107 and a half botijas (19 reales each/256 pesos). See AHCM, Cabildo, secc. Administración pecuniaria, Colecturía, Diezmo, exp. 91. We are grateful to Isla Jiménez Pérez for sharing this document.

551 The figures for 1622 are from the property inventory of the authorities of Colima, available at: AGI, México, 262 and AGI, México, 263. Those for 1631 are from Ramón López Lara, *El Obispado de Michoacán en el siglo XVII*.

552 AHMC, secc. B, caja 14, exp. 3.

553 AHCM, Cabildo, secc. Administración pecuniaria, Colecturía, Diezmo, leg. 22. Thanks to Isla Jiménez Pérez for sharing this document.

554 *Ibid*, p. 38.

555 The author distinguishes two types of chantries, one ecclesiastical, the other laic, defining the latter as "a pious foundation to which a person assigned certain real estate or upon which she/he imposed a certain amount of capital. The fruits or profits generated were used to celebrate ceremonies or masses in the conditions that the founder determined". See Alberto Carrillo Cázares, *Michoacán en el otoño del siglo XVII*, 2011, pp. 99-104.

556 Dejación (transfer) was the act of ceding rights, property, or obligations to another person.

557 AHMC, secc. B, caja 29, exp. 21.

558 AHMC, secc. B, caja 30, exp. 1.

559 *Ibid*.

560 AHMC, secc. B, caja 31, exp. 26.

561 Located today in Cofradía de Juárez, municipality of Armería, Colima.

562 AHMC, secc. B, caja 32, exp. 43.

563 Alberto Carrillo, *Michoacán en el otoño del siglo XVII*, p. 402.

564 The hacienda of San Salvador Chiamilan covered three towns in the alcaldía mayor of Colima (Santa Ana Ecautlán, Ixtlahuacán de los Reyes, San Miguel Tamala) and three more in the alcaldía mayor of Motines (San Salvador Chiamilan, San Francisco Jolotlán, San Juan Zinacamitlán).

565 At least the first four owners were residents of the villa of Colima.

566 Alberto Carrillo, *Michoacán en el otoño del siglo XVII*, p. 427.

567 Alberto Carrillo, *Michoacán en el otoño del siglo XVII*, pp. 692-694.

568 José Miguel Romero, *Clérigos, encomenderos, mercaderes y arrieros*, p. 14. See also the study by Magdalena Escobosa Haas, *Los mercedarios en Colima. Haciendas y trapiches*, 1999.

569 AHMC, secc. B, caja 32, exp. 23.

570 AHMC, secc. B, caja 35, exp. 27.

571 Paulina Machuca, *Elites y gobierno en Colima de la Nueva España. Siglo XVII*, 2016, pp. 207-209.

572 AHEC, Fondo colonial, caja 17, carpeta 16.

573 AGN, Indiferente virreinal, caja 2949, exp. 52, f. 1v.

574 AHCM, Diocesano, Justicia, Testamentos, Capellanías y Obras pías, caja 98.

575 Arnaldo Issasy, *Demarcación y descripción*, p. 174.

576 AGN, Tierras, vol. 3624, exp. 2 and 3. See also Déborah Oropeza, "Los indios chinos", p. 93.

577 AHEC, Fondo colonial, caja 17, carpeta 1, f. 40 v.

578 The original title of the document is: "Planta y mapa de la hacienda de palmas donde pretende licencia para fundar trapiche Francisco Martínez de Moscoso en el valle de Nahualapa en esta jurisdicción de la villa de Colima". In the lower part we read: "in the center of this map [are] the houses of said hacienda with others for its service and people for the [plantation] and the others in the places [indicated by the] letter in the margin of the annotations declared. The passage ends with these words: "Those towns and haciendas are the ones most contiguous with the hacienda of Francisco Martínez de Moscoso, who cultivates it, and its form is what I have described, and to verify this I signed it in the presence of witnesses in said Nanualapa valley on the thirtieth day of the month of November of the year one thousand six hundred and eighty-eight".

Vino de Cocos, the Pilgrim Beverage

579 AHMC, secc. B, caja 33, exp. 19.
580 AHEC, Fondo colonial, caja 17, carpeta 16.
581 AHEC, Fondo colonial, caja 17, carpeta 1.
582 Ibid.
583 AHMC, secc. B, caja 34, exp. 4.
584 AHEC, Fondo colonial, caja 17, carpeta 4, f. 33 v.
585 Ibid., f. 36 v.
586 Luis Gabriel Gómez Azpeitia, "El ordenamiento territorial en la provincia de Colima durante el siglo XVIII", 2000, p. 215.
587 Ibid., p. 156.
588 AHMC, secc. C, caja 1, exp. 19. We return to this figure and his trip to Zacatecas in the next chapter.
589 Henry J. Bruman, "The culture history of Mexican vanilla", *The Hispanic American Historical Review*, vol. 28, no. 3, August, 1948, pp. 360-376.
590 Enrique Florescano and Lydia Espinosa, *Fuentes para el estudio*, vol. 2, p. 458.
591 AHMC, secc. C, caja 6, exp. 44.
592 AGI, México, 262, N. 51; AGI, México, 262, N. 265.
593 In 1602, the colimense Diego de Monroy sent a load of 76 botijas (874 kg) of Cassia fístula to Mexico City at a price of 7 pesos per botija: AHEC, Fondo colonial, caja 7, carpeta 1, f. 57.
594 AHEC, Fondo colonial, caja 11, carpeta 5, f. 111.
595 AGI, México, 262, N. 51.
596 Enrique Florescano and Lydia Espinosa, *Fuentes para el estudio*, vol. 1, p. 244.
597 Arnaldo Issasy, *Demarcación y descripción*, p. 174.
598 Déborah Oropeza, Los "indios chinos", pp. 156-158.
599 AHMC, secc. C, caja 1, exp. 19, f. 14 f.; AHMC, secc. C, caja 2, exp. 38, f. 6 f. It is important to note that each load could include up to 18 dozen coconuts; that is, 216 pieces.
600 Enrique Florescano and Lydia Espinosa, *Fuentes para el estudio*, vol. 1, p. 248; vol. 2, p. 454.
601 Gerardo Sánchez. *Los cultivos tropicales*, pp. 86-87.
602 Luis Alonso Álvarez, "Mascar, aspirar y fumar. Pautas de consumo y cambio tecnológico: la evidencia del tabaco en España, 1735-1886" in Luis Alonso Álvarez, Lina Gálvez, and Santiago de Luxán (eds.), *Tabaco e Historia Económica. Estudios sobre fiscalidad, consumo y empresa (siglos XVIII-XX)*, 2006, pp. 247-270.
603 Domingo Lázaro de Arregui, *Descripción de la Nueva Galicia*, 1980, p. 106.
604 José J. Hernández Palomo, *El aguardiente de caña*, p. 7.
605 Teresa Lozano Armendares, *El chinguirito vindicado. El contrabando de aguardiente de caña y la política colonial*, 2005, p. 25.
606 On commerce in wine and aguardiente from Parras, see Archivo Histórico de Mazapil (hereinafter AHM), Fondo colonial, caja 23, no. 173 (1762); on the sale and prohibitions of mezcals, see AHM, Fondo colonial, caja 25, unnumbered (1771), and AHM, Fondo colonial, caja 30, unnumbered (1787).
607 Sergio Corona, *La vitivinicultura en el pueblo de Santa María*, p. 217.
608 Domingo Lázaro de Arregui, *Descripción de la Nueva Galicia*, p. 106.
609 Teresa Lozano, *El chinguirito vindicado*, p. 136.
610 Juan de Montenegro, "Descripción de Colima. 1744" in José Antonio Calderón Quijano (dir.), *Documentos para la Historia del Estado de Colima*, 1979, p. 160.
611 Miguel José Pérez Ponce de León, "Descripción de Colima. 1776-1777" in José Antonio Calderón Quijano (dir.), *Documentos para la Historia del Estado de Colima*, 1979, p. 200.
612 AHMC, secc. F, caja 2, pos. 1, f. 38.
613 AHEC, Fondo colonial, caja 30 A, carpeta 9.

Endnotes

614 José Antonio Villaseñor y Sánchez, *Theatro Americano*, p. 187.

615 Jorge Alberto Ruiz and María Concepción Gavira, "Mezclas y desorden en la población de una provincia fronteriza: Zacatula-México en el siglo XVIII", *Cuadernos interculturales*, año 11, no. 21, segundo semestre 2013, p. 146.

616 *Ibid.*, p. 156.

617 Felipe Castro Gutiérrez, "Alborotos y siniestras relaciones: la república de indios de Pátzcuaro colonial", *Relaciones. Estudios de Historia y Sociedad*, vol. XXIII, no. 89, invierno 2002, p. 204.

618 Document entitled "Memoria del vino que se va haciendo en la hacienda de Zinacamitlán desde veintiséis de octubre de mil seiscientos y treinta y ocho años que murió doña Catalina de Alarcón, mujer que fue de Antonio Carrillo de Guzmán, que es a su cargo como su albacea testamentario, que es como sigue", held in AHMC, secc. B, caja 18, exp. 1.

619 AHMC, secc. B, caja 18, exp. 1, f. 7-8v.

620 AHEC/Reyes, regs. 1215, 1216. Other notarial references in AHEC/Reyes are: 1587, 1588, 1589, 1590.

621 Evidenced by the jailing of the merchant Miguel López in 1630 for selling vino de cocos in Ahuaculco. The corregidor of Tala fined him 50 pesos and spilled all his aguardiente: ARAG, progr. 198, caja 4, exp. 49.

622 Equivalent to approximately 0.5 liters.

623 AHMC, secc. B, caja 63, exp. 1.

624 AHMC, secc. B, caja 10, exp. 5.

625 AHMC, secc. B, cajas 54, exp. 12, pos. 3; 57, exp. 7, pos. 3; 63, exp. 1.

626 Especially the alcabala tax ledgers for 1653-1684, in AHMC, secc. B, caja 28, exp. 20.

627 Juan Carlos Reyes, *La antigua provincia de Colima*, p. 202.

628 Gerardo Sánchez mentions this route in *Los cultivos tropicales*, p. 89.

629 AHAP, caja 9, carpeta 16.

630 AHAP, caja 9, carpeta 1.

631 AHAP, caja 9, carpeta 7.

632 AHEC, Fondo colonial, caja 11, carpeta 6, f. 60-61.

633 AHMC, Fondo Sevilla del Río, caja 5, exp. 22.

634 AGN, General de parte, vol. 7, f. 128v.

635 AGN, General de parte, vol. 7, f. 129.

636 AHAP, caja 12, carpeta 1.

637 AHAP, caja 8, carpeta 4, f. 160 and ff.

638 We have a photocopy of the band issued by don Lope Diez de Armendariz, Marqués de Cadereyta, which granted the 1637 license that added Maquili, dated 20 February 1637, reproduced in Felipe Sevilla del Río, *Provança*, Anexos.

639 AGN, General de parte, caja 2949, exp. 52, f. 3v.

640 José J. Hernández Palomo, *La renta del pulque en Nueva España (1663-1810)*, 1979, p. 37.

641 Gerardo Sánchez, *Los cultivos tropicales*, p. 83.

642 Óscar Mazín, *Archivo capitular de administración diocesana Valladolid-Morelia. Catálogo I*, 1991, p. 188, reg. 1283.

643 *Ibid.*, p. 162, reg. 1015.

644 With information from Gerardo Sánchez, *Los cultivos tropicales*, p. 83.

645 Peter Bakewell, *Minería y sociedad en el México colonial: Zacatecas, 1546-1700*, 1976, p. 108.

646 AHMC, secc. A, caja 15, exp. 21.

647 José Miguel Romero, *Andariegos y pobladores*, pp. 141-142.

648 Felipe Sevilla del Río, *Provança*, p. 60.

649 María Luisa Pazos Pazos and Justina Sarabia Viejo, "Orden y delincuencia. Los alguaciles de las ciudades novohispanas, siglos XVI-XVII" in Rey Tristán et al., *Actas del XIV Encuentro de Americanistas Españoles*, 2010, pp. 684-698, 692.
650 AGN, General de parte, caja 6716, exp. 57.
651 AGN, Indiferente virreinal, caja 6366, exp. 48.
652 AHEC/Reyes, reg. 498.
653 Felipe Sevilla del Río, *Provança*, p. 59.
654 We addressed this topic in Paulina Machuca, "Alcohol, mineros y operarios en la Nueva España, siglos XVI-XVIII" in Patricio Herrera and Juan Carlos Yáñez (coords.), *Alcohol y trabajo en América Latina, siglos XVII-XIX. Experiencias económicas, políticas y socioculturales*, 2019, pp. 17-39.
655 Carlos Sempat Assadourian, *El sistema de la economía colonial: el mercado interior. Regiones y espacio económico*, 1983, p. 115.
656 Archivo Histórico del Estado de Zacatecas (hereinafter AHEZ), Fondo Ayuntamiento de Zacatecas, Reglamentos y bandos, caja 1.
657 José Arturo Burciaga Campos, *El prisma en el espejo. Clero secular y sociedad en la Nueva Galicia. Guadalajara y Zacatecas, siglo XVII*, 2012, p. 261.
658 Felipe Sevilla del Río, *Provança*, p. 64.
659 Ibid., p. 61.
660 Chantal Cramaussel, "El camino real de tierra adentro. De México a Santa Fe" in Chantal Cramaussel (ed.), *Rutas de la Nueva España*, 2006, p. 306.
661 A botija of vino de cocos sold for 18-20 reales in Zacatecas; that is, 2.25-2.5 pesos, while a load was offered in up to 5 pesos; see AHMC, secc. C, caja 1, exp. 19, f. 14.
662 Matthew J. Furlong, "Peasants, servants, and sojourners", p. 434.
663 AHMC, secc. B, caja 31, exp. 34, f. 16.
664 Archivo Histórico del Estado de San Luis Potosí (hereinafter, AHESLP), Fondo Alcaldía mayor de San Luis Potosí, 1655, 2, caja 353, exp. 17, f. 1.
665 In November 1652, Captain Alonso Orejón was ordered to pay half an anata for his post as alcalde mayor of Colima, AGN, Reales Cédulas Duplicadas, vol. D 18, exp. 402, f. 234 v. In 1653, he appeared as the alcalde mayor of that place; Paulina Machuca, *Elites y gobierno*, p. 99.
666 Primo Feliciano Velázquez, *Historia de San Luis Potosí*, vol. 1, 2004, p. 638.
667 Louisa Schell Höberman, *Mexico's Merchant Elite, 1590-1660: Silver, State and Society*, 1991, p. 124.
668 AHESLP, Fondo Alcaldía mayor de San Luis Potosí, 1655, 2, caja 353, exp. 17, f. 1.
669 Ibid.
670 Matthew J. Furlong, "Peasants, servants, and sojourners", p. 434.
671 AHMC, secc. C, caja 1, exp. 19.
672 AHEZ, Ayuntamiento de Zacatecas, Reglamentos y Bandos, caja 1, f. 1-1v.
673 In another article, we discussed the dynamics of the vino de cocos and mezcal royal monopoly in Guadalajara. We take some relevant aspects from that text for this book; see Paulina Machuca et al., "El estanco de vino de cocos y mezcal en la Nueva Galicia, siglos XVII-XVIII", *Letras Históricas*, no. 8, primavera-verano 2013, pp. 71-99.
674 Thomas Calvo, *Guadalajara y su región en el siglo XVII, población y economía*, 1992.
675 René de León Meza, "El sistema productivo y comercial de la Nueva Galicia, siglos XVI y XVII", 2010, p. 248.
676 It is interesting to note that, during this history, the diverse authorities and actors involved in the royañ monopoly called mezcal by several names: mezcale, mezcate, mezcali, mexcalillo, even mezcala. This term and indigenous reality penetrated slowly into the Hispanic universe. The word cocos always appears in plural.
677 *Actas de cabildos de la Guadalajara. Volumen segundo del 1º de enero de 1636 al 18 de junio del año de 1668*, 1984, pp. 26-37.

Endnotes

678 Manuel López Cotilla states that in 1640 the ayuntamiento of Guadalajara presented to the King its proposal for conducting water from Rancho del Álamo to the city at a cost of 16,000 pesos, but because the author of the regulations on the use of water and the plans for the aqueduct, Custodio de la Higuera, was absent, work had to be suspended. See Manuel López Cotilla, Historia de la introducción de agua en Guadalajara desde su fundación hasta la fecha en la cual se han refundido todas las noticias importantes que existen en la Secretaría del Ayuntamiento y otras que se han adquirido en lo particular, 1842, pp. 17-18.

679 Actas de cabildos, pp. 26-37.

680 On Luis de Encío, see Thomas Calvo's text, "Japoneses en Guadalajara", and Melba Falck and Héctor Palacios, El japonés que conquistó Guadalajara.

681 Interestingly, in the Philippines, the place of origin of vino de cocos, the creation of a distribution center for the drink was not approved until the 1760s. AGI, Filipinas, 335, L. 17, f. 393 R.

682 Thomas Calvo, Poder, religión y sociedad en la Guadalajara del siglo XVII, Guadalajara, 1992, p. 66.

683 See Manuel López Cotilla, Historia de la introducción.

684 Actas de cabildos, p. 141.

685 AHMC, caja 14, exp. 3.

686 ARAG, Ramo civil, caja 331, exp. 10, progresivo 4787.

687 Thomas Calvo, Poder, religión y sociedad, p. 14.

688 Actas de cabildos, p. 140.

689 Ibid., p. 141.

690 AHMC, Fondo Sevilla del Río, caja 2, exp. 18.

691 Ibid.

692 AHMC, Fondo Sevilla del Río, caja 2, exp. 18.

693 For more information on this figure, see Thomas Calvo, Poder, religión y sociedad, pp. 14-16.

694 José Arturo Burciaga, El prisma en el espejo, pp. 261-262.

695 The topic of discourses on vino de cocos and other alcoholic drinks is addressed in the next chapter.

696 AGI, Guadalajara, 231, L. 4. The Real Academia de la Historia in Madrid also holds a copy of this decree, Colección Mata Linares, t. C., f. 104-105.

697 AGI, Guadalajara, 15, R.1, N. 26.

698 AGI, Contaduría, 875.

699 AGI, Guadalajara, 15, R. 1, N. 26.

700 Based on John TePaske and Herbert S. Klein, Ingresos y egresos de la Real Hacienda de Nueva España, 1988, 2 vols.

701 Archivo Histórico Municipal de Sombrerete (hereinafter, AHMS), Fondo Colonial, exp. 3234. Emphasis added. We thank Tomás Dimas for localizing this document.

702 Ibid.

703 For more information, see the article by Paulina Machuca et al., "El estanco de vino de cocos y mezcal".

704 AHEC, Fondo Colonial, caja 30 A, exp. 9.

705 Miguel José Pérez Ponce de León, "Descripción de Colima. 1776-1777", p. 193.

706 Enrique Florescano and Lydia Espinosa, Fuentes para el estudio, vol. 2, p. 458.

707 Hernando de Vascones, "Relación de Zacatula", p. 452.

708 The information in this paragraph is from Matthew J. Furlong, "Peasants, servants, and sojourners", pp. 494-495.

709 AGI, Guadalajara, 231, L. 4.

Vino de Cocos, the Pilgrim Beverage

710 On this route, see Paulina Machuca and Maricruz Piza, "El camino de México a Acapulco (siglo XVII)" in Beatriz Rojas (coord.), *De caminos y puentes: ordenamiento territorial en la Nueva España*, 2021, pp. 129-151.

711 Carlos Paredes Martínez, "El mercado de Pátzcuaro y los mercaderes tarascos en los inicios de la época colonial" in Carlos Paredes Martínez (coord.), *Historia y sociedad. Ensayos del Seminario de Historia Colonial de Michoacán*, 1997, p. 170.

712 José J. Hernández Palomo, *La renta del pulque*, p. 68.

713 Thomas Calvo, "Algunas historias de granos en medio de fluctuaciones planetarias: México y Cartagena de Indias en 1690-1692" in Luis Alberto Arrioja and Armando Alberola Romá (eds.), *Clima, desastres y convulsiones sociales en España e Hispanoamérica, siglos XVII-XX*, 2016, pp. 269-294.

714 AGI, Patronato, 226, N. 1, R. 25.

715 Teresa Lozano discusses these arguments in her book, *El chinguirito vindicado*, pp. 32-41.

716 Felipe Sevilla del Río, *Provança*, pp. 85-86.

717 Alberto Carrillo, *Michoacán en el otoño del siglo XVII*, p. 375.

718 Óscar Cruz Barney, "El vino y el derecho", p. 173.

719 William Taylor, *Embriaguez, homicidio y rebelión*, p. 69.

720 Libro 6, título 3, ley 4, in Zorita, *Leyes y ordenanzas reales*, p. 311.

721 José J. Hernández Palomo, *La renta del pulque*, pp. 33, 68.

722 Libro 6, título 3, ley 5, in Zorita, *Leyes y ordenanzas reales*, p. 311.

723 As the 17th century advanced, figures like the priest Hernán Ruiz de Alarcón (brother of Juan, the dramaturgist) and Viceroy Juan de Palafox y Mendoza (1642) vociferated against the alcoholic drinks consumed by Indians in Mexico City, where pulque was ingested in enormous amounts because the authorities tolerated that trade. Even Carlos de Sigüenza y Góngora questioned the Viceroy's actions that allowed Spaniards, negros, mulattoes, chinos, and mestizos to fill the taverns, get drunk, and commit "offenses against God"; see Sonia Corcuera, "La embriaguez, la cocina y sus códigos morales" in Antonio Rubial García (coord.), *Historia de la vida cotidiana en México. La ciudad barroca*, vol. II, 2005, pp. 519-554. The well-known shout "Long live pulque" from the 1692 tumult in Mexico City well reflects official concern over social disorder sparked by consumption of "drinks of the land"; see José J. Hernández Palomo, *La renta del pulque*, p. 68.

724 AGN, Ordenanzas, vol. 1, exp. 144, f. 130v-131.

725 AGN, Ordenanzas, vol. 1, exp. 144, f. 130v-131.

726 José J. Hernández Palomo, *La renta del pulque*; Teresa Lozano, *El chinguirito vindicado*.

727 AHMC, secc. B, caja 49, exp. 7, pos. 8.

728 AHMC, secc. B, caja 25, exp. 12, pos. 3.

729 AHMC, secc. B, caja 31, exp. 6, pos. 3.

730 AHMC, secc. B, caja 34, exp. 1, pos. 2.

731 The original document disappeared from the Archivo Histórico del Municipio de Colima, but Felipe Sevilla del Río's book, *Provança*, contains a transcription to which we have referred previously.

732 Felipe Sevilla del Río, *Provança*, pp. 85-86.

733 Carlos Viesca Treviño, "Hechizos y hierbas mágicas en la obra de Juan de Cárdenas", *Estudios de Historia Novohispana*, vol. 9, no. 9, 1987, p. 40.

734 Felipe Sevilla del Río, *Provança*, p. 59. On the physician Enrique Tavares, see Felipe Sevilla del Río, *Prosas literarias e históricas*, 2005, p. 229.

735 Juan de Cárdenas, *Problemas y secretos maravillosos de las Indias. Compuesta por el doctor Juan de Cárdenas*, Médico, 1591, pp. 102-103.

736 For a comparative view of the medicinal practices reported in the historical chronicles with current techno-scientific analyses, see Paulina Machuca and Ana Coria Téllez, "Prácticas curativas en torno a la palma de coco (Cocos nucifera L.) en "Filipinas, la India y México. Del conocimiento tradicional a la validación técnico-científica" in Paulina Machuca Chávez and

Endnotes

Salvador Pérez Ramírez (coords.), *Enfermedades y prácticas curativas en México. Diálogos entre el pasado y el presente*, 2021, pp. 89-116.

737 We thank Heriberto Ibáñez Chávez for his aid in interpreting medical aspects of the colonial documents.
738 Victoria Yepes, *Historia natural de las islas bisayas*, p. 96.
739 G. Mondragón Preciado et al., "Identificación de bacteriocinas producidas por bacterias ácido-lácticas aisladas en tuba", *XIX Congreso Nacional de Ingeniería Bioquímica*, Mazatlán, Sinaloa, 2014.
740 Hética was an "illness consisting in chills and fever of the whole body, with various symptoms, especially external heat in the extremities, heartburn after eating, thinning of the body, nocturnal sweating, and others. It is caused by the effervescence of the most acrid and salty blood [and is] of slow evolution". *Diccionario de la Lengua Castellana* (Autoridades), 1734, vol. 4, p. 141.
741 Francisco Hernández, *Obras completas*, p. 168.
742 Francisco Hernández, *Obras completas*, p. 167.
743 Gonzalo Fernández de Oviedo, *Historia general y natural de las Indias*, pp. 336-337.
744 Francisco Hernández, *Obras completas*, p. 168
745 Victoria Yepes, *Historia natural de las islas bisayas*, p. 99.
746 Blas de la Madre de Dios, *El libro de medicinas caseras*, p. 25.
747 Manuel Blanco, *Flora de Filipinas*, p. 719.
748 Francisco Hernández, *Obras completas*, p. 167.
749 Ibid.
750 AHEC, Fondo colonial, caja 9, carpeta 1, f. 2.
751 AHEC/Reyes, reg. 1044.
752 In his historical review of this form of supplication, Víctor Tau Anzoátegui argues that the phrase " the law is observed but not obeyed" did not indicate rebelliousness or disrespect for the mandates of colonial authorities but, rather, that applying the letter of the laws decreed could harm society since those orders often came from the Iberian Peninsula, or the capital cities of the Vice-Royalties and their audiencias, whose authorities were unfamiliar with local realities; see his book, *La ley en América hispana. Del descubrimiento a la emancipación*, 1992, pp. 67-144.
753 AHEZ, Fondo Ayuntamiento, Serie Reales Cédulas y Provisiones, Reales Cédulas, f. 1 v-2. We also examine the relation of alcoholic drinks to mining zones in detail in Paulina Machuca, "Alcohol, mineros y operarios".
754 AHEZ, Fondo Ayuntamiento, Reales Cédulas y Provisiones, Reales Cédulas, f. 1v-2.
755 We followed the trail of this corregidor but failed to find any document that relates him to wine from Castille. Our conjecture derives from other experiences where the opposition of some provincial authorities in this matter reflected vested economic interests. Sáenz Izquierdo held important posts in New Spain, as corregidor and alcalde mayor in Zacatecas, Puebla, and Villa Alta de San Ildefonso (Oaxaca), and as governor of the province of Yucatán. See AGN, Tierras, no. 110, vol. 2971, exp. 57; AGN, Real Hacienda, no. 98, vol. 4, exp. 22; AGN, Real Hacienda, no. 8, vol. 454, exp. 83; and AGN, Indiferente virreinal, caja 2050, exp. 1.
756 On this topic, see José Enciso Contreras' article, "Mercado de vino, mercaderes y fraude de la sisa en Zacatecas (1583-1584)", *Estudios de Historia Novohispana*, vol. 14, no. 14, 1994, pp. 9-37.
757 AHEZ, Ayuntamiento de Zacatecas, Serie Reglamentos y Bandos, caja 1, f. 1-1v.
758 AIPJ, Libro de Gobierno, tomo I, f. 180v-184.
759 AGN, Reales Cédulas Originales y Duplicadas, no. 100, vol. D12, exp. 264.
760 AIPJ, Libro de Gobierno, tomo I, f. 180v-184.
761 AIPJ, Libro de Gobierno, tomo I, f. 183.
762 Ibid.
763 Ibid.

Vino de Cocos, the Pilgrim Beverage

764 John Jay Tepaske, *El Real Protomedicato. La reglamentación de la profesión médica en el imperio español*, Mexico, 1997, especially pp. 94-102.

765 We reviewed, for example, the catalogue of the Archivo General de la Nación, and the Índice de los ramos hospitales y protomedicato, elaborated by María Teresa Esquivel Otea and Mercedes Sánchez Sandoval, 1977.

766 AGI, Guadalajara, 231, L. 4. The Real Academia de la Historia de Madrid holds a copy of this decree, Colección Mata Linares, t. C., f.104-105.

767 Juan Pedro Viqueira Albán, ¿*Relajados o reprimidos? Diversiones públicas y vida social en la ciudad de México durante el Siglo de las Luces*, 1987, p. 173.

768 AHMC, Fondo Sevilla del Río, caja 5, exp. 22.

769 Ibid.

770 Local sources in Colima record strong tremors in 1563, 1566, 1568, 1585, 1590, 1625, 1632, and 1680, and fires in 1587, 1600, 1613, and 1658; see Abelardo Ahumada González, *Sismos, pestes y vendavales en Colima y sus alrededores*, 2006; Juan Oseguera Velásquez, *Efemérides de Colima y de México*, 1989.

771 On this topic, see Raymundo Padilla Lozoya, "Desastres en México y Filipinas: cicatrices históricas que unen a nuestras culturas" in Thomas Calvo and Paulina Machuca (eds.), *México y Filipinas: culturas y memorias sobre el Pacífico*, 2016, pp. 57-78.

772 Juan de Montenegro, "Descripción de Colima. 1744", p. 160.

773 AGN, Ordenanzas, vol. 5, exp. 21, f. 15.

774 AGN, Indiferente virreinal, caja 2949, exp. 52, f. 1v.

775 Ibid., f. 2 v.

776 Ibid, f. 3.

777 AGN, Indiferente virreinal, caja 6112, exp. 5, f. 2.

778 Ibid.

779 Ibid, f. 2-2v.

780 AGN, Reales cédulas originales y duplicadas, vol. 22, exp. 23.

781 AGN, Indiferente virreinal, caja 6112, exp. 5, f. 2 v.

782 Juan Pedro Viqueira, ¿*Relajados o reprimidos*?, p. 176.

783 Juan de Montenegro, "Descripción de Colima. 1744", p. 160.

784 For more information on the raw materials of these drinks, consult the special issue of the journal *Arqueología Mexicana* devoted to alcoholic drinks in ancient Mexico, no. 114, marzo-abril, 2012, and Bruman's book, *Alcohol in Ancient Mexico*.

785 Alberto Carrillo, *Michoacán en el otoño del siglo XVII*, p. 375.

786 AGN, Impresos oficiales, caja 3002, exp. 19, f. 1v. Emphasis added.

787 Ibid., f. 2v.

788 José J. Hernández Palomo, *La renta del pulque*, p. 106.

789 Matías de la Mota Padilla, *Historia del Reino de Nueva Galicia en la América Septentrional*, 1973, p. 102.

790 Juan de Montenegro, "Descripción de Colima. 1744", p. 160.

791 Miguel José Pérez Ponce de León, "Descripción de Colima", p. 200.

792 Ibid.

793 AHMC, secc. F, caja 2, pos. 1, f. 38.

794 Tonio Andrade, "A Chinese Farmer, Two African Boys, and a Warlord", p. 574. His analysis takes place in Taiwan in 1661, a connected world that allowed interaction among the Chinese, Dutch, and African slaves.

795 Miles Ogborn, *Global Lives*.

796 We thank Edwin Mayoral Sánchez, a student in the Doctoral Program in Social Science at El Colegio de Michoacán, for his valuable feedback on this updated Epilogue. He is currently writing his thesis, "Destilando memorias vino-mezcaleras en las tabernas del Centro Occi-

ENDNOTES

dente de México: los casos de Zapotitlán de Vadillo, Tonaya y Tuxpan (Jalisco) y de Comala y La Rosa de San José de Lumber (Colima)".

797 Carl Lumholtz, *El México desconocido: cinco años de exploración entre tribus de la Sierra Madre Occidental, en la tierra caliente de Tepic y Jalisco, y entre los tarascos de Michoacán*, 1904, pp. 181-183. Emphasis added.

798 Henry J. Bruman, "Aboriginal drink areas in New Spain", 1940; and Henry J. Bruman, *Alcohol in ancient Mexico*.

799 Henry J. Bruman, "The Asiatic origin of the Huichol Still", *Geographical Review*, vol. 34, no. 3, July, 1944, p. 423.

800 *Ibid*, p. 427.

801 Daniel Zizumbo Villarreal and Patricia Colunga García-Marín, "Early coconut distillation and the origins of mezcal and tequila spirits in west-central Mexico", *Genetic Resources and Crop Evolution*, vol. 55, 2008, pp. 493-510.

802 Ana Valenzuela Zapata et al., "Influencia asiática en la producción de mezcal en la costa de Jalisco. El caso de la raicilla", *México y la cuenca del Pacífico*, vol. 11, no. 33, septiembre-diciembre 2008, pp. 91-116.

803 Hyunhee Park, *Soju: A Global History*, 2021.

804 Mari Carmen Serra Puche and Jesús Carlos Lazcano Arce, "Etnoarqueología de mezcal: su origen y su uso en Mesoamérica", in José Luis Vera Cortés and Rodolfo Fernández, *Agua de las verdes matas. Tequila y mezcal*, 2015, pp. 23-42.

805 Daniel Zizumbo Villarreal et al., "Distillation in Western Mesoamerica before European contact", *Economic Botany*, vol. 63, no. 4, 2009, pp. 413-426.

806 Joseph Needham, *Science and Civilization in China*, vol. 5, part 4, 1980, p. 108.

807 John G. Bourke, "Distillation by early American Indians", *American Anthropologist*, vol. 7, no. 3, July, 1894, pp. 297-299; and John G. Bourke, "Primitive distillation among the Tarascoes", *American Anthropologist*, vol. 6, no. 1, January, 1893, pp. 65-70.

808 The first dictionary that defines the word "distill" is the Diccionario de la Lengua Castellana (Autoridades), 1732, p. 235, with the meaning, "To flow or run liquid drop by drop". It is only in the second definition that we find: "Also to extract the juice or sap from something by a still, reducing it to a liquor with the strength of fire". Emphasis added.

809 Zizumbo Villarreal et al., "Distillation in Western Mesoamerica before European contact", pp. 413-426. Emphasis added.

810 Serra and Lazcano, "Etnoarqueología de mezcal", p. 25. In this same tone, we can include Claudio Jiménez Vizcarra's, *El vino mezcal, tequila y la polémica sobre la destilación prehispánica*, 2013.

811 Information from Dionisio, a resident of the town of Ixcatlán in Oaxaca, Mexico, who is over 100 years old; pers. comm., 4 September 2016.

812 The word mexcalli and its variants are mentioned in diverse sources from the early colonial period. They were used to designate the cooked heads of agave plants that served as food for people. The name of the drink mezcal was derived from that term.

813 Mari Carmen Serra Puche and Jesús Carlos Lazcano Arce, *El mezcal, una bebida prehispánica. Estudios etnoarqueológicos*, 2016, p. 196.

814 *Ibid.*, p. 202.

815 Although Serra and Lazcano used early colonial sources to evidence mezcal production, the citations they include in reality allude to mezcalli as cooked agave heads that were prepared as food. Regarding the drink, there are no clear allusions to a process of distillation. Cfr. Serra and Lazcano, "Etnoarqueología de mezcal", pp. 25-32.

816 Antonio Pigafetta, *Relazione del primo viaggio*, p. 81.

817 Ludovico de Varthema, *Itinerario de Ludovico de Varthema*, p. 50.

818 John Huyghenvan Linschoten, *The voyage of John Huyghen van Linschoten*, p. 49.

819 Patrick E. McGovern et al., "Pre-Hispanic Distillation? A Biomolecular Archaeological Investigation", *Open Access Journal of Archaeology and Anthropology*, vol. 1, no. 2, 2019.

820 Zizumbo Villarreal et al., "Distillation in Western Mesoamerica before European contact".

Vino de Cocos, the Pilgrim Beverage

821 Patrick E. McGovern et al., "Pre-Hispanic Distillation? A Biomolecular Archaeological Investigation", pp. 9-10.

822 Domingo García Garza, *La revolución mezcalera. Los destilados de agave y la invención de mezcal tradicional*, 2022, p. 26.

823 Ibid., p. 33.

824 Ibid., p. 241.

825 Valenzuela et al., "'Huichol' stills: a century of anthropology, technology transfer and innovation", *Crossroads*, no. 8, October, 2013, pp. 157-191.

826 His original surname may have been Angioçar o Angiozar, of Basque origin. Thanks to Guillermo Tovar y de Teresa, we know that in 1619 he signed as a witness and resident of Guadalajara in a contract to carry out the works of the main altarpiece in the Capilla del Sagrario of the new church in Guadalajara; see his text, "Noticias acerca del retablo mayor y sillería de coro de la catedral de Guadalajara: Francisco de la Gándara Hermosa en 1619", *Boletín de Monumentos Históricos del INAH*, tercera época, no. 1, p. 14.

827 Archivo Histórico del Arzobispado de Guadalajara (hereinafter AHAG), secc. Gobierno, Cabildos, Diezmos generales, caja 3, carpeta 1616-1821, exp. Provincia de Ávalos, año de 1616. Emphasis added. We modernized the orthography of the original document, and our transcription differs slightly from the one by René de León Meza in his text "Vino de coco y vino mezcal, una historia comercial conjunta en la época colonial", *Letras Históricas*, no. 12, primavera-verano, 2015, p. 32.

828 AGN, Indios, vol. 10, exp. 212, f. 116 v., cited in Matthew J. Furlong, "Peasants, Servants, and Sojourners", p. 590; unfortunately, the method used to produce this maguey aguardiente is not specified by the author, nor the place where it was elaborated.

829 AGN, Indiferente virreinal, 5087, exp. 36, f. 4.

830 See Ch. 7 of this book.

831 Matthew J. Furlong, "Peasants, Servants, and Sojourners", pp. 588-589.

832 AGI, México, 2324, N. 6.

833 AHAG, secc. Gobierno, Cabildos, Diezmos generales, caja 3, carpeta 1616-1821, exp. Provincia de Ávalos, año de 1619.

834 Domingo Lázaro de Arregui, *Descripción de la Nueva Galicia*, p. 106.

835 This process is well documented by Diana Carrano, *Los corregidores de Tequila en la Nueva Galicia. Una institución de larga duración (1563-1789)*, 2024.

836 In 1777, a judicial process began against Domingo Lázaro and Juan García over two loads of mezcal, and against Antonio Soriana for two other loads; AHJEO, secc. Teposcolula, Civil, Despacho real, año de 1777-1778, leg. 42, exp. 25.

837 Archivo Histórico del Estado de Oaxaca (hereinafter, AHEO), Alcaldías mayores, leg. 9, exp. 11.

838 Guadalupe Pinzón, *Acciones y reacciones*, p. 193.

839 AHJEO, secc. Ejutla, Penal, Lesiones, año de 1851, leg. 10, exp. 4.

840 We discussed this topic in Paulina Machuca, "Tras las huellas del mestizaje cultural entre México y Filipinas" in Paulina Machuca and Thomas Calvo (eds.), *México y Filipinas: culturas y memorias sobre el Pacífico*, 2016, pp. 385-401.

841 Ana Valenzuela et al., "'Huichol' stills"; Valenzuela, "East Asian Stills", pp. 140-151. The original map in Valenzuela et al., 2013, Fig. 12, has legends in English. Likewise, an illustration of the diverse types of stills used to produce mezcal in Mexico can be consulted in Domingo García, *Mezcal, un espirituoso artesanal de clase mundial*, 2019.

842 Sergio Corona, *La vitivinicultura*, p. 157.

843 To understand the importance of the use and handling of agave in Zapotitlán de Vadillo through the agricultural practices of peasants and mezcal production, see Carlos Lucio, "Mezcales y biodiversidad cultural en los alrededores del Volcán de Colima. El caso de los productores tradicionales de Zapotitlán de Vadillo", *EntreDiversidades. Revista de Ciencias Sociales y Humanidades*, vol. 5, otoño-invierno, 2015, pp. 13-43.

844 AGI, Guadalajara, 231, L. 4.

Endnotes

845 The resurgence of vino de cocos by Jorge Velasco has drawn the attention of specialists in distillates, like Nicholas Stevens, who traveled from the U.S. to Colima to learn the process of elaborating tuba and vino de cocos, and published a special note in the prestigious guide, Atlas Obscura: Stevens, N. C., "Is this Mexico's Oldest Spirit?", Atlas Obscura, secc. Gastro Obscura, 18 June 2024. https://www.atlasobscura.com/articles/mexicos-oldest-spirit-vino-de-cocos

846 Fernand Braudel, *Civilización material, economía y capitalismo*, p. 200.

847 Ibid., p. 205.

848 Rob DeSalle and Ian Tattersall, *Distilled: A Natural History of Spirits*, 2022, pp. 127-211.

ARCHIVES CONSULTED

AGI: Archivo General de Indias (Seville)
AGN: Archivo General de la Nación (Mexico City)
AHAG: Archivo Histórico del Arzobispado de Guadalajara
AHAP: Archivo Histórico del Ayuntamiento de Pátzcuaro (Michoacán)
AHCM: Archivo Histórico de la Casa de Morelos (Morelia)
AHEC: Archivo Histórico del Estado de Colima
AHESLP: Archivo Histórico del Estado de San Luis Potosí
AHEO: Archivo Histórico del Estado de Oaxaca
AHEZ: Archivo Histórico del Estado de Zacatecas
AHJEO: Archivo Histórico Judicial del Estado de Oaxaca
AHN: Archivo Histórico Nacional (Madrid)
AHM: Archivo Histórico de Mazapil (Zacatecas)
AHMC: Archivo Histórico del Municipio de Colima
AHMS: Archivo Histórico del Municipio de Sombrerete
AHPB: Archivo Histórico de la Parroquia de Beaterio (Colima)
AIPJ: Archivo de Instrumentos Públicos de Jalisco (Guadalajara)
ARAG: Archivo de la Real Audiencia de Guadalajara
BNE: Biblioteca Nacional de España (Madrid)
RAHM: Real Academia de la Historia (Madrid)

BIBLIOGRAPHY

Acosta, Cristóbal de, *Tractado de las drogas, y medicinas de las Indias Orientales, con sus plantas debuxadas al bivo por Christobal de Acosta, medico y cirujano que las vio ocularmente*, Burgos: Imprenta de Martín de Victoria, 1578.

Actas de cabildos de la ciudad de Guadalajara. Volumen segundo del 1º de enero de 1636 al 18 de junio del año de 1668, Guadalajara: H. Ayuntamiento de Guadalajara, 1984.

Acuña, René (ed.), *Relaciones geográficas del siglo XVI: Tlaxcala*, Mexico: UNAM, 1985.

Acuña, René (ed.), *Relaciones geográficas del siglo XVI: Michoacán*, Mexico: UNAM, 1987.

Acuña, René (ed.), *Relaciones geográficas del siglo XVI: Nueva Galicia*, Mexico: UNAM, 1988.

Ahumada González, Abelardo, *Sismos, pestes y vendavales en Colima y sus alrededores*, Colima: Secretaría de Cultura, Gobierno del Estado de Colima, 2006 (Colección Alforja Histórica Colimense).

Albarrán González, Benigno, "La primera traducción de la Doctrina cristiana del Cardenal Belarmino al ilocano (Filipinas)", *Livius*, núm. 12, 1998, pp. 9-20.

Alcalde de Rueda, Juan, "Relación de parte de la provincia de Motín que es en la costa de la Mar del Sur en esta Nueva España" in René Acuña (ed.), *Relaciones geográficas del siglo XVI: Michoacán*, Mexico: UNAM, 1987, pp. 156-180.

Alonso Álvarez, Luis, "Los señores del *Barangay*. La principalía indígena en las islas Filipinas, 1565-1789: viejas evidencias y nuevas hipótesis" in Margarita Menegus Bornemann and Rodolfo Aguirre Salvador (coords.), *El cacicazgo en Nueva España y Filipinas*, Mexico: UNAM, Plaza y Valdés, 2005, pp. 355-406.

Alonso Álvarez, Luis, "Mascar, aspirar y fumar. Pautas de consumo y cambio tecnológico: la evidencia del tabaco en España, 1735-1886" in Luis Alonso Álvarez, Lina Gálvez and Santiago de Luxán (eds.), *Tabaco e Historia Económica. Estudios sobre fiscalidad, consumo y empresa (siglos XVIII-XX)*, Madrid: Fundación Altadis, 2006, pp. 247-270.

Andrade, Tonio, "A Chinese Farmer, Two African Boys, and a Warlord: Toward a Global Microhistory", *Journal of World History*, no. 4, vol. 21, December, 2010, pp. 573-591.

Anglería, Pedro Mártir de, *Décadas del Nuevo Mundo, por Pedro Mártir de Anglería, Primer cronista de Indias*, Estudio y apéndices de Edmundo O'Gorman, Traducción del latín por Agustín Millares Carlo, Vol. I, Mexico: Biblioteca José Porrúa Estrada de Historia Mexicana dirigida por Jorge Gurría Lacroix, Primera Serie, 1964.

Argensola, Bartolomé Leonardo de, *Conquista de las islas Malucas al rey Felipe III Nuestro Señor escrita por el Licenciado Bartolomé Leonardo de Argensola, capellán de la Magestad de la Emperatriz y Rector de Villahermosa*, Libro primero, Madrid: 1609.

Assadourian, Carlos Sempat, *El sistema de la economía colonial: el mercado interior. Regiones y espacio económico*, Mexico: Nueva Imagen, 1983.

Bakewell, Peter, *Minería y sociedad en el México colonial: Zacatecas, 1546-1700*, Mexico: FCE, 1976.

Barros, João de, *Da Asia. Dos feitos, que os portuguezes fizeram no descubrimento, e conquista dos mares, e terras do Oriente*, Decada Terceira, parte primeira, Lisbon: Regia Officina Typografica, [1563] 1777.

Bibliography

Battuta, Ibn, *A través del Islam*, Traducción del árabe, introducción y notas de Serafín Fanjul y Federico Arbós, Madrid: Alianza Editorial, 2014.

Bayle, Constantino, *Los cabildos en la América española*, Madrid: Sapientia, 1952.

Berthe, Jean-Pierre and Thomas Calvo (eds.), *Administración e imperio. El peso de la monarquía hispana en sus Indias (1631-1648)*, Zamora: El Colegio de Michoacán, Fideicomiso Felipe Teixidor y Monserrat Alfau de Teixidor, 2011.

Bertrand, Romain and Guillaume Calafat, "Global microhistory: A case to follow", *Annales*, 73, no. 1, 2018, pp. 3-17.

Blanco, Manuel, *Flora de Filipinas. Según el sistema sexual de Linneo*, Manila: Imprenta de Santo Thomas, 1837.

Bourke, John G., "Primitive distillation among the Tarascoes", *American Anthropologist*, vol. 6, no. 1, January, 1893, pp. 65-70.

Bourke, John G., "Distillation by early American Indians", *American Anthropologist*, vol. 7, no. 3, July, 1894, pp. 297-299.

Braudel, Fernand, *Civilización material, economía y capitalismo, siglos XV-XVIII, Vol. 1: las estructuras de lo cotidiano*, Madrid: Alianza Editorial, 1984.

Bruman, Henry J., "Aboriginal drink areas in New Spain", Doctoral Thesis, California: University of California, Berkeley, 1940.

Bruman, Henry J., "Some observations on the early history of coconut in the New World", *Acta Americana*, vol. 2, no. 3, 1944, pp. 200-243.

Bruman, Henry J., "The Asiatic origin of the Huichol Still", *Geographical Review*, vol. 34, no. 3, July 1944, pp. 418-427.

Bruman, Henry J., "Early coconut culture in Western Mexico, *The Hispanic American Historical Review*, no. 25, 1945, pp. 301-314.

Bruman, Henry J., "Notes and comment: a further note on coconuts in Colima", *The Hispanic American Historical Review*, vol. 27, no. 3, August, 1947, pp. 572-573.

Bruman, Henry J., "The culture history of Mexican vanilla", *The Hispanic American Historical Review*, vol. 28, no. 3, August, 1948, pp. 360-376.

Bruman, Henry J., "Relations of Carl Sauer and Research in Latin America", *Geographical Review*, vol. 86, no. 3, July, 1996, pp. 370-376.

Bruman, Henry J., *Alcohol in ancient Mexico*, Foreword by Peter T. Furst, Salt Lake City: The University of Utah Press, 2000.

Burciaga Campos, José Arturo, *El prisma en el espejo. Clero secular y sociedad en la Nueva Galicia. Guadalajara y Zacatecas, siglo XVII*, Foreword by Thomas Calvo, Zacatecas: Universidad Autónoma de Zacatecas, 2012.

Burckhardt, Titus, *La civilización hispano-árabe*, Madrid: Alianza, 2004.

Calvo, Thomas, "Japoneses en Guadalajara: 'blancos de honor' durante el seiscientos mexicano", *Revista de Indias*, vol. XLIII, no. 172, 1983, pp. 531-547.

Calvo, Thomas, *Guadalajara y su región en el siglo XVII, población y economía*, Guadalajara: Centro de Estudios Mesoamericanos y Centroamericanos, H. Ayuntamiento de Guadalajara, 1992.

Calvo, Thomas, *Poder, religión y sociedad en la Guadalajara del siglo XVII*, Guadalajara: Centro de Estudios Mesoamericanos y Centroamericanos, H. Ayuntamiento de Guadalajara, 1992.

Calvo, Thomas, "Algunas historias de granos en medio de fluctuaciones planetarias: México y Cartagena de Indias en 1690-1692" in Luis Alberto Arrioja and Armando Alberola Romá (eds.), *Clima, desastres y convulsiones sociales en España e Hispanoamérica, siglos XVII-XX*, Zamora: El Colegio de Michoacán, Universidad de Alicante, 2016, pp. 269-294.

Calvo, Thomas, *Espacios, climas y aventuras: el galeón de Filipinas y la Fragata de las Marinas en el Pacífico occidental (1680-1700)*, San Luis Potosí: El Colegio de San Luis, 2016.

Calvo, Thomas and Guillaume Gaudin (comps.), *Arar la Mar del Sur. Documentos sobre navegación y colonización de Filipinas (Siglos XVI-XVII)*, Lagos de Moreno: Universidad de Guadalajara, 2022.

Candolle, Alphonse de, *Origine des plantes cultivées*, Paris: Ancienne Librairie Germer Baillière et Compagnie, 1886.

Cárdenas, Juan de, *Problemas y secretos maravillosos de las Indias. Compuesta por el doctor Juan de Cárdenas, Médico*, Mexico: Imprenta de Pedro Ocharte, 1591.

Cardona, Nicolás de, "Descripción de la costa de Colima. 1614-1615" in José Antonio Calderón Quijano (dir.), *Documentos para la Historia del Estado de Colima*, Mexico: Novaro, 1979, pp. 115-122 (Colección Peña Colorada).

Carrano, Diana, *Los corregidores de Tequila en la Nueva Galicia. Una institución de larga duración (1563-1789)*, Guadalajara: Universidad de Guadalajara, 2024 (Colección Estudios de la Humanidad).

Carrillo Cázares, Alberto, *Partidos y padrones del Obispado de Michoacán (1680-1685)*, Zamora: El Colegio de Michoacán, Gobierno del Estado de Michoacán, 1996.

Carrillo Cázares, Alberto, *Michoacán en el otoño del siglo XVII*, Morelia: El Colegio de Michoacán, Fondo Cultural Piedadense, Morevallado Editores, 2011.

Bibliography

Carrillo Martín, Rubén, "Asians to New Spain. Asian cultural and migratory flows in Mexico in the early stages of 'globalization' (1565-1816)", Doctoral Thesis, Information and Knowledge Society Doctoral Program, Internet Interdisciplinary Institute (IN3), Universitat Oberta de Catalunya (UOC), Barcelona 2015.

Carrillo Martín, Rubén, "Los 'chinos' de Nueva España': migración asiática en el México colonial", Millars, no. 2, vol. XXXIX, 2015, pp. 15-40.

Carrillo Martín, Rubén, *Las gentes del Mar Sangley*, Mexico: Palabra de Clío, 2017.

Castro Gutiérrez, Felipe, "Alborotos y siniestras relaciones: la república de indios de Pátzcuaro colonial", *Relaciones. Estudios de Historia y Sociedad*, no. 89, invierno 2002, vol. XXIII, pp. 203-233.

Cervera, José Antonio, "A cultural bridge between East and West in the Sixteenth Century: Juan Cobo and his book *Shilu*" in Florina H. Capistrano-Baker and Meha Priyadarshini (eds), *Transpacific engagements. Trade, translation, and visual culture of entangled empires (1565-1898)*, Makati City, Los Ángeles and Florence: Ayala Foundation, Inc., Getty Research Institute, Kunsthistorisches Institut in Florenz (Max-Planck-Institut), 2020, pp. 77-89.

Chinte-Sánchez, Priscila, *Philippine fermented foods. Principles and technology*, Quezon City: The University of the Philippines Press, 2008.

Chirino, Pedro, *Relacion de las Islas Filipinas, i de lo que en ellas an trabaiado los padres de la Compañía de Iesvs*, Rome: Imprenta de Estevan Paulino, 1604.

Colín, Francisco, *Labor evangélica, ministerios apostólicos de los obreros de la Compañía de Jesús, fundación y progresos de su provincia en las islas Filipinas*, Madrid: Joseph Fernández de Buendía, 1663.

Comyn, Tomás de, *Estado de las Islas Filipinas en 1810, brevemente descrito por Tomás de Comyn, con permiso del Supremo Consejo de Indias*, Madrid: Imprenta de Repullés, 1820 (Colección Clásicos Tavera, Serie 1. Iberoamérica en la Historia, vol. 11).

Cook, O. F., "History of the coconut palm in America", *Contributions from the United States Natural Herbarium*, no. 14, Washington, 1910, pp. 271-342.

Corcuera, Sonia, "La embriaguez, la cocina y sus códigos morales" in Antonio Rubial García (coord.), *Historia de la vida cotidiana en México. La ciudad barroca*, Vol. II, Mexico: El Colegio de México, FCE, 2005, pp. 519-554.

Corona Páez, Sergio Antonio, *La vitivinicultura en el pueblo de Santa María de las Parras. Producción de vinos, vinagres y aguardientes bajo el paradigma andaluz (siglos XVII y XVIII)*, Torreón: Ayuntamiento de Torreón, Instituto Municipal de Documentación y Archivo Histórico Eduardo Guerra, 2004.

Covarrubias Orozco, Sebastián de, *Thesoro de la Lengua Castellana o Española*, Madrid: Imprenta de Luis Sánchez, 1611.

Cramaussel, Chantal, "El camino real de tierra adentro. De México a Santa Fe" in Chantal Cramaussel (ed.), *Rutas de la Nueva España*, Zamora: El Colegio de Michoacán, 2006, pp. 299-327.

Crosby Jr., Alfred W., *The Columbian Exchange. Biological and cultural consequences of 1492*, Connecticut: Greenwood Press, 1972.

Cruz Barney, Óscar, "El vino y el derecho: la regulación jurídica de la producción, comercio y consumo del vino en México (1529-1888)", *Anuario Mexicano de Historia del Derecho*, no. 16, 2004, pp. 169-186.

Cruz Domínguez, Silvana Elisa, "Conflicto entre trabajadores y mineros del Real del Monte. Antecedentes, documentos y efectos", *Contribuciones desde Coatepec*, no. 23, julio-diciembre, 2012, pp. 67-93.

Cunill, Caroline, "La alfabetización de los mayas yucatecos y sus consecuencias sociales, 1545-1580", *Estudios de cultura maya*, vol. 31, 2008, pp. 163-192.

Dampier, William, *A new voyage round the world*, vol. 1, London: Printed from James Knapton at the Crown of St. Paul's Church yard, 1699.

De Lara, Juan, "El coco de Vigo: el coco chocolatero de la Batalla de Rande, 1702", *Anales del Instituto de Investigaciones Estéticas*, vol. XVVI, no. 125, 2024, pp. 197-215.

De la Peña, José F., *Oligarquía y propiedad en Nueva España, 1550-1624*, Mexico: FCE, 1983.

Delgado, Juan José, *Historia general sacro-profana, política y natural de las islas del Poniente llamadas Filipinas*, Manila: Imprenta de El Eco de Filipinas de D. Juan Atayde, 1892.

De los Santos, Domingo, *Vocabulario de la lengua tagala. Primera y segunda parte*, Sampaloc: Imprenta de N. S. de Loreto, 1794.

DeSalle, Rob and Ian Tattersall, *Distilled: A Natural History of Spirits*, New Haven: Yale University Press, 2022.

Descalzo Yuste, Eduardo, "La compañía de Jesús en Filipinas (1581-1768): realidad y representación", Doctoral Thesis, Barcelona: Universidad Autónoma de Barcelona, 2015.

Diccionario de la Lengua Castellana (Autoridades), Madrid: Imprenta de la Real Academia Española, 1734.

Drake, Francis, *Récit des voyages (1577-1596)*, Paris: Éditions Cartouche, 2012.

Dubs, Homer H. and Robert S. Smith, "Chinese in Mexico City in 1635", *The Far Eastern Quarterly*, vol. 1, no. 4, August 1942, pp. 387-389.

Bibliography

Echevarría Arsuaga, Ana, "De cadí a alcalde mayor. La élite judicial mudéjar en el siglo XV", *Al-Qantara*, XXIV, no. 2, 2003, pp. 273-290.

Enciso Contreras, José, "Mercado de vino, mercaderes y fraude de la sisa en Zacatecas (1583-1584)", *Estudios de Historia Novohispana*, vol. 14, no. 14, 1994, pp. 9-37.

Escobosa Haas, Magdalena, *Los mercedarios en Colima. Haciendas y trapiches*, Colima: Archivo Histórico del Municipio de Colima, Ayuntamiento de Colima, Gobierno del Estado de Colima, Universidad de Colima, 1999.

Escribano Cobo, Gabriel and Alfredo Mederos Martín, "Botijas en yacimientos arqueológicos subacuáticos de las Islas Canarias. Una fuente complementaria para el análisis del comercio canario-americano" in Francisco Morales Padrón (coord.), *XII Coloquio de Historia Canario-Americana (1996)*, vol. 1, Gran Canaria, Cabildo insular de Gran Canaria, 1998, pp. 539-568.

Esquivel Otea, María Teresa and Mercedes Sánchez Sandoval, *Índice de los ramos hospitales y protomedicato*, Mexico: Archivo General de la Nación, 1977.

Falck Reyes, Melba and Héctor Palacios, *El japonés que conquistó Guadalajara. La historia de Juan de Páez en la Guadalajara del siglo XVII*, Guadalajara: Universidad de Guadalajara, 2009.

Feliciano Velázquez, Primo, *Historia de San Luis Potosí*. Vol. 1, San Luis Potosí: El Colegio de San Luis, Universidad Autónoma de San Luis Potosí, 2004.

Fernández de Oviedo y Valdés, Gonzalo, *Historia general y natural de las Indias, islas y Tierra firme del Mar Océano*, Madrid: Imprenta de la Real Academia de la Historia, 1851.

Flores Clair, Eduardo, "Minas y mineros: pago en especie y conflictos, 1790-1880" in *Historias*, no. 13, abril-junio 1986, pp. 51-57.

Florescano, Enrique and Lydia Espinosa, *Apuntes para el estudio de la agricultura colonial*, Mexico: INAH, 1987, 2 vols.

Foale, M., "An introduction to the coconut palm" in Pons Batugal et al., *Coconut Genetic Resources*, Serdang-Malaysia: International Plant Genetic Resources Institute, Regional Office for Asia, the Pacific and Oceania, 2005, pp. 1-8.

Fossey, Mathieu de, "Por los rumbos de Colima" en Servando Ortoll (comp.), *Por tierras de cocos y palmeras. Apuntes de viajeros a Colima, siglos XVIII a XX*, Mexico: Instituto Mora, 1987, pp. 45-62.

Fuchigami, Eigi, "Indios chinos en Colima, siglos XVI y XVII. Resumen rápido de los resultados de la investigación en el Archivo Municipal de Colima", n.d.

Furlong, Matthew, "Soldiers, sailors, and salesmen: Pampangan service and ethnicity in colonial Mexico, 1591-1691", XIII *Reunión de Historiadores de México, Estados Unidos y Canadá*, 26-30 October 2010, Santiago de Querétaro, Mexico, pp. 1-17.

Furlong, Matthew, "Peasants, servants, and sojourners: itinerant Asians in colonial New Spain, 1571-1720", Doctoral Thesis, Arizona: The University of Arizona, 2014.

Gama, Vasco de, *Roteiro da viagem em descobrimento da India pelo Cabo da Boa Esperança fez Dom Vasco da Gama em 1497*, Edited by Diogo Kopke, Porto: Tipographia Commercial Portuense, 1838.

Gama, Vasco de, *La relation du premier voyage aux Indes (1497-1499)*, Traduite et présenté par Paul Teyssier, Paris: Éditions Chandeigne, 1998.

García Garza, Domingo, *Mezcal, un espirituoso artesanal de clase mundial*, Oaxaca: 1450 Ediciones, 2019.

García Garza, Domingo, *La revolución mezcalera. Los destilados de agave y la invención del mezcal tradicional*, Zamora: El Colegio de Michoacán, Université de Lille, 2022.

Garone Gravier, Marina, "Nuevos retratos para las viejas palabras. Libros novohispanos en lenguas indígenas", *Istor: revista de historia internacional*, año 8, no. 31, 2007, pp. 102-117.

Geertz, Clifford, *La interpretación de las culturas*, Barcelona: Gedisa, 2003.

Gerber, James and Lei Guang, *Agriculture and rural connections in the Pacific, 1500-1900*, Aldershot: Ashgate, Variorum, 2006 (Colección The Pacific World. Lands, Peoples and History of the Pacific, 1500-1900, vol. 13).

Gerhard, Peter, *Geografía histórica de la Nueva España, 1519-1821*, Mexico: UNAM, 1986.

Ghobrial, John-Paul, "Introduction: seeing the world like a microhistorian", *Past and Present*, supplement 14, 2019, pp. 1-22.

Gibson, Charles, *Los aztecas bajo el dominio español*, Mexico: Siglo XXI, 1996.

Gil, Juan, *Los chinos en Manila. Siglos XVI y XVII*, Lisbon: Centro Científico e Cultural de Macau, 2011.

Ginzburg, Carlo, "Microhistoria: dos o tres cosas que sé de ella", *Manuscrits*, no. 12, 1994, pp. 13-42.

Giraldez, Arturo, *The Age of Trade. The Manila Galleons and the Dawn of the Global Economy*, London: Rowman & Littlefield, 2015.

Gómez Amador, Adolfo, "La presencia filipina en Colima y su aporte a la identidad regional" in Juan Carlos Reyes (ed.), *Memorias del Primer Foro de Arqueología, Antropología e Historia de Colima*, Colima, Gobierno del Estado de Colima, 2005.

Bibliography

Gómez Azpeitia, Luis Gabriel, "El ordenamiento territorial en la provincia de Colima durante el siglo XVIII", Doctoral Thesis, Mexico: División de estudios de posgrado, Facultad de Arquitectura, Universidad Nacional Autónoma de México, 2000.

Gonzalbo Aizpuru, Pilar, *Vivir en Nueva España. Orden y desorden en la vida cotidiana*, Mexico: El Colegio de México, 2009.

González de Mendoza, Juan, *Historia de las cosas notables, ritos y costumbres, del Gran Reyno de la China, sabidas assi por los dichos libros de los mesmos Chinas, como por relación de los religiosos y otras personas que an estado en el dicho Reyno...* Antwerp: Casa de Pedro Bellero, 1596.

González Heras, Natalia, "Retazos americanos en las residencias madrileñas de los servidores virreinales", *Anales del Museo de América*, no. XXV, pp. 222-228.

Gourou, Pierre, *Introducción a la Geografía humana*, Madrid: Alianza, 1979.

Granados Sánchez, D. and G. F. López Ríos, "Manejo de la palma de coco (Cocos nucifera L.) en México", *Revista Chapingo*, Serie Ciencias Forestales y del Ambiente, vol. 8, no. 1, enero-junio 2002, pp. 39-48.

Gschaedler, Anne Cristine et al., "Fermentación. Etapa clave en la elaboración del Tequila" in *Ciencia y Tecnología del Tequila. Avances y Perspectivas*, Guadalajara, CIATEJ, 2004, pp. 63-120.

Guijo, Gregorio M. de, *Diario (1648-1664)*, Vols. I and II, Edited by Manuel Romero de Terreros, Mexico: Porrúa, 1953.

Gunn, Bee F. et al., "Independent origins of cultivated coconut (Cocos nucifera L.) in the old world tropics", *Plos One*, vol. 6, Issue 6 (e21143), June 2011, pp. 1-8.

Harries, H. C., "The Cape Verde region (1499 to 1549); the key to coconut culture in Western hemisphere?", *Turrialba*, no. 3, 1977, pp. 227-231.

Harries, H. C., "The evolution, dissemination & classification of Cocos nucifera L., *The Botanical Review*, vol. 44, no. 3, July-September 1978, pp. 265-319.

Hernández, Francisco, *Obras completas. Historia Natural de Nueva España*, Vol. 1, Mexico: UNAM, 1959.

Hernández Palomo, José Jesús, *El aguardiente de caña en México*, Seville: Escuela de Estudios Hispanoamericanos, Consejo Superior de Investigaciones Científicas, 1974.

Hernández Palomo, José J., *La renta del pulque en Nueva España (1663-1810)*, Seville: Escuela de Estudios Hispanoamericanos, CSIC, 1979.

Hernández Santana, José R. et al., "Regionalización morfoestructural de la Sierra Madre del Sur, México", *Investigaciones Geográficas*, no. 31, 1995, pp. 45-67.

Hespanha, António Manuel, *Cultura jurídica europea: síntesis de un milenio*, Madrid: Tecnos, 2002.

Israel, Jonathan I., *Razas, clases sociales y vida política en el México colonial 1610-1670*, Mexico: FCE, 1980.

Issasy, Francisco Arnaldo, *Demarcación y descripción de el Obispado de Michoacán y fundación de su Iglesia Cathedral* (1649), Biblioteca Americana, vol. 1, no. 1, Florida: University of Miami Station, Coral Gables, 1982.

Jagor, Fedor, *Viajes por Filipinas*, Madrid: Imprenta de Aribau y Cia., 1875.

Jiménez Vizcarra, Claudio, *El vino mezcal, tequila y la polémica sobre la destilación prehispánica*, Guadalajara: Benemérita Sociedad de Geografía y Estadística del Estado de Jalisco, 2013.

Ju-Kua, Chau, *His work on the Chinese and Arabe trade in the twelfth and thirteenth centuries, entitles Chu-fan-chï*, Translation and notes by Friedrich Hirth y W.W. Rockhill, San Petersburgo: Imperial Academy of Sciences, 1911.

Landers, Jane G. and Barry M. Robinson, *Slaves, subjects and subversives*, Albuquerque: University of New Mexico Press, 2006.

Lavrin, Asunción, "La mujer en la sociedad colonial hispanoamericana", *Historia de América Latina. América Latina colonial: población, sociedad y cultura*, vol. 4, 1990, pp. 109-137.

Lázaro de Arregui, Domingo, *Descripción de la Nueva Galicia*, Preliminary study by François Chevalier, Guadalajara: Unidad Editorial del Gobierno del Estado de Jalisco, 1980.

Lebrón de Quiñones, Lorenzo, "Relación sumaria de la visita que hizo en Nueva España el Licenciado Lebrón de Quiñones a doscientos pueblos" in José Antonio Calderón Quijano (dir.), *Documentos para la Historia del Estado de Colima, siglos XVI-XIX*, Mexico: Novaro, 1979 (Colección Peña Colorada).

Lemoine Villicaña, Ernesto, "Relación de agravios de los naturales de la provincia de Colima de los motines contra su alcalde mayor y juez congregador, 1603-1604", *Boletín del Archivo General de la Nación*, t. 1, no. 2, Mexico, Archivo General de la Nación, 1960, pp. 201-212.

León Meza, René de, "El sistema productivo y comercial de la Nueva Galicia, siglos XVI y XVII", Mexico: El Colegio de México, Doctoral Thesis, 2010.

León Meza, René de, "Vino de coco y vino mezcal, una historia comercial conjunta en la época colonial", *Letras Históricas*, no. 12, primavera-verano 2015, pp. 15-36.

Levi, Giovanni, *Le pouvoir au village. Histoire d'un exorciste dans le Piémont du XVIIe siècle*, París: Gallimard, 1989.

Bibliography

Linschoten, John Huyghen van, *The voyage of John Huyghen van Linschoten to the East Indies. From the old translation of 1598*, Edited by Mr. P. A. Tiele, London: Hakluyt Society, 1885.

López Cotilla, Manuel, *Historia de la introducción de agua en Guadalajara desde su fundación hasta la fecha en la cual se han refundido todas las noticias importantes que existen en la Secretaría del Ayuntamiento y otras que se han adquirido en lo particular*, Guadalajara: Imprenta del Estado de Jalisco, 1842.

López de Gómara, Francisco, *Historia de la conquista de México*, Mexico: Océano, 2003.

López de Legazpi, Miguel, "Expedición" en *Colección de documentos inéditos relativos al descubrimiento, conquista y organización de las antiguas posesiones españolas de ultramar: Segunda serie. De las Islas Filipinas*, Vol. 3, II, Documento 39, Madrid: Impresores de la Real Casa, Sucesores de Rivadeneyra, 1887.

López Lara, Ramón, *El Obispado de Michoacán en el siglo XVII. Informe inédito de beneficios, pueblos y lenguas*, Morelia: Fimax Publicistas, 1973.

López Razgado, Irma, "Dulce Nombre de Jesús: iglesia y cofradía de los mulatos y pardos en la villa de Colima, siglo XVIII", unpublished document.

López Razgado, María Irma and María del Carmen Ochoa Gutiérrez (coord.), *Archivo Histórico Parroquial de San Felipe de Jesús, "El Beaterio". Libro de bautismos siglo XVII*, t. I, Colima: Gobierno del Estado de Colima, 2021.

Lozano Armendares, Teresa, *El chinguiritos vindicado. El contrabando de aguardiente de caña y la política colonial*, Mexico: UNAM, 2005.

Lucio, Carlos, "Mezcales y biodiversidad cultural en los alrededores del Volcán de Colima. El caso de los productores tradicionales de Zapotitlán de Vadillo", *EntreDiversidades. Revista de Ciencias Sociales y Humanidades*, vol. 5, otoño-invierno 2015, pp. 13-43

Luis, Diego Javier, *The first Asians in the Americas. A Transpacific History*, Cambridge and London: Harvard University Press, 2024.

Lumholtz, Carl, *El México desconocido: cinco años de exploración entre tribus de la Sierra Madre Occidental, en la tierra caliente de Tepic y Jalisco, y entre los tarascos de Michoacán*, Translated by Balvino Dávalos, New York: Charles Scribner's Sons, 1904.

Macarro, Sebastián, "Relación de Tancítaro" in René Acuña (ed.), *Relaciones geográficas del siglo XVI: Michoacán*, Mexico: UNAM, 1987, pp. 285-309.

Machuca, Paulina, "Cabildo, negociación y vino de cocos: el caso de la villa de Colima en el siglo XVII", *Anuario de Estudios Americanos*, enero-junio 2009, vol. 66, no. 1, pp. 173-192.

Machuca, Paulina, "El alcalde de los chinos en la provincia de Colima durante el siglo XVII: un sistema de representación en torno a un oficio", *Letras Históricas*, no. 1, otoño-invierno 2009, pp. 95-115.

Machuca, Paulina et al., "Introducción y difusión temprana de recursos fitogenéticos en la región Balsas-Jalisco durante el siglo XVI: una perspectiva agro-histórica", *Geografía Agrícola. Estudios regionales de la agricultura mexicana*, no. 45, julio-diciembre 2010, pp. 77-96.

Machuca, Paulina, "De porcelanas chinas y otros menesteres. Cultura material de origen asiático en Colima, siglos XVI-XVII", *Relaciones, estudios de historia y sociedad*, no. 131, verano 2012, vol. XXXIII, pp. 77-134.

Machuca, Paulina et al., "El estanco de vino de cocos y mezcal en la Nueva Galicia, siglos XVII-XVIII", *Letras Históricas*, no. 8, primavera-verano 2013, pp. 71-99.

Machuca, Paulina, "El arribo de plantas a las Indias Occidentales: el caso del Balsas-Jalisco a través de las Relaciones geográficas del siglo XVI", *Relaciones, estudios de historia y sociedad*, no. 136, otoño 2013, vol. XXXIV, pp. 73-114.

Machuca, Paulina, *Hacer tuba en México y Filipinas: cuatro siglos de historia compartida*, Documental (material audiovisual), Zamora: El Colegio de Michoacán, PACMYC Colima, Secretaría de Cultura del Gobierno del Estado de Colima, H. Ayuntamiento de Colima, Archivo Histórico del Municipio de Colima, 2013.

Machuca, Paulina, "El arte de hacer *tuba* en México y Filipinas: una aproximación etnohistórica" in Angela Schottenhammer (coord.), *Tribute, trade, and smuggling: commercial, scientific and human interaction in the Middle Period and Early Modern World*, Wiesbaden: Harrassowitz Verlag, 2014, pp. 247-267.

Machuca, Paulina, "Les 'Indiens chinois' *vinateros* de Colima: processus d'insertion sociale dans les haciendas de palmes du XVIIè siècle", *Diasporas. Histoire et sociétés*, no. 25, CNRS, Université de Toulouse Le Mirail, 2015, pp. 121-137.

Machuca, Paulina, "La palma de coco: regalo de Filipinas a México (siglos XVI-XVII)" in Thomas Calvo and Paulina Machuca (eds.), *México y Filipinas. Culturas y memorias sobre el Pacífico*, Zamora: El Colegio de Michoacán, Ateneo de Manila University Press, 2016, pp. 321-340.

Machuca, Paulina, "Tras las huellas del mestizaje cultural entre México y Filipinas" in Paulina Machuca and Thomas Calvo (eds.), *México y Filipinas: culturas y memorias sobre el Pacífico*, Zamora: El Colegio de Michoacán, Ateneo de Manila University Press, 2016, pp. 385-401.

Machuca, Paulina, "Medrar entre palmares. Francisca Martha, una 'india china' en el Colima del siglo XVII" in Thomas Calvo and Armando Hernández (coords.), *Medrar para sobrevivir. Individuos presos en la fragua de la sociedad*, San Luis Potosí: El Colegio de San Luis, 2016, pp. 337-362.

Bibliography

Machuca, Paulina, *Elites y gobierno en Colima de la Nueva España. Siglo XVII*, Colima: Secretaría de Cultura del Gobierno del Estado de Colima, Archivo Histórico del Municipio de Colima, 2016.

Machuca, Paulina, "Alcohol, mineros y operarios en la Nueva España, siglos XVI-XVIII" in Patricio Herrera and Juan Carlos Yáñez (coords.), *Alcohol y trabajo en América Latina, siglos XVII-XIX. Experiencias económicas, políticas y socioculturales*, Valparaíso: Universidad de Valparaíso, 2019, pp. 17-39.

Machuca, Paulina, "Microhistoria global de una escritura peregrina: el alfabeto filipino baybayin en Colima de la Nueva España (1600-1604)", *Allpanchis*, no. 90, año XLIX, julio-diciembre 2022, pp. 85-121.

Machuca, Paulina, "Francisca Martha, une petite propriétaire de palmiers entre deux mondes: Philippines-Mexique, XVIIe siècle" in Sophie Dulucq et al. (coords.), *Au coeur des empires. Destins individuels et logiques impériales XVIe-XXIe siècle*, Paris: CNRS Éditions, 2023, pp. 41-57.

Machuca, Paulina and Ana Coria Téllez, "Prácticas curativas en torno a la palma de coco (*Cocos nucifera* L) en Filipinas, la India y México. Del conocimiento tradicional a la validación técnico-científica" in Paulina Machuca Chávez and Salvador Pérez Ramírez (coords.), *Enfermedades y prácticas curativas en México. Diálogos entre el pasado y el presente*, Zamora: El Colegio de Michoacán, 2021, pp. 89-116.

Machuca, Paulina and Maricruz Piza, "El camino de México a Acapulco (siglo XVII)" in Beatriz Rojas (coord.), *De caminos y puentes: ordenamiento territorial en la Nueva España*, Mexico: Instituto Mora, El Colegio de Michoacán, 2021, pp. 129-151.

Madre de Dios, Blas de la, *El libro de las medicinas caseras de Fr. Blas de la Madre de Dios. Manila, 1611*, Edited by Francisco Guerra y María del Carmen Sánchez Téllez, Madrid: Ediciones Cultura Hispánica, 1984.

Malinowski, Bronislaw, "Prólogo" in Fernando Ortiz, *Contrapunteo cubano del tabaco y el azúcar*, Barcelona: Ariel, 1973.

Marcus, George, "Ethnography in/of the World System: The Emergence of Multi-Sited Ethnography", *Annual Review of Anthropology*, vol. 24, 1995, pp. 95-117.

Mas y Sanz, Sinibaldo de, *Informe sobre el estado de las Islas Filipinas en 1842. Escrito por el autor del Aristodemo, del sistema musical de la lengua castellana etc.*, Madrid: 1842.

Mazín, Óscar, *Archivo capitular de administración diocesana Valladolid-Morelia. Catálogo I*, Morelia: El Colegio de Michoacán, Gobierno del Estado de Michoacán, 1991.

McGovern, Patrick E. et al., "Pre-Hispanic Distillation? A Biomolecular Archaeological Investigation", *Open Access Journal of Archaeology and Anthropology*, vol. 1, no. 2, 2019, DOI: 10.33552/OAJAA.2019.01.000509.

Mena García, Carmen, "Nuevos datos sobre bastimentos y envases en armadas y flotas de la Carrera", *Revista de Indias*, vol. LXIV, no. 231, 2004, pp. 447-484.

Mercado, Ignacio, *Declaración de las virtudes de los árboles y plantas que están en este libro. Manuscrito del siglo XVII, copia del original del P. Ignacio de Mercado y propiedad de esta corporación…* Introducción y adiciones de D. J. Madrid Moreno, Madrid: Academia Nacional de Medicina, 1936.

Mercado, Ignacio, *Declaración de las virtudes de los árboles y plantas que están en este libro* (Plantas medicinales filipinas), Edited by Blas Sierra de la Calle, Valladolid: Museo Oriental, 2023.

Miller, Christopher, "Filipino Cultural Heritage in the UST Archives. Baybayin script in 17th century land deeds", *International Conference on the Heritage and History of the University of Santo Tomas*. Manila: Universidad de Santo Tomás, 2011a.

Miller, Christopher, "Linguistic insights into the history of Philippine script: graphonomic structure, sociolinguistic variation, and contact phenomena". Paper presented in *Philippine Linguistics Conference*. Quezon City: Universidad de Filipinas Diliman, 2011b.

Mojarro, Jorge, "Los primeros libros impresos en Filipinas (1593-1607)". *Hispania sacra*, vol. LXXII, no. 145, enero-junio, 2020, pp. 231-240.

Mombelli Pierini, María Inés, "La formación histórica del paisaje en el corredor Acapulco-Zihuatanejo", *Investigaciones geográficas. Boletín del Instituto de Geografía de la UNAM*, no. 72, 2010, pp. 120-138.

Mondragón Preciado, G. et al., "Identificación de bacteriocinas producidas por bacterias ácido-lácticas aisladas en tuba", Paper presented at the XIX *Congreso Nacional de Ingeniería Bioquímica*, Mazatlán, Sinaloa, del 9-11 April 2014.

Montenegro, Juan de, "Descripción de Colima. 1744" in José Antonio Calderón Quijano (dir.), *Documentos para la Historia del Estado de Colima*, Mexico: Novaro, 1979, pp. 157-163 (Colección Peña Colorada).

Morga, Antonio de, *Sucesos de las islas Filipinas*, Mexico: FCE, 2007.

Mota Padilla, Matías de la, *Historia del Reino de Nueva Galicia en la América Septentrional*: Guadalajara, Instituto Jalisciense de Antropología e Historia, 1973.

Mota y Escobar, Alonso de la, *Descripción geográfica de los reinos de Nueva Galicia, Nueva Vizcaya y Nuevo León*, Guadalajara: Instituto Jalisciense de Antropología e Historia, 1993.

Needham, Joseph, *Science and Civilization in China*. Vol. 5, Cambridge: Cambridge University Press, 1980.

Novillo, Miguel, "Tinajas arqueológicas del sitio Los Guachimontones, sector Talleres, durante el Posclásico (900-1521 d.C.): una aproximación a su uso y funcionalidad", Master's Thesis, La Piedad: Centro de Estudios Arqueológicos, El Colegio de Michoacán, 2014.

Obispado, Kristyl, "The Pacific sailors: global workers at and on the edge of the Spanish empire (1580-1640)", Doctoral Thesis, Mexico: Centro de Estudios Históricos, El Colegio de México, 2021.

Ogborn, Miles, *Global Lives. Britain and the World, 1550-1800*, Cambridge: Cambridge University Press, 2008.

Olveda, Jaime, (coord.), *Relaciones intercoloniales. Nueva España y Filipinas*, Zapopan: El Colegio de Jalisco, 2017.

Oropeza Keresey, Déborah, "Los 'indios chinos' en la Nueva España: la inmigración de la Nao de China, 1565-1700", Doctoral Thesis, Mexico: Centro de Estudios Históricos, El Colegio de México, 2007.

Oropeza Keresey, Déborah, "La esclavitud asiática en el virreinato de la Nueva España, 1565-1673", *Historia Mexicana*, vol. XLI, no. 1, julio-septiembre 2011, pp. 5-57.

Oropeza, Déborah, *La migración asiática en el virreinato de la Nueva España: un proceso de globalización (1565-1700)*, Mexico: El Colegio de México, 2020.

Orta, Garcia da, *Colquios dos simples e drogas da India*, Dirigida e annotada pelo Conde de Ficalho, Lisbon: Academia Real das Sciencias de Lisbon, Imprenta Nacional, [1563] 1891.

Orta, Garcia da, *Colóquios dos simples e drogas e coisas medicinais da Índia*, Edited by Rui Manuel Loureiro and Teresa Nobre de Carvalho, Lisbon: Cátedra de Estudos Sefarditas Alberto Benveniste, 2024.

Oseguera Velásquez, Juan, *Efemérides de Colima y de México*, Guadalajara: Impre-Jal, 1989.

Pacheco Olvera, Reyna María, "El intercambio de plantas en la Nao de China y su impacto en México" in Janet Long Towell and Amalia Attolini Lecón (coords.), *Caminos y mercados de México*, Mexico: UNAM, INAH, 2010, pp. 593-607.

Padilla Lozoya, Raymundo, "Desastres en México y Filipinas: cicatrices históricas que unen a nuestras culturas" in Thomas Calvo and Paulina Machuca (eds.), *México y Filipinas: culturas y memorias sobre el Pacífico*, Zamora: El Colegio de Michoacán, Ateneo de Manila University, 2016, pp. 57-77.

Paredes Martínez, Carlos, "El mercado de Pátzcuaro y los mercaderes tarascos en los inicios de la época colonial" in Carlos Paredes Martínez (coord.), *Historia y sociedad. Ensayos del Seminario de Historia Colonial de Michoacán*, Morelia: UMSNH, 1997, pp. 143-182.

Park, Hyunhee. *Soju: A Global History*, Cambridge: Cambridge University Press, 2021.

Patiño, Víctor Manuel, *Plantas cultivadas y animales domésticos en América equinoccial. Plantas introducidas*, Vol. IV, 14a edition, Cali: Imprenta Departamental, 1963.

Patiño de Ávila, Álvaro, "Descripción de la ciudad de Veracruz y su comarca" in René Acuña (ed.), *Relaciones geográficas del siglo XVI: Tlaxcala*, Mexico: UNAM, 1985, pp. 299-374.

Pazos Pazos, María Luisa and Justina Sarabia Viejo, "Orden y delincuencia. Los alguaciles de las ciudades novohispanas, siglos XVI-XVII" in Rey Tristán et al., *Actas del XIV Encuentro de Americanistas Españoles*, Santiago de Compostela: Universidad de Santiago de Compostela, Centro Interdisciplinario de Estudios Americanistas Gumersindo Bustos, Consejo Español de Estudios Iberoamericanos, 2010, pp. 684-698.

Pennington, Terence D. and José Sarukhán, *Árboles tropicales de México*, Mexico: UNAM, FCE, 2005.

Pérez Ponce de León, Miguel José, "Descripción de Colima. 1776-1777" in José Antonio Calderón Quijano (dir.), *Documentos para la Historia del Estado de Colima*, Mexico: Novaro, 1979, pp. 176-207 (Colección Peña Colorada).

Pérez Zamora, Octavio, "Fertilización nitrogenada y potásica del cocotero en Colima", *Tierra Latinoamericana*, vol. 21, no. 3, julio-septiembre 2003, pp. 401-408.

Pigafetta, Antonio, *Relazione del primo viaggio attorno al mondo*, Testo critico e commento di Andrea Canova, Padova: Editrice Antenore, 1999.

Pinzón Ríos, Guadalupe, *Acciones y reacciones en los puertos del Mar del Sur. Desarrollo portuario del Pacífico novohispano a partir de sus políticas defensivas, 1713-1789*, Mexico: UNAM, Instituto Mora, 2012.

Pinzón Ríos, Guadalupe, "Desde tierra y hacia el horizonte marítimo. Una reflexión sobra la relevancia de los establecimientos portuarios del Pacífico novohispano", *México y la Cuenca del Pacífico*, año 17, no. 50, mayo 2014, pp. 67-87.

Piza López, Maricruz, "Acapulco y sus alrededores: herencia filipina a partir del Galeón de Manila", B.A. Thesis, Guerrero: Universidad Autónoma de Guerrero, 2019.

Polo, Marco, *Libro de las cosas maravillosas*, Introducción de Stéphanie Yerasimos, Prólogo de Rafael Benítez Claros, Barcelona: Medievalia, 2002.

Ponce, Fray Alonso, *Viajes de fray Alonso Ponce al occidente de México*, Corresponsalía del Seminario de Cultura Mexicana, Guadalajara: n.d.

Potet, Jean-Paul G., "La pétition tagale: *Caming manga alipin* (1665)", *Cahiers de Linguistique. Asie Orientale*, vol. 16, no. 1, Juin, 1987, pp. 109-157.

Bibliography

Potet, Jean-Paul G., *Tagalog linguistics and miscellanies*, Raleigh: Lulu Press, Inc., 2013.

Potet, Jean-Paul G., *Baybayin. The Syllabic Alphabet of the Tagalogs*, Raleigh: Lulu Press, Inc., 2014.

Prado Ramírez, Rogelio, "Destilación" in *Ciencia y Tecnología del Tequila. Avances y Perspectivas*, Guadalajara: CIATEJ, 2004, pp. 123-170.

Rendón Garduño, Isolda, "Catálogo de los fondos del siglo XVII del Archivo Histórico del Municipio de Colima", B.A. Thesis in Ethnohistory, Mexico: Escuela Nacional de Antropología e Historia, 2000.

Restall, Matthew, "Heirs to the hieroglyphs: indigenous writing in colonial Mesoamerica", *The Americas*, vol. 54, no. 2, October, 1997, pp. 239-267.

Retama Ávila, Julio, *Testamentos de "indios" en Chile colonial: 1564-1801*, Santiago: Universidad Andrés Bello, 2000.

Revel, Jacques, "L'histoire au ras de sol" in Giovanni Levi, *Le pouvoir au village. Histoire d'un exorciste dans le Piémont du XVIIe siècle*, Paris: Gallimard, 1989, pp. I-XXXIII.

Revel, Jacques and Antonella Romano (dirs.), *Penser global? Dix variations sur un thème*, Paris: Éditions de l'École des Hautes Études en Sciences Sociales, 2024.

Reyes Garza, Juan Carlos, *La antigua provincia de Colima, siglos XVI al XVIII*, Colima: Universidad de Colima, Gobierno del Estado de Colima, Conaculta, 1995.

Reyes Garza, Juan Carlos, *Al pie del volcán. Los indios de Colima en el virreinato*, Mexico: CIESAS, INI, Gobierno del Estado de Colima, 2000 (Colección Historia de los pueblos indígenas de México).

Reyes Garza, Juan Carlos, *Por mandato de su Majestad. Inventario de bienes de las autoridades de Colima, 1622*, Colima: Secretaría de Cultura del Gobierno del Estado de Colima, 2000.

Rojas, Beatriz, "Repúblicas de españoles: Antiguo régimen y privilegios", *Secuencia*, no. 53, mayo-agosto 2002, pp. 7-47.

Romero de Solís, José Miguel, *Andariegos y pobladores. Nueva España y Nueva Galicia (siglo XVI)*, Zamora: El Colegio de Michoacán, Archivo Histórico del Municipio de Colima, Universidad de Colima, Conaculta, Fonca, 2001.

Romero de Solís, José Miguel, *Conquistas e instituciones de gobierno en Colima de la Nueva España (1523-1600)*, Zamora: Archivo Histórico del Municipio de Colima, Universidad de Colima, El Colegio de Michoacán, 2007.

Romero de Solís, José Miguel, *Clérigos, encomenderos, mercaderes y arrieros en Colima de la Nueva España (1523-1600)*, Colima: Archivo

Histórico del Municipio de Colima, Universidad de Colima, El Colegio de Michoacán, 2008.

Ruiz, Jorge Alberto and María Concepción Gavira, "Mezclas y desorden en la población de una provincia fronteriza: Zacatula-México en el siglo XVIII", *Cuadernos interculturales*, año 11, no. 21, segundo semestre 2013, pp. 141-160.

Rzedowsky, Jerzy, *Vegetación de México*, Mexico: Limusa, 1983.

Sánchez Díaz, Gerardo, *La costa de Michoacán. Economía y Sociedad en el siglo XVII*, Morelia: UMSNH, Morevallado Editores, 2001.

Sánchez Díaz, Gerardo, *Los cultivos tropicales en Michoacán. Época colonial y siglo XIX*, Morelia: Fundación Produce, A.C., Centro de Investigación y Desarrollo del Estado de Michoacán, Fondo Editorial Morevallado, UMSNH, 2008.

Santamaría, Alberto, "El 'Baybayin' en el Archivo de Santo Tomás. Algo de paleografía tagala", UNITAS, vol. XVI, no. 8, 1938, pp. 441-480.

Schell Höberman, Louisa, *Mexico's merchant elite, 1590-1660: Silver, State and Society*, Durham: Duke University Press, 1991.

Scott, William Henry, *Prehispanic Source Materials for the Study of Philippine History*. Quezon City: New Day Publishers, 1984.

Scott, William Henry, *Barangay. Sixteenth-century Philippine culture and society*, Quezon City: Ateneo de Manila University Press, 2010.

Seijas, Tatiana, "The Portuguese Slave Trade to Spanish Manila: 1580-1640", *Itinerario*, vol. XXXII, no. 1, 2008, pp. 19-38.

Seijas, Tatiana, *Asian slaves in colonial Mexico. From chinos to Indians*, New York: Cambridge University Press, 2015.

Serra Puche, Mari Carmen and Jesús Carlos Lazcano Arce, "Etnoarqueología del mezcal: su origen y su uso en Mesoamérica" in José Luis Vera Cortés and Rodolfo Fernández, *Agua de las verdes matas. Tequila y mezcal*, Mexico: Artes de México y del Mundo S.A. de C.V., INAH, 2015, pp. 23-42.

Serra Puche, Mari Carmen and Jesús Carlos Lazcano Arce, *El mezcal, una bebida prehispánica. Estudios etnoarqueológicos*, Mexico: UNAM, 2016.

Sevilla del Río, Felipe (ed.), *Provança de la villa de Colima en su defensa ante un mandamiento de la Real Audiencia de México, que ordenaba la tala total de los palmares colimenses. Año de 1612*, Introducción, paleografía y notas de Felipe Sevilla del Río, Mexico: Jus, 1977.

Sevilla del Río, Felipe, *Prosas literarias e históricas*, Colima: Universidad de Colima, 2005.

Bibliography

Sicardo, Fray Joseph, *Vida y Milagros del glorioso San Nicolás de Tolentino, religioso del orden de los ermitaños de nuestro padre San Agustín*, Madrid: Imprenta de Manuel Ruiz de Murga, 1701.

Slack, Jr., Edward R., "The Chinos in New Spain; A Corrective Lens for a Distored Image", *Journal of World History*, no. 1, vol. 20, 2009, pp. 35-67.

Stevens, N. C., "Is this Mexico's Oldest Spirit?", *Atlas Obscura*, secc. Gastro Obscura, 18 June 2024. https://www.atlasobscura.com/articles/mexicos-oldest-spirit-vino-de-cocos

Tau Anzoátegui, Víctor, *La ley en América hispana. Del descubrimiento a la emancipación*, Buenos Aires: Academia Nacional de la Historia, 1992.

Taylor, William B., *Embriaguez, homicidio y rebelión en las poblaciones coloniales mexicanas*, Traducción de Mercedes Pizarro de Parlange, Mexico: FCE, 1987.

Tello, Fray Antonio, *Crónica miscelánea de la Sancta Provincia de Xalisco...* Guadalajara: Gobierno del Estado de Jalisco, Universidad de Guadalajara, Instituto Nacional de Antropología e Historia-Instituto Jalisciense de Antropología e Historia, 1985.

Tepaske, John and Herbert S. Klein, *Ingresos y egresos de la Real Hacienda de Nueva España*, Mexico: INAH, 1988, 2 vols.

Tepaske, John Jay, *El Real Protomedicato. La reglamentación de la profesión médica en el imperio español*, Mexico: UNAM, 1997.

Teyssier, Paul, "Introduction" en Vasco de Gama, *La relation du premier voyage aux Indes (1497-1499)*, Traduite et présenté par Paul Teyssier, Paris: Éditions Chandeigne, 1998, pp. 7-25.

Tovar y de Teresa, Guillermo, "Noticias acerca del retablo mayor y sillería de coro de la catedral de Guadalajara: Francisco de la Gándara Hermosa en 1619", *Boletín de Monumentos Históricos del INAH*, tercera época, no. 1, pp. 7-15.

Trota José, Regalado, "Don Luis Castilla Offers to Sell Land in Manila (1629)" in Christina H. Lee and Ricardo Padrón (eds). *The Spanish Pacific, 1521-1815*. Amsterdam: Amsterdam University Press, 2020, pp. 91-113.

Urquiola Permisán, José Ignacio, *Trabajadores de campo y ciudad. Las cartas de servicio como forma de contratación en Querétaro (1588-1609)*, Querétaro: Gobierno del Estado de Querétaro, Archivo Histórico de Querétaro, 2001.

Valenzuela Zapata, Ana et al., "Influencia asiática en la producción de mezcal en la costa de Jalisco. El caso de la raicilla", *México y la cuenca del Pacífico*, vol. 11, no. 33, septiembre-diciembre 2008, pp. 91-116.

Valenzuela, Ana et al., "'Huichol' stills: a century of anthropology, technology transfer and innovation", *Crossroads*, no. 8, October 2013, pp. 157-191.

Valenzuela Zapata, Ana G., "East Asian Stills: Distillation influences in Mezcal Production in Mexico" in Angela Schottenhammer (ed.), *Tribute, Trade and Smuggling. Commercial, Scientific and Human Interaction in the Middle Period and Early Modern World*, Wiesbaden: Harrassowitz Verlag, 2014, pp. 140-151.

Varthema, Ludovico de, *Itinerario de Ludovico de Varthema Bolognese nello Egitto, nella Soria nella Arabia deserta, & felice, nella Persia, nella India, & nela Ethyopia. Le fede el vivere, & costumi delle prefate Provincie. Et al presente agiontoui alcune Isole novamente ritrovate*, Venezia: Francesco di Alessandro Bindone & Mapheo di Pasini Compani, 1535.

Vascones, Hernando de, "Relación de Zacatula" in René Acuña (ed.), *Relaciones geográficas del siglo XVI: Michoacán*, Mexico: UNAM, 1987, pp. 449-462.

Viesca Treviño, Carlos, "Hechizos y hierbas mágicas en la obra de Juan de Cárdenas", *Estudios de Historia Novohispana*, vol. 9, no. 9, 1987, pp. 37-50.

Villamor, Ignacio, *La antigua escritura filipina*. Manila: Tip. Pontificia del Colegio de Santo Tomás, 1922.

Villaseñor y Sánchez, José Antonio, *Theatro Americano. Descripción General de los Reinos y Provincias de la Nueva España y sus jurisdicciones*, Mexico: Imprenta de la viuda de don Joseph Bernardo de Hogal, 1746.

Viqueira Albán, Juan Pedro, *¿Relajados o reprimidos? Diversiones públicas y vida social en la ciudad de México durante el Siglo de las Luces*, Mexico: FCE, 1987.

Widmer, Rolf, *Conquista y despertar en las costas de la Mar del Sur (1521-1684)*, Mexico: Conaculta, 1990.

Yepes, Victoria, *Historia natural de las islas bisayas del padre Alzina*, Madrid: CSIC, 1996.

Yepes, Victoria, *Una etnografía de los indios bisayas del padre Alzina*, Madrid: CSIC, 1996.

Zavala, Silvio, *Ordenanzas del trabajo, siglo XVI y XVII*, Mexico: Centro de Estudios del Movimiento Obrero Mexicano, 1980.

Zizumbo Villarreal, Daniel, "History of coconut (*Cocos nucifera* L.) in Mexico: 1539-1810", *Genetic Resources and Crop Evolution*, no. 43, 1996, pp. 505-515.

Zizumbo Villarreal, Daniel and Patricia Colunga García-Marín, "Early coconut distillation and the origins of mezcal and tequila spirits in west-central Mexico", *Genetic Resources and Crop Evolution*, vol. 55, 2008, pp. 493-510.

Zizumbo Villarreal, Daniel et al., "Distillation in Western Mesoamerica before European contact", *Economic Botany*, vol. 63(4), 2009, pp. 413-426.

Bibliography

Zizumbo, Daniel et al., "Archaeological Evidence of the Cultural Importance of *Agave spp.* in Pre-Hispanic Colima, Mexico", *Economic Botany*, vol. 63, no. 3, 2009, pp. 288-302.

Zorita, Alonso, *Leyes y ordenanzas reales de las Indias del Mar Océano* (1574), Mexico: SHCP, 1974.

Glossary

alcalde de los chinos: Advocate of the Asians.
alcalde mayor: Provincial magistrate.
alcalde ordinario: Local judge on the *cabildo* (town council).
alférez: Military officer.
alguacil: Constable.
alquitaras: Stills, distillers.
arroba de vino: A volume measurement equivalent to 16 liters.
asientos: Deposits.
audiencia: Tribunal.
ayuntamiento: Municipal council.
bando: Decree, edict.
beneficiado: A beneficed priest, meaning a clergyman with a fixed income from church revenues.
botijas: Clay vessel for storing wine of approximately 16 liters.
caballerías: Unit of land measurement, equivalent to around 43 hectares (100 acres).
cabecera: Administrative center.
cabildo: Municipal council.
cacahuanantzin: Mother of cacao in Náhuatl.
caja real: Royal Treasury.
calabacillo: Small gourd or squash.
calabazos: Gourds.
cántaros: Vessels, pitchers, jugs.
cañutos: Tubes.
capote: Palm leaf raincoat.
carrizo: Reed.
casas reales: Royal houses.
chicha: Maize-based beverage.
chinguirito: Sugarcane aguardiente.

Vino de Cocos, the Pilgrim Beverage

cocos chocolateros:	Decorative cups for drinking chocolate.
cofradía:	Catholic lay organization for pious activities.
corregimiento:	Administrative district governed by a Corregidor.
coyota:	One of the many castes in colonial New Spain.
cuartillo:	Unit of measure equivalent to approximately 0.5 liters.
depositario general:	Official responsible for managing and safeguarding assets, funds, and properties held in trust by the government.
diezmeros:	Tithe collectors.
diezmo:	Tithe.
encomendero:	Man who held an *encomienda*.
encomiendas:	Royal grants of indigenous labor and tribute.
enganches:	Advance payments that bound workers to haciendas.
estanco:	Royal monopoly.
fanegas:	Unit of dry volume used primarily for measuring grain, maize, and other agricultural commodities. It was roughly equivalent to 55.5 liters
gobernadorcillos:	Town official in the colonial Philippines.
hacienda:	Agricultural unit.
hijodalgo:	Nobleman.
indios laboríos:	Free Indian workers.
jícara:	Small cup or bowl.
libranzas:	Letters of exchange.
mayordomo:	Official of a religious fiesta.
Mar del Sur:	South Seas, referring to the Pacific Ocean.
Mezcal:	Distilled beverage made from the agave plant.
milpa:	Cornfield.
moriscos:	One of the many castes in New Spain.
oidor:	Judge of an Audiencia.
padrinazgo:	Ritual co-parenthood.
pago a partido:	Payments made partly in money and partly in goods.

Glossary

panocha:	Unrefined sugar.
principales:	Indigenous noblemen.
protomédico:	Royal physician from the Protomedicato Tribunal.
pueblos de indios:	Indian towns.
pulque:	Fermented beverage made from the maguey plant.
pulquería:	Establishment that sold *pulque*.
reales derechos:	Royal rights
reales:	Unit of money, ratio of 8 *reales* to 1 peso.
repúblicas de indios:	Indian towns.
tecomates:	Gourds.
tecomatillo:	Small gourd.
tejuino:	A traditional fermented corn beverage in Mexico.
tepache:	A traditional fermented beverage made from pineapple rinds, piloncillo (unrefined cane sugar), and spices.
tianguis:	Market.
tresalbos:	One of the many castes in New Spain.

Thematic Index

Key Names

Agustín (chino vinatero): 15, 166, 169, 205, 211, 212, 213, 214, 219.

Alarcón, Catalina de: 171, 178, 239, 269, 270, 314.

Alcalde de Rueda, Juan: 112, 276.

Alzina, Francisco Ignacio: 31, 32, 41, 43, 45, 47, 48, 71, 73, 85, 86, 211, 371, 372, 373.

Anglería, Pedro Mártir de: 52.

Arbide, Bartolomé de: 410.

Arregui, Domingo Lázaro de: 307, 413.

Báez, Sebastián: 339, 340, 344, 345, 346.

Barros, João de: 40, 42, 44, 47, 49.

Battuta, Ibn: 39, 43, 44, 49.

Blanco, Manuel: 41, 42, 46, 48, 73, 371, 374.

Bravo Lagunas, Bartolomé: 173, 174, 237, 317.

Brizuela, Rodrigo de: 113, 118, 133, 135, 264, 266, 269, 275, 284.

Bruman, Henry J.: 55, 56, 226, 301, 400, 401, 402, 414.

Calderón y Romero, Fernando: 378, 379, 380.

Canseco y Quiñones, Juan de: 338, 340.

Cárdenas, Juan de: 369, 370.

Carrillo de Guzmán, Jorge: 113, 180, 181, 182, 193, 263, 264, 266, 268, 275.

Carrillo de Guzmán, Juan: 113, 118, 263, 266, 274, 292, 297.

Casafuerte, Marquis de: 259, 307, 386, 387, 388.

Caviedes, Luis de: 344, 345.

Ceballos, Hilario: 299.

Chirino, Pedro: 89, 198, 199, 204, 207, 211, 216, 219.

Cook, Orator Fuller: 50.

Correa Gudiño, Diego: 143, 155, 156, 158.

Cruz, Juan de la (chino from Sengayan): 124-125, 148, 153, 154, 155, 177, 183, 193, 220, 221, 238, 296, 297.

Cruz, Sebastián de la: 142, 143, 145, 146, 148, 149, 156, 187, 188.

Vino de Cocos, the Pilgrim Beverage

Dampier, William: 42, 43, 45, 56.

Dávalos Vergara, Jerónimo: 133, 135, 217, 262.

Encío, Luis de: 205, 339, 340.

Escudero de Figueroa, Francisco: 136, 167, 168, 231, 239, 366.

Fernández de Baeza, Pedro: 340, 343, 345, 378.

Fernández de Oviedo, Gonzalo: 51, 372, 373.

Filipinos: 14, 16, 24, 60, 63, 71, 89, 91, 94, 109, 115, 124, 127, 139, 160, 161, 174, 175, 176, 184, 194, 197, 199, 205, 206, 211, 215, 219, 222, 223, 231, 238, 239, 240, 247, 248, 396, 400, 411.

Francisca Martha (china): 14, 24, 94, 96, 123, 124, 138, 139, 140, 142, 143, 144, 145, 146, 147, 148, 149, 150, 152, 153, 154, 155, 156, 157, 158, 183, 184, 187, 397, 417.

Franciscans: 206, 208.

Furlong, Matthew J.: 124, 128, 162, 190, 251, 274, 353.

García de Grijalva, Álvaro: 113, 118, 166, 167, 168, 209, 216, 230, 263, 267.

García Garza, Domingo: 407.

Gómez Machorro, Hernán: 61, 114, 117, 135, 267, 330.

González de Mendoza, Juan: 42, 47, 72.

Harries, Hugh C.: 35, 36, 57.

Hernández, Francisco (protomédico): 35, 66, 369, 371, 372, 373.

Indios chinos: 17, 23, 24, 60, 91, 93, 105, 120, 123, 124, 125, 126, 127, 128, 129, 131, 132, 133, 136, 137, 138, 142, 143, 144, 145, 150, 152, 153, 159, 162, 168, 171, 173, 180, 183, 184, 185, 187, 188, 192, 193, 194, 197, 198, 205, 209, 216, 218, 219, 220, 221, 222, 223, 226, 229, 230, 231, 232, 234, 238, 240, 244, 247, 248, 250, 252, 366, 370, 411.

Issasy, Francisco Arnaldo: 115, 118, 276, 281, 282, 294.

Jesuits: 203, 206, 207.

Juan (*vinatero* who signed in Baybayin): 16, 205, 206, 207, 208, 209, 212, 214, 215.

Legazpi, Miguel López de: 88, 205, 206, 219.

Linschoten, John Huyghen van: 45, 83, 406.

Lumholtz, Carl: 399, 400, 402.

Magallanes, Fernando de (Ferdinand Magellan): 41, 87, 88, 406.

Mananquel, Nicolás: 182, 183, 186, 187, 188, 221, 222.

THEMATIC INDEX

Mendaña y Neira, Álvaro de: 55, 56, 58, 59, 91.
Miller, Christopher: 199, 203.
Morga, Antonio de: 81, 89, 126, 127.
Orta, Garcia da: 32, 40, 41, 42, 43, 44, 47.
Parrales, Juan Martín: 95, 233, 234, 237, 317, 366.
Patiño, Víctor Manuel: 51, 56, 57.
Pigafetta, Antonio: 41, 44, 46, 48, 87, 88, 89, 373, 406.
Pineda, Sebastián de: 144, 159, 160, 161, 163, 260.
Ponce, Alonso: 55, 56, 91.
Rodríguez, Nicolás: 137, 162, 175, 214.
Rosales, Andrés: 180, 181, 182, 184, 193, 221, 222.
Sáenz Izquierdo, Pedro: 376, 377.
Sangleys: 201.
Scott, William H.: 199, 219.
Serra Puche, Mari Carmen: 402, 403, 405.
Sigüenza y Góngora, Carlos de: 359.
Solís, Miguel de: 148, 149, 154, 155, 156, 157, 247.
Tello, Antonio: 97, 100.
Tinbán, Pedro (chino): 215, 216, 217.
Tumbaga, Sebastián (chino): 173, 174, 175, 187, 188, 221, 222, 244, 245.
Valenzuela, Ana: 401, 408, 414, 415.
Varthema, Ludovico de: 39, 40, 41, 44, 46, 52, 68, 71, 83, 406.
Velasco, Luis de (El Joven): 257, 259, 260, 364, 365, 366, 367, 376.
Vera, Santiago de: 63, 332, 369.
Vera, Sebastián de: 31, 61, 63, 117, 331, 333, 369.
Villalobos, Domingo de (chino): 162, 182.

KEY PLACES

Acámbaro: 318.
Acapulco: 9, 11, 19, 20, 21, 23, 58, 59, 65, 104, 105, 107, 108, 109, 110, 111, 119, 120, 128, 129, 131, 132, 135, 136, 137, 141, 144, 159, 161, 163, 184, 190, 191, 194, 195, 222, 226, 229, 251, 273, 281, 294, 295, 303, 310, 352, 353, 354, 355, 356, 368, 396, 414.

Achiotlán: 107, 115, 172, 173, 280.

Africa: 37, 57.

Aguacatitlán Valley: 107, 113, 114, 175, 250, 266, 275, 279, 289, 290, 302.

Agualulco: 315, 316, 318.

Aguascalientes: 318, 351.

Ajuchitlán: 353.

Aklan: 90, 127.

Alima: 59, 106, 107, 113, 115, 138, 172, 232, 259, 266, 280, 288, 294, 295, 323.

Almoloyan: 106, 107, 115, 235, 240, 279.

Amula: 413.

Apasagualcos (Apuzagualcos): 108, 109, 115, 160, 260, 274, 281.

Apatzingán: 59, 304, 353.

Arantza, Arantzan: 313, 318, 354, 361, 388.

Armería River: 105, 106, 211, 295, 311, 401.

Atlantic Ocean: 36, 37, 57, 229.

Atoyac: 108, 274, 287.

Autlán: 318, 400.

Ávalos, Province of: 305, 339, 409, 411, 413.

Azores: 37.

Batangas: 90, 127, 199, 208.

Bohol: 75, 88, 116.

Borica: 51.

Borneo: 125, 126.

Brunei: 126.

Calicut (India): 37, 38, 44, 52.

Campeche: 57.

Cape Verde: 40, 57.

Cavite: 127, 132, 159, 162, 213.

Caxitlán: 15, 58, 95, 106, 107, 113, 114, 118, 138, 139, 140, 150, 151, 155, 156, 166, 167, 168, 180, 183, 209, 210, 211, 214, 222, 230, 231, 234, 243, 247, 248, 249, 250, 251, 252, 259, 263, 266, 267, 275, 279, 282, 288, 289, 293, 295, 296, 297, 298.

Cebu: 88, 127, 131, 136, 152, 219, 220.

Thematic Index

Celaya: 318, 321.

Chiamila: 106, 107, 115, 118, 234, 240, 279, 280, 282, 291, 314, 322.

Chilchota: 228, 229, 318, 321, 327.

China: 42, 43, 47, 63, 65, 72, 124, 125, 162, 182, 201, 217, 251, 295.

Churintzio: 318.

Churumuco: 353.

Coalcomán: 59, 106, 107, 321.

Cochin: 52, 126, 205.

Cocula: 318.

Colima (Villa and Province): 14, 15, 16, 17, 18, 19, 20, 21, 22, 24, 25, 26, 31, 55, 56, 58, 59, 60, 61, 62, 63, 64, 65, 66, 91, 92, 93, 94, 95, 97, 100, 101, 102, 104, 105, 106, 107, 111, 113, 114, 116, 117, 118, 119, 120, 123, 124, 125, 127, 128, 129, 130, 131, 132, 133, 134, 135, 136, 137, 138, 139, 140, 141, 143, 144, 145, 147, 150, 151, 154, 155, 156, 157, 158, 160, 161, 162, 163, 164, 165, 166, 167, 168, 169, 170, 171, 172, 173, 174, 176, 180, 182, 183, 184, 185, 186, 188, 189, 190, 192, 193, 194, 195, 197, 205, 207, 209, 213, 214, 215, 217, 218, 219, 221, 222, 226, 227, 228, 229, 231, 232, 233, 234, 235, 236, 237, 238, 239, 240, 241, 242, 245, 246, 247, 248, 249, 250, 257, 258, 259, 260, 261, 262, 263, 264, 265, 266, 268, 269, 271, 272, 274, 275, 276, 277, 278, 279, 281, 282, 283, 284, 285, 286, 287, 288, 289, 290, 291, 292, 293, 294, 295, 296, 298, 299, 300, 301, 302, 303, 304, 305, 307, 308, 309, 310, 311, 313, 314, 315, 316, 317, 318, 319, 320, 321, 322, 323, 324, 325, 326, 328, 330, 331, 332, 333, 334, 335, 336, 337, 338, 339, 340, 341, 342, 344, 345, 346, 352, 354, 355, 355, 356, 357, 361, 364, 366, 367, 368, 369, 370, 371, 374, 375, 379, 380, 381, 382, 383, 384, 386, 388, 390, 391, 396, 397, 400, 401, 402, 406, 407, 408, 409, 410, 416, 417, 419.

Comala: 237, 246, 416, 419.

Coquimatlán: 106, 107, 233, 235, 236, 237, 295, 297, 366.

Costa Grande (Guerrero): 107, 190, 193, 251, 260, 274.

Coyuca: 65, 108, 109, 111, 144, 190, 191, 194, 195, 274, 353.

Cuencamé: 318.

Cuitseo: 318.

Cuyutlán: 296.

Durango: 318, 333, 351.

Ecautlán: 107, 234, 241, 242, 243, 244, 245.

Goa (India): 42, 126, 133, 134.

Vino de Cocos, the Pilgrim Beverage

Guachinango: 316, 318, 351.

Guadalajara: 20, 26, 106, 132, 175, 193, 194, 205, 218, 220, 285, 305, 315, 316, 318, 319, 331, 332, 333, 334, 338, 339, 340, 341, 343, 344, 345, 346, 347, 348, 349, 351, 352, 356, 367, 369, 377, 378, 379, 380, 410.

Guadiana: 318, 333.

Guanajuato: 318, 321, 333, 334, 356.

Gujarat: 126.

Hostotipaquillo (Ostotipaque): 134, 135, 316, 318.

Huaniqueo: 318.

India: 32, 35, 36, 38, 39, 40, 41, 43, 44, 45, 46, 52, 67, 68, 71, 83, 84, 125, 126, 133, 134, 135, 205, 406.

Indian Ocean: 32, 35, 36, 37, 38, 71, 370.

Indonesia: 125, 126, 183.

Irapuato: 318.

Ixcatlán: 404, 412.

Ixtlahuacán: 106, 107, 150, 151, 152, 231, 234.

Jacona: 318.

Jala: 106, 107, 114, 279, 295.

Jalisco: 97, 98, 129, 227, 248, 309, 316, 419.

Japan: 63, 80, 125, 201, 401.

Java: 126.

Jiquilpan: 318, 320, 321, 352.

Juchipila: 318, 333, 351.

La Guagua: 127.

La Huacana: 59, 353.

La Navidad, Port of: 128, 129, 130, 131, 219.

La Piedad: 318, 320.

Laguna de Bay: 83, 162.

León: 58, 318, 334.

Lisbon: 37, 38.

Los Ramos: 318, 333.

Luzon: 21, 22, 73, 74, 80, 81, 90, 127, 128, 199, 206, 212.

Thematic Index

Madeiras: 37.

Malabar (costa): 126.

Malacca: 35, 126, 153.

Maldives: 35, 39, 40, 42, 43, 44, 47, 68.

Manila: 9, 11, 15, 18, 23, 65, 84, 126, 127, 128, 131, 132, 134, 144, 152, 153, 159, 162, 176, 194, 201, 203, 205, 212, 213, 219, 220, 223, 332.

Maquilí: 59, 106, 107, 114, 115, 118, 134, 172, 235, 267, 279, 280, 281, 282, 304, 325, 326.

Maravatío: 318.

Mariana Islands (Guam): 41, 42, 48, 373.

Mazapil: 20, 306, 318, 335, 336, 351.

Mexcala: 107, 115, 280.

Mexico City: 20, 26, 62, 101, 108, 128, 129, 130, 131, 132, 135, 137, 139, 152, 153, 166, 188, 203, 205, 213, 260, 273, 302, 303, 304, 306, 313, 318, 319, 320, 321, 324, 327, 328, 330, 331, 335, 348, 350, 355, 356, 359, 367, 386, 411.

Michoacán, Bishopric of: 20, 106, 108, 134, 228, 229, 282, 283, 291, 311, 313, 318, 320, 321, 326, 334, 337, 352, 356, 361, 410.

Mindanao: 127, 128, 133, 134.

Moluccas: 49, 126.

Motines, Province of: 20, 21, 24, 58, 92, 104, 105, 106, 107, 108, 111, 113, 114, 117, 119, 120, 132, 138, 163, 171, 176, 179, 184, 192, 229, 232, 234, 235, 239, 258, 259, 260, 261, 264, 265, 266, 268, 271, 276, 279, 280, 281, 282, 283, 285, 287, 291, 294, 298, 301, 302, 303, 304, 305, 310, 311, 314, 315, 318, 319, 320, 321, 322, 323, 325, 326, 328, 330, 331, 345, 356, 396.

Mozambique: 37, 57.

Nahualapa: 106, 107, 141, 142, 146, 154, 155, 247, 295, 296, 297, 298, 311.

New Guinea: 35, 125, 126.

New Spain: 15, 17, 18, 19, 20, 21, 23, 24, 25, 26, 32, 35, 47, 55, 58, 59, 65, 66, 68, 69, 71, 72, 84, 91, 92, 93, 96, 97, 99, 100, 101, 103, 104, 110, 115, 120, 123, 124, 125, 126, 127, 128, 129, 130, 131, 132, 135, 137, 141, 142, 144, 147, 151, 153, 157, 159, 160, 161, 162, 164, 166, 169, 172, 175, 176, 182, 184, 188, 192, 193, 195, 207, 208, 219, 220, 222, 225, 226, 228, 239, 252, 257, 258, 262, 273, 275, 276, 278, 286, 302, 303, 306, 307, 308, 317, 318, 320, 323, 325, 330, 331, 332, 333, 334, 335, 337, 338, 345, 346, 351, 352, 354, 356, 359, 360, 361, 362, 363, 367, 368, 370, 377, 380, 385, 386, 387,

388, 391, 392, 395, 396, 397, 402, 406, 409, 411, 412, 413, 414, 415, 416, 417, 419, 420.

Nombre de Dios: 318, 333.

Nueva España: 13, 14, 66, 130, 278, 373, 380.

Nueva Vizcaya: 100, 313, 337.

Oaxaca: 55, 129, 228, 335, 362, 404, 405, 412, 413, 414.

Ormuz: 39, 43.

Pachuca: 135, 171, 318, 333, 334.

Pacific Ocean: 9, 13, 16, 19, 23, 35, 36, 53, 72, 97, 104, 120, 141, 142, 198, 205, 222, 223, 302.

Pampanga: 127, 128, 162, 182, 199.

Panama: 51, 52, 55.

Pangasinan: 90.

Papua: 126.

Parañaque: 15, 127, 212, 213.

Parras, Santa María de las: 100, 101, 306, 332, 337, 377, 416.

Pátzcuaro: 20, 134, 236, 237, 313, 318, 321, 322, 325, 326, 353, 354, 356, 402.

Peru: 51, 161, 169, 265.

Petatlán: 109, 119, 274, 294, 353.

Popoyutla: 93, 100, 107, 114, 267.

Portugal: 37.

Puebla de los Ángeles: 128, 129, 132, 317, 405.

Puerto Rico: 57.

Puruándiro: 318.

Querétaro: 133, 175, 228, 318, 321, 343.

Río Grande: 165, 184, 236, 318.

Salagua, Port of (Manzanillo): 15, 55, 56, 58, 59, 100, 104, 128, 129, 130, 131, 220, 385.

Salamanca: 318.

Salvatierra: 318.

San Blas: 194.

San José del Parral: 318.

San Juan de los Lagos: 334.

Thematic Index

San Juan Parangaricut: 319.

San Luis Potosí: 20, 319, 321, 333, 334, 335, 336, 346.

San Miguel el Grande: 334.

Santa Ana Pacueco: 319, 334.

Santa Clara del Cobre: 353.

Santo Domingo: 57.

Sayula: 131, 154, 155, 309, 318, 346, 352.

Sengayan: 125, 126, 183, 184, 193.

Sierra Madre del Sur: 104, 355.

Solomon Islands: 16, 58, 59, 91.

Sombrerete: 20, 318, 333, 336, 351.

Spain: 20, 41, 43, 50, 58, 62, 68, 92, 160, 161, 203, 260, 265, 308, 332, 381, 391, 409, 411.

Sri Lanka (Ceylon): 35, 84, 125, 126.

Suchitzi: 107, 114, 267.

Tamazula: 319, 320.

Tangancícuaro: 319.

Tarecuato: 319.

Taxco: 134, 135.

Taximaroa: 319, 321.

Tayabas: 74, 80, 83, 90, 162.

Tecolapa: 107, 118, 131, 140, 143, 150, 151, 155, 156, 180, 240, 248, 279, 280, 282.

Tecpan: 59, 108, 115, 119, 274, 281, 286, 287, 294, 303.

Tecuciapa: 107, 114, 236, 279, 295.

Teocaltiche: 319.

Tepalcatepec: 59, 106, 319, 321.

Tepuxtitlán: 107, 115, 280.

Tequila: 13, 79, 309, 316, 319, 339, 343, 351, 352, 400, 413, 420.

Tingüindin: 319.

Tlajomulco: 319, 343.

Tlaltenango: 319.

Tlazazalca: 319.

Toluca: 319, 321, 355.

Topia: 318, 333, 336.

Tuxcacuesco: 228, 309, 352, 400, 413.

Tuxpan: 319, 320, 400.

Ucareo: 319.

Valladolid (Morelia): 26, 282, 283, 294, 313, 319, 320, 321, 322, 324, 325, 328, 329, 334, 352, 353, 355, 356, 363, 367.

Valle de Santiago: 319.

Veracruz: 57, 129, 132, 301.

Villa de la Purificación: 319, 351.

Visayas: 21, 22, 32, 75, 85, 87, 88, 89, 90, 116, 124, 127, 198, 199, 406.

Xicotlán: 107, 114, 166, 171, 211, 267, 279, 295.

Xolotlán: 107.

Zacatecas: 20, 25, 129, 132, 135, 301, 304, 319, 332, 333, 336, 337, 345, 346, 351, 354, 356, 376, 377.

Zacatula, Province of: 20, 21, 59, 92, 104, 105, 106, 107, 108, 109, 110, 111, 113, 114, 119, 120, 132, 144, 184, 190, 191, 226, 229, 251, 257, 259, 260, 273, 281, 286, 287, 292, 294, 301, 302, 303, 304, 305, 310, 311, 334, 352, 353, 354, 355, 356, 364, 396.

Zamboanga: 127.

Zamora: 319, 320, 337.

Zapotitlán de Vadillo: 97, 98, 419.

Zapotlán: 162, 182, 294, 319, 346, 351, 352.

Zapotlanejo: 107, 113, 114, 266, 279, 295, 298.

Zinacamitlán: 106, 107, 171, 176, 178, 179, 220, 235, 239, 298, 314, 315, 317, 343.

Zinapécuaro: 319.

KEY CONCEPTS

Acculturation: 144, 153.

Agave (Maguey): 13, 20, 68, 97, 110, 227, 228, 229, 252, 307, 397, 400, 401, 402, 403, 404, 405, 406, 407, 409, 410, 411, 412, 416, 419.

Agency: 13.

Thematic Index

Aguardiente: 21, 25, 63, 68, 71, 76, 79, 81, 83, 84, 91, 92, 93, 96, 97, 100, 101, 103, 105, 106, 118, 142, 145, 149, 164, 166, 167, 169, 173, 180, 213, 217, 218, 222, 230, 232, 236, 237, 238, 239, 242, 243, 247, 250, 251, 259, 260, 261, 264, 268, 269, 271, 273, 274, 278, 279, 281, 282, 283, 284, 286, 287, 291, 292, 294, 295, 298, 300, 303, 304, 305, 306, 307, 308, 309, 310, 314, 315, 317, 318, 320, 322, 325, 328, 330, 331, 332, 335, 341, 343, 344, 351, 352, 354, 356, 357, 366, 367, 369, 370, 373, 374, 375, 376, 381, 383, 385, 387, 388, 390, 391, 411, 413, 414, 419.

Alcabala (sales tax): 137, 271, 306, 318, 323, 327, 334, 341, 345, 385.

Alcalde de los chinos: 182, 184, 186, 188, 189.

Alembic (Alquitara): 80, 98, 99, 100, 101, 307.

Arrak (Alak, Uraca): 46, 79, 83, 87, 406.

Arroba (unit of measure): 118, 264, 265, 278, 279, 281, 282, 283, 287.

Asian-Mexican stills: 414, 415.

Balché: 226.

Banana: 91, 92, 103, 199, 228, 239, 304, 413.

Baybayin (Filipino alphabet): 14, 16, 24, 25, 167, 195, 197, 198, 199, 200, 201, 202, 203, 204, 205, 206, 207, 208, 215, 216, 223, 396.

Biocultural transfers: 22, 29, 395.

Botija perulera (jar): 233, 265, 283.

Branding iron: 182, 183.

Cacahuanantzin (mother of cacao): 24, 68, 111, 112, 120.

Cacao (Theobroma cacao): 15, 20, 23, 24, 63, 68, 103, 104, 105, 109, 110, 111, 112, 113, 114, 115, 116, 117, 118, 119, 120, 132, 137, 166, 190, 191, 211, 258, 260, 263, 264, 268, 269, 270, 272, 274, 275, 276, 277, 278, 281, 283, 284, 285, 286, 294, 295, 302, 303, 310, 311, 320, 323, 330, 353, 356, 382.

Chantry (capellanía): 150, 151, 152, 153, 251, 276, 289, 290, 291, 293, 294.

China poblana: 139.

Chinguirito: 25, 232, 305, 306, 307, 308, 365, 391.

Cimarrones: 188.

Cocada: 116.

Coconut Palm (Cocos nucifera): 15, 16, 17, 18, 19, 23, 24, 25, 31, 32, 33, 35, 36, 37, 38, 39, 40, 41, 42, 44, 46, 47, 48, 49, 50, 51, 52, 53, 54, 55, 56, 57, 58, 59, 60, 61, 62, 63, 64, 66, 67, 68, 70, 73, 74, 84, 85, 86, 91, 92, 93, 95, 96, 102, 103, 104, 105, 108, 111, 112, 113, 115, 116, 117, 118, 119, 120, 132, 137, 162, 165, 166, 180, 192, 211,

222, 229, 239, 257, 259, 264, 271, 273, 277, 282, 288, 294, 299, 307, 309, 368, 372, 375, 392, 395, 411.

Coconut water: 16, 45, 46, 48, 371.

Cofradía (confraternity): 150, 153, 289.

Columbian Exchange: 22.

Compadrazgo (ritual co-parenthood): 139.

Conquistadores: 261, 275, 368.

Copra: 34, 39, 43, 44, 119, 368.

Corn (Maíz): 23, 32, 56, 109, 110, 118, 119, 176, 178, 193, 195, 227, 228, 229, 230, 235, 257, 270, 284, 285, 303, 310, 336, 340, 346, 359, 360, 379, 404, 413.

Cosmogony: 32, 68.

Cotton: 91, 92, 103, 110, 118, 119, 126, 177, 195, 300, 303, 305, 310.

Debt peonage: 164, 173, 178, 192, 193, 244.

Diezmo (tithe): 260, 265, 270, 282, 283, 284, 285, 286, 287, 302, 304, 311, 313, 320, 321, 322, 334, 347, 352, 356, 385, 387, 388, 409, 410, 413.

Distillation: 20, 25, 26, 79, 80, 81, 83, 84, 85, 90, 96, 97, 98, 100, 101, 106, 144, 225, 229, 248, 252, 253, 396, 399, 400, 401, 402, 403, 405, 406, 407, 408, 409, 411, 413, 414, 415, 419.

Dowry: 142, 143, 145, 146, 149.

Drunkenness (embriaguez): 71, 89, 161, 167, 169, 171, 215, 226, 229, 230, 231, 232, 235, 258, 260, 322, 323, 324, 325, 352, 354, 360, 361, 362, 363, 364, 379, 388, 390.

Encomienda: 108.

Enganche (advance payment): 164, 172.

Estanco (royal monopoly): 285, 305, 325, 333, 338, 339, 340, 341, 343, 344, 345, 346, 347, 348, 349, 351, 377, 378, 379, 380, 411, 414, 415.

Evangelization: 201, 206, 208, 220, 258.

Fermentation: 21, 79, 80, 83, 85, 101, 403, 412.

Filipino-style still: 20, 98.

First Globalization: 19, 24, 25, 121, 123, 197, 205, 222, 223, 395, 397.

Gliricidia sepium (cacahuanantzin): 24, 68, 111, 112, 120.

Global microhistory: 14, 18, 19, 222, 395.

Grape: 72, 100, 363, 409, 411, 419.

Thematic Index

Hacienda (cacao, sugarcane, palm): 17, 18, 24, 27, 58, 60, 84, 95, 100, 103, 104, 105, 106, 107, 108, 109, 110, 111, 113, 114, 117, 118, 119, 120, 123, 124, 132, 133, 136, 137, 139, 140, 141, 142, 143, 144, 145, 146, 147, 148, 149, 154, 155, 156, 157, 160, 161, 163, 167, 168, 170, 171, 173, 174, 175, 176, 178, 179, 180, 181, 183, 185, 186, 190, 191, 192, 193, 194, 197, 211, 216, 217, 218, 220, 222, 226, 230, 231, 234, 238, 240, 242, 243, 244, 245, 247, 248, 249, 250, 251, 252, 259, 260, 262, 263, 264, 268, 269, 270, 271, 272, 274, 275, 276, 277, 278, 279, 281, 282, 286, 288, 289, 290, 291, 292, 293, 294, 295, 296, 297, 298, 299, 300, 301, 302, 304, 307, 308, 311, 313, 314, 315, 317, 322, 323, 325, 326, 331, 341, 343, 345, 352, 353, 356, 375, 382, 384, 385, 391, 396, 411, 417.

Hijodalgo: 275.

Historiography: 13, 17, 24, 132, 206, 395.

Humors (Galenic theory): 62, 369, 370, 372.

Idolatry: 258, 364.

Indio chino (term): 17, 23, 24, 60, 91, 93, 105, 120, 123, 124, 125, 126, 127, 128, 129, 131, 132, 133, 136, 137, 138, 142, 143, 144, 145, 150, 152, 153, 159, 162, 168, 171, 173, 180, 183, 184, 185, 187, 188, 192, 193, 194, 197, 198, 205, 209, 216, 218, 219, 220, 221, 222, 223, 226, 229, 230, 231, 232, 234, 238, 240, 244, 247, 248, 250, 252, 366, 370, 411.

Indios laboríos: 185, 186, 187, 188, 209, 230, 270.

Justice (clement): 17, 57, 165, 166, 172, 186, 187, 317, 323, 326, 327, 346, 362, 381.

Ladino: 217, 220.

Lambanog: 9, 11, 21, 46, 79, 83, 84, 90, 278, 396.

Lease contracts: 262, 263.

Libranza (letter of exchange): 337.

Maestro de hacer vino (master winemaker): 15.

Maguey: 68, 92, 227, 228, 229, 257, 306, 357, 362, 363, 387, 391, 401, 402, 404, 405, 409, 410, 411, 412.

Manananggot (tuba gatherer): 21, 72, 75, 76, 80.

Mangrove: 85, 101.

Manila Galleon (Nao de China): 11, 13, 18, 19, 23, 26, 32, 48, 68, 103, 108, 123, 129, 130, 132, 133, 141, 143, 163, 198, 207, 213, 222, 273, 302, 310, 367, 368, 395, 397.

Mestizaje: 123, 138.

Mezcal: 13, 20, 21, 25, 26, 79, 84, 97, 98, 100, 226, 227, 232, 248, 252, 285, 286, 305, 306, 307, 308, 309, 333, 336, 337, 338, 339, 340, 343, 344, 345, 346, 347, 348, 349, 350, 351, 352, 357, 376, 377, 378, 379, 387, 391, 395, 397, 399, 400, 401, 402, 403, 404, 405, 407, 408, 409, 410, 411, 412, 413, 414, 415, 416, 419, 420.

Milpa: 110, 243.

Muleteers (arrieros): 137, 291, 304, 318, 336, 337, 346.

Multi-sited ethnography: 21.

Nipa Palm (*Nypa fruticans*): 81, 85.

Palapa: 16, 47, 64.

Palm haciendas: 17, 24, 27, 58, 60, 84, 100, 103, 104, 105, 106, 107, 108, 109, 110, 113, 114, 118, 119, 120, 123, 124, 132, 139, 140, 141, 144, 145, 154, 161, 163, 167, 168, 173, 175, 176, 180, 181, 183, 185, 186, 191, 192, 193, 211, 220, 222, 226, 231, 234, 238, 242, 244, 245, 247, 248, 249, 250, 259, 262, 263, 264, 268, 269, 270, 272, 278, 281, 282, 288, 289, 290, 291, 292, 293, 295, 296, 297, 298, 300, 301, 302, 304, 307, 308, 311, 313, 317, 323, 352, 356, 384, 385, 396, 411.

Partido (payment in kind): 164, 167, 168, 169, 170, 171, 172, 173, 176, 193, 238.

Pirates: 367, 368, 385.

Prohibition: 25, 26, 232, 257, 258, 259, 260, 306, 310, 317, 322, 330, 357, 359, 362, 363, 364, 365, 367, 377, 379, 387.

Protomedicato (medical tribunal): 346, 380, 384, 411.

Public health: 362, 376, 378, 392.

Pulque: 69, 101, 102, 226, 227, 258, 325, 327, 331, 345, 359, 360, 362, 363, 364, 365, 381, 386, 387, 390, 391, 392, 402, 406, 411, 413.

Rice: 23, 43, 62, 86, 88, 119, 137, 195, 285, 302, 303, 310.

Salt: 110, 166, 182, 193, 245, 260, 261, 270, 283, 291, 292, 296, 307, 310, 318, 320, 330, 333, 334, 337, 353, 362, 372.

Savoir faire (know-how): 24, 68, 170, 192, 195, 238, 240.

Sisa (tax): 327, 328, 329, 330, 344.

Slavery: 133, 173, 193.

Still (distilling apparatus): 20, 26, 79, 80, 81, 82, 83, 97, 98, 99, 100, 101, 159, 161, 269, 307, 397, 399, 400, 401, 402, 405, 407, 409, 412, 414, 415, 416, 417.

Sugar: 38, 40, 43, 44, 46, 57, 79, 80, 118, 238, 285, 295, 297, 301, 305, 334, 353, 368, 372, 392.

Thematic Index

Sugarcane: 21, 25, 86, 103, 149, 227, 232, 238, 239, 286, 297, 302, 303, 305, 306, 346, 357, 379, 382, 384, 387, 397, 413, 414.

Tamarind: 23, 59, 119, 303, 304.

Tecomate (gourd vessel): 48, 93, 166, 191, 211, 270, 295, 317.

Tepache: 228, 308, 387, 391, 413.

Tesgüino: 226, 227.

Tribute: 136, 137, 185, 186, 187, 188, 189, 215, 244, 289.

Tuba: 16, 21, 22, 25, 39, 40, 45, 46, 48, 49, 62, 69, 72, 73, 74, 75, 76, 77, 79, 80, 81, 82, 83, 84, 85, 87, 90, 91, 92, 93, 94, 95, 96, 97, 101, 102, 112, 116, 117, 120, 139, 149, 164, 171, 181, 183, 190, 191, 194, 195, 238, 240, 241, 243, 245, 246, 247, 248, 252, 263, 268, 270, 295, 298, 300, 306, 307, 308, 370, 371, 372, 376, 391, 392, 400, 401, 406, 411, 416, 417, 419.

Tubero (tuba gatherer): 22, 72, 73, 74, 76, 77, 78, 80, 83, 85, 90, 91, 94, 96, 102, 248, 307.

Tuna-mezquite: 226.

Vanilla: 118, 119, 294, 301, 303, 353.

Vinatero (winemaker): 14, 15, 24, 25, 123, 124, 127, 128, 132, 136, 145, 149, 159, 163, 164, 166, 167, 168, 170, 171, 172, 173, 174, 175, 176, 178, 179, 180, 181, 182, 183, 184, 190, 191, 192, 193, 194, 195, 197, 198, 205, 209, 214, 215, 218, 219, 220, 222, 225, 226, 238, 239, 240, 241, 243, 244, 245, 246, 247, 248, 252, 269, 297, 301, 366, 396.

Vino de cocos: 11, 13, 14, 15, 16, 17, 17, 18, 19, 20, 21, 22, 24, 25, 26, 27, 33, 45, 46, 49, 62, 63, 69, 71, 72, 73, 76, 79, 82, 83, 84, 87, 88, 89, 91, 93, 94, 96, 97, 98, 100, 101, 103, 106, 107, 108, 109, 112, 117, 118, 119, 120, 123, 124, 133, 134, 138, 139, 142, 145, 146, 147, 148, 149, 152, 157, 159, 160, 161, 163, 164, 165, 166, 167, 170, 171, 172, 173, 174, 175, 180, 181, 182, 183, 184, 189, 190, 191, 192, 193, 194, 197, 205, 207, 209, 211, 212, 213, 215, 216, 217, 218, 223, 226, 227, 230, 231, 232, 233, 234, 235, 236, 237, 238, 239, 240, 241, 243, 244, 247, 248, 250, 251, 252, 253, 257, 258, 259, 260, 261, 262, 263, 264, 265, 266, 267, 268, 270, 271, 272, 274, 276, 277, 278, 279, 281, 282, 283, 284, 285, 286, 287, 288, 289, 292, 294, 295, 296, 298, 300, 301, 302, 303, 304, 305, 306, 307, 308, 309, 310, 311, 313, 314, 315, 316, 317, 318, 319, 320, 321, 322, 323, 324, 325, 326, 327, 328, 329, 330, 331, 332, 333, 334, 335, 336, 337, 338, 339, 340, 341, 342, 343, 344, 345, 346, 347, 348, 349, 350, 351, 352, 353, 354, 355, 356, 357, 359, 361, 362, 364, 365, 366, 367, 368, 369, 370, 372, 373, 374, 375, 376, 377, 378, 379, 380, 381, 382, 384, 385, 386, 387, 388, 389, 390, 391, 392, 395, 396, 397, 399, 400, 401, 402, 406, 408, 409, 410, 411, 415, 416, 417, 418, 419.

Vino de Cocos, the Pilgrim Beverage

Wine (from Castille): 69, 120, 160, 161, 63, 258, 259, 260, 332, 336, 337, 360, 362, 364, 365, 366, 368, 377.

INDEX OF MAPS

Map 1.	Route of the dispersion of the coconut palm toward America.	54
Map 2.	Dispersion of the coconut palm in the Pacific region of New Spain.	59
Map 3.	Palm haciendas in the Colima-Motines nucleus.	107
Map 4.	Palm haciendas in the Zacatula-Acapulco nucleus.	110
Map 5.	Origins of the *indios chinos* who settled in New Spain.	125
Map 6.	The settlement of *indios chinos* in New Spain.	129
Map 7.	Palm haciendas in Colima (17th century).	141
Map 8.	Records of writing in Baybayin in diverse repositories in the world.	202
Map 9.	The Caxitlán Valley (17th century).	210
Map 10.	The Island of Luzon (The Philippines).	212
Map 11.	*Pueblos de indios* in Colima (17th century).	241
Map 12.	Places where *vino de cocos* from the Colima-Motines nucleus was consumed.	320
Map 13.	Places where *vino de cocos* from the Zacatula-Acapulco nucleus was consumed.	354
Map 14.	The route from Acapulco to Mexico City (17th century).	355
Map 15.	Asian-Mexican stills and their distribution.	415

THEMATIC INDEX

INDEX OF TABLES

Table 1.	The coconut palm and its benefits, according to chroniclers (12th-19th centuries).	44
Table 2.	Benefits of the coconut palm according to residents of Colima (1612).	61
Table 3.	Estimated current *lambanog* production in Laguna, the Philippines (2008).	84
Table 4.	Principal fermented drinks derived from palm trees in the Philippines.	86
Table 5.	Residents of Colima who owned cacao and palm haciendas in Colima-Motines (1622).	113
Table 6.	Cacao and palm haciendas in Colima, Motines, and Zacatula (1631 and 1649).	114
Table 7.	Purchase/sale of *indios chinos* slaves in Colima (17th century).	133
Table 8.	Properties of Francisca Martha and Sebastián de la Cruz (1652).	143
Table 9.	Comparison of Francisca Martha's properties (1652-1664).	149
Table 10.	Chantries in the province of Colima (17th century).	151
Table 11.	Trajectory of Francisca Martha.	156
Table 12.	*Indios chinos vinateros* in Colima (1604).	168
Table 13.	Debts of *chinos* on the hacienda of Zinacamitlán, Motines (1638-1639).	179
Table 14.	Voting for the *alcalde de los chinos*, mulattos and *indios laboríos* (1642).	186
Table 15.	Election of the *alcalde de los chinos*, *indios laboríos*, free mulattos, and free negros (1651).	188
Table 16.	Chinos, *tuba*, and *vino de cocos* on the hacienda of Nuestra Señora del Buen Suceso in Coyuca (fragment).	191

Table 17.	Sentences imposed on the *chinos vinateros* (1600).	214
Table 18.	Signatures of *indios chinos* in Colima (17th century).	221
Table 19.	*Indios vinateros* on the palm hacienda of Ecautlán (1638).	244
Table 20.	Census of the palm haciendas in Caxitlán, Colima (1681, 1683).	249
Table 21.	Annual *vino de cocos* production in the Colima-Motines nucleus (1622).	266
Table 22.	Administration costs on the cacao and palm hacienda of the Del Valle family (1625-1626).	269
Table 23.	Administration costs on the palm hacienda of doña Catalina de Alarcón (1639).	270
Table 24.	Distribution of investments in Colima, 1622.	272
Table 25.	Annual *vino de cocos* production in the Colima-Motines nucleus (1631).	279
Table 26.	Annual *vino de cocos* production in the Zacatula-Acapulco nucleus (1631).	281
Table 27.	Tithes paid on *vino de cocos* from Colima (17th century).	284
Table 28.	Tithes paid on *vino de cocos* from Zacatula (17th century).	287
Table 29.	Chantries and palm haciendas in Colima-Motines (1680).	291
Table 30.	Record of *vino de cocos* production on the hacienda of Zinacamitlán (1638-1639).	315
Table 31.	Market for *vino de cocos* in the Colima-Motines nucleus (17th century).	318
Table 32.	Licenses for the free production and sale of *vino de cocos* (17th century).	324
Table 33.	*Sisa* tax on *vino de cocos* in Valladolid (1633).	329

Thematic Index

Table 34.	Loads of *vino de cocos* sent from Colima to other provinces (1637).	342
Table 35.	Tithe collectors for *vino de cocos* and mezcal (1674-1701).	347
Table 36.	Revenue to the Royal Treasury (*Real Caja*) of Guadalajara from the royal monopoly on *vino de cocos* and mezcal (1680-1699).	349
Table 37.	Revenue to the Royal Treasury (*Real Caja*) of Mexico for the concept of *vino de cocos* and mezcal (1683-1697).	350
Table 38.	Medicinal properties of the coconut palm and its derivatives.	372

INDEX OF PHOTOGRAPHS

Photograph 1.	Raincoat known as a *china* (Colima).	65
Photograph 2.	Bamboo bridges among palm trees for extracting *tuba*.	74
Photograph 3.	Preparing the inflorescence to extract *tuba*.	75
Photograph 4.	Bees in *tuba* most.	80
Photograph 5.	Rustic still for elaborating *vino de nipa*.	82
Photograph 6.	Cacao tree under the shade of a coconut palm (Bohol, the Philippines).	116
Photograph 7.	Cooked agave heads recently removed from the oven (Ixcatlán, Oaxaca).	404
Photograph 8.	Fermentation of agave heads in bull hides (Ixcatlán, Oaxaca).	412
Photograph 9.	Public presentation of the *vino de cocos*, "La china mestiza".	418

INDEX OF ILLUSTRATIONS

| Illustration 1. | Morphology of *Cocos nucifera* L. | 34 |

Illustration 2.	Coco *chocolatero* from San Luis Beltrán (ca. 1671).	67
Illustration 3.	Materials used to store *tuba*.	77
Illustration 4.	A Filipino *tubero* or *indio mananguetero* (1847).	78
Illustration 5.	*Lambanog* and *tuba* today in the Philippines.	90
Illustration 6.	Materials used in the collection and storage of *tuba* in Colima.	94
Illustration 7.	Filipino-style still for mezcal production (Zapotitlán de Vadillo, Jalisco, Mexico).	98
Illustration 8.	Arab-style still made of copper.	99
Illustration 9.	Signature of Juan Martín, a *chino*, Francisca Martha's father.	145
Illustration 10.	Variants of the Baybayin alphabet according to Sinibaldo de Mas y Sanz (1843).	200
Illustration 11.	Baybayin alphabet according to Pedro Chirino (1604).	204
Illustration 12.	Signature of don Juan [de Chávez?].	206
Illustration 13.	Signature of Pedro Tinban.	216
Illustration 14.	Signature of Juan de Chávez.	217
Illustration 15.	Signature of Pedro García elaborated by Juan de Chávez.	218
Illustration 16.	Document in Nahuatl from the town of Ecautlán (1638).	242
Illustration 17.	Plan of the palm haciendas in the Nahualapa Valley (1688).	296
Illustration 18.	Plan of the house of don Hilario Ceballos (1720).	299
Illustration 19.	A common landscape in Colima with coconut palms (1802).	309

Table of Contents

Presentation	9
Foreword	11
Preface to the English Edition	13
Introduction	15
Part I. Biocultural Transfers Across the Pacific	29
1. The World the Coconut Palm Created	31
2. Vino de cocos: A Traveling Technique from the Philippines to New Spain	71
Part II. Actors of the First Globalization: A View "From Below"	121
3. Francisca Martha and the Indios Chinos in the Mar del Sur	123
4. Indios Chinos Vinateros: Rural Connections Across the Pacific	159
5. The Vinateros Who Signed in Baybayin	197
6. Indian Vinateros and Other Castes	225
Part III. The Pilgrim Beverage	255
7. Prohibition, Apogee, and Decline of Vino de cocos	257
8. Commercial Routes of Vino de cocos	313

9. Vino de cocos and Prohibitionist Policies	359
Conclusions	395
Epilogue. Mezcal: The Heir of Vino de cocos?	399
Endnotes	423
Archives Consulted	455
Bibliography	455
Glossary	477
Thematic Index	481
Key Names	481
Key Places	483
Key Concepts	490
Index of Maps	496
Index of Tables	497
Index of Photographs	499
Index of Illustrations	499

Made in the USA
Coppell, TX
15 February 2026

71336234R00291